Klaus Roth, Robert Hayden (Eds.)

Migration in, from, and to Southeastern Europe
Part 1

Migration in, from, and to Southeastern Europe

Part 1
Historical and Cultural Aspects

edited by

Klaus Roth and Robert Hayden

Ethnologia Balkanica

Journal for Southeast European Anthropology
Zeitschrift für die Anthropologie Südosteuropas
Journal d'anthropologie du sud-est européen

Volume 13/2009

LIT

ISSN 1111-0411

Printed in Germany

The journal is published by the International Association for Southeast European Anthropology (InASEA). It publishes articles by members of InASEA as well as by non-members. All articles are anonymously reviewed.
Languages of publication: English, French, German
Contributions must be supplied with a short abstract in English.

Cover:

A spatio-temporal shift: a German-Turkish couple in Berlin. Photograph taken in a studio in Berlin, in March 2002, on the day of the couple's wedding ceremony. Neither the Ottoman fez, nor the nargile or the background reflect present Turkish culture, and likewise the posture of the couple refers to a culture that is not part of their biographies. The photograph manifests how migration expands the boundaries of both time and space, referring to imaginations, feelings of belonging, values, and material aspects of culture (see article by Gülsüm Depeli).

Subscription: Subscription price (one volume per year): Students: 10€, Individuals: 16€, Institutions: 20€
Individuals and institutions in Southeast Europe: 10€.

Bibliographic information published by the Deutsche Nationalbibliothek
The Deutsche Nationalbibliothek lists this publication in the Deutsche Nationalbibliografie; detailed bibliographic data are available in the Internet at http://dnb.d-nb.de.

ISBN 978-3-643-10895-1

A catalogue record for this book is available from the British Library

Fresnostr. 2 D-48159 Münster
Tel. +49 (0) 2 51-620 320 Fax +49 (0) 2 51-922 60 99
e-Mail: lit@lit-verlag.de http://www.lit-verlag.de

Distribution:

In Germany: LIT Verlag Fresnostr. 2, D-48159 Münster
Tel. +49 (0) 2 51-620 32 22, Fax +49 (0) 2 51-922 60 99, e-mail: vertrieb@lit-verlag.de

In Austria: Medienlogistik Pichler-ÖBZ, e-mail: mlo@medien-logistik.at

In Switzerland: B + M Buch- und Medienvertrieb, e-mail: order@buch-medien.ch

In the UK: Global Book Marketing, e-mail: mo@centralbooks.com

In North America by:

Transaction Publishers
New Brunswick (U.S.A.) and London (U.K.)

Transaction Publishers
Rutgers University
35 Berrue Circle
Piscataway, NJ 08854

Phone: +1 (732) 445 - 2280
Fax: + 1 (732) 445 - 3138
for orders (U. S. only):
toll free (888) 999 - 6778
e-mail: orders@transactionpub.com

Contents

Editorial

Migrations have shaped Balkan societies in past and present. Historically, the long-standing integration of Southeast Europe in large empires facilitated various kinds of migration. In the modern period, the agrarian crisis, the lack of jobs, and migrant networks stimulated millions of people to go abroad, whether as overseas emigrants before World War One, as so-called *Gastarbeiter* in the 1960s and 70s, or as economic migrants after the collapse of socialism. In the 19th and 20th centuries, many people were also forced to leave their homes as victims of ethnic cleansing, as refugees from war or political persecution. On the other hand, Balkan countries are also hosts to immigrants and refugees - and they have witnessed large-scale domestic migration processes, mainly from village to urban centres, since the 1950s.

Migrations, thus, became typical experiences in many a Southeast European life-course and established transnational linkages providing important resources. Apart from its socio-economic and political dimensions, migration is also a complex cultural phenomenon. Migrants are often faced with cultural alterity and have to develop new ways of communication, resulting in strategies of assimilation or integration, but also of segregation or marginalisation. The evidence of 19th century overseas emigration as well as of recent migrations shows that they lead to complex processes of social and cultural change both in the country of origin and in the host country. The same holds true for the changes that take place between the generations of migrants, particularly in our days of transnational mobility and of new media of communication.

In view of this high relevance of migration for the Balkan Peninsula, the 5th conference of InASEA, the International Association for Southeast European Anthropology, was devoted to the topic "Migration in, from, and to Southeastern Europe. Intercultural Communication, Social Changes, Transnational Ties". The conference took place at Hacettepe University in Ankara, Turkey, on 21–24 May, 2009. It was splendidly organised by Asker Kartarı and his team of the Communications Department at Hacettepe University and attracted more than 130 participants from Southeast Europe and beyond. The conference received the generous financial support of the Wenner Gren Foundation for Anthropological Research, the Promotion Fund of the Turkish Prime Ministry, Hacettepe University, the German Science Foundation (DFG), and the Agence Universitaire de la Francophonie.

This volume of Ethnologia Balkanica, the journal of InASEA, presents the first part of a selection of conference papers. It was the goal of the conference, and it is the goal of the two volumes, to promote the ethnological study of migration in, from, and to Southeast Europe in view of the fact that the significance of migration for the region continues to be very high. Both volumes present papers which analyse aspects of the causes and the social, political, and above all cultural consequences of the various migration processes affecting the region – and the entire European Union. Most contributors to both volumes are ethnologists, but there is also a sizable number of authors from other disciplines such as history, sociology, political science, communication studies, language teaching, et al. With their focus on the socio-cultural dimensions of migration, their papers shall contribute to the main goal of InASEA, the advancement of a cross-disciplinary and transnational dialogue.

Last but not least, the president of InASEA and the editor-in-chief want to express their gratitude to all those who contributed to the success of the conference, in the first place to Asker Kartari; likewise we want to thank all authors of the two volumes and the reviewers.

Klaus Roth, editor-in-chief Munich, June 2010
Ulf Brunnbauer, president of InASEA

Migrationen haben in Geschichte und Gegenwart die Gesellschaften Südosteuropas nachhaltig geprägt. Historisch gesehen hat die lange Einbindung Südosteuropas in große Reiche verschiedenste Formen der Migration hervorgebracht. In der Moderne haben dann vor allem die Agrarkrise, der Mangel an Lohnarbeit und migrantische Netzwerke Millionen von Menschen dazu bewogen, ins Ausland zu gehen, sei es als Auswanderer nach Übersee vor dem Ersten Weltkrieg, als sogenannte *Gastarbeiter* in den 1960er und 70er Jahren oder als Wirtschaftsmigranten nach dem Zusammenbruch des Sozialismus. Im 19. und 20. Jahrhundert waren zudem viele Menschen gezwungen, als Opfer ethnischer Säuberungen oder auf der Flucht vor Krieg und politischer Verfolgung ihre Heimat zu verlassen. Andererseits haben die Balkanländer auch Immigranten und Flüchtlinge aufgenommen – und sie haben gewaltige innere Migrationsströme erlebt, vor allem die Landflucht von Millionen seit den 1950er Jahren.

Migration wurde damit zu einer typischen Erfahrung zahlreicher südosteuropäischer Lebensläufe und erzeugte transnationale Verbindungen, die wichtige Ressourcen bildeten. Neben ihren sozio-ökonomischen und politischen Dimensionen ist Migration auch ein komplexes kulturelles Phänomen. Migranten sind zumeist mit kultureller Alterität konfrontiert und müssen neue Kommunikationsweisen entwickeln, was zu Strategien der Assimilation oder Integration, aber auch der Segregation oder Marginalisierung führt. Sowohl die Auswanderung im 19. Jahrhundert als auch neueste Migrationsbewegungen zeigen, dass Migration stets zu komplexen Prozessen des sozialen und kulturellen Wandels sowohl im Herkunfts- als auch im Gastland führt. Das Gleiche gilt für jenen Wandel, der zwischen den Generationen von Migranten stattfindet, ganz besonders in unserer Zeit der transnationalen Mobilität und der neuen Kommunikationsmedien.

Vor dem Hintergrund dieser hohen Bedeutung von Migration für die Balkanhalbinsel war die 5. Konferenz der InASEA, der International Association for Southeast European Anthropology, dem Thema „Migration in, von und nach Südosteuropa. Interkulturelle Kommunikation, sozialer Wandel, transnationale Bindungen" gewidmet. Die Konferenz fand statt an der Hacettepe Universität in Ankara, Türkei, vom 21. bis 24. Mai 2009. Sie war hervorragend organisiert von Asker Kartarı und seinem Team von der Fakultät für Kommunikation an der Hacettepe Universität und sie zog mehr als 130 Teilnehmer aus Südosteuropa und weit darüber hinaus an. Die Konferenz wurde großzügig finanziell unterstützt von der Wenner Gren Foundation for Anthropological Research, dem Promotion Fund of the Turkish Prime Ministry, der Hacettepe Universität, der Deutschen Forschungsgemeinschaft und der Agence Universitaire de la Francophonie.

Der vorliegende Band von Ethnologia Balkanica, der Zeitschrift der InASEA, präsentiert den ersten Teil einer Auswahl von Konferenzbeiträgen. Es war das Ziel der Konferenz und es ist das Ziel der beiden Bände, die ethnologische Erforschung der Migration in, aus und nach Südosteuropa zu fördern angesichts der Tatsache, dass die Bedeutung der Migration für die Region weiterhin sehr hoch ist. Beide Bände legen Arbeiten vor, die Aspekte der Ursachen und der sozialen, politischen und vor allem kulturellen Folgen der verschiedenen Migrationsprozesse analysieren, die die Region und damit auch die ganze Europäische Union betreffen. Die meisten Beiträger der Bände sind Ethnologen, doch stammt eine beachtliche Zahl der Autoren aus anderen Disziplinen wie der Geschichte, der Soziologie, der Politologie, der Kommunikationswissenschaft, der Sprachdidaktik u.a. Mit ihrer Ausrichtung auf die sozio-kulturellen Dimensionen der Migration sollen ihre Artikel beitragen zum Hauptziel der InASEA, der Förderung des interdisziplinären und transnationalen Dialogs.

Schließlich ist es dem Präsidenten der InASEA und dem Herausgeber ein wichtiges Anliegen, allen, die zum Erfolg der Konferenz beigetragen haben, an erster Stelle jedoch Asker Kartari ganz herzlich zu danken; unser Dank gebührt aber auch den Autoren der beiden Bände und den Rezensenten.

Klaus Roth, Herausgeber München, Juni 2010
Ulf Brunnbauer, Präsident der InASEA

Les migrations ont modelé les sociétés balkaniques hier et aujourd'hui. Historiquement, la longue intégration de l'Europe du Sud-Est dans des empires a facilité différents genres de migration. Dans la période moderne, la crise agraire, le manque de travail et les réseaux migratoires ont stimulé des millions de gens à partir à l'étranger, soit en qualité d'émigrants d'outre-mer (avant la première guerre mondiale), soit en tant que Gastarbeiter (pendant les années 1960 et 1970) ou en tant que migrants après la chute du socialisme. Aux IXème et XXème siècles, beaucoup de gens ont été forcés de quitter leurs pays puisque ils étaient victimes de nettoyages ethniques, ou en tant que réfugiés de persécutions. D'un autre côté, les Balkans sont aussi des pays d'accueil pour des immigrants et des réfugiés et ont été témoins de grands processus de migration domestique, surtout de la campagne vers les centres urbains, et ce depuis les années 1950.

Les migrations, donc, sont devenues des expériences courantes dans la vie de nombreux européens du Sud-Est et elles ont établi des liens transnationaux qui ont fourni d'importantes ressources. Mis à part ses dimensions socio-économique et politique, la migration est également un phénomène culturel complexe. Les migrants sont souvent confrontés à l'altérité culturelle et doivent développer de nouveaux moyens de communication qui entraînent des stratégies d'assimilation ou d'intégration, mais aussi de ségrégation ou de marginalisation.

À ce propos, l'émigration vers les Etats-Unis au IXème siècle, tout comme les migrations récentes, montrent qu'elles conduisent à des processus compliqués de changement culturel et social tant dans le pays d'origine que dans le pays hôte. Ceci peut être également affirmé pour les changements qui ont lieu entre les générations de migrants, en particulier pour notre époque, elle-même caractérisée par la mobilité transnationale et par les nouveaux moyens de communication.

En corollaire à la haute importance de la migration pour la péninsule balkanique, la 5ème conférence de l'InASEA, l'International Association for Southeast European Anthropology, a été consacrée au thème « Migration dans, depuis et vers l'Europe du Sud-Est. Communication interculturelle, changements sociaux, liens transnationaux ». La conférence a eu lieu à l'université Hacettepe de Ankara, Turquie, du 21 au 24 mai 2009. Elle a été organisée de main de maître par Asker Kartarı et son équipe du Département de Communication à l'Université Hacettepe. Elle a attiré plus que 130 participants de l'Europe du Sud-Est et d'ailleurs. La conférence a reçu une importante aide financière de la part de la Wenner Gren Foundation for Anthropological Research, de la Promotion Fund of the Turkish Prime Ministry, de l'Université Hacettepe, de la Fondation de Recherche Allemande (DFG) et de l'Agence Universitaire de la Francophonie.

Ce numéro de Ethnologia Balkanica, le journal de l'InASEA, présente la première partie d'une sélection de contributions de la conférence. Le but de la rencontre ainsi que le but des deux volumes est de promouvoir l'étude ethnologique de la *Migration dans, depuis et vers l'Europe du Sud-Est* suite à l'importance de la migration pour la région. Les deux volumes présentent des contributions qui analysent les causes et les conséquences sociales, politiques et surtout culturelles des différents processus migratoires qui affectent la région, ainsi que l'Union Européenne tout entière. La plupart des scientifiques qui ont contribué aux deux volumes sont des ethnologues, mais parmi eux, il y a également un nombre important d'auteurs provenant d'autres disciplines, telles que l'histoire, la sociologie, les sciences politiques, l'étude de la communication, l'enseignement des langues, etc.

Grâce à leur focalisation sur les dimensions socioculturelles de la migration, leurs travaux vont contribuer à atteindre le principal objectif de l'InASEA, c'est-à-dire la suite d'un dialogue interdisciplinaire et transnational.

Enfin, le président de l'InASEA et le rédacteur en chef veulent exprimer leur gratitude à tous ceux qui ont contribué au succès de la conférence, en premier lieu à Asker Kartarı ; par la même occasion, nous voulons remercier tous les auteurs des deux volumes ainsi que les relecteurs.

Klaus Roth, rédacteur en chef — Munich, juin 2010
Ulf Brunnbauer, président de l'InASEA

Towards a Comparative History of Migration and Membership in Southeast Europe (1500–1900)

Leo Lucassen, Leiden

Abstract

This article is a plea for more rigorous and systematic comparisons of migration and settlement processes in general and in Southeast Europe in particular. Which definitions or typologies are helpful in such an exercise of course depends on the research questions. The three dominant approaches to migration (political, social-economic or cultural) all have their strengths and weaknesses, but focus on different aspects of the migration process. It is important that scholars be explicit in their choice of which to use. In principle these three approaches do not fundamentally distinguish between free and unfree, or labour versus refugee, migration. Unfortunately however, such dichotomies too easily lead to myopic and in the end unsatisfactory analyses. Without denying differences between forms and contexts of migration, such differences should first be charted and compared explicitly before jumping to conclusions.

Introduction

For migration historians, Southeast Europe presents a fascinating puzzle. Fascinating, because the area has been bustling with movement of the most varying types for centuries, from people captured as slaves to work elsewhere to those who converted to Islam in order to reach high positions within the Ottoman Empire, often far from where they were born. At the same time the constant warfare between the Habsburg and Ottoman empires, with the Venetians at times involved as well, led to various forms of colonization along both sides of the military border that separated the two empires. These widely different forms of migration, as well as the identity formations inextricably linked to them, however, are not well understood and only partially studied. Moreover, most of the available studies tend to be rather isolated and lack a coherent analytical framework. This is not only true for migration, but also for the ensuing settlement process and group formation. So far, much knowledge is hidden in numerous subfields, which all have their own questions, paradigms, discussions and approaches: military history, urban history, Ottoman history, Jewish history, and so on.

In this article I will first discuss the various typologies and definitions of migration, suggest a solution to the fragmentation of migration studies and apply this solution to the history of Southeast Europe. In the second part of this paper I shift to the consequences for group formation in this part of Europe and propose a unifying heuristic model that enables comparisons between seemingly very different forms of settlement processes of migrants and their descendants.

The need for a comparative migration history

In order to make these historiographies compatible and "legible", to use James Scott's term (1998), we need a systematic approach that enables rigorous comparisons, both in time and in space. In the field of migration history, it is clear that this problem of scattered knowledge cannot be solved easily. First of all, like the landscape in Southeast Europe itself, the scholarly terrain that deals with migration and group formation is characterized by massive mountain ranges, separated by fast running rivers, which makes comparing not self evident. Particularly unfruitful are the many typologies, often solidified in mutually exclusive dichotomies (Lucassen, Lucassen 1997). The most important of these are the distinctions between free and unfree migrations and between labour migrants and refugees. Although there are important differences between these forms of migration, it is too easily forgotten that they are parts of long continua, with many different expressions in between. Moreover, even the extremes have in common concerns with people who experience geographical mobility, whereas the impact on receiving societies reveals unexpected similarities. For the functioning of labour markets, for example, it does not really matter whether people are taken against their will or whether they migrate freely. Some, like the Ottoman Janissary recruits, may have been forced, but they or their parents also fully realized that the Ottoman army offered interesting career possibilities, so that the Janissaries have much in common to what is known as career migration, which is usually associated with free migration. Although we should have a keen eye for different expressions of the multifaceted migration phenomenon, a comprehensive interpretative framework is much needed.

Definitions

A second problem that stands in the way of structural comparisons is the lack of theoretical and conceptual clarity about what exactly constitutes "migration". As Leslie Page Moch (1992) once aptly remarked, of all demographic phenomena migration is the most unruly. Unlike birth, marriage and death, which are fairly uniform and consistent, migration has many expressions which tend to escape rigorous conceptual delineation. In historiography at least three dominating approaches can be distinguished: political, socio-economic and cultural.

The *political approach* uses the nation state as point of departure and defines migrants as those who cross national boundaries, often with the aim to settle for a longer period, thus excluding tourists, visitors, and transmigrants. This perspective is dominant, not least because nation states since the 19th century have produced numerous statistics to make all kind of social facts visible, among which is geographical mobility (Porter 1986, Scott 2009). Given the interest of states in defining those whom each considers as its citizens and those who are members of other states, people who cross national boundaries are seen as more relevant and important than citizens who move within the territory of the state. As the state became more dominant in the 20th century, especially after World War I, it increasingly offered more services to its citizens, such as welfare, and expected taxes, loyalty, administrative and linguistic unity, and prescribed moral behaviour in return. This mix of economic, social, political and cultural ties between the nation state and its citizens had a homogenizing effect that highlighted differences with citizens of other states. By crossing national borders people immediately became the object of state scrutiny and sometimes restrictive and exclusionary practices (Torpey 2000, Lucassen 1998, Fahrmeir 2007).

However logical such an obsession with national boundaries may be from the perspective of the nation state, for the study of migration this political approach is rather myopic and leads to a quite unsatisfying approach, as it focuses only on one dimension of the migration process. Moreover this definition is very arbitrary and leads to absurd outcomes occasionally. Thus, within the international definition, migrants who move very short distances but cross a state boundary, for example Belgians who settled in the textile area of Northern France, around Lille, Valenciennes and Roubaix, immediately show up on the radar screen, whereas Russians (or Chinese) who travel for thousands of miles remain invisible (fundamentally criticized by McKeown 2004). For those who are primarily interested in state attitudes and policies versus members of other states, this may not constitute a problem, but those who want to understand the relation between mobility and labour, for example, or who are primarily interested in the early modern period and before, are left in the dark. In other words the political approach is of little value for most of human history (for recent overviews Manning 2005 and Hoerder 2002).

Even more myopic and arbitrary is the definition of migration as intercontinental moves, often requiring migrants to cross seas and oceans. This perspective has become prominent from the 1860s onwards, when millions of Europeans left their continent to settle in the Americas and in the so-called white settlement colonies. Enabled by the transport revolution, these huge migrations were regarded as so spectacular that for many observers intercontinental moves are the ultimate expression of migration and overshadow intra-continental moves. A good example can be seen in the history of Italian emigration since the end of the 19th century, when indeed millions left for overseas destinations, both in North and South America as well as Australia. At least 50 % of Italian migrants, however, remained in Europe and settled in France, Germany, the Austrian-Hungarian empire and beyond (Gabaccia 2000, Bertagna, Maccari-Clayton 2007). Yet by far the most attention of migration historians has been paid to Italians who left Europe, reflecting this – often implicit – hierarchy.

In reaction to this political focus social and economic historians developed other approaches, of which the *household perspective* is most dominant. Here the focus is not on the relation between state and citizen, but on a much lower level of analysis, that of the household and its members. Decisions to migrate are often taken within households and stem from the need to pool the incomes of their members by looking for work elsewhere, often temporarily. How this works out for these members very much depends on (gendered) institutional arrangements that are intertwined with both family systems and labour market institutions. In North-west Europe, nuclear families became dominant already in the Middle Ages within a relatively free labour market that offered employment for both men and women (for family systems see Kok 2010). This development was closely related to early forms of proletarianisation and urbanization that hugely stimulated migration to centres of "capital", be they commercial farming areas, mines or cities (Van Bavel 2007, Van Zanden 2008; see also Tilly 1978 and De Vries 1984). Migration as a survival and income pooling strategy within households can be observed over both short and long distances. Men who worked as seasonal labourers part of the year, before returning to their wives and children, for example often travelled hundreds of kilometres, frequently crossing state boundaries (Lucassen 1987).

The emergence of the household perspective has played a key role in the realization that early modern European societies were much more mobile than had often been assumed. This led the well-known American historian and sociologist Charles Tilly to come up with a typology of migration that went beyond the nation state. Tilly, struck by early manifestations of proletarianisation in Western Europe, realized that this process had far-reaching consequences for the mobility of Europeans at least since the 16th century, forcing people to migrate to places with a (high) demand for labour. This realization brought him to propose a socio-economic typology that put labour markets at the centre and that defined migration basically as all moves over municipal borders, thus linking migration from between villages to intercontinental movements (Tilly 1978; see figure 1).

The great advantages of this socio-economic typology over the nation-state approach are that it can be applied to a much longer time period, and that its focus on the household enables interesting and often surprising comparisons in

Form	Function	Range
Local migration	Finding work and marriage partners	Limited to the region
Seasonal migration	Temporarily earning money in areas with a high demand for labour and high wages	Within a range of some 300 kilometres
Chain migration	Finding support and information by joining relatives and acquaintances from the same place/region of origin	From short to very long distances
Career migration	In function of large organizations (state, private of church) and often moving up the career ladder	Both within and between states
Colonial	Finding employment in overseas colonies	Intercontinental

Figure 1: Social-economic migration typology pertaining to the history of Western Europe since 1500 (Source: Tilly 1978).

time and space. Young men who nowadays leave their families and villages in Western Africa, for example, and who risk their lives in small and often ramshackle boats hoping to find illegal work in Spain or Italy, may seem very different from local migrants in Europe's past. When we use the household perspective, however, systemic similarities strike the eye. Men and women who left their families to work as farm hands or domestics in a neighbouring village or town did not run the risk of drowning or deportation, but their motives and the function of their migrations were quite similar to that of today's "boat refugees". In both cases the aim has been to earn as much money as possible and send this back and thus to contribute to the household economy. That the reality may be different because of death, the lack of employment or turning ones back to the household, is immaterial.

Another example that shows the comparative power of Tilly's typology is that of seasonal labour. If one were to use a nation-state definition of migration, most early modern seasonal migrants would not qualify as migrants, in stark contrast to Italians who left for Argentina to do the harvest, enabled by fast and cheap transport from the 1860s onwards, and then returned to their own peasant farms. From the household perspective, however, distance is irrelevant and both internal Italian and transcontinental seasonal migrants can be studied, understood and explained within the same conceptual framework.

Finally it is clear that the other three forms of migration in Tilly's typology, which has been very fruitfully applied to the history of Western Europe in Leslie Page Moch's seminal book *Moving Europeans*, also lend themselves to comparison across time and space. Ukranian women who for a decade or so can be found in many Greek villages earning money by taking care of the elderly, or Albanians working in Italy since the early 1990s, migrate in very much the same way and for similar reasons as did local migrants in Europe's past.

Those interested in the cultural impact of migrants on both sending and receiving societies may have some difficulties with both the political (nation-state) and the socio-economic (household) approaches. Although the first one at least implicitly does acknowledge cultural difference, it ignores all expressions that escape the gaze of the state, be they religious, regional or linguistic. The socio-economic perspective on the other hand does not use culture as a criterion and includes all migrations irrespective of cultural distance between migrants and natives.

A typology that combines social, economic, political and cultural perspectives and enables broad comparisons in time and place is proposed by Patrick Manning in his recent book *Migration in world history* (2005). In this study he stresses the importance of migration for the forging of connections and exchanges between various parts of the world since *homo sapiens* left Africa some 60000 years ago. Manning argues that migration is not limited to humans (think of birds, whales etc.), but that only humans can cross cultural boundaries. The unique development of fully inflected languages among *homo sapiens* played a key role. As humans started to migrate, first within Africa, in isolation they not only developed different solutions to ecological challenges, they also developed different languages which enabled them to communicate ideas, values, world views and technologies among one another. Thus unlike other species, in the diaspora process human language communities created unique cultures. In the "out of Africa" movement this proliferation of languages and cultures increased dramatically. This diversification was further stimulated by encounters with often very different ecological circumstances, especially when humans moved to colder climate zones, which demanded new solutions in order to survive. In contrast to other species the spread of humans over the entire globe between (roughly) 60000 and 30000 years before the current era thus produced not only differences in phenotype but also in cultures. Migration between culturally distinct language communities therefore often led to the confrontation with new ideas and practices. According to Manning, this constant fusion can be considered the engine of human development (figure 2).

These cross community migrations, with people from one (language) community moving to another, has different expressions of which the following four are the most important:

Type	Function	Range	Who?
Home community migration	Broaden gene pool	Within one's own community	All species
Colonisation migration	Extend range of species	Within similar ecological settings	Most species
Whole community migration	Alternate among ecological settings	Within a restricted territory	Some species
Cross community migration	Share community experience	The entire world	Only humans

Figure 2: Cultural migration typology pertaining to the history of mankind (Source: Manning 2005: 7).

- settlers (joining a new community with the aim to stay for good);
- sojourners (joining a new community with the aim to return);
- itinerants (moving between different communities without a community of their own to return to);
- invaders (moving to another community and taking control).

Applying the cultural migration typology to European history

If we want to identify (and quantify) cross-community migrations in European history over the last half century, and more specifically within Southeast Europe, we need to "translate" Manning's typology into categories that cover the relatively recent European experience (this paragraph is based on Lucassen, Lucassen 2009). These categories should have minimal overlap and cover the entire spectrum of cross-community migrations. If we apply these conditions to Europe as a whole (from the British Isles in the West to the Urals in the East), the following six forms of cross-community migration should be considered:

- people leaving Europe (emigration),
- people entering Europe (immigration),
- people settling in rural areas (colonisation),
- people moving from rural to urban areas (migration to cities),
- people moving on a seasonal basis (migratory labour),
- soldiers and sailors (multi-annual migration).

This typology differs from conventional classifications which distinguish, for example, between refugees and labour migrants, or free and unfree. Both divisions are incorporated in the six-fold typology, however. Refugees, for example, show up in various categories, as the example of the Huguenots shows. With the revocation of the Edict of Nantes in 1685 almost a million French Protestants were forced to convert to Catholicism, which most of them indeed did. Some 150000, however, chose to leave France illegally and settle in countries where they could practice their religion (Asche 2007: 635). Most of them moved to cities (like Geneva, Amsterdam and Berlin), but others settled in rural areas (colonisation), while a number of families ended up in North America and South Africa (emigration). Some of them, finally, became soldiers, thus carrying on the profession they had carried out earlier in the French army of Louis XIV.

As for unfree migrants, they also show up in most of the six categories. Thus, from the 15th century onwards millions of people in what is now Poland, the Baltic States and Russia were captured by Caucasian and Circassian slave raiders and taken to Central Asian slave markets (emigration) (Fisher 1972). Others, like hundreds of thousands of West African slaves, were taken to Spain and Portugal, making up 10 % of the population of Lisbon and Valencia in the 16th century (Saunders 1982, Phillips 2007). Other forms of unfree migration have been studied by military and maritime historians. Well known are the slave raids in the Balkans, both by the Ottomans and the Venetians, who until well in to the 17th century both were constantly in need of oarsmen to man their galleys in the Mediterranean (Frauenstädt 1896, Lucassen 1996: 49–51).

When we apply this typology to the history of Europe in the period 1500–1900 for which we have enough data, it becomes clear that the assumption that Europeans only became mobile in the 19th century, the era of industrialisation, urbanisation and massive overseas emigration, cannot be upheld. Since the 1980s many migration historians have argued against this modernisation paradigm, and more specifically against the idea of a fundamental "mobility transition" in the 19th century (Moch 1992, Hochstadt 1999, Hoerder 2002), but so far a solid quantitative foundation was lacking. A recent quantitative reconstruction of cross-community migrations in Europe between 1500 and 1900 suggests that Europe was already highly mobile long before 1800 and that the increase in the second half of the 19th century, when tens of millions of Europeans left for the Americas and other continents, should not be interpreted as a confirmation of the modernisation paradigm. That paradigm assumes that Europe only became mobile in the 19th century caused by a concerted combination of commercialisation, industrialisation, globalization and urbanisation. In fact migration rates were already quite high and the increase after 1850 is not caused by modernisation, but is simply a consequence of the transport revolution (steam ships and trains) and the ensuing lowering of transport costs (Lucassen, Lucassen 2009). A conservative interpretation of the available evidence, in which we calculated the chance of a European in a given period of 50 years to make a cross-cultural move in his or her life, is presented in the next figure (3).

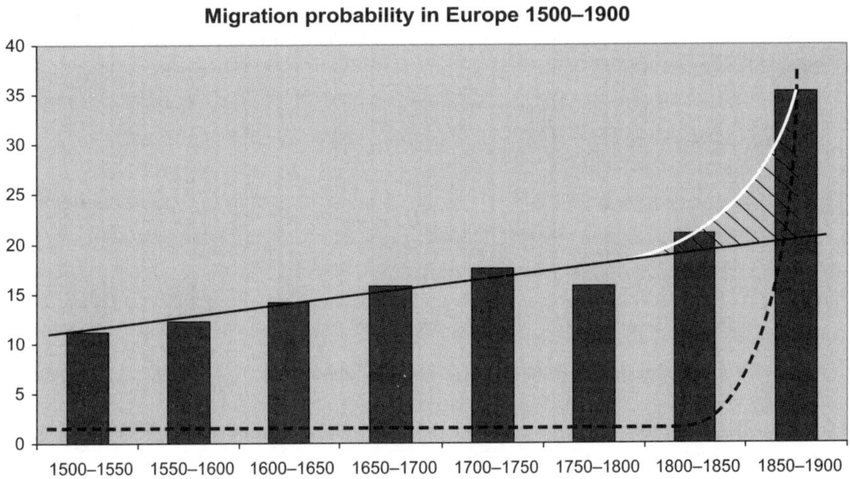

Figure 3: Migration rates 1500–1900 (Source: Lucassen and Lucassen 2009).
Legend: Migration probabilities per period. Both the black and the white lines are merely aids for the eye. The straight black line indicates the trend one would naively expect from the data in the period 1500–1850. The white line shows a clear deviation from this trend, denoted by the shade area. The dotted line is our interpretation of the classical mobility transition idea.

If we want to understand better in what kind of cross-cultural moves people were involved and how the six different forms developed over time, we need to break these aggregate figures down (figure 4).

Figure 4 first of all makes clear the importance in the early modern period of migration by soldiers and sailors, which is ignored by most migration scholars. Our own calculations only consider those soldiers and sailors who crossed a cultural boundary, which explains the decrease in their share in the 19th century, when standing armies became the norm and most soldiers – except those who left for the colonies (Bosma 2009) – did not leave their countries during their service. This was quite different before 1800 when soldiers, often mercenaries like Scotts and Swiss, were hired by other states and many of them were deployed throughout Europe. Prior to the introduction of general military conscription, most soldiers in Europe were long-distance migrants (Mallet, Hale 1984: 1–2, Pfister 1994: 53–54, Asche 2008: 15–25).[1]

[1] For military recruitment systems see Lucassen, Zürcher 1999. The mobility of occasional militias was very low, see Brewer 1989: 32–33.

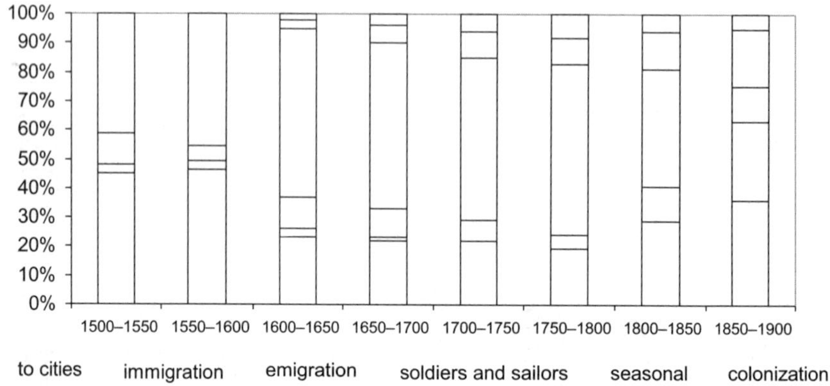

Figure 4: The share of migration types in the total migration rate 1500–1900 (in percent) (Source: Lucassen, Lucassen 2009).

The large share of soldiers (and to a lesser extent sailors) reflects the more general history of Europe, which is characterised by a constant interstate competition, which led Charles Tilly (1990) to conclude that the history of European state formation in the last millennium is one in which "war makes states and states make war". This insight reminds us of the fact that migration history should be regarded as an integral part of European (and world) history, as is illustrated by the next figure (5) in which the six types of cross-community migration are linked to major historical processes since 1500.

Cross-community migrations in Southeast Europe

As Holm Sundhaussen has argued recently (2007), Southeast Europe from the early modern period onwards and probably even before, has been an extremely mobile part of Europe. So far, however, this history is badly known and only studied in a very partial way. Most studies concentrate on the 20th century, starting with the demise of the Ottoman Empire, the Balkan wars of 1912–1913 and the population exchange between Turkey, Russia and Greece in the beginning of the 1920s, and ending with the downfall of the communist regimes and the tragic Yugoslav civil wars at the end of the 20th century. Others, who go further back in time, also tend to view migration primarily as the result of political disruption and war. Although war and state formation more generally have indeed had a grave impact on cross community migration patterns in Southeast Europe,

Historical Process	Cross-community migration types
Commercialisation and proletarianisation	Migration to cities Seasonal migration
State Formation	Soldiers Colonization (both in Russia and the Balkans)
Globalization (including the phase "thin globalisation" starting with discovery of the Americas by Columbus at the end of the 15th century (Flynn, Giráldez 2004; see also Manning 2005)	Sailors Emigration Immigration (from Africa to Italy and the Iberian Peninsula since 1400; Tinhorão 1988, Casares 2000, Davis 2007, Mendes 2008, McKee 2008)

Figure 5: The relationship between major historical processes and migration in European history since 1500.

they do not cover the whole migration story. In the remainder of this paper I take stock, with no claim to be exhaustive, of the manifold expressions of cross community migrations, by applying the six-fold migration categorisation presented above to Southeast Europe since the end of the Middle Ages.

Emigration

In the period before 1800 we can distinguish various forms of emigration, that is of people leaving this region for non-European destinations. Most of them concerned men who were drafted into the Ottoman army as a result of institutional arrangements, such as the levy of young boys *(devşirme)*. The *devşirme* is a phenomenon well-known since the 14th century, although seldom analysed within a migration framework. To understand this phenomenon, we have to realize that the Ottomans, like other states in the Mediterranean, used slave labour for all kind of tasks, including the army. As Muslims could not be enslaved, the Ottomans were dependent on Christians and Jews. In the Balkans the Ottomans aimed especially at the Christian Slavic population (few Greeks and Armenians were taken), and when the need for new soldiers arose the Ottomans would collect boys and young men, ranging in age from seven to twenty, from Christian parents (in principle one fifth of the Christian boys), who showed little resistance. These boys were taken to training camps in Anatolia and Islamized. The more intelligent among them were educated in palace schools to occupy high and prestigious functions in the Ottoman administration. These educational perspectives may have been attractive to parents, and Albanian and Bosnian Muslim parents tried at times to bribe recruiters to take their children as well, provided they could enter the palace schools (Clarence-Smith 2006: 37). From 1564 onwards it became legally possible for Muslim children to enlist (Lucassen, Zürcher 1999). The soldiers became part of the Sultan's new army *("yeni eri")*, the Janissaries, with an average strength of 70000 men (Peters 2003: 276–277, Lucassen, Zürcher 1999), and in the period 1400–1650 some 200000 Balkan youths were recruited through the *devşirme* system (Clarence-Smith 2006: 1).

Immigration

Notwithstanding the conflicts between the Habsburg and Ottoman empires, from the 15th to the 17th century many migrants from non-European regions also found Southeastern Europe to be an attractive region to settle or work in for a period of time. In regard to the Balkans, most entered from the east. From the mid 14th century some 50000 nomadic Turcoman migrants from Anatolia settled in Macedonia and Thrace, and most of them had become sedentary by the mid-16th century (Inalcik 1994: 34–37; see also Todorov 1983: 47–49). By that time the population belonging to this group of (former) immigrants is estimated at some 160000 (Zhelyazkova 2002: 232). Others were taken by force, as slaves and impressed soldiers, in both the European and Asian parts of the Ottoman empire (Toledano 1998, Davis 2003, Clarence-Smith 2006, Dávid, Fodor 2007).

Colonization

Migrants who moved to "empty" rural areas within Southeast Europe have been noted, but are not easy to quantify. We know that tens of thousands moved because of the shifting (military) borders between the two major empires, first non-Muslims like Serbs to the North, and then from the 17th century onwards Christian migrants to the South, in the wake of the slow retreat of the Ottoman empire. A special case is the so-called "Militärgrenze" *(confinium militare)*, which was created in 1553 under direct authority of Vienna (Kaser 2007, Sundhaussen 2007). In this shifting buffer zone of some 20000 square kilometres between the two empires, colonists were offered land in exchange for farming and fighting. In just the first half of the 18th century this involved at least some 350000 people (Hoerder 2002: 285).

	1500	1600	1700	1750	1800	1850
Albania	—	30	36	24	60	68
Romania	30	25	87	104	153	399
Bulgaria	97	94	126	143	277	299
Greece	29	83	53	67	252	174
Hungary	12	12	33	109	254	828
Yugoslavia	145	170	127	89	193	275
Total	313	414	462	536	1189	2043
Total Population	6500	7450	8300		18374*	
percent urban population	4.8	5.6	5.6		8.8**	

Source for the population of cities: Bairoch et al. 1988.
Source for the total population: A. Maddison: Historical Statistics of the World Economy 1–2006 AD (http://www.ggdc.net/maddison/).
* in 1820.
** We have used the average of the population in 1800 and 1850.

Figure 6: Total population of cities >9999 inhabitants in Southeast Europe (in 000s)

The most well-known colonists, however, were migrants coming from an array of Southern German states (Hesse, Bavaria, Baden, Palatinate, Swabia), soon lumped together under the heading of *Schwaben* (Hungarian *Sváb*). They were invited by the Habsburg authorities to settle in Southeast Europe, in the mercantilist hope that their qualities as farmers would develop the economy and stimulate agriculture and industry (Fata 2007). Luring German settlers to Transylvania, the Banat and Bačka in Serbia was justified on the grounds that "they come with good determination and their own means, and they behave exceedingly well". The recruitment started in 1689 with the *Impopulationspatent* of the emperor and the newcomers enjoyed freedom of movement and temporary exemption of taxes. In the first half of the 18th century it has been estimated that 350000–400000 Germans were present in Southeast Europe, which in 1773 had increased to 637000, and to over a million in 1840 (Fata 2007). These migrants, who were from both Catholic and Protestant regions, were spread over the areas of settlement alongside Hungarians, Rumanians, Slovaks, and Southern Slavs. Although colonists, they were in constant contact with their neighbours. Only in the Banat and along the military border did German-speakers live more segregated.

To cities

Southeast Europe did not have large urban areas, with the exception of Istanbul, which in the mid 16th century already boasted half a million inhabitants. In the 1520s the number of 400000 inhabitants is mentioned which increased to 700000 (Behar 1996: 5). Until the 19th century 5 % of the population lived in cities larger than 10000 inhabitants (figure 6). Until 1550 only Edirne, Salonika and Sarajevo reached this threshold, with Athens, Vidin, Nikopol and maybe Sofia joining in the second half of the 16th century (Todorov 1983: chapter 2). Only in the 19th century did the share of the urban population increase, albeit modestly. Given the high mortality rates in cities until 1800 we may assume that urban growth was only possible through immigration, and moreover that migrants were also needed to make up for negative growth (De Vries 1984). Most of them came from the surrounding countryside, but others like Sephardic Jews and some of the German immigrants – including Christian renegades from German states who converted to "the light of Islam" (Krstić 2009) – arrived from other parts of Europe. Taken together, cities in this part of Europe did not "produce" a large number of migrants, especially when compared with the highly urbanised North-western part of Europe, with the Western part of the Dutch Republic (50 % of the population in cities around 1700) as absolute peak (De Vries 1984).

As slavery was widespread in the Ottoman Empire it does not come as a surprise that part of the urban population in the Balkans was comprised of slaves or freedmen with roots in Russia, Georgia and the Ukraine. Thus, in 1570 four percent of the Muslim households in Sarajevo were established by former slaves (Zhelyazkova 2002: 246).

One of the most well-known group of migrants coming from outside Southeast Europe were Sephardic Jews who escaped persecution by the Catholic Spanish and Portuguese kings at the end of the 15th century and in the 1530s. How many chose the Eastern Mediterranean as their destination is not quite clear, but most scholars agree that a considerable part of the 150000 Jews who left Spain and Portugal ended up in the Ottoman empire, either directly or after a brief stay in Italy. In the mid 16th century both Salonika and Istanbul housed some 20000 Jewish inhabitants (Bell 2008: 36). The second wave of refugees from Portugal in the 1530s brought many to Istanbul, where 30350 Sephardim were counted in 1535, most of whom stayed there only briefly and then settled in smaller Ottoman cities (Rozen 2002: 49–51). Although, like Christians, they were discriminated against and not treated as full citizens, as "people of the book" they had the right to practice their religion and enjoyed certain privileges (like exemption from the *devşirme*), provided they paid their taxes. In general the tolerance of religious difference in the Ottoman empire was considerably greater than in most Christian states that in principle only allowed one religion, like France after 1685 and most German states after 1648 (Parker 2006).

Finally, we should not forget that part of the German migrants who left for the Balkans did not settle in villages, but became part of the urban fabric. In contrast to their rural counterparts, most Germans assimilated much quicker to their Hungarian, Romanian and Slavic environments. Class influenced the pace of assimilation as well. While German farmers and artisans preserved their culture in their new surroundings, most young "Swabian" men from the countryside who went to universities, especially in the 19th century, assimilated quickly. In Hungary this integration was further stimulated by the dominance of the Hungarian nobility and the ensuing Magyarization of the bourgeoisie (Fata 2007).

Soldiers and sailors[2]

Earlier we briefly mentioned the "emigration" of young boys and men to the Asian part of the Ottoman Empire as a consequence of the forced levy for the army. This phenomenon also fits the last migration category proposed in this paper, that of multi-annual labour migrants who are recruited for the army or the (merchant) navy. Given the crucial importance of warfare between the Ottoman and Habsburg empires in Southeast Europe, it is clear that the army and navy exerted a structural pull on the available manpower in this region. The demand for these kind of labour migrants varied considerably over time and was linked to the intensity of warfare.

Until the end of the 19th century the Ottomans deployed the largest army in the Balkans. An important part were the Janissaries, consisting of Islamized men who were drafted as children and raised as professional soldiers. Hammer estimated that in total half a million Christian children were seized by the Ottoman army (Todorov 1983: 51, 503). For the late medieval period one can distinguish between the *Kapikulu Corps* (consisting of infantry units of Janissaries, elite cavalry and artillery) and the provincial *Sipahi* cavalry (Nicolle 1995). Moreover, there were auxiliary cavalry called *Akincis* and vassals' troops from the Balkans, Southern Russia, and the Kurdish and Arab parts of the Empire. In the 15th and 16th centuries the Sipahi cavalry numbered around 40000 men, half of whom came from "Rumeli", i. e., the European provinces, and the others from Anatolia (Nicolle 1983: 11, cf. 29 [85000 for the Turkish army in 1402]).

---

2 This paragraph is based on the elaborate reconstruction and account of Lucassen and Lucassen (2009), to be published on the website of the International Institute of Social History.

From a total of 90000 Ottoman soldiers in the first half of the 16th century, 40000 men at least must have originated from Europe.

In 1649 the Habsburg standing army was founded, which mobilised large numbers of soldiers to fight in the Southeast. Next to this there were the so-called "Grenzer" also known as *Uskoks* (literally: escapees). These refugees from the Turkish lands agreed to lifetime military service as a sort of border patrol or militia in exchange for land grants (Boerke 2009: 68–79, Kaser 2007).

While the recruitment of soldiers was organised in a more or less orderly and institutionalised fashion, although by no means without coercion, finding enough men for the fleet was quite another matter. As in Western Europe this is explained by the high risks at sea, but in the case of the Mediterranean this was aggravated by the nature of warships, which depended on oarsmen instead of sails. Most ships of the Ottoman, Genoese, Venetian and French forces were manned by a mix of free and slave labour. The Ottomans preferred free oarsmen to slaves (who were tied by chains to their benches) because they could also be used as soldiers for boarding actions. They used mercenaries from Greece and the Balkans, but most also had a minority of Christian slaves (Nolan 2006, under "galley"). A more violent form of slave taking involved regular raids along the Balkan shores of what is now Greece, Albania and Croatia by both the Ottomans and their Christian enemies, who all looked for young men for their war galleys, or for the French Mediterranean navy (Bamford 1973: 170–173).

Quantitative data for the Balkans are hard to come by because the part of its population in the total Ottoman fleet is unknown. This is unfortunate, because we know that the Ottoman Empire was able to mobilize many sailors. The Turkish fleet of more than a hundred ships is believed to have had 37000 men (Glete 2000: 149). On the Ottoman side the battle of Lepanto probably involved more than 80000 sailors and soldiers, many of whom came from Albania and Greece (Scammell 1981: 134 [230 Ottoman ships]; Parker 1988: 89 [400 galleys on both sides, which carried, between them, some 160000 men]; Glete 2000: 105). Very provisionally, we might suppose that maritime employment in the Balkans was greatest in the 16th century, declined in the 17th century and stabilized in the following centuries.

Galleys were used in the Mediterranean until the beginning of the 18th century, although they were gradually replaced in the course of the 17th century. Overcrowding caused high death rates and therefore a constant demand for rowers, which was satisfied by sending condemned criminals to the galleys, but also by kidnapping one's own citizens (Faroqhi 2004: 127–128). This involved not only Christians. As the power of the Ottomans increased the number of slaves needed increased accordingly, especially in the Black Sea area, so that also Muslims were enlisted, both voluntarily and coerced (Dávid, Fodor 2007: XVII).

Migration and membership

Notwithstanding the high population mobility in the Balkans during the early modern period, sketched only very roughly above, from the 19th century onwards most of its inhabitants increasingly viewed and defined themselves in static ethnic and nationalist terms. In contrast to Western Europe this "ethnicisation" was not per se incompatible with collective memories of migration, as the nationalist interpretation of Serbian history testifies. The migration history of "Serbs" is viewed through the lens of collective forced northbound migrations from the Kosovo heartland following the defeat against the Ottomans in 1389 at Kosovo Polje. The centuries of forced wanderings explained why only 20 % of the Serbs in the post-Ottoman Serbian kingdom were native-born, as the famous anthropologist and geographer Jovan Cvijić showed around 1900. At the same time, however, Cvijić used his scholarly work, which enjoyed an international reputation, to bolster Serbian nationalist claims (Sundhaussen 2007: 290–291; see also Kaser 1998).

The idea of Serbs as a centuries-old ethnic group is highly problematic, however, and is the product of an essentialist interpretation of collective identities that spread quickly in the 19th century. Before that time identities were much more layered, contextual, multiple, and less fixed, as Holm Sundhaussen has convincingly argued recently (Sundhaussen 2007).[3] Terms used in early modern sources, like "Greeks", "Serbs" or "Turks" are far from straightforward and may have many meanings. Depending on the specific context, terms could refer to ethno-linguistic, religious or occupational affiliations and seldom did these converge and solidify into stable ethnic markers (Sundhaussen 2007: 292). Moreover, Sundhaussen (2007: 291) concludes that so far no real attempt has been made to systematize the migration history of Southeast Europe and in doing so transcend national-historiographical interpretation schemes.

To move beyond the present unsatisfactory state of the art and reach a better understanding of how identities changed through time, we need to combine and integrate new theoretical perspectives from both migration and religious studies which emphasize human agency at the micro and meso level, without ignoring the influence of institutional arrangements. With respect to the most well-known minority groups (Jews and Gypsies, or Roma), their history is mostly written from a *top down* perspective with a central role for the state and religious institutions.[4] Furthermore most scholars hardly ever theorise beyond their specific case study, with a few exceptions (Van Arkel 1985, 2009; Lucassen et al. 1998,

---

[3] For Western Europe, see the exemplary study on France by Weber (1976); for a global perspective see Bayly (2004) and Manning 2005).

[4] For the Roma see Barany 1995, Ladányi, Szelényi 2003, Achim 2004, Crow 2007.

Lucassen, Willems 2003). A more *bottom up* approach is found in recent contributions in the field of early modern religious and toleration studies, including Ottoman Europe. With a particular focus on conversions, processes of "passing" and inter-group dynamics, especially at the local and individual level, this methodology is a welcome addition to our understanding of minority formation.[5] The concept of "passing" is especially interesting, because it highlights how individuals can cross group boundaries while the group category itself remains intact.

Crucial analytical tools have been developed by studies on inter-group relations, in the fields of migration, minority and religious studies, which emphasise the importance of day-to-day contacts between people with different identities and group labels. In defiance of institutional barriers at the macro level, embodied by official rules of the prevailing membership regimes (Benhabib 2004), these studies show that on the meso and micro levels, borders between groups were less rigid than one would assume. Even those migrants who to some extent developed parallel societies, like the Germans in Russia and in the Habsburg-Ottoman border region (Eberl 1983), at least partially adapted to the surrounding majority society (Brandes 2007, Parker 2006). These meso and micro processes are in line with recent research on religious toleration in Early Modern Europe at the local level (Parker 2006, Kaplan 2007). Historians of the Balkans therefore should pay much more attention to the social and cultural implications of ordinary day-to-day interactions between various groups to determine to what extent institutional borders could be overcome in the shorter and longer terms, leading to processes of mutual adaptation.

In this regard the ideas developed by the American sociologists Alba and Nee (2003: 60–61) concerning the long term sociological process of assimilation of immigrants in the United States are relevant. Instead of *crossing* boundaries (for example by "passing", and conversion), with individuals moving to another group while the boundary remains intact, boundaries can also *blur*, making the social distinction less clear and breaking down rigid categorisations. Ultimately, boundaries can even *shift*, transforming former outsiders into insiders, or producing new outsiders. In most research on migration and settlement, especially in Southeast Europe, the crossing, blurring and shifting of boundaries between groups are understudied or completely ignored, which greatly simplifies and distorts our understanding what really went on.

---

[5] See Bennassar, Bennassar 1989, Stewart 1997, Hsia, Lehmann 1995, Faroqhi 2000, Minkov 2004, Dursteler 2006, Parker 2006, Kaplan 2007, Hrstic 2009.

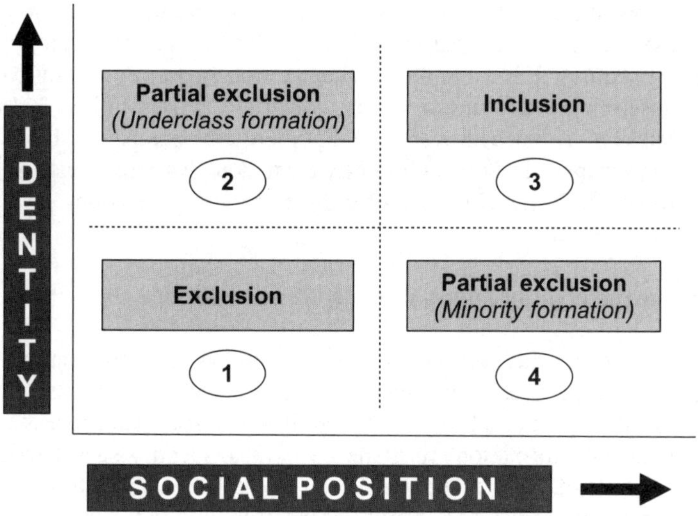

Scheme 1: Varieties of settlement in Europe since 1500

Applying the settlement model to Europe since 1500

Although most theorising about settlement processes, like that of Alba and Nee, is rooted in the nation-state experience of the last 200 years, with some caution it can be applied to early modern Europe as well. We should, however, avoid simplistic, linear and modernist (anachronistic) interpretations and realise that the outcome of settlement processes can differ widely, depending on the prevailing migration and membership regime. To systematise the manifold variations in time and place, a simple model which distinguishes between a *structural (social position)* and an *identificational* domain can be fruitful, as applied in Lucassen (2005) and Lucassen et al. (2006). The structural focuses on the social position of migrants and their descendants: the work they do, where they live and patterns of social mobility. The identificational domain refers to the extent migrants and their descendants identify with the receiving (local/regional/national) society and how they are viewed by those already there. How the settlement process in these two domains develops over time and over generations depends not only on their own characteristics and preferences (including intra-group barriers), but also on the extent of "openness" (or barriers) in the society in which they settle. The dimensions can be summarised in the model presented in scheme 1.

This model is by no means static: groups can move to different positions over time, and even move back into previous positions, as happened with many assimilated Jews in the 1930s and 1940s. Although a certain position may be the end result after a long period has passed, it can also be an intermediary snapshot of changing statuses. For example, Huguenots who fled to Protestant countries found themselves initially in box 4, but, over time, moved to box 3. In many cases, "inclusion" is reached over time, but there are examples of both "exclusion" (Roma groups) and "partial minority formation" (various Jewish migrants; many Germans in Eastern Europe) after three or more generations.

Divergent membership regimes in Early Modern Europe

Scheme 1, however, does not include institutional barriers, both on the side of the migrants and the receiving society. In practice such barriers played an important role. In order to understand the multifaceted historical processes of minority and identity formation we therefore have to identify such barriers and measure their effect, both at the macro and micro levels. In early modern Europe, legal stratifications which could thwart structural and identificational assimilation were firmly in place. Full citizenship in early modern cities, for example, was limited to a minority of well-off male inhabitants (class, gender) and other markers (e. g. religion) often produced partial exclusion too (Hahn 2008). The remaining question, then, is how did Southeast Europe compare with membership regimes in the rest of Europe, starting with the early modern period?

As argued by Hoerder, Lucassen and Lucassen (2007), before 1800 in *Western and Southern European dynastic territorial states* (such as Spain, France, the United Kingdom and the German states) religion was much more salient than origin or ethnicity. The inclusion of co-religionists was, therefore, quickly accomplished. Those subjects who deviated from the dominant religion were forced to convert or leave the territory of the state. In the long run, inclusion in the receiving society followed religious (and gendered) class lines. Origin did matter, but only temporarily. The admittance of immigrants to local institutions (e. g. guilds) and the granting of rights took time, but due to an implicit *ius soli* principle, the second generation often encountered the same chances and restrictions, depending on class and gender, as did the rest of the population. The most important barriers, then, were to be found along the identificational axis, only to be overcome by either conversion or migration to states with the 'right' religion. Option 4 in scheme 1, therefore, was virtually impossible because of the enforced religious homogeneity *(cuius regio, eius religio)*.

Exceptions to this rule were small republics and city-states, such as the *Dutch Republic* and the *Venetian city-state*, which opted for a practical form of toleration (Davids, Lucassen 1995, Parker 2006). This membership regime was exceptional but very influential, due to its overall successes in the 16th and 17th centuries. These European regions were characterised by high levels of urbanisation, and by low entrance levels for immigrants. The immigrants they attracted were not required to belong to the official religion of Venice (Catholicism) or of Holland (Protestantism). Even Jews and Armenians, and sometimes Muslims, were welcome. The difference between the two republics lies in Venice's inability to rely solely on free immigrants. As we saw earlier, from the middle of the 16th century its navy employed unfree labour at the oars of its ships, whereas other kind of slave labour was common in this major maritime port as well. Such forced labour was absent in Amsterdam, which depended heavily and exclusively on free migrants. The other early maritime power in Europe, Portugal, depended even more than Venice did on the importation of (African) slaves and might be seen as a subcategory within this group.

In the *Habsburg* and *Russian Empires* membership regimes were also constructed differently from those in Western Europe. Societies were much more segregated according to class (free versus unfree) or estate and ethnicity/language. This was especially true in the Habsburg Empire, where the difference between the German-speaking groups and the Slavonic, Hungarian and Romanian populations was often considerable. This segregation also manifested itself spatially, with different living quarters in cities and in ethnically fairly homogeneous villages. As a consequence of this structural and pluralist segregation, there was a less clear-cut mainstream to adapt to, although the elites of the empire were German speakers. Moreover, migrants often developed parallel societies of their own, as was the case with German-speaking colonists who settled as farmers and artisans in Eastern Europe and who often retained their ethnic identity for a prolonged period (Brandes 2007). In Russia, Germans were also often allowed to retain their cultural, religious and linguistic identity, but over the generations various forms of acculturation did occur, without leading necessarily to full-scale inclusion (Maurer, Auch 2000).

Finally, we distinguish these previous modes of settlement from the *Ottoman model*, which bears a number of similarities to the Dutch-Venetian type. In the Ottoman Empire, patterns of cultural interaction constituted a special case. Its Eurasian territories – the Balkans, parts of Hungary, the south Russian plains, Asia Minor and the cultures of the eastern and southern Mediterranean – formed an integrated migration region. The top levels of the state were composed of voluntary and involuntary elite migrants. As we saw earlier, future administrators were not only recruited from the Muslim population but also from a forced levy *(devşirme)* of young Christian boys who were educated and raised as Muslims and from established ethnically Greek *Phanariots* (Zürcher 1999, Nicolle 1995, Goodwin 1994). The wives of the sultans and of high-ranking administrators came from slave catchment areas – Circassia, North Africa, or a few other areas – and they, too, were highly educated. This bound service elite spoke a *lingua nullius*, the *Ottomanlica*, an artificial language created in order to ensure that all ethnicities were equal within the civil service of the empire.

Ottoman society was split along religious lines (Braude 1982, Masters 2001, Parker 2006), with each group (Jews, Greek orthodox, Armenians etc.), being allowed their own set of judicial rules and institutional settings. As in Southern and Western European dynastic states, it was religion rather than ethnicity that was the master category. The difference was that the Islamic East was less exclusive and more tolerant when it came to religion than was, for example, the competing Habsburg Empire, where Jews and Muslims were sporadically persecuted. Nevertheless, tolerance had its limits. Non-Muslims had a clear subordinate status in society. Whether migrants were easily included in the dominant (Muslim) society, therefore, depended on religion or their readiness to convert to Islam. Those who stuck to their own religion were excluded, especially in the identificational domain. Furthermore, inclusion depended on the legal position of the migrant. Many were taken to the Ottoman Empire as slaves and only gradually, or over generations, could reach a more or less free status. We have to realize that there were many slave-statuses, however, so that the extent and nature (identificational/structural) of exclusion could differ considerably.

This short description of various membership regimes in Eastern Europe before 1800 shows that, the different kinds of institutional barriers notwithstanding, the basics of the settlement model in scheme 1 can still be applied, albeit with caution. In most cases, there was a dominant society in which people, migrants or not, could become (partial) members.

The convergence of membership regimes in Europe since the 19th century

With the emergence of the national state in the 19th century and the shrinking of the Ottoman territory in Southeast Europe, the nation model gained ground and, with it, the greater stress on (alleged) origin (Brubaker 1996, Sundhaussen 2007, Barkey 2009). This was also the case within the Habsburg Empire, in which the romantic notion of a people with a common origin, language, territory – frequently cast in racial terms – began to gain acceptance and became an important divisive element. Thus, in this part of Europe, the national discourse furnished ammunition for a number of conflicts and for the final disintegration of the multi-ethnic empires (Ottoman, Habsburg) that followed immediately before and during the First World War (Barkey, von Hagen 1997).

From the second half of the 19th century, growing nationalist fervour culminated in World War One, when (social, economic and political) citizenship rights became much more salient and, as a consequence, the line between citizens and immigrants was drawn much more firmly.[6] Not only was migration more regulated and monitored, but states also became more interested in the "assimilability" of immigrants.

Conclusion

This article is a plea for more rigorous and systematic comparisons of both migration and settlement processes in general and in Southeast Europe in particular. Which definitions or typologies are helpful in such an exercise of course depends on the research questions. The three approaches to migration (political, social-economic or cultural) all have their strong and weak sides and focus on different aspects of the migration process. Most important is that scholars be explicit in their choice among them. In principle these three approaches do not fundamentally distinguish between free and unfree, or labour versus refugee, migration. Unfortunately, however, such dichotomies too easily lead to myopic and ultimately unsatisfactory analyses. Without denying differences between forms and contexts of migration, such differences should first be charted and compared explicitly before jumping to conclusions.

Recent advances in the study of settlement processes and the refinement of theories of integration can also be of use for Southeast Europe, both in the modern and the early modern period. Notwithstanding differences in state (and broader opportunity) structures, settlement processes have a number of characteristics in common. This article is therefore no plea for a simple application of modern (democratic) nation state models to other regions and periods. The main argument is that a nuanced and thoughtful application of models that distinguish between structural and identificational integration, in the broader institutional context, can be very helpful and an efficient tool to compare apparently very different settlement processes. In this respect, Nancy Green's distinction between divergent and convergent comparisons can be very helpful as well (Green 1997). In doing so, one should be aware of the specific 'membership regimes' in which such developments take place, especially because such regimes define the rules of the game and thereby the nature of barriers that may stand in the way of (full) inclusion.

Finally, it strikes me that insights in migration and area studies could and should be much better integrated. Migration scholars can learn much from specialists on, for example, the Habsburg and Ottoman empires, while theoretical

---

6 Caplan, Torpey 2001, Fahrmeir et al. 2003, Fahrmeir 2007, Rosenberg 2006, Lucassen 1998.

insights from migration studies could be implemented much more systematically. As I hope to have made clear in this article, both areas have a lot to win by gaining more in-depth knowledge of each others expertise.

Literature

Achim, Viorel 2004: The Roma in Romanian History. Budapest: CEU Press.

Alba, Richard D., Victor Nee 2003: Remaking the American Mainstream: Assimilation and Contemporary Immigration. Cambridge/Mass.: Harvard University Press.

Arkel, Dik van 1985: The Growth of the Anti-Jewish Stereotype: An Attempt at a Hypothetical-Deductive Method of Historical Research. In: International Review of Social History 30, 3: 270–306.

Arkel, Dik van 2009: The Drawing of the Mark of Cain. A Social-Historical Analysis of the Growth of Anti-Jewish Stereotypes. Amsterdam: Amsterdam University Press.

Asche, Matthias 2007: Hugenotten in Europa seit dem 16. Jahrhundert. In: Klaus J. Bade, Pieter Emmer, Jochen Oltmer, Leo Lucassen (eds.), Enzyklopädie Migration in Europa vom 17. Jahrhundert bis zur Gegenwart. Paderborn, München: Fink/Schöningh, 635–643.

Asche, Mattias 2008: Krieg, Militär und Migration in der frühen Neuzeit. Einleitende Beobachtungen zum Verhältnis von horizontaler und vertikaler Mobilität in der kriegsgeprägten Gesellschaft Alteuropas im 17. Jahrhundert. In: Matthias Asche et al. (eds.), Krieg, Militär und Migration in der frühen Neuzeit. Münster: Lit, 11–36.

Bairoch, Paul, Jean Batou, Pierre Chèvre 1988: La Population des Villes Européennes: Banque de données et analyse sommaire des résultats, 800–1850 [The population of European cities: Data bank and short summary of results, 800–1850] Geneva: Publications du Centre d'Histoire Economique Internationale de l'Université de Genève.

Bamford, Paul W. 1973: Fighting Ships and Prisons. The Mediterranean Galleys of France in the Age of Louis XIV. London: Oxford University Press.

Barany, Zoltan 1995: The Roma in Macedonia: Ethnic Politics and the Marginal Condition in a Balkan State. In: Ethnic and Racial Studies 18, 3: 515–531.

Barkey, Karen, Mark von Hagen (eds.) 1997: After Empire: Multi-ethnic Societies and Nation-Building: The Soviet Union and the Russian, Ottoman, and Habsburg Empires. Boulder: Westview Press.

Barkey, Karen 2009: Empire of Difference: The Ottomans in Comparative Perspective. Cambridge: Cambridge University Press.

Bavel, Bas van 2007: The Transition in the Low Countries: Wage Labour as an Indicator of the Rise of Capitalism in the Countryside, 1300–1700. In: Past and Present 2: 286–303.

Bayly, C. A. 2004: The Birth of the Modern World 1780–1914. Oxford: Blackwell.

Behar, Cem 1996: Osmanlı İmperatorluğu'nun ve Türkiye'nin Nüfusu, 1500–1927 [The population of the Ottoman Empire and Turkey]. Ankara: T. C. Başbakanlık Devlet İstatistik Enstitüsü.

Bell, Dean Phillip 2008: Jews in the Early Modern World. Plymouth: Rowman & Littlefield.

Benhabib, Seyla 2004: The Rights of Others. Aliens, Residents and Citizens. Cambridge: Cambridge University Press.

Bennassar, Bartolomé, Lucile Bennassar 1989: Les Chrétiens d'Allah: L'histoire extraordinaire des renégats, xvie et xviie siècles. Paris: Perrin.

Bertagna, Federica, Marina Maccari-Clayton 2007: Italien. In: Klaus J. Bade, Pieter Emmer, Jochen Oltmer, Leo Lucassen (eds.), Enzyklopädie Migration in Europa. Vom 17. Jahrhundert bis zur Gegenwart. Paderborn, München: Schöningh, 205–219.

Boerke, Arthur Mark 2009: Conscription in the Habsburg Empire to 1815. In: Donald Stoker, Frederick C. Schneid, Harold D. Blanton (eds.), Conscription in the Napoleonic Era. A Revolution in Military Affairs? London, New York: Routledge, 66–83.

Bosma, Ulbe 2009: European Colonial Soldiers in the Nineteenth Century: Their Role in White Global Migration and Patterns of Colonial Settlement. In: The Journal of Global History 4, 2: 317–336.

Brandes, Detlev 2007: Deutsche Siedler in Russland seit dem 18. Jahrhundert. In: Klaus J. Bade, Pieter Emmer, Leo Lucassen, Jochen Oltmer (eds.), Enzyklopädie Migration in Europa. Vom 17. Jahrhundert bis zur Gegenwart. Paderborn, München: Schöningh/Fink, 514–520.

Braude, Benjamin 1982: Foundation Myths of the Millet System. In: Benjamin Braude, Bernard Lewis (eds.), Christians and Jews in the Ottoman Empire: The Functioning of a Plural Society. New York, London: Holmes & Meier, 69–88.

Brewer, John 1989: The Sinews of Power. War, Money and the English State, 1688–1783. London: Unwin Hyman.

Brubaker, Rogers 1996: Nationalism Reframed: Nationhood and the National Question in the New Europe. Cambridge: Cambridge University Press.

Caplan, Jane, John Torpey (eds.) 2001: Documenting Individual Identity. The Development of State Practices in the Modern World. Princeton: Princeton University Press.

Casares, Aurelio Martín 2000: La Esclavitud en la Granada del Siglo XVI: Género, Raza y Religión. Granada: Universidad de Granada.

Clarence-Smith, William G. 2006: Islam and the Abolition of Slavery. London: Hurst.

Crowe, David M. 2007: A History of the Gypsies of Eastern Europe and Russia. Basingstoke: Palgrave Macmillan.

Dávid, Géza, Pál Fodor (eds.) 2007: Ransom Slavery along the Ottoman Borders: Early Fifteenth–Early Eighteenth Centuries. Leiden, Boston: Brill.

Davids, Karel, Jan Lucassen (eds.) 1995: A Miracle Mirrored: The Dutch Republic in European Perspective. Cambridge: Cambridge University Press.

Davis, Robert 2003: Christian Slaves, Muslim Masters: White Slavery in the Mediterranean, the Barbary Coast, and Italy, 1500–1800. New York: Palgrave Macmillan.

Dursteler, Eric 2003: Venetians in Constantinople: Nation, Identity, and Coexistence in the Early Modern Mediterranean. Baltimore: Johns Hopkins University Press.

Eberl, Immo (ed.) 1983: Die Donauschwaben: Deutsche Siedlungen in Südosteuropa. Stuttgart.

Fahrmeir, Andreas 2007: Citizenship. The Rise and Fall of a Modern Concept. New Haven: Yale University Press.

Fahrmeir, Andreas, Olivier Faron, Patrick Weil (eds.) 2003: Migration Control in the North Atlantic World. The Evolution of State Practices in Europe and the United States from the French Revolution to the Inter-War Period. New York: Berghahn.

Faroqhi, Suraiya 2000: Subjects of the Sultan: Culture and Daily Life in the Ottoman Empire. London: Tauris.

Faroqhi, Suraiya 2004: The Ottoman Empire and the World around it. London: I. B. Tauris.

Fata, Márta 2007: Donauschwaben in Südosteuropa seit der frühen Neuzeit. In: Klaus J. Bade, Pieter C. Emmer, Leo Lucassen, Jochen Oltmer (eds.), Enzyklopädie Migration in Europa vom 17. Jahrhundert bis zur Gegenwart. Paderborn, München, 535–540.

Fisher, Alan 1972: Muscovy and the Black Sea Trade. In: Canadian-American Slavic Studies 6, 4: 582–593.

Flynn, Dennis O., Arturo Giráldez 2004: Path Dependence, Time Lags and the Birth of Globalisation: A Critique of O'Rourke and Williamson. In: European Review of Economic History 8, 1: 81–108.

Forrest, Alan 1990: Soldiers of the French Revolution. Durham, London: Duke University Press.

Frauenstädt, P. 1896: Zur Geschichte der Galeerenstrafe in Deutschland. In: Zeitschrift für die gesamte Strafrechtswissenschaft, 518–546.

Gabaccia, Donna R. 2000: Italy's Many Diasporas. London: UCL Press.

Glete, Jan. 2000: War at Sea, 1500–1650. Maritime Conflicts and the Transformation of Europe. London: Routledge.

Goodwin, Geoffrey 1994: The Janissaries. London: Saqi Books.

Green, Nancy L. 1997: The Comparative Method and Poststructural Structuralism: New Perspectives for Migration Studies. In: Jan Lucassen, Leo Lucassen (eds.), Migration, Migration History, History: Old Perspectives and New Paradigms. Bern et al.: Peter Lang, 57–72.

Hahn, Sylvia 2008: Migration - Arbeit - Geschlecht: Arbeitsmigration in Mitteleuropa vom 17. bis zum Beginn des 20. Jahrhunderts. Göttingen: V & R unipress.

Hochstadt, Steven 1999: Mobility and Modernity: Migration in Germany, 1820–1989. Ann Arbor: University of Michigan Press.

Hoerder, Dirk 2002: Cultures in Contact. World Migrations in the Second Millennium. Durham, London: Duke University Press.

Hoerder, Dirk, Jan Lucassen, Leo Lucassen 2007: Terminologien und Konzepte in der Migrationsforschung. In: Klaus J. Bade, Pieter Emmer, Leo Lucassen, Jochen Oltmer (eds.), Enzyklopädie Migration in Europa vom 17. Jahrhundert bis zur Gegenwart. Paderborn, München: Fink/Schöningh, 28–53.

Hsia, Ronnie Po-Chia, Hartmut Lehmann (eds.) 1995: In and Out of the Ghetto: Jewish-Gentile Relations in Late Medieval and Early Modern Germany. Washington, DC, Cambridge: German Historical Institute and Cambridge University Press.

Inalcik, Halil 1994: The Ottoman State: Economy and Society, 1300–1600. In: Halil Inalcik, Donald Quataert (eds.), An Economic and Social History of the Ottoman Empire, 1300–1914. Cambridge: Cambridge University Press, 9–380.

Kaplan, Benjamin 2007: Divided by Faith: Religious Conflict and the Practice of Toleration in Early Modern Europe. Cambridge Mass.: The Belknap Press of Harvard UP.

Kaser, Karl 1998: Anthropology and the Balkanization of the Balkans. Jovan Cvijic, Dinko Tomašic. In: Ethnologia Balkanica 2: 89–99.

Kaser, Karl 2007: Siedler an der Habsburgischen Militärgrenze seit der frühen Neuzeit. In: Klaus J. Bade, Pieter Emmer, Leo Lucassen, Jochen Oltmer (eds.), Enzyklopädie Migration in Europa vom 17. Jahrhundert bis zur Gegenwart. Paderborn, München: Fink/Schöningh, 985-990.

Kok, Jan 2010: The Family Factor in Migration Decisions. In: Jan Lucassen, Leo Lucassen, Patrick Manning (eds.), Migration History in World History. Multidisciplinary Approaches. Leiden, Boston: Brill, 215–250.

Krstić, Tijana 2009: Illuminated by the Light of Islam and the Glory of the Ottoman Sultanate: Self-Narratives of Conversion to Islam in the Age of Confessionalization. In: Comparative Studies in Society and History 51, 1: 35–63.

Ladányi, János, Iván Szelényi 2003: The "Social Construction" of Roma Ethnicity in Bulgaria, Romania, and Hungary during the Period of Transformation to a Market Society. In: Zeitgeschichte 30, 2: 64–75.

Lucassen, Jan 1987: Migrant Labour in Europe. The Drift to the North Sea. London: Croom Helm.

Lucassen, Leo 1996: Zigeuner. Die Geschichte eines polizeilichen Ordnungsbegriffes in Deutschland 1700–1945. Köln: Böhlau.

Lucassen, Jan, Leo Lucassen 1997: Introduction. In: Jan Lucassen, Leo Lucassen (eds.), Migration, Migration History, History: Old Paradigms and New Perspectives. Bern: Peter Lang, 1–38.

Lucassen, Leo 1998: The Great War and the Origins of Migration Control in Western Europe and the United States (1880–1920). In: Anita Böcker, Kees Groenendijk, Tetty Havinga, Paul Minderhoud (eds.), Regulation of Migration. International Experiences. Amsterdam: Spinhuis, 45–72.

Lucassen, Leo, Wim Willems, Annemarie Cottaar 1998: Gypsies and Other Itinerant Groups. A Socio-Historical Approach. London, New York: MacMillan/St. Martin's Press.

Lucassen, Jan, Erik Jan Zürcher 1999: Introduction: Conscription and Resistance. The Historical Context. In: E. J. Zürcher (ed.), Arming the State. Military Conscription in the Middle East and Central Asia 1775–1925. London, New York: I. B. Tauris.

Lucassen, Leo, Wim Willems 2003: The Weakness of Well-Ordered Societies: Gypsies in Western Europe, the Ottoman Empire, and India, 1400–1914. In: Review 26, 3: 283–314.

Lucassen, Jan, Leo Lucassen 2004: Alte Paradigmen und neue Perspektiven in der Migrationsgeschichte. In: Mathias Beer, Dittmar Dahlmann (eds.), Über die trockene Grenze und über das offene Meer. Binneneuropäische und transatlantische Migrationen im 18. und 19. Jahrhundert. Essen: Campus, 17–44.

Lucassen, Leo 2005: The Immigrant Threat: The Integration of Old and New Migrants in Western Europe since 1850. Urbana, Chicago: The University of Illinois Press.

Lucassen, Leo, David Feldman, Jochen Oltmer (eds.) 2006: Paths of Integration. Migrants in Western Europe (1880–2004), Imiscoe Research. Amsterdam: Amsterdam UP.

Lucassen, Jan, Leo Lucassen 2009: The Mobility Transition Revisited, 1500–1900: What the Case of Europe Can Offer to Global History. In: The Journal of Global History 4, 4: 347–377.

Mallet, M. E., J. R. Hale 1984: The Military Organization of a Renaissance State: Venice, C. 1400 to 1617 Cambridge: Cambridge University Press.

Manning, Patrick 2005: Migration in World History. New York and London: Routledge.

Masters, Bruce 2001: Christians and Jews in the Ottoman Arab World: The Roots of Sectarianism. Cambridge: Cambridge University Press.

Maurer, Trude, Eva-Maria Auch (eds.) 2000: Leben in zwei Kulturen: Akkulturation und Selbstbehauptung von Nichtrussen im Zarenreich. Wiesbaden: Harrassowitz.

McKee, Sally 2008: Domestic Slavery in Renaissance Italy. In: Slavery and Abolition 29, 3: 305–326.

McKeown, Adam 2004: Global Migration 1846–1940. In: Journal of World History 15, 2: 155–189.

Mendes, António Almeida 2008: Les réseaux de la Traite Ibérique dans l'Atlantique Nord (1440–1640). In: Annales HSS 63, 4: 739–768.

Minkov, Anton 2004: Conversion to Islam in the Balkans. Kisve Bahasi Petitions and Ottoman Social Life, 1670–1730. Leiden, Boston: Brill.

Moch, Leslie Page 1992: Moving Europeans. Migration in Western Europe since 1650. Bloomington: Indiana University Press.

Nicolle, David 1983: Armies of the Ottoman Turks 1300–1744. Oxford: Osprey Publishing.

Nicolle, David 1995: The Janissaries. Oxford: Osprey Publishing.

Nolan, Cathal J. 2006: The Age of Wars of Religion, 1000–1650. An Encyclopedia of Global Warfare and Civilization, vol. I. Westport: Greenwood Press.

Parker, Charles H. 2006: Paying for the Privilege: The Management of Public Order and Religious Pluralism in Two Early Modern Societies. In: The Journal of World History, 17: 267–296.

Peters, F. E. 2003: The Monotheists. Jews, Christians and Muslims in Conflict and Competition. vol. I. Princeton: Princeton University Press.

Pfister, Christian 1994: Bevölkerungsgeschichte und historische Demographie 1500–1800. München: Oldenbourg.

Phillips, William D. 2007: Afrikanische Sklaven auf der iberischen Halbinsel in der frühen Neuzeit. In: Klaus J. Bade, Pieter C. Emmer, Leo Lucassen, Jochen Oltmer (eds.), Enzyklopädie Migration in Europa. Vom 17. Jahrhundert bis zur Gegenwart. Paderborn, 364–366.

Porter, Theodore M. 1986: The Rise of Statistical Thinking, 1820–1900. Princeton: Princeton University Press.

Rosenberg, Clifford 2006: Policing Paris. The Origins of Modern Immigration Control between the Wars. Ithaca, London: Cornell University Press.

Rozen, Minna 2002: A History of the Jewish Community in Istanbul: The Formative Years, 1453–1566. Leiden: Brill.

Saunders, A. C. de C. M. 1982: A Social History of Black Slaves and Freedmen in Portugal, 1441–1555. Cambridge: Cambridge University Press.

Scammell, G. V. 1981: The World Encompassed: The First European Maritime Empires, C. 800–1650. Berkeley: University of California Press.

Scott, James C. 1998: Seeing Like a State: How Certain Schemes to Improve the Human Condition have Failed. New Haven: Yale University Press.

Scott, James C. 2009: The Art of Not Being Governed. An Anarchist History of Upland Southeast Asia. New Haven: Yale University Press.

Stewart, Michael 1997: The Time of the Gypsies. Boulder: Westview Press.

Sundhaussen, Holm 2007: Südosteuropa. In: Klaus J. Bade, Pieter Emmer, Leo Lucassen, Jochen Oltmer (eds.), Enzyklopädie Migration in Europa. Vom 17. Jahrhundert bis zur Gegenwart. Paderborn, München. 285–313.

Tilly, Charles 1978: Migration in Modern European History. In: William H. McNeill, B. Adams (eds.), Human Migration. Patterns and Policies. Bloomington: Indiana UP, 48–72.

Tilly, Charles 1990: Coercion, Capital and European States, AD 990–1992. Cambridge: Cambridge UP.

Tinhorão, José Ramos 1988: Os Negros em Portugal. Lisbon: Editorial Caminho.

Todorov, Nikolai 1983: The Balkan City 1400–1900. Seattle, London: University of Washington Press.

Toledano, Ehud 1998: Slavery and Abolition in the Ottoman Middle East. Seattle: University of Washington Press.

Torpey, John 2000: The Invention of the Passport. Surveillance, Citizenship and the State. Cambridge: Cambridge University Press.

Vries, Jan de 1984: European Urbanization 1500–1800. London: Methuen.

Weber, Eugen 1976: Peasants into Frenchmen: The Modernization of Rural France, 1870–1914. Stanford: Stanford University Press.

Zanden, Jan Luiten van 2008: The Road to the Industrial Revolution: Hypotheses and Conjectures about the Medieval Origins of the "European Miracle". In: Journal of Global History 3, 3: 337–359.

Zhelyazkova, Antonia 2002: Islamization in the Balkans as a Historiographical Problem: The Southeast-European Perspective. In: Fikret Adanir, Suraiya Faroqhi (eds.), The Ottomans and the Balkans. A Discussion of Historiography. Leiden: Brill, 223–266.

Zürcher, E. J. (ed.) 1999: Arming the State: Military Conscription in the Middle East and Central Asia, 1775-1925. London: Tauris.

Families Immigrating from Bulgaria to Turkey Since 1878

Seher Cesur-Kılıçaslan, Istanbul, R. Günsel Terzioğlu, Ankara

Abstract

The importance of migration can be understood by looking at Turkey's social structure. Anatolia is a historical migration centre. During the foundation period, the Ottoman State implemented a settlement policy from the east to the west in order to increase the Balkan population and maintain social order. This policy helped to Turkify conquered lands by importing large groups of people from Anatolia. Bulgaria is the Balkan country which has the most concentrated Turkish population. Immigrants from Bulgaria revert to the customs they had left; however, this does not mean that they do not also manifest differences. After they emigrated to Bulgaria, they lived in interaction with a different culture for centuries. Some family lifestyle practices have been found to differentiate Bulgarian immigrants from Anatolian natives. Some of these practices are distinct among immigrants who arrived in specific years, while others remain consistent regardless of the immigrants' time of arrival. Previous studies indicate that the differences between Bulgarian immigrants and local families can be analyzed with regard to the following aspects: "practices regarding marriage", "women's status", "level of education", "economic status" and "adaptation to the community". Thus, Bulgarian immigrant families who came from different places and settle in Turkey will be considered in terms of these aspects.

Introduction

Migration is an ancient phenomenon of human history. It is defined as the change of one's living place and social environment for another, unfamiliar community. The purpose of migration may be to improve one's life opportunities under new conditions, or to escape from natural, economic, political or other pressures. What distinguishes migration from other manners of replacement in a community is the fact that the migrant replaces her/his former society and economy with other ones in the new place (Akkayan 1979: 23).

It is generally thought that migration is one of the basic elements of economic, political and social dynamics shaping the world since the end of the 1990s. There is a consensus among social scientists that migration will have new dimensions in the 21st century (Toksöz 2006: 1, 11), and some claim that migration and migrants are highly important foreign and domestic policy issues (Zlotnik 1999).

The importance of migration can be well understood by looking at Turkey's social structure. Above all, Anatolia is a historical migration centre. After Turkish people immigrated into the region, migration movements both from inside to outside and vice versa continued, resulting in today's social structure. According to Akkayan (1979: 23), immigration and immigrants have been among the leading issues in Turkey during the last three centuries. During its foundation stage, the Ottoman State implemented a settlement policy from the east to the west in order to increase the Balkan population and maintain social order. This policy helped to Turkify conquered lands by importing large groups of people from Anatolia. While Bulgaria is the Balkan country which now has the most concentrated Turkish population, immigration from Bulgaria to Anatolia began in 1806 with the outbreak of the Ottoman-Russian War, and individual or mass migration has continued sporadically from 1878 until today (Doğanay 1997: 197).

The history of the Bulgarian Turks is in one sense a long history of migration (Şimşir 1985: 47–48). During the enlargement period of the Ottoman Empire, Turkish people emigrated to the conquered Balkan lands. The situation was reversed later in the regression and dissolution periods, when Turkish people living in the lands which were lost had to resettle in the shrinking Ottoman territories. However, despite the migrations, the Turkish population continued to live in some of the mentioned areas (Doğanay 1997: 97). Even after the withdrawal of the Ottoman Empire from the Balkans and the empire's dissolution, large masses of Turks continued to live in some of these lands. The immigration of Turkish families from Bulgaria to Anatolia has continued since the 19th century. Immigration movements increased or decreased at various times, but never ceased. The issue of Turkish immigrants from Bulgaria is still of current interest (Şimşir 1985: 47–48).

Immigration from Bulgaria constituted 48.0 % (790 717 people) of total immigration movements into Turkey during the Republican Era, and immigrants from Bulgaria still take the lead among total immigrants arriving in Turkey (Doğanay 1997: 97). Thus, it is preferable to study immigrants from Bulgaria specifically in order to better understand their internal dynamics and their impact on the overall social fabric of Turkey.

Memoğlu-Süleymanoğlu (2004: 1) divides all Bulgarian migratory events into four sub-groups by the dates they took place: immigration before the Ottoman-Russian War of 1877–1878; immigration due to the Ottoman-Russian War of 1877–1878; immigration following the Balkan Wars of 1912–1913; and finally immigration that took place during the Republican Era. Doğanay (1997: 197) considers immigration events during the Republican Period in four sub-groups: during the first stage, a total of 218 998 people arrived, 75 877 being subject to the settlement procedures. The other 143 121 immigrated independently to Turkey until 1949, following the conclusion of the Turkish-Bulgarian Residence Agreement signed in 1925. Another 154 393 people immigrated to and settled in Turkey as settling immigrants due to the forced migration and deportation imposed by Bulgarian authorities between the years 1950 and 1952. Between 1968 and 1979 another 116 521 immigrants came from Bulgaria to Turkey within the framework of the Turkey-Bulgaria Agreement on Close Relatives Migration. According to this agreement, close relatives of a majority of the immigrant families arriving between 1950 and 1952 were allowed to freely move from Bulgaria to Turkey, so that scattered families could be reunited. The latest immigration movement from Bulgaria began in 1989, when Turkish-origin Muslim inhabitants of Bulgaria were forced by the Bulgarian Government to emigrate to Turkey. As a result, within only 3 months, Turkey had to absorb the most intensive and forced migration in Europe since the period immediately following World War II. During these three months 226 863 people came to Turkey as independent immigrants. Since then, the number of independent immigrants who intermittently arrived in Turkey reached 73 957 by 1995 (Doğanay 1997: 197). Around 100 000 immigrants who arrived in and after 1989 returned to Bulgaria later due to reasons such as not being satisfied with their place of settlement, economic challenges and regaining their rights in Bulgaria (Eren 1993: 373).

International migration does not necessarily result in interaction of culturally different communities. As in the case of Britons in Australia or Austrians in Germany, some immigrants are hardly different from the host community into which they are accepted (Castles, Miller 2008: 21). In fact, immigrants from Bulgaria revert to the customs their ancestors had left; however, this does not mean that they do not demonstrate differences. After they emigrated to Bulgaria, Turks kept living in interaction with a different culture for centuries. From time to time, they were exposed to pressure due to their religion, language and traditions. It must be remembered that, as Sloane (1987: 40) suggests, the Balkans host such an unusual mosaic of Europe, in that a myriad of religions and nationalities are represented there. In fact, Sloane (1987: 40) states that the Balkans resembles a large anthropology museum due to the variety of nationalities and religions present. Thus, Turkish groups in the Balkans can be expected to differ from the Anatolian communities because they lived as part of such a sophisticated mosaic, or "anthropological museum", for centuries. It is therefore not surprising that immigrants from Bulgaria formed a culturally distinct society upon their return to Anatolia. Yet it is also obvious that such a difference will bring about interactions. Türkarslan (1997) draws attention to this interaction and says that there is still an acculturation process between the immigrants and local people with the same cultural roots.

From 1878 up to date, there has been regular research on immigrants from Bulgaria to Turkey during various periods. These investigations show that immigrants from Bulgaria, although exhibiting Turkish cultural characteristics, bring their own particular cultural fabric and lifestyle. Some family lifestyle practices were found to differentiate Bulgarian immigrants from the natives. Some of these practices are distinct among immigrants who arrived in specific years, while others remain consistent, regardless of the immigrants' time of arrival. Previous studies indicate that the differences between Bulgarian immigrants and local families can be analyzed under the following topics: "practices regarding marriage", "women's status", "level of education level", "economic status" and "adaptation to the community". Thus, Bulgarian immigrant families who came from different places and settle in Turkey should be considered in terms of these topics.[1]

Practices concerning marriage

Seeking an immigrant prospective spouse

According to research carried out by Kocacık (1978) on people immigrating from Bulgaria to Turkey between the years 1878–1900, these people, during the pre-marital stage, did not necessarily look for immigrants as prospective spouses. On the other hand, Arı (1960), in his study carried out on immigrants arriving between the years 1950 and 1951, found that these immigrants preferred to marry other immigrants even though people in Turkey are Muslim as well. Arı (1960) explains this as a tradition of endogamy which they acquired in Bulgaria because for centuries they refused to marry Christians there. The study carried out by Özönder (1979) on immigrants, which focuses mainly on those arriving between 1950, 1951 and 1953, revealed that girls marry native Turkish boys while vice versa is not prevalent. This is related to the fact that the proportion of women in business among immigrants is higher than that among the native population. Native families living in the area do not want their daughters to work. The immigrant men marry immigrant girls who work because they think that they cannot make a living on a single income.

Research conducted by Türkarslan (1997) on immigrants arriving between 1950 and 1951, 1970–1978 and 1989–1990 also reveals an interesting fact in this area: although groups that immigrated to Turkey between 1950 and 1978 are in great harmony with the local society, marriage with native girls has not been seen at all. Dimitrova's (2002) study of immigrants arriving in 1989 confirms that immigrants prefer marrying amongst themselves. A father who wants his

---

[1] Arı 1960, Kocacık 1978, Özönder 1979, Erdentuğ 1980, Toğrol 1989, Pakdemir 1992, Türkarslan 1997, Dimitrova 2002, Zhelyazkova 2002, Kıroğlu 2002, Çağlayan 2005, Cesur-Kılıçaslan 2006.

son to marry an immigrant girl explains his case as follows: "I want him to do so because they are identical with us. We have everything in common. But native girls and women do not work; only men are in business." He adds that his son can marry an immigrant from any other European country. Dimitrova (2002) points out that Bulgarian immigrants, like those coming from the other Balkan States, marry European immigrants only. These people indicate divergent cuisines as another reason for preferring marriage within immigrant groups.

Some of the immigrants arriving in Turkey between 1878 and 1900 married non-immigrants; thus it can be suggested that the gap between the natives and immigrants was not so wide to prevent their co-existence as a consequence of the acculturation process. As for the immigrants arriving from 1950 to the present, it is understood that boys are not allowed to marry native girls, largely due to economic concerns. Immigrants who had to leave all their properties in Bulgaria can start a totally new life only if all capable family members work. The research concerning the immigrants who arrived in Turkey between 1878 and 1900 was conducted after a long time elapsed. Such a long time increased the influences of the acculturation process. Also all members of the group on which research was conducted were probably born in Turkey although they came from Bulgaria. It makes sense to consider this as a factor affecting the research result. On the other hand, studies of immigrants arriving since 1950 were carried out only shortly after their arrival. Doubtlessly, other effects of the acculturation process will come to light if research continues.

Lack of kinship ties as a prerequisite for prospective spouses

Bulgarian immigrants are attentive not to marry their relatives on the maternal or paternal side. According to Özönder (1979), the majority of people who arrived in 1950, 1951 and 1953 avoided marrying relatives of their parents back to the 7th and even 9th generation. Certainty of a lack of kinship tie is regarded as a marital prerequisite among them. The research carried out by Türkarslan (1997) on those who immigrated from Bulgaria between 1950–1951, 1970–1978 and 1989–1990 revealed that these groups pay particular attention to the absence of blood kinship between the spouses. Similarly, in a study carried out by Cesur-Kılıçaslan (2006) regarding immigrants that arrived after 1989 and later, it was found out that only 0.9 % of the spouses are blood related. In those cases, it was interesting to note that the spouses could not express their closeness by using the common kinship terms. According to the results of the Family Structure Survey 2006 (T. C. Başbakanlık Türkiye İstatistik Kurumu, 2006), in Turkey among the married people over the age of 18, the rate of kin marriage was 20.9 %. This ratio decreased to 4.8 % in western areas; however increased to 40.4 % in South Eastern Anatolia Region. These remarkable differences in the kin marriage rates may be the result of ethnic, cultural and religious dissimilarities in Turkey. If this rate was high in Anatolia during the period when Bulgarian immigrants moved to Bulgaria, the immigrants may have avoided this sort of marriage due to their acculturation in the Balkans. In Cesur-Kılıçaslan's (2006) research, relevant questions provoked responses that show that immigrants also find kin marriage immoral. Functional or structural causes of such reactions can be investigated separately.

Family type and structure of kinship in extended families

Arı's (1960) research of 1950 and 1951 found that the number of immigrant families with two to five members increased while that of the families with six to ten members decreased as they arrived in Turkey. Moreover, Arı (1960) showed that the custom of living with the husband's parents declined, and couples more frequently chose to live with the wife's parents when they arrived in Turkey. Another study conducted by Özönder (1979) on a group whose majority is composed of immigrants who arrived in 1950, 1951 and 1953, found that 81.13% of married children adopt a nuclear family type while the rest of the sample group represent "temporary extended families" living together with parents of either husband or wife. Türkarslan (1997) found in his research that most of the immigrant families of 1950–1951, 1970–1978 and 1989–1990 (except for farmers) had had a nuclear family type before they immigrated and thus maintained the same after immigration. According to the research carried out by Toğrol (1989) in 1989, parents and single sister/brother, if any, of either bride or groom, depending on the case, join the new family in immigrant communities. Consequently, a new extended family takes shape like among rural families, where the bride joins the groom's family. The case of immigrant families differs from the rural example in that it is not clear which new family the elders join, and it depends on the specific case. According to Dimitrova's (2002) study about immigrants arriving in 1989, immigrants can adapt easily to the Anatolian marital practices upon their arrival in Turkey. In Turkey, young couples usually live separately from their parents, even in rented flats. In Cesur-Kılıçaslan's (2006) study of immigrants who arrived in and after 1989, it was found that 72.9 % of the immigrants live in nuclear families and 76.7 % of the extended families live with the husband's relatives.

Research shows that most of the immigrant families in Turkey are nuclear families. As Toğrol (1989) also emphasizes, the kinship structure among immigrant families differs from that of native families. Among Bulgarian immigrants, joining the household of the wife's relatives is as common as living with the husband's parents. Though this result can be explained by the improved status of women in immigrant families, further specific investigations are required for the clearer understanding of the issues that determine these arrangements.

Decision regarding choice of marriage partner
Kocacık's (1978) research showed that among immigrants of 1878–1900, marriage partner selection was based on the parents' decisions. Nonetheless, the young man's preference is now influential in choosing his marriage partner. In the case of girls, first the father's opinion is decisive, followed by the mother's and girl's opinions. Özönder's (1979) research demonstrates that 58.49 % of the immigrants of 1950, 1951 and 1953 made their own decision about marriage partner selection. According to the research carried out by Türkarslan (1997), immigrants of 1950–51, 1970–78 and 1989–90 decided on their own marriage partner, later approved by the parents. The study shows that immigrant families' tolerance of girls and boys meeting is an important factor that enhances the possibility for young people to choose their own marriage partner. The research carried out by Cesur-Kılıçaslan (2006) also revealed that 49.3 % of the immigrants arriving in and after 1989 married "upon their own decision, approved by parents" and 30.8 % did so "upon their own decision only".

Differences were identified regarding marriage partner selection between the immigrants arriving from 1878 until 1900 and those arriving since 1950. Again, this can be explained with the longer period of time that elapsed after arrival of the early group and implications of the acculturation between the generations that were born in Turkey and those who were not. Furthermore, the practices regarding marriage partner selection in Turkey during the period between 1878 and 1900 might have been the same in Bulgaria as those groups immigrated in that period of time.

Women's status in the family

Participants in Arı's (1960) study of immigrants who arrived in 1950 and 1951 reported that it is compulsory for women in Turkey to work. According to the results of Pakdemir's (1992) research on immigrants arriving after 1989, very few women report a desire to be housewives. In the research conducted by Türkarslan (1997), it was found that immigrant women who arrived between 1950–51, 1970–78 and 1989–1990 usually worked. Kıroğlu's (2002) data regarding immigrants who arrived in and after 1989 show that the patriarchal approach towards women's responsibilities such as housework and childcare was still valid, but that philosophy has partially changed. The report shows that women are not prevented from studying and working and a majority of men help with childcare and housework "as much as they can" when their women are away. But childcare and housekeeping still remain women's primary responsibilities. According to the study carried out by Zhelyazkova (2002) pertaining to immigrants who arrived in 1989, one of the obvious differences between immigrants and the local population is that an immigrant woman is an equal family member who is well-educated and has a profession with certain qualifications. The research carried out by Cesur-Kılıçaslan (2006) on immigrants who arrived in and after 1989 found that 53.8 % of women work and 12.2 % are retired. The same study observed the manner of certain family practices such as preparing meals, cleaning the house, washing dishes and laundry, ironing, shopping, regulating domestic budget and childcare. Considering the task distribution of all these activities in families, it seems that traditional task distribution is dominant in both immigrant and native families. Furthermore, among immigrants a higher participation rate of other family members in common responsibilities implies that immigrant families adopted a more modern task distribution. Another implication of these findings is that the process of acculturation is not yet complete, since both groups have not gone through a long-lasting and intensive interaction. The fact that the level of education of both sexes among immigrants is high and a majority of women are in business might be the reason for this.

The effectiveness of family members in issues regarding "decision making" was assessed in Cesur-Kılıçaslan's (2006) research. Decision-making methods within the family were examined in the cases of girls' and boys' education, marriage partner selection and marriage; visitation of the spouses' relatives; holiday locations; holiday activities; the person/persons to be met; people to visit; location and features of lodgings; and items on which to spend family income. Bearing in mind all issues regarding domestic decision making, the fact that members of immigrant families take their own decisions and make other decisions in the company of their spouses or families to a greater extent than native people implies that the immigrants have a more modern family type.

Level of education

A study by Arı (1960) on immigrants arriving in 1950 and 1951 reported that the number of literate individuals and the number of individuals who can only read was quite high among immigrants during the period when the literacy rate was low in Turkey. In Özönder's (1979) study of a sample of immigrants, the majority of whom arrived in 1950, 1951 and 1953, it was apparent that immigrants attach a lot of importance to higher education. In other research carried out by Türkarslan (1997) regarding immigrants in Bursa who arrived in Turkey between 1950–1951, 1970–1978 and 1989–1990, data show that 70.0 % of men and

70.7 % of women were graduates of secondary schools. In the overall population of Bursa, while the ratio of people with only primary school in males in 25–44 age group was 55.0 %, it was 2.0 % among Bulgarian immigrants. Similarly, among men between 25–44 years old, 30.0 % of the native men are high school graduates, while the rate was 70.0 % among their immigrant counterparts.

Among immigrants, it was also found that the education level of children is higher than that of their parents. Furthermore, it was found that the number of girls who graduated from high school or university was higher than that of their parents while the number of boys who graduated from high school or university was less than that of their parents. According to this finding, it was deduced that children of the families which immigrated to Turkey between 1950–1951 and 1970–1978 preferred employment over education. According to the statistics kept by the State Ministry in charge of the immigrants coming from Bulgaria in 1989 (İlgili Devlet Bakanlığı İstatistik Bilgileri, 1990), the majority of immigrants received education, and those who graduated from secondary school constitute a majority. Toğrol's (1989) study of immigrants arriving in 1989 found that more than half of them obtained an associate's degree or undergraduate degree. Similarly, Pakdemir's (1992) study carried out on immigrants arriving in 1989 revealed that 72.56 % of them received secondary education. In the research carried out by Cesur-Kılıçaslan (2006) regarding immigrants who arrived in and after 1989, it was concluded that 85.5 % of women and 89.1 % of men received secondary education.

The occurrence of a higher level of education among Bulgarian immigrants than that of the active local population can be explained by the fact that the period of compulsory education in Bulgaria was longer than that in Turkey in the years when the research was conducted. Additionally, education may have been promoted as a way of overcoming the minority complex.

Economic status

Arı's (1960) study of immigrants of 1950 and 1951 indicates that immigrant families usually belong to the middle class, considering the overall status of their homes and furnishing. Arı (1960) showed that their social status was higher than that of the social environment in which they lived in Istanbul. Many of them save money in Turkey. 50 % and 68 % of the immigrants in Bursa and Istanbul, respectively, said that all eligible family members must work. Türkarslan (1997) found that the number of families with two working persons is highest (44.0 %) among those arriving in 1950–51, 1970–78 and 1989–1990, followed by families in which from one to three persons work. Türkarslan (1997) also found that those reporting a single working person in the family were among the earlier immigrants. Most of the families have a medium income level and spend their income sparingly to buy or build houses; furthermore, even families given a house by the government bought their own house within five years. 94 % of Bulgarian immigrant families live in their own private houses. In the study carried out by Pakdemir (1992) regarding immigrants who arrived after 1989, 28.92 % could buy their own houses despite the short period between their arrival and the research time. According to Dimitrova's (2002) study of immigrants who arrived in 1989, these people attach considerable importance to having private homes, and they accept many difficulties to achieve this end. Dimitrova (2002) relates immigrants' efforts to acquire their own homes with a belief they imported from Bulgaria: "Whoever does not have or build one's own house is of low social level and marginal." According to the research carried out by Cesur-Kılıçaslan (2006) regarding immigrants arriving in and after 1989, dual income households make up 43.9 % of the sample and single income households are 24.4 % of the sample. When examining the native population, 44.3 % are single income households and 39.3 % of those families have two wage earners. 90.5 % of immigrants and 69.7 % of the native people are homeowners.

Social Solidarity and Support Funds were invested in the construction of 23 495 houses in 17 provinces all over Turkey for immigrants forced from Bulgaria in 1989 (T. C. Cumhurbaşkanlığı Devlet Denetleme Kurulu, 2006). Those applying for houses, depositing a certain amount of money and being nominated for a house, were given long-term loans (Cesur-Kılıçaslan 2006). Immigrants may have been motivated to own a home because of the hardships of being uprooted and being forced to restart life after the heavy loss. Home ownership may be seen as a way to gain permanent residency in Turkey (Cesur-Kılıçaslan, Terzioğlu 2008).

Adaptation to the community

Emigrating to Turkey has been a desire of ethnic Turkish Bulgarians for many years. But as Türkarslan (1997) has stressed, Bulgarian immigrants faced relative poverty after their arrival in Turkey. Thus, both men and women had to work in order to overcome this situation, which facilitated their adaptation to the Turkish socio-cultural environment.

Those with relatives and close friends in Turkey could escape the shock experienced by those staying in refugee camps or shelters donated by foreign families, and thus they could easily restart their lives. Moreover, aid centrally administered by the Turkish government and supported by international organizations contributed to mitigating the effects of the shock that immigrants went through as a result of leaving their lands, properties and acquaintances (Zhelyazkova 2002).

On the other hand, Erdentuğ's (1980) research indicates that despite their Turkish origin, Bulgarian immigrants regard themselves as a minority in Turkey as a result of the environment in which they had grown up. Also, their ethnocentric understanding led them to consider their own values superior to those of the "native people". In contrast, local people showed an ethnocentric attitude by underestimating the immigrants' values and considering their own ones to be superior. Türkarslan (1997), in her immigrant studies of 1950–51, 1970–78 and 1989–90, found that immigrants had incompatible relationships with local people, but that such incompatibility did not turn into visible conflict but rather remained as mutual discomfort that gradually disappeared as immigrants harmonized their lives with the vicinity.

The most obvious difference between early and late immigrants is the fact that those immigrating between 1951 and 1978 could adapt to both target country and region, reach an order of life and regard themselves as integral parts of Turkey in that period of time. Thus, the newcomers consider the early immigrants as native people. The first generation that was born in Bulgaria could adapt to their new location to a considerable extent in the course of time, while their children born in Turkey could entirely adapt to the Turkish socio-cultural structure. Immigrants arriving between 1989 and 1990 restricted their relationships with the local people around them and faced some challenges in adapting to the new locality except for their participation in economic activities. In the research carried out by Zhelyazkova (2002) regarding immigrants who arrived after 1989, the social harmonization process of the immigrants was found to be closely connected with their having an occupation and income level. Having higher education or vocational high school training is the factor that enables the fastest and smoothest transition to social and economic harmony. Immigrants with sought-after occupations in Turkey (such as technician, engineer, health staff, etc.) could easily find a job and start their own business once they had established a regular life that could meet their daily needs. The ones facing the greatest problems are those with only a primary or secondary school education and immigrants from rural areas. They can hardly find a good and reliable job. Still, the unemployment rate sharply decreased among Bulgarian immigrants because they accepted working conditions refused by the local population. In Çağlayan's (2005) study of immigrants arriving in and after 1989, it was found that native people and the immigrants in the region had a tendency each to regard their own values as superior to those of the others. According to the research carried out by Cesur-Kılıçaslan (2006), 84.6 % of immigrants arriving in and after 1989 are happy to live together with the native population, and 91.8 % of the native population are glad to live together with immigrants. This implies that the native people are tolerant and show little resistance against the acculturation process.

Conclusion

The studies carried out regarding family-related issues between immigrants arriving in Turkey from 1878 to the present reveal that there are differences in practices. Some of them vary depending on the year that immigrants arrived in Turkey while others remain valid and vivid regardless of the arrival date.

While immigrants who arrived between 1878 and 1900 did not insist on immigrant spouses, those arriving since 1950 consider this a prerequisite for marriage. This finding can be explained by the fact that research regarding those arriving after 1950 was done shortly after their arrival. For yet another survey of 19th century immigrants it is probable that the participants were not among the first generation of immigrants. Many years elapsed after the migration, and the process of acculturation with the native population in the region may have influenced the findings. Among the 19th century immigrants, the decision on a suitable marriage partner was first made by family elders and the boy's opinion. For girls, the parents' decision was paramount. For the immigrants arriving since 1950, however, it was common for individuals to choose their marriage partners themselves. Such a differentiation can again be explained by the longer time that elapsed since arrival of the first group in comparison to the time elapsed since the second group's arrival. In addition, we must bear in mind that the practices of marriage partner selection in Turkey in the 19th century may have been identical to the ones in Bulgaria.

Bulgarian immigrants attach importance to not selecting spouses from among their relatives, regardless of their arrival date. They shun kin marriage and consider it totally immoral, so we assume that this will remain unchanged in the next generations as well. Functional or structural causes of such reactions need to be investigated separately in order to obtain more information about the subject. The importance Bulgarian immigrants attach to education can also be taken into consideration, since it may not only increase the number of those taking the marriage decision for themselves but also discourage kin marriage.

Immigrants usually live in nuclear families. In terms of family structure, living together with a wife's relatives is as common as living with the husband's parents. No difference was found regarding immigrants' family characteristics depending on the years in which the research was conducted. However, these characteristics may have changed for new generations as more years elapse after their arrival. Therefore, we think that the research must be repeated on the first generation immigrants who can be contacted and on the new generations who were born in Turkey.

The education level among Bulgarian immigrants is higher than that of the native population. Despite the probability that children who had to immigrate during their school years decreased this rate, factors such as economic shortcomings, lack of official documents for school enrollment and their inadequate Turkish language skills may have prevented them from carrying on their education.

Regardless of their arrival date, immigrant women have usually worked outside the home. Since particularly the first generation had to leave all their property in Bulgaria, all eligible family members are expected to gain income for the family. In subsequent generations, women married to local men may not enjoy employment outside. This is a separate issue of research that deserves particular attention.

All assessments made so far show that the most notable difference between the immigrant and native families is that in immigrant families women have more economic authority and responsibility. This, in turn, increases the rate of their participation in all decision making processes in the family. Also, the sharing of their traditional responsibilities with the other family members mitigates their burden.

Literature

Arı, Oğuz 1960: Bulgaristanlı Göçmenlerin İntibakı. 1950–1951 Senelerinde Bulgaristan'dan Tehcir Edilen Türk Göçmenlerinden Yalnız Bursa'da Hürriyet Mahallesinde ve İstanbul'da Taşlıtarla'da İskan Edilenlerin İntibakı ile İlgili Sosyolojik Problemler [The adaptation of Bulgarian immigrants. The sociological problems related to the adaptation of those inhabiting only in Bursa Hürriyet neighbourhood and Istanbul Taşlıtarla among the Turkish immigrants who were deported from Bulgaria between 1950 and 1951]. Ankara: Rekor Matbaası.

Akkayan, Taylan 1979: Göç ve Değişme [Migration and Change]. Istanbul: Istanbul University Edebiyat Fakültesi Yayın No. 2573.

Castles, Stephen, Mark J. Miller 2008: Göçler Çağı. Modern Dünyada Uluslararası Göç Hareketleri [The age of migration. International population movements in the modern world]. Istanbul: Istanbul Bilgi University Press.

Cesur-Kılıçaslan, Seher 2006: İnegöl Bölgesi'nde Yaşayan Bulgaristan Göçmeni ve Yerli Ailelerin Aile Yapısı [The family structure of the Bulgarian immigrants and the local residents living in Inegol region]. Ankara: Hacettepe University, PhD thesis.

Cesur-Kılıçaslan, Seher, R. Günsel Terzioğlu 2008: The Effects of Immigration and Emigration on the Family Structure in Turkey. In: The International Journal of the Humanities 6, 1: 239–244.

Çağlayan, Savaş 2005: Göç Yağmurdan Kaçarken Doluya Tutulmak. 1989 ve Sonrası Bulgaristan Göçmeni Türkler Üzerine Yapılmış Bir Çalışma [Out of the frying pan of migration into the fire. A study on the Turkish people emigrating from Bulgaria in 1989 and post-1989]. In: Erişim, 28. 3. 2005, URL: http://155.223.1.158/edergi/sosyoloji/2004/s1213/5.pdf.

Dimitrova, Donka 2002: Between Adaptation and Nostalgia: The Bulgarian Turks in Turkey. Bulgarian Turkish Immigrants of 1989 in the Republic of Turkey. In: Erişim, 4. 2. 2002, URL: http://www.omda.bg/imir/studies/nostalgia_2.html.

Doğanay, Filiz 1997: Türkiye'ye Göçmen Olarak Gelenlerin Yerleşimi [The settlement of those who came to Turkey as immigrants]. In: II. Ulusal Sosyoloji Kongresi [2nd National Sociology Congress]. Toplum ve Göç [Society and Migration]. Ankara: Devlet İstatistik Enstitüsü Matbaası, 194–205.

Erdentuğ, Aygen 1980: Bursa Pamuk İpliği Sanayindeki Bir Fabrikada Çalışan Bir Grup Kadın İşçinin Fabrika İçi ve Aileyle Olan Sosyal İlişkileri [The social relationships of a group of women workers, who are employed in a factory of cotton yarn in Bursa, within their families and within the factory]. Ankara: H.Ü.M.S.E.F. PhD thesis.

Eren, Halit 1993: Cumhuriyet Döneminde Göç ve İltica [Migration and asylum in the Republic period]. In: Tarih Boyunca Türklerde İnsani Değerler ve İnsan Hakları [Human values and human rights for Turkish people throughout history]. Istanbul: Türk Kültürüne Hizmet Vakfı, vol. 3: 357–381.

İlgili Devlet Bakanlığı İstatistik Bilgileri 1990: [The statistical data obtained from the related ministry of state]. Ankara.

Kıroğlu, M. Meryem 2002: Bulgaristan Göçmeni Kadınların İş Yaşamına İlişkin Tutum ve Davranışları [The attitudes and behaviours of female immigrants from Bulgaria towards business life]. Ankara: Ankara University, MA thesis.

Kocacık, Faruk 1978: Bulgaristan'dan Anadolu'ya Yönelik Göçler (1878–1900) Karşılaştırmalı Yerli ve Göçmen Köyü Monografileri [Migrations from Bulgaria to Anatolia (1878-1900). Comparative native and immigrant village monographs]. Ankara: Hacettepe University, PhD thesis.

Memoğlu-Süleymanoğlu, Hayriye 2004: Edebiyatımızda Balkan Türklerinin Türkiye'ye Göçleri [The migration of Balkan Turks to Turkey in our literature]. In: EJOS VII, 4: 1–53.

Özönder, M. Cihat 1979: Manisa İli Salihli İlçesi Kurtuluş Mahallesinde Meskün Göçmenlerin Sosyal Bünyeye İntibakları [The adaptation of the immigrants living in Manisa, Salihli district, Kurtuluş neighbourhood, to the social structure]. Ankara: Hacettepe University, PhD thesis.

Pakdemir, Hasan 1992: Bulgaristan'dan Gelen Göçmenlerin Türkiye'nin Sosyal Yapısına Etkileri (Eğitim, İstihdam, İskan) [The effects of the immigrants from Bulgaria on Turkey's social structure (education, employment, housing)]. Istanbul: Istanbul University, MA thesis.

Sloane, William, M. 1987: Bir Tarih Laboratuvarı Balkanlar [A history laboratory: The Balkans]. Istanbul: Süreç Yayınları.

Şimşir, Bilal N. 1985: Bulgaristan Türkleri ve Göç Sorunu [Bulgarian Turks and the migration question]. In: Bulgaristan'da Türk Varlığı [Existence of Turks in Bulgaria]. Ankara: Türk Tarih Kurumu Basımevi, 47–66.

T. C. Başbakanlık Türkiye İstatistik Kurumu, 2006: Aile Yapısı Araştırması 2006 [Family structure survey 2006]. Türkiye İstatistik Kurumu Matbaası, Ankara: Yayın no: 3046. In: Erişim, 13. 2. 2010, URL: http://www.aile.gov.tr/images/arastirmalar/AileYapısı.pdf.

T. C. Cumhurbaşkanlığı Devlet Denetleme Kurulu 2006: T. C. Cumhurbaşkanlığı Devlet Denetleme Kurulu. Toplu Konut İdaresi Başkanlığının 2002, 2003 ve 2004 Yılları Eylem ve İşlemlerinin Araştırılıp Denetlenmesine İlişkin Rapor Özeti [The Republic of Turkey presidency, the state supervisory council. Report summary related to the investigation and assessment of the 2002, 2003 and 2004 activities and operations of the housing development administration of Turkey]. In: Erişim, 10. 9. 2006, http://www.cankaya.gov.tr/tr_html/DDK/tkonut.htm.

Toğrol, Beğlan 1989: 112 Yıllık Göç. 1989 Yazındaki Üç Aylık Göç'ün Tarihi Perspektif İçinde Psikolojik İncelemesi [112-year-old migration. The psychological analysis of the migration in the summer of 1989, which lasted three months, within a historical perspective]. Istanbul: Boğaziçi University.

Toksöz, Gülay 2006: Uluslararası Emek Göçü [International labour migration]. Istanbul: İstanbul Bilgi University Press.

Türkarslan, Nesrin 1997: Bursa İlinde Meskun Bulgaristan Göçmenlerinin Etno-Sosyolojik İncelenmesi [The ethno-sociological analysis of the immigrants from Bulgaria living in Bursa province]. Ankara: Hacettepe University, PhD thesis.

Zhelyazkova, Antonina 2002: The Social and Cultural Adaptation of Bulgarian Immigrants in Turkey. In: Erişim, 4. 2. 2002, URL: http://www.omda.bg/imir/studies/nostalgia_1.html.

Zlotnik, H. 1999: Trends of International Migration since 1965: What Existing Data Reveal. In: International Migration 37, 1: 21–62.

Setting the Limits of the Nation: Greek Migrants and Religious Faith in Egypt at the Turn of the 20th Century[1]

Marios Papakyriacou, Berlin

Abstract

It has often been assumed that modern Greeks have been an exclusively (Orthodox) Christian population. Religion was supposed to be a decisive factor of differentiation, especially for Greeks living in countries predominantly populated by Muslims or ruled by them. In the present text, the relation between national affiliation and religious belief is examined through the case study of a migrant community; it concerns a time crucial for the process of formulating a Greek national ideology. On the one hand, the complexity of the relation of religious and national communities are presented. Furthermore, the consequences of a shift of Greek migrants in Egypt to Islam are explored. It is claimed that national ideology, although supposed to be a secular one promoting equality among all the members of the nation based either on a belief of a common origin and/or on participation in a common political project, in fact carried with it various religious - not to mention social - classifications.

Nation and religion

The view of certain scholars that nationalism emerged as a secular ideology succeeding religion - the system of beliefs of traditional societies - has been criticized as reproducing an axiomatic dichotomy between "traditional" and "modern" (van der Veer, Lehmann 1999: 3–6). Other authors insist that some cultural resources, and predominantly religious symbols, were not just "invented" by nationalists, but constituted the "sacred foundations" of national ideologies (Smith 2003). The following case study begins with the assumption that although *nation* became an important framework of social organization and the major subject of political claims in the long 19th century, there have not existed two absolutely distinct epochs, one of the "traditional" religions and one of nations. Furthermore, it is assumed that religious belief and symbols were not merely "nationalized" by national ideologies, although they often became part of discourses

[1] The material presented here is part of an ongoing dissertation on the Greeks in colonial Egypt, carried out at the *Free University of Berlin* with the financial support of *I.K.Y.*, the Greek *State Scholarships Foundation*.

through which the nation and its limits were set. A variety of religious choices and definitions of nation co-existed at the turn of the 20th century, the period of focus of the present text. They influenced each other in different ways and sometimes following particular political needs, although pre-existing prejudices and contemporary antagonisms might be responsible for difficulties in setting limits according to the aspirations of certain diplomats and intellectuals.

In the Greek case in the period of Enlightenment and afterwards, even intellectuals and activists who started with a radical critique of religion, often chose to avoid a complete rupture with the faithful, because of the specific conditions of the revolutionary period and their need for broader alliances (Iliou 1985, Chatzopoulos 2009). Religion became one criterion for defining the subject of the Greek state which emerged in the late 1820s. In the first years of independence, the the new-born kingdom accepted a group of Muslim youth only as far as they would be perceived as "apoplanithentes Ellinopaides" ("enticed Greek-boys", as the descendants of local population who had shifted to Islam in an earlier period were described by Greek authorities), whereas Turkish women who shifted to Orthodox Christian faith had no problem with being recognized as Greeks and thus remaining on their land (Vogli 2007: 200–204). This indicated the close relationship between national and religious definitions at the time. The creation of an independent archdiocese in Athens with the king as its political leader signified the attempt of the kingdom to gain control over religious institutions (ibid: 181–191). The discourse of "ethno-martyrs" (i. e., martyrs of the nation), as Christians suffering because of their religious beliefs during the Ottoman period were called, offered a unifying symbol not just of a "nationalised" religion, but of nation (Tzedopoulos 2002).

More than a mere spiritual issue or an individual choice, conversion from one religion to the other might easily have been interpreted as a disruption of the political status in the Ottoman Empire, where peaceful co-existence was maintained through religious segregation (Chatziiosif 2005: 40–43). At the period when the "Eastern Question", i. e., the future status or succession of the late Ottoman Empire, was a major issue in politics, religious choice gained the further significance of indicating population groups which could be claimed as justifying antagonistic national projects. For example, it was the period when the discovery of "crypto" Christian population groups, only superficially practicing Islam, was used to facilitate Greek claims on Ottoman territories, combined with an argument of common origin (Souliotis 1921, Skalieris 1922). On the other hand, among the non-Muslim population, being loyal to one or another Orthodox Christian religious institution signified participation in a national community in the Ottoman Balkans (Matalas 2003). An influential intellectual and activist of the time, Neoklis Kazazis, explained in a speech concerning the "Greek Patriarchates of Antioch, Jerusalem and Alexandria" (Kazazis 1901: 3), that "religious idea and political interest coincide" (ibid: 62). This was a view shared even by Sofronios, Orthodox Patriarch of Alexandria during the last three decades of the 19th century. From his perspective of maintaining an influential position for religion under the new conditions emerging with the dissolution of the Ottoman Empire and the flow of secular ideas, he explained that "our national revival and progress depends on the strengthening of religious feelings and on the reliance of public education on the bases of Christian morality" (Ragkavis 1888: 513). Thus, "depending on the point of view, the nation could be praised as the safeguard of religion, or religion as the safeguard of the nation" (Skopetea 1988: 123).

Extent of identification of Orthodox Christians and Greeks

Although exact calculations are unavailable, it can be safely assumed that there were at least 100 000 Greeks in Egypt at the turn of the century, a great part of them being Ottoman subjects. In later texts on the Egyptian Greeks of that time, it has often been implied that Greeks were an exclusively (Orthodox) Christian population in a Muslim country, with religion seen as an "insuperable wall" preventing Greeks in Egypt from "assimilation" (Malanos 1971: 360, 376, Gialourakis 2006: 388). By the first half of the 20th century, influential Egyptian Greek intellectuals already considered the church as one of the means for sustaining the future of the Greeks in Egypt (Michailidis 1927: 17); and recently Egyptian Greek intellectuals have stated a similar view (Kottis 2004: 59, n. 1). However, according to this argument, religious difference did not lead to a conflict with Egyptians, as it did with the Turks. At least since the 1920s and the model offered by Christoforos Nomikos (Nomikos 1927), Egyptian Greek intellectuals studied Egyptian culture and history much more than they had before and also tried to re-appreciate the Egyptian contribution to world culture and show that the past can provide examples of peaceful relations between Greeks and Arabs. Leading Egyptian Greek intellectuals were also engaged in showing how Greeks, the "pioneers of civilization" in modern Egypt, contributed to its progress (Politis 1930). It should be mentioned that this was at the same time that the Greeks understood that their future in Egypt was seriously threatened.

Let us return to the discourses at the turn of the century, before the need to provide a viable model for the future had made religious difference acceptable and not necessarily confrontational. Religion had a political importance for migrants during the late 19th and early 20th century, even though Egypt was not a part of the territories to which Greeks aspired at the time of the "Eastern Question" and was only nominally a part of the Ottoman Empire. Greco-Turkish conflicts had an echo among migrants in Egypt, a considerable number of whom were recruited or even volunteered during the wars. Celebrations in the streets of Egyptian towns by Greeks of Egypt or by Egyptians, depending on the winner of a battle at the Balkan war front, were often reported in the press. For some Egyptians, the wars were perceived as a religious encounter, with Greeks presented as enemies of Islam. Even an Egyptian nationalist intellectual much influenced by secular ideas, Moustafa Kamel Pacha, when speaking to an Egyptian audience on the occasion of the 1897 war in the Balkans, mentioned that, even though the "patriotism" of the Greeks should be admired, certain Greek "anti-Muslim sentiments" could not be approved by Egyptians (Kamel Pacha 1906: 165).

Greeks in Egypt, however, were not in fact identified with Christians, or even with Orthodox Christians. The Greek consul in Egypt mentioned a number of 5000 to 6000 Syrians of Orthodox faith in Egypt, to which he juxtaposed a number of 120000 Greeks in Egypt, Sudan and the rest of Africa, all of them being the flock of the Orthodox Patriarch in Alexandria (HAGMFA 1918, B/35.2). The possibility of extending the limits of the Greek nation to include Syrians or Albanians, mainly those of Orthodox Christian religion, was vivid in Egyptian Greek discourses at least until the beginning of the 20th century. Until then a few hundred Syrians in Egypt were protected by the Greek state, some of them even claiming a Greek origin and publicly identifying themselves with Greek national interests (Tachydromos 6/19. 5. 1914). There were Greek intellectuals and diplomats in Egypt who claimed that the abandonment of the protection provided to Syrians or Albanians would be a national catastrophe, as Greeks would lose an actual or potential part of the nation (Metarrythmisis 16/28. 11. 1888; Syndesmos 7/20. 7. 1903; HAGMFA 1912, 115: 8; Tachydromos 6/19. 5. 1914). Others, however, considered Albanians and Syrians as non-Greeks and, furthermore, as agents of foreign powers (Tilegrafos 27/8. 11. 1895; HAGMFA 1918, B/35.2).

Compared to the cases of Albanians and Syrians of Orthodox Christian faith, the participation in Greek institutions in Egypt of Jews coming from the Greek state and of Greek-speaking Ottoman Jews was even less self-evident. An intellectual criticized in an Egyptian Greek newspaper the exclusion of non-Orthodox Christians from a Greek brotherhood in Zagazig, arguing that Greeks of Catholic faith or Jews should be considered as much a Greek as anyone at that "epoch of liberty of religion and conscience" (Tilegrafos 1/14. 7. 1905). It was probably under the burden of prejudice and the fear of exclusion, connected with an anti-Semitic discourse which was intense in Corfu during the 1880s (Gekas 2004: 187), that a group of Jews from there felt the need to insist on the loyalty of Jews to Greek national aims (Ton en Aleksandreia Eptanision 1889: 34–35). It is noteworthy, however, that the "national celebration" in which those Greek Jews participated together with other Greeks of Egypt started, as in most similar occasions, with a doxology at the biggest Orthodox church in Alexandria, *Evangelismos*. Participation in the *Greek Community of Orthodox in Cairo*, established from all of the *"omogeneis"* (= people of the same origin) in 1856 (Soulogiannis 2001: 40), theoretically still depended upon religious faith, even if that was not absolutely clear in the regulation. This institution was succeeded in 1904 by a *Greek Community of Cairo*, which still defined its possible members as *"omogeneis"* (ibid: 95). As clarified in an individual case of 1919, though, a Greek citizen of Jewish religious affiliation could become a member of it (AGCC 1919, A21/4 Incomings 24, Memorandum N. 329).

Greek subjects of Muslim faith also existed in Egypt, not only coming from the provinces added to Greece after the 1910s decade of wars (Kerkinos 1930: 162–163). It proved more difficult to find any signs of their participation in Greek institutions even when no formal limitation due to religion was posed. In the *Brotherhood of Cretans in Cairo* dedicated to the interests of the *"patrida"* (the fatherland) and the aid to every Cretan in Egypt (Adelfotis ton en Kairo Kriton 1910), no sign of participation by Muslim Cretans was detected, such as, for example, a Muslim name. Even though incidents of a Cretan Muslim speaking Greek and possessing some kind of emotional affiliation with Greeks in Egypt were occasionally reported (Paraskeuopoulos 1899: 475, Slip 1915: 41), at a time of instability in Crete, for which migrants in Egypt were explicitly informed and mobilized (Tachydromos 6/18. 2. 1897; Kritiki Efimeris 1. 1. 1901; Embros 6. 6. 1910), it may have been difficult for Cretan Muslims to identify themselves as Greeks in Egypt, as well as for the Cretan Orthodox to accept Cretan Muslims as Greeks. As pointed out in a short story of the famous Egyptian Greek writer Stratis Tsirkas, in reference to the 1919 Egyptian revolt, for (obviously Orthodox Christian) Cretans, "all Muslims are Turks" (Tsirkas 1994: 21).

The *Brotherhood of Ipeirotes in Egypt* did try to attract Albanians to become members. Following a trend in Greek policy at the turn of the century, the Brotherhood's regulation underlined that its possible members would be accepted irrespective of religion and language (Ipeirotiki Adelfotita 1904). However, Muslim Albanians were considered by some Greeks as a hostile or inferior group, even as a bunch of fortune-seekers who adopted Islam only to satisfy material interests (Syndesmos 1/14. 7. 1903). It may thus have been difficult both to attract Albanians of Muslim religion to join Greek political projects, as well as to have them accepted by other Greeks in their institutions. A solution was to provide and promote a story of Albanian Muslims as being only superficial Muslims who were forced to shift to Islam in Ottoman times, yet "remained essentially unchanged, respectfully maintaining the traditions of their ancestors" (Mekios 1909: appendix: ε'). The history book in which Mekios posed the matter this way won a contest that the *Brotherhood of Ipeirotes in Egypt* organized, and was published with the financial support of the brotherhood.

Evangelos Achillopoulos is presented as one of the wealthy Egyptian Greek benefactors who not only supported various Greek institutions, as was usually the case, but even financed a Muslim benevolent society in Cairo, an action interpreted as a sign of the "incorporation" of Greeks in "the social and religious setting of Egypt" (Tomara-Sideri 2002: 26, 36). The case was exceptional, however, if compared to the amounts given by Egyptian Greek benefactors to Greek institutions, either in the Balkans or in Egypt. Furthermore, it came from a person who left a great legacy to his own sons, on condition they would marry only Orthodox Christian Greek women (ibid: 37). In 1929, the secretary of the *Cairo Council of the Greek Brotherhood of Cypriots in Egypt*, while suggesting the creation of a fund for the protection of widows and orphans, proposed that this right would be awarded provided the widow of a Cypriot was not of another religion and origin (than Orthodox and Greek) and did not remarry, exhibit bad conduct or leave the city of her dead husband (Elliniki Adelfotis ton en Aigypto Kyprion 1929: 7). Orthodox Christians and Greeks were not identified, even though that was often implied, but certainly Islam was considered beyond any possible definition of "Greekness". It should be mentioned that in 1923, the dissolution of the Ottoman Empire and the attempt to create nationally homogeneous Greek and Turkish states was supposed to be achieved with an exchange of population not depending on some kind of definition of the nation, but only on religious faith.

Migrants shifting to Islam in Egypt

At a period of relatively high mobilization in the name of nation, and considering the advantages of claiming protection from a capitulatory state and of entering networks of commercial activity in which Greeks had a great role and connections, it might be expected that the choice of a Greek migrant to shift to Islam would be unattractive, if not absolutely unthinkable. However, Greek newspapers report a few dozen cases of individuals shifting from Christianity to professing Islam after moving to Egypt at the end of 19th and the beginning of 20th century. The people involved in those incidents were mainly poor migrants and the majority of them originated from islands with a significant Greek population but outside the limits of the Greek State, extending from Cyprus up to the northeastern Aegean islands. As will be seen, even for those who were not Greek subjects, some responsibility would be sought in Greek communal and diplomatic authorities. King George was, after all, proclaimed king of the Greeks and not just of his kingdom, and regulations of various Greek institutions in Egypt had to be approved and signed by him.

According to the information available from reporters covering such stories, a common motivation for converting to Islam was a love affair and marriage, which would be considered problematic if the involved pair was of a different religion, in Egypt (Peters 2008) as well as elsewhere in the Ottoman Empire (Chatziiosif 2005: 71–74). A second motivation was poverty, as some migrants assumed that they might improve their chances of finding a job by entering certain Egyptian networks, a strategy made easier if they were Muslims. One might expect that those cases would occur in small, relatively isolated places and not in the main cities of Egypt, where most Greeks were living. In the latter, Greek institutions and networks would provide relatively more opportunities through which to find a job, socialize with Greeks and get married to a Greek woman. On the other hand, the pressure of the social setting to prevent a religious shift may have been smaller in big urban centres, due to their size and the possibility of anonymity. Some of the reported stories of religious shift took place indeed not only in small towns of the Delta or isolated parts of southern Egypt, but even in Alexandria and Cairo. It may, however, be assumed that in places with only a few Greek residents the pressure was greater, resulting even in incidents of violence towards "renegades". In one such case reported in Kafr el Dawar, a Greek reporter described such an incident that took place without any sign of disapproval or even the slightest surprise (Tilegrafos 4/17. 6. 1902).

Journalists describing conversion to Islam usually considered the renegade as someone who, by losing his or her religion, was also stepping out of the Greek national community. The act would be usually described as an *"eksomosia"* (Metarrythmisis 3/15. 6. 1892; Omonoia 16/29. 2. 1904), an apostasy from the religious oath. It might also be characterized as an "aponenoimeno diavima" (Omonoia 10/23. 2. 1903), a desperate, out of mind action, an expression usually reserved for people who commit suicide. In this understanding, choosing to adopt the Muslim religion was not just an individual choice concerning spiritual matters, but additionally signified giving away "tin thriskeian kai ton ethnismon", both religion and "national essence" (Metarrythmisis 3/15. 6. 1892). People who took such a decision were the people who "tourkeuoun", who "become Turks", an expression applied even when referring to people shifting to Islam in Egypt (Metarrythmisis 30/12. 5. 1891; Alitheia 3/15. 11. 1895). The use of this expression is an example of what has been called "Ottoman thinking", according to which Muslims and Turks are conflated, and was even popular many years after the dissolution of the Ottoman Empire (Hirschon 2001: 171). Sometimes journalists took the chance to criticize the inefficiencies of the Greek communal institutions in Alexandria which shared responsibility, "since it was about the loss of a Greek girl" (Tilegrafos 21/3. 6. 1904). Parents were also considered responsible for their indifference. When the journal of the Orthodox Patriarchate of Alexandria referred to an incidence of a boy of Syrian origin in Mansoura converting to Islam in order to satisfy his love for a Muslim woman, the author of the article, claiming to have some information about the boy's family, took the opportunity to comment that "since even his parents and brothers ignored the temple of their religion, what could one expect from him?" (Pantainos 1913: 587–588).

In other cases responsibility was attributed mainly if not exclusively to the renegade, the personality of whom was diminished. When a sergeant of the Greek army decided to convert to Islam, the journalist of *Tachydromos* commented that "he was not mentally balanced" and the consul of Greece added that it was good not only for the religion but also for the nation "to get rid of such creatures" (Tachydromos 2/14. 9. 1897). In the case of her conversion to Islam because of a love affair with an Egyptian man, a Greek woman in Damanhour was criticized for being motivated by her "bestial impulses" to sacrifice "her religion and national essence". The local Greeks reacted against her decision and expanded her case into a national matter, since it could become an example to be followed by others and should therefore be prevented, as if it was a disease, from diffusion. Describing their reaction, the journalist claimed that on the contrary a "faulovia", a corrupted woman like that, who would sacrifice values such as religion and nation to satisfy her passion which "only the hearty young fellah could extinguish," should be gladly released from the nation (Metarrythmisis 3/15, 8/20 and 9/21. 6. 1892). The nation had no place for "faulovioi", corrupted members, as was repeated in the case of a Greek man in Sohag who wanted to convert to Islam in order to marry an Egyptian woman. He was characterized as "not of blameless morality", while the Egyptian woman was described as a "monster" and a "monkey" (Metarrythmisi 30/12. 5. 1891). In contrast, when a Greek girl from Chios working as a servant in Ramleh decided on a similar motivation for conversion to Islam but finally yielded to pressures from her relatives and compatriots and married a religious (Orthodox Christian) gardener from her island, the reporter of a Cypriot Greek newspaper in Egypt described her as "blond, white, a real beauty" (Alitheia 3/15. 11. 1895).

Leaving aside the stereotypes certain Greek journalists carried with them, it should be pointed out that instead of, or together with, blaming the institutions of the nation and complaining about the loss of a member of it, the strategy of degrading the renegades, who were mainly of lower social strata, was maintained by reversing the wrath to contentment at the fact that those "corrupted" people automatically "exited" the national community by converting to Islam. We might recall a passage by Lord Cromer, British consul for many years at the turn of the century and informal ruler of Egypt, considered by many Greeks of Egypt as their arch-enemy. Cromer commented that he had no problem with the Greek presence in Egypt, "an unmixed benefit for the country"; his problem was with "a portion of the Greek colony", consisting of "low-class Greeks exercising the professions of usurer, drink-seller, etc". Paraphrasing a saying of his time concerning Europe and Turks, Cromer concluded that "It would be an excellent thing for Turkey and its dependencies if some of the low-class Greeks who inhabit the Ottoman dominions could be turned bag and baggage out of Turkey" (Cromer 1908: 250–252). Apparently, there were also Greeks in Egypt who shared a similar view about some of the possible members of the Greek nation.

It was even suggested that some of the poor migrants were peddling their intention to convert to Islam to the Greek press in order to find a job, expecting to profit from the sentiments of wealthier Greeks of Egypt willing to support them financially, at least to get a ticket to return to their place of origin (Omonoia 14/27. 3. 1903). A story of a migrant from the island of Limnos, resident in Tanta, who had economic difficulties and was convinced by Egyptians to convert to Islam so as to resolve them, may be an indication of this. The mobilized Greeks of the town convinced him not to change his faith on the condition he would receive 50 francs to go away. It proved, however, difficult to collect this amount. The journalist of the Athenian newspaper touring in Egypt and describing the event commented that many of the Greek merchants of the town were wealthy, probably reproducing one of the typical clichés about Greeks in Egypt. But, according to the same reporter, they preferred spending their money on golden bracelets for local women of low morality, and so the sum was mainly collected by the Greek intellectuals of the town, so that the poor man managed to leave Egypt (Embros 23. 10. 1897). That is probably the story of a journalist of Athens, to which the Greeks of Tanta, mainly originating from the same island as the poor protagonist, reacted by calling it absurd (Paraskeuopoulos 1899: 426–427). They did so because of being presented collectively not only as immoral, but also as unconcerned for the loss of a member of the nation. It did not seem so absurd that "saving" Greeks before changing their faith was a priority, irrespective of motives and wishes an individual might have.

Cases of conversion to Islam for reasons other than a love affair or the hope of economic survival have also been found, such as the story of a young orphan girl. The girl was brought up by an Egyptian woman, described by the Greek journalist as an "Othomanis", an Ottoman lady, a qualification differing from the usual description of "Egyptian" and probably meant to emphasize her negative characteristics to the sensitive readers. The step-mother, according to the interpretation of the Greek journalist, had been treating the girl like her own daughter simply in order to convince her to become a Muslim, something she would have probably achieved had the Greek ladies of Alexandria not been informed about the story on time. With the intervention of the consul himself, the girl was separated from her step-mother and confined in a Greek girls school in Alexandria. The "Othomanis", plotting the whole time, helped the girl escape from the school twice and, when the girl was discovered for the second time by Greeks of Alexandria, it was decided to send her immediately to Athens, where the police would find a "good family" to take care of her upbringing (Omonoia 16/29. 2. 1904). What an individual might choose did not necessarily count. This would also be the case for a 16 year old Greek boy working at the tobacco shop of another Greek in Port Said, who also spent his time in the "coffee shops of the natives", according to the description of the reporter. The boy was convinced by an Egyptian friend to convert to Islam, but he was arrested by the Greek consular authorities to whom he "insolently" responded to the questions of his interrogators that he was already a Muslim. Although he finally admitted, or pretended to do so, of having regretted this action, the Greek consul thought proper to send him back to Limnos, the island of his origin, at the time still Ottoman (Tilegrafos 2/15. 10. 1908).

Greek newspapers, even those in Egypt, did not hesitate to expose any incidence of violence committed against Greek migrants by Egyptians, in order to justify their complaints against either Egyptian or British authorities concerning the security of Greeks in Egypt. The discourse of Greeks in danger due to the religious fanaticism or criminality of the "natives" was frequently present in reports, especially those coming from the southern interior of Egypt. Still, almost no incidents of counter-reactions of Egyptian Muslims to Greek protests against renegades were detected, with the exception of the case of a young boy from Cyprus who would have adopted Islam had other Cypriots of Alexandria not mobilized the Patriarchate. Even then, nothing more than an "irritation of the natives" was reported (Embros 21. 7. 1907), whereas a comparable incident in ottoman Thessalonika in 1876 had led to considerable violence (Mazower 2004: 171–173). The incident in Thessalonika was known among Greeks in Egypt from a newspaper describing a similar case in Tanta, in 1876. There, a Greek woman of lower social class believed initially that her lover was a Christian of Coptic faith, but later found out that he was an "Ottoman", a Muslim who initially had lied to her and now wanted to persuade her to convert to Islam. With the co-operation of the Greek vice-consul of Tanta and the local governor, the incident was resolved and the girl regained her freedom without any further disturbances, even though Tanta was believed to be a place of many fanatic Muslims (Kairon 8/20. 5. 1876).

Religious and social factors for drawing the limits of nation

The boundaries of nation were often drawn through the process of migration and the needs of classification of both state bureaucrats and migrant institutions. Greeks in Egypt mostly identified nation and religion and used expressions such as "tourkeuo" (to become a Turk) to describe people shifting to Islam in Egypt. Rather than being "closer" to Egyptians in comparison to (other) "Europeans", Greeks in Egypt conceived religion as an element of conflict against the Ottoman Empire during the long 19th century. In this context, a change of religion was understood as a symbol of breaking away from the nation. National ideology held the right of (collective) self-determination among its main values during the 19th and 20th centuries, but did not consider this right to be self-evident concerning individual choice. A field of normative presuppositions, not exclusively based on the belief of a common origin, were invoked instead in order to define the limits of participation in the nation. Religion was one of those presuppositions in the Greek case at the turn of the century. Rather than being just an individual choice concerning spiritual matters, religion turned into a statement of participation in a political community.

Albanian and Syrian Orthodox Christians as well as Greek Jews composed part of the occupational and other networks of Greek migrants in Egypt even though confronted with difficulties due to prejudices and antagonism, especially from migrants of middle and lower social strata (Prantis 1880: 58–64, Anonymous 1902, Chatziiosif 1990). Political and material factors may thus be of some importance in setting formal and informal boundaries, as shown by groups, such as Jews and Armenians, who were excluded by state authorities in Greece with different criteria used each time (Hirschon 2001). The fact that Jews, Albanians and Syrians who were observed participating in Greek social activities, institutional or not, were usually (and contrary to the cases of Greeks converting to Islam) lawyers, doctors or engaged in financial and commercial activities, indicates that the limits of nation were not set exclusively through religious choices. Tasos Neroutsos, an Egyptian Greek doctor and intellectual, himself originating from an old Albanian family of Athens (Neroutsos-Hartinger 1992: 126), pointed out in 1888 that Albanian-speaking people were considered the lower strata of modern Greek society, whereas those using the Greek language, even when their Albanian or Slavic origin was obvious, were perceived as real Greeks, descendants of the glorious ancient Greeks (ibid: 128–129). After all, even in the late 20th century, participation in the Greek nation might still be based on social status and achievements, as shown by the kind of "honorary Greekness" attributed to certain migrants, as opposed to the threat posed by "uncultured foreigners" (Tzanelli 2006: 31–36). As has been shown, a renegade was often equated with a "faulovios", a corrupted man or woman, a typical expression of the time when a diplomat or a journalist referred to people of lower social strata. He or she would be described as "immoral", having refused to be a part of the nation, with the act of religious shift understood even as suicide.

References

Unpublished sources:
AGCC: Archives of Greek Community of Cairo
HAGMFA: Historical Archive of Greek Ministry of Foreign Affairs

Press:
Metarrythmisis, Omonoia, Pantainos, Tachydromos, Tilegrafos (Alexandria)
Embros (Athens)
Kairon (Cairo)
Alitheia (Limassol)
Syndesmos (Port Said)
Kritiki Efimeris (Rethymno)

Literature

Adelfotis ton en Kairo Kriton to Arkadion 1910: Kanonismos tis Adelfotitos ton en Kairo Kriton [Regulation of the brotherhood of Cretans in Cairo]. Cairo.

Anonymous 1902: I Koinotis Kairou kai to syllalitirion tis Megalis Tetartis [The Community of Cairo and the demonstration of spy Wednesday], Cairo.

Chatziiosif, Christos 1990: Pascha stin Aleksandreia: laikes prokatalipseis kai diakoinotikes diamaches stin Aigypto sta teli tou 19ou aiona [Easter in Alexandria: popular prejudice and intercommunal discords in late 19th century Egypt]. In: Ta Istorika 7, 12–13: 121–148.

Chatziiosif, Christos 2005: Synasos, istoria enos topou choris istoria [Synasos, history of a place without history]. Irakleio: Panepistimiakes Ekdoseis Kritis.

Chatzopoulos, Marios 2009: From Resurrection to Insurrection: "Sacred" Myths, Motifs, and Symbols in the Greek War of Independence. In: Roderick Beaton, David Ricks (eds.), The Making of Modern Greece: Nationalism, Romanticism & the Uses of the Past (1797–1896). London: Ashgate, 81–93.

Cromer, Earl of 1908: Modern Egypt. Vol. 2. London: Macmillan and Co.

Elliniki Adelfotis ton en Aigypto Kyprion 1929: Tameion perithalpseos chiron kai orfanon. Eidikos kanonismos [Relief fund for widows and orphans. Special regulation]. Cairo.

Gekas, Sakis 2004: The Port Jews of Corfu and the "Blood Libel" of 1891: A tale of many centuries and of one event. In: David Cesarani, Gemma Romain (eds.), Jewish Culture and History. Special Issue: Jews and Port Cities, 1590–1990. Valentine Mitchell Journal 7, 1–2: 171–196.

Gialourakis, Manolis 2006 [1967]: I Aigyptos ton Ellinon. Synoptiki istoria tou Ellinismou tis Aigyptou [Egypt of the Greeks. A concise history of Egypt's hellenism]. Athens: Kastaniotis.

Hirschon, Renée 2001: Identity and the Greek State: Some Conceptual Issues and Paradoxes. In: Richard Clogg (ed.), The Greek Diaspora in the Twentieth Century. Basingstoke et al.: Palgrave, 158–180.

Iliou, Filippos 1985: I siopi gia ton Christodoulo Pampleki [The silence about Christodoulos Pamplekis]. In: Ta Istorika 2, 4: 387–404.

Ipeirotiki Adelfotita 1904: Kanonismos tis Ipeirotikis Adelfotitos Aigyptou en Kairo [Regulation of brotherhood of the Ipeirotes of Egypt in Cairo], Cairo.

Kamel, Moustafa Pacha (Juliette Madame Adam, ed.) 1906: Égyptiens et Anglais. Paris: Librarie Académique Didier.

Kazazis, Neoklis 1901: To dinarion tis Orthodoksias. Peri ton kindyneuonton propyrgion tis Ellinikis Orthodoksou Ekklisias kai peri ton meson tis enischyseos auton [The dinar of Orthodoxy. About the endangered strongholds of the Greek Orthodox Church and about the means of enforcing them]. Athens: Etaireia o Ellinismos.

Kerkinos, Pantelis 1930: I elliniki ithageneia en Aigypto [Greek citizenship in Egypt]. Alexandria: Grammata.

Kottis, Spyros 2004: I Aigyptos ton Ellinon pou agapisame. Anamniseis kai provlimatismoi, chthes, simera, aurio [The Egypt of the Greeks we loved. Memories and reflections, yesterday, today, tomorrow]. Athens: Taksideutis.

Malanos, Timos 1971: Anamniseis enos Aleksandrinou [Memories of an Alexandrian]. Athens: Mpoukoumanis.

Matalas, Paraskeuas 2003: Ethnos kai Orthodoksia. Oi peripeteies mias schesis. Apo to "elladiko" sto voulgariko schisma [Nation and Orthodoxy. The adventures of a relation. From the "Hellenic" to Bulgarian schism]. Irakleio: Panepistimiakes Ekdoseis Kritis.

Mazower, Mark 2004: Salonica, city of ghosts, Christians, Muslims and Jews, 1430–1950. London: Harper Collins.

Mekios, Konstantinos 1909: Istoria tis Ipeirou apo ton archaiotaton chronon mexri ton kath' imas. Meta parartimatos peri Alvanon kai Vlachofonon Ellinon [History of Ipeiros from the ancient times until our time. With an appendix about Albanian and Vlach-speaking Greeks]. Cairo.

Michailidis, Eugenios 1927: O aigyptiotis ellinismos kai to mellon tou [The Egyptian Hellenism and its future]. Alexandria: Grammata.

Neroutsos-Hartinger, Helga 1992: Der Briefwechsel zwischen Tassos Neroutsos Bey und Gustav Meyer. Ein Beitrag zur Geschichte der Albanologie. In: Südost-Forschungen 51: 105–148.

Nomikos, Ch[ristoforos] A. 1927: Eisagogi eis tin istoria ton Aravon. To Islam – Oi kataktiseis (570–750) [Introduction to the history of Arabs. Islam – the Conquests (570–750)]. Alexandria: Grammata.

Paraskeuopoulos, G[eorgios] P. 1899: I Megali Ellas [Great Greece]. Athens.

Peters, Rudolph 2008 [1998]: The infatuated Greek: social and legal boundaries in nineteenth-century Egypt. In: Égypte/Monde arabe 34/1998. http://ema.revues.org/index1490.html, visited on 22 October 2008.

Politis, Athanasios G. 1930: O Ellinismos kai i neotera Aigyptos. Symvoli tou Ellinismou eis tin anaptyksin tis neoteras Aigyptou [Hellenism and modern Egypt. Contribution of Hellenism in the evolution of modern Egypt], vol. 2. Alexandria-Athens: Grammata.

Prantis, Euthimios St. 1880: Alvanika parapona [Complaints of Albanians]. Athens: Typografeion tou Mellontos.

Ragkavis, Alexandros Rizos 1888: Ekdromi eis Aigypton [Excursion to Egypt]. In: Estia Eikonografimeni 14. 8. 1888, 513–517.

Skalieris, Georgios Kleanthis 1922: Laoi kai fylai tis Mikras Asias [People and tribes of Asia Minor]. Athens.

Skopetea, Elli 1988: To "protypo vasileio" kai i Megali Idea. Opseis tou ethnikou provlimatos stin Ellada (1830–1880) [The "model kingdom" and the Great Idea. Aspects of the national problem in Greece (1830–1880)]. Athens.

Slip [Pissaridis] 1915: O Eleutherios Venizelos en Aigypto [Eleutherios Venizelos in Egypt]. Alexandria.

Smith, Anthony D. 2003: Chosen Peoples, New York: Oxford University Press.

Souliotis, Athanasios 1921: Oi katoikoi tis Mikras Asias [Inhabitants of Asia Minor]. Athens.

Soulogiannis, Euthymios 2001: I Elliniki Koinotita tou Kairou (1856–2001) [The Greek Community of Cairo (1856–2001)]. Athens: Kotinos.

Tomara-Sideri, Matoula 2002: Euergetismos kai prosopikotita. Euergetes Ellines tou Kairou [Benefaction and personality. Greek benefactors of Cairo]. Vol. 1. Athens: Papazisis.

Ton en Aleksandreia Eptanision 1889, Enthymion tou eortasmou tis eikosipentaetiridos tis enoseos tis Eptanisou [Remembrance of the celebration of the 25 years since the union of Eptanisos]. Alexandria: Typografeion Metarrythmiseos.

Tsirkas, Stratis 1994 [1957]: Nouredin Boba, Athens: Kedros.

Tzanelli, Rodanthi 2006: "Not my flag!" Citizenship and Nationhood in the Margins of Europe (Greece, October 2000/2003). In: Ethnic and Racial Studies 29, 1: 27–49.

Tzedopoulos, Giorgos 2002: Ethniki omologia kai symvoliki stin Ellada tou 19ou aiona. Oi ethnomartyres [National confession and symbolic in 19th century Greece. The martyrs of the nation]. In: Mnimon 24: 107–143.

van der Veer, Peter, Hartmut Lehmann (eds.) 1999: Nation and Religion: Perspectives on Europe and Asia. Princeton, New Jersey: Princeton University Press.

Vogli, Elpida 2007: "Ellines to genos". I ithageneia kai i tautotita sto ethniko kratos ton Ellinon (1821–1844) ["Greeks in origin". Citizenship and identity in the national state of the Greeks (1821–1844)]. Irakleio: Panepistimiakes Ekdoseis Kritis.

Ethnologia Balkanica 13 (2009)

Refugees in Greece (1922): The Attitude of the Press Towards Their Arrival

Georgia Eglezou, Bournemouth, UK

Abstract

The present article examines the attitude of the local press to the thousands of refugees who arrived in Piraeus in 1922 after the "Asia Minor Disaster": the defeat of the Greek Army in Asia Minor in 1922 by the Turkish Nationalist Army and the violent uprooting of the Orthodox population of Greek origin from their homeland. It focuses on how two leading Piraeus newspapers represented the response of politicians, the church, the local business community and the general population to the refugees' arrival. However, as a newspaper is not simply a mirror reflecting public attitudes but also an opinion former, the ideological stance adopted by the two newspapers towards the refugees is examined and found to be conflicted. Initially articles encouraged the local people to offer help to the refugees but gradually they became hostile towards the presence of the refugees in the heart of the local community. The negative language employed by the local press, which construed the refugees as threatening and undesirable elements, was a powerful contributor towards the marginalisation of and discrimination against the refugees, and led to the creation of an imaginary union of the local population which was hostile to the continued presence of the refugees in Piraeus.

Introduction

The defeat of the Greek Army in Asia Minor in 1922 ended the Greco-Turkish War that had started in 1919 and resulted in what became known to the Greeks as the "Asia Minor Disaster" *[Mikrasiatiki Katastrofi]:* the violent uprooting of the Orthodox population of Greek origin from their homeland. Thousands of people were compelled to emigrate from Asia Minor to Greece, a "forced migration caused by war" (Hirschon 2004: 11). The forced migration had two phases: the first the "initial flight of the mass of refugees under emergency conditions" immediately following the Greek army's defeat, and the second between the years 1923 and 1926 when the remaining Orthodox Christians left Anatolia following the signing of the Treaty of Lausanne.[1] Simultaneously, hundreds of

[1] In Greek as in English the term "refugee" *[prosfygas]* denotes a particular form of migration, the forced exodus from the fatherland (Hirschon 1989: 4). By referring to themselves

thousands of Muslims were forced to emigrate from Greece to Turkey.[2] The result was a population exchange of Christians and Muslims which excluded only those specified by the Treaty of Lausanne.[3] Here we will discuss the first phase in 1922, when thousands of Christians were forced to move from Asia Minor to Greece under emergency conditions.

The native Greeks and the newly arrived refugees were two fundamentally similar groups. Most of the Christians from Asia Minor had the same national aspirations and ideals as the native Greeks and were faithful to Greek tradition. At the same time the refugees were, and recognised that they were, different (Pentzopoulos 2002: 200). By calling themselves *Mikrasiates* [from Asia Minor] "they conveyed a particular cultural endowment associated with their place of origin and their unique heritage" (Hirschon 1989). Most significantly of all the refugees shared among themselves the collective experience of the loss of home and place, a traumatic experience which not only determined their lives and influenced their decisions (Gounaris, Michailidis 2004: 9) but also moulded the ways they perceived themselves and the others.

Piraeus was one of the Greek ports at which a large number of refugees arrived. According to the press in Piraeus, it is estimated that around 60000 refugees landed there in September 1922.[4] Piraeus at that time "consisted of a port, a small commercial centre and a few industrial establishments on the edge of a limited residential area, surrounded by open land and fields" (Hirschon 1989: 49). As autumn began the refugees found themselves living in warehouses, school buildings, churches, railway sheds, factory store-rooms and tents all over Piraeus. The Greek state, as a result of its constant participation in wars since the Balkan Wars of 1912–13, found itself in an extremely bad financial situation and was unable to meet the cost of the refugees' upkeep. Therefore much of the early relief work had to be undertaken by international organizations such as the Red Cross and Save the Children Fund while the Greek government merely formed an *ad hoc* body, the Refugee Relief Fund (Hirschon 1989: 36).

---

as "refugees" the newly arrived people distinguished themselves from the local Greek populace. The Greek population used the term to refer to the Orthodox newcomers to Greece (Hirschon 2004: xii).

[2] The Lausanne Convention legitimized the exchange of 1104216 Orthodox Christians and 388146 Muslims (Yildirim 2006: 105).

[3] The text of the Lausanne Convention regarding the Exchange of Greek and Turkish Populations can be found in Hirschon (2004: 281–287).

[4] *Simea*, 17 December 1922, p. 3.

The refugees in historiography

The issue of the population exchange between Greece and Turkey has been examined by numerous scholars. From the Greek side a leading study of the Lausanne convention was Dimitri Pentzopoulos's PhD thesis at Princeton University which was published in 1962 and republished in 2002 as *The Balkan Exchange of Minorities and its impact on Greece*. His detailed work was based mainly on the study of Greek, British, American and the League of Nations archives. Among the scholars who have examined the social effects of the population exchange from an anthropological perspective and challenged some of the pre-existing views is Renée Hirschon, in her book, *Heirs of the Greek Catastrophe: The Social Life of the Asia Minor Refugees in Piraeus* (1989), which is based on her dissertation at Oxford. Hirschon, who focused on the Greek side, conducted her research in the 1970s in a suburb of Piraeus where thousands of refugees from Asia Minor had settled. Also noteworthy is Elisabeth Kontogiorgi's *Population Exchange in Greek Macedonia: the Rural Settlement of Refugees 1922–1930*, which examines the issue of the settlement of refugees in post-Ottoman Macedonia. Her main contribution is that she examined the multiple aspects of the settlement from a social, economic and ethnological perspective rather than from an exclusively political perspective.

It is also worth noting the existence of thousands of oral testimonies provided by refugees who settled in Greece which have been collected by the Kentro Mikrasiatikon Spoudon [Centre of Asia Minor Studies] in Athens. Some of the most representative testimonies were published in Greek in two volumes in 1980 and 1982 under the titles *I Exodos: Martiries Apo tis Eparchies ton Ditikon Paralion tis Mikras Asias* [The Exodus: Testimonies from the Provinces of the Western Coast of Asia Minor] and *I Exodos: Martiries Apo tis Eparchies tis Kentrikis kai Notias Mikrasias* [The Exodus: Testimonies from the Provinces of Central and South Asia Minor], respectively.

From the Turkish side, Onur Yildirim's 2002 doctoral thesis at Princeton University is an excellent work, based on extensive research conducted in Greek, Turkish and British archives. This was published in 2006 as *Diplomacy and Displacement: Reconsidering the Turco-Greek Exchange of Populations, 1922–1934*. Yildirim's aim is "to open up a previously neglected area in the historiography of Turkey and to show its importance for the history of the country as a whole" (Yildirim 2006: 21). Oral histories from Muslim refugees forced out of Greece in the compulsory population exchange remain for the most part unrecorded (ibid: 23). However, the Turkish NGO The Foundation of the Lausanne Treaty Emigrants has attempted to fill the gap and collect the memories of elderly refugees before it is too late. The Foundation has organized many conferences on the topic and has edited the proceedings, providing an invaluable source of information. Also from the Turkish side, one of the best accounts of the exchange of the population is Kemal Ari's book *Büyük Mübadele: Türkiye'ye Zorunlu Göc 1923–25* [The Great Exchange: Forced Migration to Turkey] 1995. The work was based on extensive research conducted in the Turkish archives.

All the above studies focus exclusively on either the Greek or the Turkish side of the story. The sole work which examines the effects of the population exchange on both societies is Renée Hirschon's (ed.) *Crossing the Aegean: An Appraisal of the 1923 Compulsory Population Exchange Between Greece and Turkey*, which was published in 2003. This collection grew out of papers presented at a conference in Oxford which had examined the consequences of the Lausanne convention for both countries.

The present article focuses, as stated above, on the Christian Orthodox refugees forced to emigrate from Asia Minor to Greece. Although the issue has been examined from the diplomatic and the social perspectives, no work has yet been done on the contemporary attitude of institutions such as the press towards the refugees. The early 20th century Greek press was closely allied to the movement of Greek irredentist nationalism and played a leading role in forming Greek public opinion, especially during the last and most disastrous phase of the realisation of the *Megali (Great) Idea,*[5] by providing the technical means of "representing" the kind of imagined community that is formed into a nation (Anderson 1991: 25). After the signing of the Armistice of Mudros, the Greek press played a leading role in the campaign for the support of the Greek claims in the negotiations in the Paris Peace Conference (Eglezou 2009: 47). In this campaign the Orthodox Christians in Asia Minor were labelled "brothers" who were suffering at the hands of the Turks.[6] After the disastrous defeat of the Greek Army by the Nationalist Kemalist Army in 1922 the Greek press remained a vehicle for nationalistic ideas which created an imaginary internal union against the external enemy (ibid: xviii, 177). However, initially the press supported the refugees in Greece, labelling them "victims of the external enemy" and organising fundraising campaigns. Soon, though, articles were published that were not only critical towards the Greek state for not adequately providing for the settlement of the refugees but also of the refugees themselves, who began to be classified as "outsiders" who put in danger "the well being of the local community". In

[5] The *Megali Idea*, the romantic but unrealistic dream of the revival of the Byzantine Greek Empire which would unite within the bounds of a single state all the areas of substantial Greek population, was the dominant ideology of the Modern Greek State following its creation and up to 1922. The he term has been attributed to the leader of the French Party, Ioannis Kolettis, a Hellenised Vlach. However, similar sentiments had been expressed earlier (Clogg 1988: 253–255).

[6] *Ethnos*, 1 February 1919.

this way the press helped create a new imaginary union against the new "internal enemy": the refugees.

Aims and methodology

The present article explores the attitude of the local Piraeus press to the thousands of refugees who arrived in Piraeus. It especially investigates how the press construed the reaction of groups and individuals who held important positions in public life, such as politicians, the church and the local business community, to the refugees' arrival. It also investigates press representations of the attitude of the general population towards the refugees.

Media scholars claim that the language which is used in newspapers is not neutral, but influences ideas and beliefs. If we analyse the language in the press we can reveal ideologies "which are not necessarily stated and ... which dominated the structure of presentation" (Fowler 1991: 1–2). The goal here is to show that the press in Piraeus, in reporting on reactions towards the arrival of the refugees, used language which played a powerful role in marginalising the refugees by representing them as threatening and undesirable elements. This resulted in the formation of an imagined union of the local population which discriminated against the refugees.

The first newspaper to be examined was *Sfera* (Sphere), the oldest daily newspaper in Piraeus, founded by secondary school teacher, writer and journalist Ioannis Kalostypis in 1880, which continued until 1941 when it ceased publication as a result of the German occupation. *Sfera* was influenced by the Athenian newspaper *Acropolis*. The newspaper belonged to the sphere of political influence of Dimitrios and Trifonas Moutsopoulos, who had been mayors of Piraeus for 25 years (Droulia, Koutsopanagou 2008, 4: 156–157). The second paper analyzed, *Simea* (Flag), was published for the first time in 1917 and stopped publishing in 1941 for the same reason as *Sfera*. Its owner and managing editor was P. Th. Logothetis. *Simea* claimed on its front page to have the highest circulation of all Piraeus newspapers. It was an organ of the anti-Venizelist politician Nikolaos Stratos, but expressed criticism of the Royalist government under Gounaris as "clumsy and timid".[7]

The two newspapers were examined for the period September – December 1922, when a significant number of refugees arrived in Piraeus. Their arrival was a significant event which naturally received extensive newspaper coverage, since it touched the lives not only of the refugees but also of the local people

---

[7] *Simea*, 17 March 1922, leader.

in the country of settlement and had the required intensity, continuity and unexpectedness to guarantee prolonged media coverage. In the analysis, emphasis was given to two columns located on the front page of each newspaper, which provided local news reports or commented on local Piraeus news. *Sfera*'s column was named *Epikera* [Well-Timed] and *Simea*'s column was named *Simiomata* [Notes]. During the four months under review 65 columns of *Epikera (Sfera)* and 55 columns of *Simiomata (Simea)* reported on the refugees or on issues connected to the refugees. Frequently the newspapers published more than one report regarding the refugees.

The majority of the reports in *Epikera* (14) referred to issues regarding the housing of the refugees, followed by reports referring to acts of charity by foreign countries, international organizations and Greek companies, unions and individuals. Eight reports referred to health issues such as the spread of epidemics and the lack of sanitation which was, according to the newspaper, the cause of epidemics. In *Simiomata* the majority of reports referred to health and to dangers towards public health which resulted from the poor sanitary conditions caused by the accumulation of too many people in churches, schools and squares. This topic was followed by reports on the housing of refugees and by reports regarding charity. A smaller number of reports referred to the local people and to their indifference or their hostility towards the refugees. Other topics were the transfer of refugees out of the city and the increase in criminality which, according to the press, coincided with the arrival of the refugees (Figure 1).

Before examining how different groups received the arrival of the refugees, it is worth examining how the press itself presented their arrival and what language it used to describe the refugees who were arriving in Piraeus.

The refugees through the pages of the press

On 3 September 1922 *Sfera* wrote in the column *Epikera* describing the first refugees who had arrived in Piraeus:

> Mothers without children and children without mothers, wives without husbands, all out of their mind, naked, hungry, left one with the impression of horror and terror but also of the tremendous despair for their future, are piling up down there. They parade in distressing and mourning escorts which break the toughest and most indifferent heart.

There was no major difference in the language used by both newspapers to describe the refugees. Evaluative adjectives were widely employed: the refugees

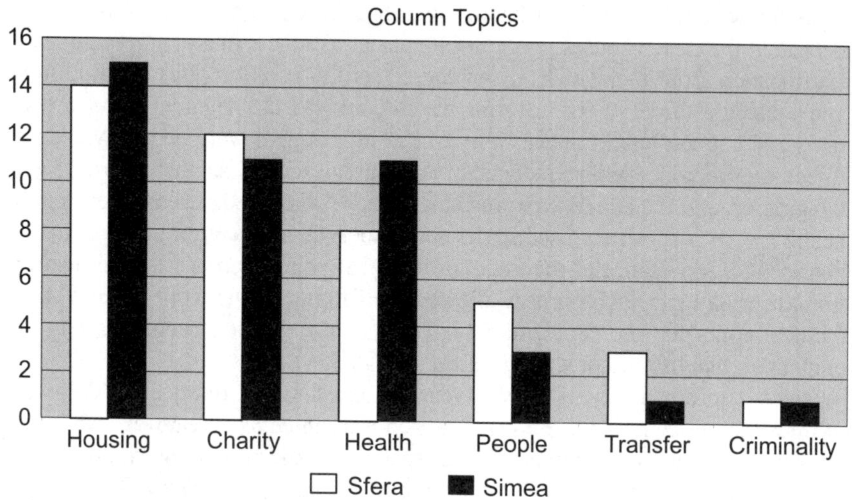

Fig. 1: Column topics in the Piraeus newspapers *Sfera* and *Simea* (1922)

were "the unfortunate and tragic victims", "the tragic victims of fate",[8] the victims of "this inhuman uprooting of Hellenism", "the wretched",[9] "the afflicted and desperate beings",[10] "the poor refugees"[11] who were "brothers, homogenous and of the same blood [with the local people]", they were "the unlucky refugees", the "unfortunate creatures who, frail and dilapidated, were losing their minds desperate to protect themselves from the rain" who presented "the sad spectacle of the most heartbreaking misfortune",[12] and who "were naked in full winter and hungry and dying from hardships and mental anxiety"[13].

At the same time the refugees were considered to be the cause of much trouble and an excess of negative feeling was expressed. They were presented as responsible for "all this dangerous refugee throng"[14] and for the "noise" inside the churches which was caused by their "talking, arguing, joking in the area set

[8] *Sfera*, 10 October 1922, Column *Epikera*.
[9] *Simea*, 28 November and 9 December 1922, Column *Simiomata*.
[10] *Sfera*, 5 October 1922, Column *Epikera*.
[11] *Simea*, 5 September 1922, Column *Simiomata*.
[12] *Sfera*, 5 September and 1, 5 October 1922, Column *Epikera*.
[13] *Simea*, 29 November 1922, Column *Simiomata*.
[14] *Sfera*, 1 November 1922, Column *Epikera*.

aside for women"[15]; and as behaving in public in the same manner they would behave in their own houses, using public places as toilets in a manner that led to "suffocation from the stench". They were "setting cooking fires day and night and causing a threat of fire". Terms which could denote negative emotive reactions and connote malevolence were used. The refugees were people who could infect the populace with epidemics "on a great scale", as they were "freely hanging around the streets carrying smallpox"[16]. The words "health" or "public health" were very widely used in the newspapers in a variety of contexts to emphasise the importance of the issue for the local population and to highlight the immanent danger. Such phrases allowed the linking of the word "health" with medical concepts like "epidemic" or social concepts like "people's safety" to emphasise the "unsafe practices" of the refugees.

Such "unsafe practices" were even attributed to the refugee children; the "threat" came from them, too. They were represented as "creatures" who were "begging" presenting the most "pitiful spectacle" and who were "more annoying than mosquitoes and flies", according to the newspaper *Sfera*. They had to be taken into custody as "begging was a branch of petty theft"[17].

The above words and phrases were used by the press to categorize the refugees and their attributes. As Fowler argues, categorization is the basis for practices of discrimination (Fowler 1991: 93). The refugees were represented in a way that separated them from the locals. They were a distinct body who were considered a marginalised group occupying an abnormal position removed from the rest of the population. They were victims, desperate, poor, unlucky, hungry, naked and insane. Some rather offensive and abusive terms were used not only to describe them but also to undermine them: they had no manners as they were making noise inside churches, or they were behaving in yards as they would behave inside their houses. Even worse, they were considered a threat, spreading epidemics to the locals. Even terms which were dehumanizing were used: their children were labelled "creatures" who were more annoying than mosquitoes and flies.

In the following section we focus on how the Piraeus newspapers reported the attitudes and the feelings of the local people towards the newly arrived refugees. Emphasis is given to how the public attitude changed from one of indifference or initial sympathy to one of hostility and negative feelings.

---

15 *Simea*, 18 November 1922, Column *Simiomata*.

16 *Sfera*, 21 September and 21, 28 December 1922, Column *Epikera*.

17 *Sfera*, 17, 21 October 1922, Column *Epikera*.

The people in general

With the arrival of the refugees the local press invited its readers to help the Greek State raise private money for them. The initial reaction was sympathy from the local population (Hirschon 2004: 19). Some people responded to the call and offered money or services. The majority of the people, though, remained indifferent, an issue which was overtly stigmatized by the press.

Private offers were extensively reported, in an effort to encourage more people to contribute assistance for the refugees; a lawyer gave for free the house he was renting for the settlement of "poor refugee families" and took over himself the responsibility of paying the rent.[18] Even offers of little importance, like the man who offered 500 drachmas to buy sweets for the children as Christmas was approaching, were reported in detail. The offer of a pair of shoes was news considered worth reporting, as there was no other major offer available for inclusion in the newspapers. We read in the newspaper *Sfera* on 23 September 1922:

> A truly sensitive and philanthropic lady, made a nice and gentle gesture; meeting in front of the door of her house an unlucky refugee from a good family who was barefoot and shivering. She took off her elegant court shoes and gave them to the refugee who cried because of gratitude. She walked up the stairs of her house satisfied.

However, it seems that there were local people who instead of offering assistance were interested in making money at the refugees' expense. The press reported cases of people who asked unreasonable rents for their houses: "for their hovels the prices are higher than the prices of the Hotel Grande Bretagne[19]" wrote *Sfera*. The press condemned such people as "exploiters of the unfortunate victims"[20]. Similar comments were published in the Athenian press about the behaviour of the people in Piraeus towards the refugees.[21]

It seemed, however, that the majority of the local population had little if any interest in helping the refugees. On the contrary, they were spending a lot of money on their own entertainment. The press reported:

> At a time that all the night clubs are absolutely full and the nouveaux riches spend their money – better, they throw it away – on the satisfaction of ridiculous whims, are there no drachmas left for the relief of our

[18] *Simea*, 29 September 1922, Column *Epikera*.
[19] Grande Bretagne was the most expensive and prestigious hotel in Athens.
[20] *Sfera*, 6 September 1922, Column *Epikera*.
[21] *Eleftheron Vima*, 4 September 1922, Column *Eleftheron Vima*.

> brothers who are suffering the most heart-breaking misfortune and are under the shelter of our hospitality? What a shame![22]

Gradually the locals felt threatened by the refugees and started openly to express their hostility. They felt that the refugees were taking their jobs. On 19 October 1922, the newspaper *Simea* wrote that the workers in the Custom Service objected when they were informed that some refugees would be hired to work alongside them. "They decided that they would block in every way and by every means the hiring of the refugees and they asked for the help of other unions." It seemed that the workers had the support of the other unions, according to the press, as they did not want "the same thing to happen to other professions"[23].

More outbursts of hostility by the locals followed the decree of "forced housing" according to which every family had to house homeless refugees. This was an issue which received wide coverage in the press. The newspapers not only directly addressed their readers, but also presumed to speak on their behalf and presented the measure as a threat to local families as "a person of unknown character, morality and upbringing" would be a witness "to intimate family relationships and secrets". Additionally there was hostility because the refugees were occupying schools. High school students complained in a letter they sent to the managing editor of *Sfera* of the requisitioning of their schools for the refugees' use, which they claimed reduced their studies to a quarter of the usual teaching hours. They argued that "when they will leave school, they will make no progress in any higher study" wrote the newspaper.[24]

In the following section the attitude of the local business community as reported in the Piraeus press is examined. Although it might be expected that the local business community would offer generous donations to the refugees, this was not the case. On the contrary, a hostile attitude, similar to the hostility of the local population in general, was reported.

Local business community

Offers for the support of the refugees from the local business community, despite its important role in local public life, were not frequent. The local press, instead of stigmatising such an attitude of neglect, chose to mention any contribution in an effort to encourage more businesses to assist the refugees. Any offer was considered newsworthy and was reported.

---

[22] *Sfera*, 9 September 1922, Column *Epikera*.
[23] *Simea*, 19 October 1922, Column *Simiomata*.
[24] *Sfera*, 27 October 1922, Column *Epikera*.

The union of the tobacconists in Piraeus made one of the first financial donations. Although the sum donated, 500 drachmas, was paltry, the newspaper *Sfera* published the letter which the president of the union, Giannopoulos, the secretary Liberis and the treasurer Pelianakos wrote to the newspaper in which they stated that although their funds were limited they offered the amount for "our brothers, refugees of Asia Minor". The insurance company *Athinaiki* offered ten thousand drachmas for the refugees. The newspaper *Sfera* reported that representatives of two foreign insurance companies in Piraeus, Manousis and Gialistras, offered an unspecified sum of money for the "sacred mission of the care of the unfortunate refugees"[25].

The newspapers in Piraeus, as businesses, did not follow the example of leading Athenian newspapers, such as *Eleftheron Vima* and *Kathimerini*, which used their power to organize fund-raising campaigns for the refugees.[26] Perhaps due to the limited circulation the Piraeus newspapers had in comparison with the Athenian ones, they chose to let the most powerful and influential newspapers take the leading role.

Conversely, there were cases of local businesses which tried to increase their profits by raising the prices of their products, an issue which was repeatedly criticised by the local press. We read in the newspaper *Simea*:

> Profiteering, taking advantage of the increasing need of the increasing population, raises the prices of the essential products daily and hourly without justification ...[27]

The hostility by the local people and the business community towards the refugees was not expressed by the politicians. The politicians were the organs of the government whose main role was to follow faithfully the official state policy to settle the refugees. Their measures, though, were criticised by the press as a cause of serious disturbance for the local community.

---

25 *Sfera*, 8 and 12 September 1922, Columns *Epikera* and *Grammata Pros tin Sferan* [Letters to Sfera].

26 The newspaper *Eleftheron Vima* had started the campaign in early September 1922 and daily it published on the front page the amount of money which had been raised to that point. Indicatively I mention that by 23 October 1922 the amount was 1 594 000 drachmas. The newspaper *Kathimerini* followed the example of *Eleftheron Vima* and started a separate campaign on 7 September 1922.

27 *Sfera*, 17 September 1922, Column *Epikera*.

Politicians

Politicians had authority and were therefore represented in the press as agents with the power to take decisions which could improve the refugees' living conditions. The newspapers in Piraeus appealed to the politicians at a very early stage in an effort to persuade them to take the necessary decisions.

The politicians who were primarily involved in the project for the resettlement of the refugees, such as the Minister of Care, Doxiadis, the Major of Piraeus Panagiotopoulos, the Minister of Foreign Affairs, Politis, members of the city council of Piraeus such as Sakalis, Kaberos, Vourvoulis did not, however, make any statements in the press concerning the refugees. The press kept the issue in the public domain by reporting on the responsibility and shortcomings of the government. Decisions that were taken by the politicians, such as transferring the refugees to empty factories far from the city centre, provided temporary housing and offered "relative thinning and spaciousness" to places where before there had previously been an "unbearable throng", but according to the newspapers such measures did not solve the refugee problem.[28] What the press constantly demanded of the politicians was a radical solution: to transfer the refugees away from the cities, preferably to other parts of Greece.

What was most criticised by the press was the decree by the Minister of Care for "forced housing". This measure was lambasted as spreading all kinds of problems to a wider range of areas where it could produce collective reactions such as a "social revolution and dislike against the refugees"[29]. In addition, by highlighting the criticism against the decree the press reproduced the beliefs of the community, that the presence of an outsider inside the family could only cause serious trouble.

The Church

In a religious country like Greece it might be expected that the church would play a very active role in the campaign supporting the integration of the refugees into Greek society. This, however, did not happen. In addition to the indifference of the clergy, the local press criticised the presence of the refugees occupying churches, as though the refugees' presence was their own fault.

What was notable about the church as an institution was that it failed to use its considerable power and influence to appeal to the locals to support the refu-

[28] *Simea*, 20 September 1922, Column *Simiomata*.

[29] *Sfera*, 24 September 1922, Column *Epikera*.

gees. No members of the local clergy used the Piraeus press to encourage the populace to help the refugees. The church made no effort to donate money to them. Nor did it encourage people to raise money for the refugees during the period under examination. This lack of initiative by the clergy was not stigmatized by the local press. In contrast, the Ecumenical Patriarch Meletios appealed in the Athenian press to the population to help the refugees.[30] The only reference made to a church-based initiative in the Piraeus press was to praise one from a female religious fraternity called "O Kalos Samaritis" [The Good Samaritan] who in addition to taking care and comforting sick refugees made clothes for the refugee children.

Church buildings were used as temporary housing for the refugees, but only after a decision taken by the local authorities. Most of the churches in Piraeus, especially those which were in the centre, were full of refugees.[31] The local newspapers repeatedly asked the state and the city council to remove the refugees from the churches, which they considered to be not only an important indicator of religious identity but also to form a major part of everyday local life. The local press claimed that the refugees' presence not only interfered with the running of the church but also put in danger the sense of security that the church was supposed to offer. The press even went so far as to claim that the refugees' presence in the churches endangered their own health and the health of neighbouring residents. The refugees, according to the newspapers presented "a disgusting spectacle" which carried the "stigma of stink and excrement and endangered public health" and the churches became "the most disgusting centre of contamination"[32]. The newspapers further implied that the gathering of the refugees in churches damaged public morality as "the gathering of a mixed population of males and females inside the churches" was, "somehow sacrilegious" because of "the physical and carnal needs and desires of such people"[33].

The myth of the internal enemy

The press and the media in general have "the power to place people and events into the pre-existing categories of hero, villain, good or bad, and thus to invest their stories with the authority of mythological truth" (Carey 1988: 80). A myth has its own coherence and is itself a complete and cohesive system. Myths interpret a complicated reality in a simplistic way. They place individuals in groups

[30] *Eleftheron Vima*, 7 September 1922.

[31] The churches of St Nicholas, of Holy Trinity, of St. Vasilios, of St Sofia.

[32] *Sfera*, 26, 28 September and 1 November 1922, Column *Epikera*.

[33] *Simea*, 21 November 1922, Column *Simiomata*.

and define them as enemies or friends. Especially in periods of crisis, when collective insecurity dominates and may reach the level of collective obsession, the activation of a myth is determined by the juncture between the crisis and the collective insecurity (Eglezou 2009: 43–44). This is what happened in 1922. The press mobilized the myth of the "internal enemy" in order to provide an explanation for the crisis for which the Greek state was incapable of finding a prompt solution. The refugees were at first represented by the press as victims of the Turks, a view which agreed not only with the long-established popular imagery that Greeks held of Turks but also with the nationalistic irredentist aspirations of the Greeks. Such a representation initially encouraged donations and stigmatized local indifference. However, gradually the newspapers altered their representation of the refugees. From "brothers" the refugees came to be represented as enemies. They were construed as a marginalised group which endangered the stability of the country by occupying schools, churches, competing with the local populace for work, and even worse by "intruding" into local houses as a result of the measure of "forced housing". Therefore negative evaluative adjectives dominated the description of the refugees.

Conclusion

With the arrival of the refugees in Piraeus as well as in other parts of Greece, the local had a story which was maintained at a high level of coverage for several months, contributing to the high emotive level of the discourse. Evaluative adjectives had a prominent role in the description of the refugees, who were considered "unfortunate victims". After the initial sympathy of the people towards them, the language in the press changed and the refugees were considered responsible for all kinds of trouble, which gradually justified and increased public indifference, which eventually mutated into hostility. Politicians took decisions, though not effective ones. Measures like the decree on "forced housing" were highly criticised as causing serious disturbance to local family life. While the church as an institution remained silent in the local press, the isolated initiatives of local businesses were widely reported. The general population at an early stage regarded the refugees as hostile intruders. Their hostility was openly reported and reached hysterical levels, especially when the press voiced "public opinion" that accused the refugees of taking their jobs, occupying their schools and infecting them with epidemics.

The press's use and reporting of evaluative language hostile to the refugees succeeded in marginalising them and in construing the refugees as threatening and undesirable elements. The mobilisation of the myth of the "internal enemy" resulted in the creation of an imagined union of the local population directed against the refugees.

Bibliography

Primary Sources: Newspapers

Eleftheron Vima, September - October 1922
Ethnos, February 1919
Kathimerini, September - October 1922
Sfera, September - December 1922
Simea, September - December 1922

Literature

Anderson, Benedict 1991: Imagined Communities. 2nd ed. London: Verso.

Apostolopoulos, Fotis (ed.) 1980, 1982: I Exodos: Martiries apo tis Eparchies ton Ditikon Paralion tis Mikras Asias [The exodus: testimonies from the provinces of the Western Coast of Asia Minor] and: I Exodos: Martiries Apo tis Eparchies tis Kentrikis kai Notias Mikrasias [The exodus: testimonies from the provinces of central and south Asia Minor]. Athens: Kentro Mikrasiatikon Spoudon, vol. 2.

Ari, Kemal 1995: Büyük Mübadele: Türkiye'ye Zorunlu Göc 1923–25 [The great exchange: forced migration to Turkey 1923–25]. Istanbul. Tarih Vakti.

Carey, James C. (ed.) 1988: Media, Myth and Narratives. London: Sage Publications.

Clogg, Richard 1988: The Byzantine Legacy in the Modern Greek World: The Megali Idea. In: Lowell Clucas (ed.), The Byzantine Legacy in Eastern Europe. New York: Boulder, 253–255.

Droulia, Loukia, Gioula Koutsopanagou (eds.) 2008: Encyclopaedia tou Ellinikou Typou 1784–1974 [Encyclopaedia of the Greek press 1784–1974]. Athens: Institouto Neoellinikon Erevnon, Ethniko Idryma Erevnon 4: 156–157.

Eglezou, Georgia 2009: The Greek Media in World War I and its Aftermath: The Athenian Press on the Asia Minor Crisis. London: I. B. Tauris.

Fowler, Roger 1991: Language in the News. Discourse and Ideology in the Press. London: Routledge.

Gounaris, Vasilis, Iakovos Michailidis (eds.) 2004: Prosfyges sta Valkania. Mnimi ke Ensomatosi [Refugees in the Balkans: memory and integration]. Athens: Ekdosis Patakis.

Hirschon, Renée 1989: Heirs of the Greek Catastrophe. The Social Life of Asia Minor Refugees in Piraeus. Oxford: Clarendon Press.

Hirschon, Renée 2004: "Unmixing Peoples" in the Aegean Region and the Consequences of the Lausanne Convention. In: Renée Hirschon (ed.), Crossing the Aegean. Oxford: Berghahn, 3–20.

Kontogiorgi, Elisabeth 2006: Population Exchange in Greek Macedonia: the Rural Settlement of Refugees 1922–1930. Oxford: Clarendon Press.

Pentzopoulos, Dimitri 2002: The Balkan Exchange of Minorities and its Impact on Greece. London: Hurst & Co.

Yildirim, Onur 2006: Diplomacy and Displacement. Reconsidering the Turco-Greek Exchange of Populations, 1922–1934. New York: Routledge.

„Nur ein paar Lumpen, die Ihren Judaslohn in Alkohol umsetzen“
Streikbrecher vom Balkan in der Schweiz im frühen 20. Jahrhundert und ihre Wahrnehmung

Christian Koller, Bangor

Abstract: „Just a few rogues spending their traitor's reward on alcohol“: Strike-breakers from the Balkans in Switzerland in the early 20th century and their perception

The article analyses the use of migrant workers from the Balkans as strike-breakers in Swiss labour conflicts in the early 20th century. It especially focuses on the 1909/10 Winterthur construction workers' strike, the outcome of which was strongly influenced by the deployment of foreign strike-breakers. Whilst in Swiss strike discourses the bourgeois press usually stressed that most of the strikers were foreigners and that they behaved in a manner quite different from "civilised Swiss citizens", though, the labour press countered that there was no difference between Swiss and foreign workers, discourses on Southeast European strike-breakers somehow saw a reversal of these patterns of argument. The labour movement depicted them as "first rate rabble-proletarians" from "culturally backward countries". Employers, on the other hand, would try to hide them from public discussions. On the other side, Swiss perceptions of migrant workers from the Balkans in the early 20th century show many features which are still common in the late 20th and early 21st century. However, one crucial shift can be identified: Whilst in the years before 1914 (and again in the 1960s and 70s) Italians were the main target of Swiss xenophobia and at the very centre of the notion of "overforeignization", people from the Balkans, although always having been perceived overwhelmingly negatively, came to be seen as a threat to Switzerland's cultural identity only towards the end of the 2nd millennium.

Spricht man heute über Migration von Südosteuropa in die Schweiz, so denkt man in erster Linie an das letzte Drittel des 20. und den Beginn des 21. Jahrhunderts. Hatte sich der Anteil von Migrantinnen und Migranten vom Balkan an der ausländischen Wohnbevölkerung in der Schweiz bis 1960 im Promillebereich bewegt, so stieg er danach rasant an. Am markantesten war die Immigration von Menschen aus Jugoslawien beziehungsweise Ex-Jugoslawien, deren Anteil von 0,2 Prozent (1960) über 2,3 Prozent (1970), 6,4 Prozent (1980) und 12,5 Prozent (1990) auf 24,0 Prozent (1998) wuchs, um dann bis 2008 auf 18,4 Prozent zurückzugehen. In absoluten Zahlen war der Zuwachs noch markanter, von etwa 1000 Menschen im Jahre 1930 über 5000 zum Ende des Zweiten Weltkrieges (von denen nur etwa 700 Personen, die meisten davon Tschetniks, in der Schweiz blieben) auf 200000 im Jahre 1990 und 320000 im Jahre 2008. Damit überholte diese Gruppe um die Jahrtausendwende erstmals die Italiener, die seit dem Zweiten Weltkrieg stets das mit Abstand größte Ausländerkontingent in der Schweiz gestellt hatten. Im gleichen Zeitraum stieg auch der Anteil der Türken stark an, von 0,1 Prozent (1960) über 1,1 Prozent (1970) und 4,1 Prozent (1980) auf 5,8 Prozent (1990), um dann bis 2008 auf 4,1 Prozent zurückzugehen. Insgesamt lebten im Jahre 2008 405357 Menschen vom Balkan und der Türkei in der Schweiz, das waren 5,2 Prozent der gesamten beziehungsweise 23,2 Prozent der ausländischen Wohnbevölkerung (Vuilleumier 2006, Steffen-Gerber 2008, Bundesamt für Migration 2009).1 Hinzu kam noch eine nicht unbeträchtliche Zahl von Menschen mit entsprechendem Migrationshintergrund, die inzwischen die schweizerische Staatsangehörigkeit erworben hatten.

Die soziale, kulturelle und politische Auswirkung dieser Migrationsbewegungen auf die schweizerische Gesellschaft war und ist enorm. Die ab den 1960er Jahren als Arbeitsmigranten und in den 1990er Jahren vermehrt auch als politische Flüchtlinge in die Schweiz kommenden Menschen vom Balkan gliederten sich zum großen Teil in die eingewanderten Unterschichten ein, die seit dem Zweiten Weltkrieg zunächst vor allem von Italienern und anderen Südeuropäern gebildet worden waren und für deren soziale Verortung die Soziologie schon in den 1970er Jahren den Begriff „Unterschichtung" geprägt hatte (Hoffmann-Nowotny 1973). Die Immigranten aus dem Balkanraum avancierten spätestens in den 1990er Jahren zum Feindbild Nummer Eins der helvetischen Xenophobie.[2] Hatte sich diese in den 1960er und 70er Jahren hauptsächlich auf die als „Tschinggen" diffamierten Italiener fokussiert,[3] so wurden – nach einer kurzen Popularität des Schimpfens gegen Lederjacken tragende tamilische Flüchtlinge in der Boulevardpresse und an den Stammtischen in den späten 1980er Jahren – nun „Jugos" in Trainingsanzügen, „balkanesische" Autoraser und ge-

---

1 Aufgeschlüsselt nach Herkunftsländern: Serbien: 179996; Türkei: 71692; Makedonien: 59664; Bosnien-Herzegowina: 37488; Kroatien: 36125; Griechenland: 6088; Rumänien: 4306; Kosovo: 3482; Slowenien: 2325; Bulgarien: 2224; Albanien: 1096; Moldova: 608; Montenegro: 263. Vgl. zu Aspekten dieser Migrationsbewegungen Kämpf 2008, Boškovska 2000, Mikić/Sommer 2003 und 2007, Mäder 2007, Riedi/Haab 2007, von Aarburg/Gretler 2008, Dahinden 2005, Tezgören 2008.

2 Vgl. allgemein dazu: Tanner 1994. Für die politische Instrumentalisierung der Xenophobie: Buomberger 2004.

3 Der seit dem späten 19. Jahrhundert gebräuchliche Begriff „Tschingg" ist vermutlich abgeleitet vom italienischen Zahlwort „cinque", insbesondere von dem im norditalienischen Spiel Morra oft vorkommenden Ausruf „cinc a la mora", aus dem die Schweizer „Tschinggalamorä" und „Tschingg" machten (Rovere 1977: 5).

walttätige „Secondos“ aus Südosteuropa zu hauptsächlichen Steinen des „gutschweizerischen“ Anstoßes.

Dies setzte das Thema auch auf die politische Agenda. Im Vorfeld des Referendums über die Ausdehnung des Personenfreizügigkeitsabkommens zwischen der Schweiz und der Europäischen Union auf Rumänien und Bulgarien im Februar 2009 malte die rechtspopulistische „Schweizerische Volkspartei“, aktuell die stärkste Partei des Landes, eine Invasion aus dem Balkan und die Überflutung der Alpen mit Fahrenden an die Wand.[4] Mit Plakaten, die auf die Schweiz hackende schwarze Raben zeigten, vermochten die Gegner der Personenfreizügigkeit immerhin 40,4 Prozent der Stimmenden zu überzeugen. Neun Monate später hießen gar 57,5 Prozent der Stimmenden eine von Exponenten derselben politischen Kreise eingereichte Volksinitiative für ein verfassungsmäßiges Verbot des Baus von Minaretten gut. Auf der anderen Seite machte etwa die Presse seit der Jahrtausendwende mit Schlagzeilen wie „Der Schweizer Nationalspieler der Zukunft kommt aus dem Balkan“ (Neue Zürcher Zeitung, 7.5.2003) oder - den traditionellen dialektalen Anfeuerungsruf „Hopp Schwyz“ mit dem für serbokroatische Namen typischen Suffix „-ić“ verbindend - „Hopp Schwiic“ (Facts, 15.7.2004) am Beispiel des Fußballs wiederholt auf den Nutzen aufmerksam, den die Schweiz aus der erfolgreichen Integration von Jugendlichen aus dem Balkanraum ziehen konnte (vgl. Koller 2006, 2008, 2008b).

Für die Zeit vor dem Zweiten Weltkrieg ist hingegen punkto Migration aus Südosteuropa in die Schweiz wenig bekannt. In den Statistiken erscheinen solche Migranten, wenn überhaupt, als unbedeutende Größen. Die wenigen Studien, die sich mit ihnen befassen, fokussieren auf elitäre Personengruppen wie Wissenschafter, Politiker und Studenten (vgl. Čičić 1982, Nuić o.J., Kieser 2003 und 2005, Staikov 2005). Über mögliche Vorläufer der Arbeitsmigration aus dem Balkanraum des späten 20. Jahrhunderts findet sich hingegen in der einschlägigen Literatur zur schweizerischen Migrations- wie auch zur Arbeitergeschichte kaum etwas. Dieser Artikel beleuchtet ein bislang nicht beachtetes Phänomen, nämlich die Verwendung von Streikbrechern aus Südosteuropa bei Arbeitskämpfen im schweizerischen Baugewerbe im ersten Viertel des 20. Jahrhunderts als Beispiel der zu dieser weit verbreiteten Praxis der Rekrutierung von „Arbeitswilligen“ in gewerkschaftlich noch wenig organisierten Gebieten. Da es sich dabei um eine lediglich temporäre Migration handelte und die Streikbrecher teilweise sogar ohne Arbeitsbewilligung eingesetzt wurden, lässt sich der quantitative Umfang dieses Phänomens nicht beziffern. Hingegen erlauben die Streikakten einzelner Arbeitskämpfe eine qualitative Analyse dieses verges-

[4] Generell zum schweizerischen Antiziganismus vgl. Meier/Wolfensberger 1998, Egger 1982, Huonker/Ludi 2001, Leimgruber 1998.

senen Kulturkontaktes. Im Folgenden sollen insbesondere die schweizerischen Wahrnehmungsmuster untersucht und zu ihren Nachfolgern um die Jahrtausendwende in Beziehung gesetzt werden.

Streiks und Immigration in der Schweiz

Zählt die Schweiz seit den 1950er Jahren zu den streikärmsten Industriestaaten der Welt, so besitzt sie für die Zeit davor eine ereignisreiche und zuweilen gar blutige Streikgeschichte (vgl. Koller 2008a, 2009). Dies gilt insbesondere für die Periode von 1880 bis zum Ausbruch des Ersten Weltkrieges, als insgesamt 2426 Streiks stattfanden (Hirter 1988: 846). Zur Mitte des ersten Jahrzehnts des 20. Jahrhunderts etwa erschütterte eine große Streikwelle das Land, auf deren Höhepunkt im Jahre 1907 sich 52777 Personen an 282 Arbeitsniederlegungen beteiligten, woraus der Verlust von 923792 Arbeitstagen resultierte.

Zeitgleich mit der raschen Zunahme der Streiktätigkeit verzeichnete die Schweiz auch eine beträchtliche Zuwanderung ausländischer Arbeitskräfte. Zwischen 1850 und 1910 stieg der Ausländeranteil von 3 auf 14,7 Prozent. Die eingewanderten Arbeiter, die sich vor allem auf die Grenzregionen sowie industrielle und urbane Ballungsräume konzentrierten, kamen dabei insbesondere aus den Nachbarländern Italien und Deutschland. Im Jahrzehnt vor dem Ersten Weltkrieg besaßen in einigen industriellen Zentren bis zu 40 Prozent der Metallarbeiter und gar bis zu 90 Prozent der Bauarbeiter keinen Schweizer Pass. Städte mit hohem Ausländeranteil befanden sich sowohl in der deutschsprachigen[5] als auch in der lateinischen[6] Schweiz (Vuilleumier 2006). Erst der Ausbruch des Ersten Weltkrieges brachte einen scharfen Einschnitt. Der Ausländeranteil ging massiv zurück, um erst in der langen wirtschaftlichen Wachstumsphase nach 1945 allmählich wieder das Niveau von 1914 zu erreichen und ab den späten 1960er Jahren gar zu übertreffen. Seit dem späten 19. Jahrhundert mehrten sich Stimmen, die die schweizerische Identität bedroht sahen und um 1900 kam das Schlagwort „Überfremdung" auf, das dann in den 1960er und 70er Jahren eine Renaissance erleben sollte (vgl. Kury 2003).

Die schweizerische Arbeiterbewegung und mit ihr das Streiken waren von Beginn an stark von Einflüssen aus den Nachbarländern geprägt (vgl. Gruner 1968, Koller 2009a). Dies führte zu einer starken Vermischung antisozialistischer und ausländerfeindlicher Diskurse. Auf Seite der Arbeitgeber und der mit ihnen sympathisierenden Presse vermutete man die Ursachen der Streiks prak-

---

[5] Z.B. Arbon (46,1 Prozent), Rorschach (41,5 Prozent), Basel (37,8 Prozent), Schaffhausen (33,9 Prozent), Zürich (33,8 Prozent).

[6] Z.B. Lugano (50,5 Prozent), Genf (42 Prozent).

tisch durchgehend im Ausland. So war etwa während des Zürcher Schlosserstreiks von 1886 mit Blick auf die deutschen Exilsozialdemokraten in der liberalen „Neuen Zürcher Zeitung“ von „fremden berufsmäßigen Agitatoren“ die Rede und von „unlautern Elementen, welche gekommen sind, im Trüben zu fischen“ (Neue Zürcher Zeitung, 11. 5. 1886, 16. 5. 1886, 6. 7. 1886). Der konservative „Stadtbote“ sah im selben Kontext sogar eine weltweite Streikverschwörung am Werke (Stadtbote, 9. 5. 1886).[7] Im Streiksommer 1906 sprach die „Neue Zürcher Zeitung“ von „Ausländerei“: „Sie ist in allem erkennbar, in der Presse, im taktischen Vorgehen: nirgends eine Spur schweizerischer Bodenständigkeit, nichts als Kopie ausländischer Muster“ (Neue Zürcher Zeitung, 22. 9. 1906). Die konservative „Freitagszeitung“ hatte im selben Jahr „nachgerade das Gefühl, einer neuen Art von Fremdherrschaft ausgeliefert zu sein, [...] nicht weniger drückend [...], als es diejenige der fremden Vögte für unsere Vorfahren war“ (Freitagszeitung, 17. 8. 1906). Im Kontext des Winterthurer Bauarbeiterstreiks von 1909/10 schrieb der freisinnige Nationalrat, Unternehmer und führende Arbeitgeberpolitiker Eduard Sulzer-Ziegler vom „Terror der italienischen Arbeiterorganisation“ und von einer „Brandschatzung“ der Schweiz, die durch höhere Löhne für die zu einem großen Teil ausländischen Bauarbeiter „dem Ausland tributpflichtig“ werde (Neues Winterthurer Tagblatt, 12. 6. 1909).

Streikbrecher vom Balkan

Diese xenophoben Töne hinderten die Schweizer Arbeitgeber indessen nicht daran, im Bedarfsfall auch jenseits der Staatsgrenzen nach Streikbrechern Ausschau zu halten. Sie waren damit keine Ausnahme. Der Einsatz von ortsfremden „Arbeitswilligen“ war zu jener Zeit eine übliche Arbeitskampfmethode der Arbeitgeberseite. Kamen diese zuweilen aus benachbarten Regionen, so war die Rekrutierung von Streikbrechern im Ausland oder, in größeren Ländern, in weiter entfernten und nach Möglichkeit soziokulturell differenten Landesteilen ebenfalls gang und gäbe. Beliebt waren dabei insbesondere Regionen, in denen die Gewerkschaften noch wenig Fuß gefasst hatten und eine Arbeiterklasse „für sich“ kaum existierte. Diese Praxis löste ab etwa 1890 einen Wettlauf zwischen Arbeitgebern und Gewerkschaften aus. Während erstere immer häufiger mit international agierenden Streikbrecheragenten zusammenarbeiteten, versuchten letztere, die grenzüberschreitende Rekrutierung von „Arbeitswilligen“ durch internationale Kooperationsabkommen zu erschweren, die ihrerseits wieder Übereinkünfte der Arbeitgeberorganisationen nach sich zogen (vgl. Koller 2009a).

[7] Vgl. zu den Verschwörungstheorien im Streikkontext Koller 2004.

Diese Transnationalisierung des Arbeitskampfes erreichte ihren Höhepunkt im letzten Jahrzehnt vor dem Ausbruch des Ersten Weltkrieges.

Die Anwerbung ausländischer Streikbrecher für den Einsatz in der Schweiz geschah etwa durch Inserate in der in- und ausländischen Presse (z. B. Landbote, 26. 8. 1909; Heuberger-Bote, 22. 2. 1910),[8] aber auch durch die Entsendung von Streikbrecheragenten in die Nachbarländer[9] und die Zusammenarbeit mit grenzüberschreitend tätigen Vermittlungsagenturen wie dem 1906 in Hamburg gegründeten „Internationalen Arbeitsnachweis".[10] In der Regel wurden dabei „Arbeitswillige" in Süddeutschland, Norditalien, Vorarlberg und Tirol rekrutiert, also in den an die Schweiz grenzenden Regionen, aus denen auch die sonstigen Arbeitsmigranten kamen. Allerdings wurde diese Praxis ab der Jahrhundertwende aufgrund des wachsenden gewerkschaftlichen Organisationsgrades auch in diesen Regionen erschwert. So konnte es vorkommen, dass die Angeworbenen, sobald sie vom Streik an ihrem Destinationsort erfuhren, ebenfalls die Arbeit niederlegten und zu den Streikenden „überliefen" (vgl. Arbeiter-Zeitung Töss, 21. 6. 1909). Die Rekrutierung von Streikbrechern in geographisch wie linguistisch weiter entfernten und gewerkschaftlich weniger gut erschlossenen Gebieten erschien deshalb, zumindest für unqualifizierte Streikbrucharbeit, als ein probates Mittel.

Der Einsatz von Streikbrechern aus dem Balkanraum ist am besten für den großen Winterthurer Bauarbeiterstreik dokumentiert, der vom 1. Juni 1909 bis zum 2. Juni 1910 dauerte und bis heute der längste Arbeitskampf der schweizerischen Streikgeschichte ist. Der Konflikt entzündete sich an der Verlängerung des Kollektivvertrags für das lokale Baugewerbe und endete mit einer Niederlage der Streikenden, dies nicht zuletzt aufgrund des massiven Zuzugs auswärtiger Streikbrecher (vgl. Schneider 1960: 103–109 und 112 f., Koller 2007 und 2009: 158–178). Diese kamen nicht nur aus Deutschland, Italien und dem Tirol, sondern auch aus Slowenien und Kroatien, vereinzelt auch aus Galizien, Bosnien, Serbien und Makedonien in die Ostschweizer Industriemetropole.[11] Die Arbeitgeber nahmen es dabei mit den gesetzlichen Vorschriften nicht immer ganz genau und versäumten es in einigen Fällen, für die „Arbeitswilligen" eine Arbeits-

[8] Vgl. auch Stadtarchiv Winterthur, Baumeisterverband 2, Copie des Lettres, S. 84.

[9] Vgl. z. B. Holzarbeiter-Zeitung, 26. 6. 1909; Bau- und Holzarbeiterzeitung, 9. 8. 1923; Basler Arbeiter-Zeitung, 15. 8. 1923; Staatsarchiv Basel-Stadt, Handel und Gewerbe AA 23: Polizeirapporte vom 13. 8. 1923 und 14. 8. 1923; ebd. Abl. 1998/7, Kiste 4, Zimmerleute: Protokolle, 9. Apr. 1920 - 6. Jan. 1924, 10. 8. 1923.

[10] Vgl. Stadtarchiv Winterthur, Baumeisterverband 4.

[11] Vgl. z. B. Schweizerisches Sozialarchiv (Zürich), Ar 21.20.1 Undatierte Notiz Arbeitersekretariat Winterthur; ebd. Arbeiterunion der Bezirke Winterthur, Pfäffikon und Uster an Bundeskomitee des Schweiz. Gewerkschaftsbundes, 25. 5. 1910.

bewilligung einzuholen.[12] Zudem monierte das k. u. k. österreichisch-ungarische General-Konsulat in Zürich im März 1910 in einem Schreiben an das Statthalteramt Winterthur, dass angeworbenen Arbeitern aus der Donaumonarchie, die keine Streikbrucharbeit verrichten und wieder abreisen wollten, von einem Bauunternehmen die Herausgabe ihrer Effekten verweigert wurde.[13]

Um den Zuzug fremdsprachiger Streikbrecher zu bekämpfen, nahm das Winterthurer Arbeitersekretariat mit italienischen Arbeiterorganisationen sowie dem Gewerkschaftssekretariat in Zagreb Kontakt auf und ließ mit deren Hilfe Flugblätter und Plakate auf Serbokroatisch, Slowenisch und Italienisch produzieren und verbreiten.[14] Auch mit dem bulgarischen Gewerkschaftsbund wurde Korrespondenz geführt.[15] Im Frühjahr 1910 reiste Franz Pechota, ein böhmischstämmiger Redaktor der Winterthurer „Arbeiter-Zeitung“, sogar durch Kroatien, Slawonien, Dalmatien und Krain, um die dortige Arbeiterschaft über den Streik zu informieren und vor der Anwerbung durch Streikbrecheragenten zu warnen.[16] In Winterthur selber stellte die Streikorganisation, um die Umgehung des von Streikposten „bewachten“ Hauptbahnhofs mit Fuhrwerken und Autos zu verhindern, ein Automobil in ihren Dienst (vgl. Der Bauhandwerker, 4. 6. 1910). Gemäß einem nach Streikabbruch verfassten Artikel der Streikkommission konnten insgesamt über 2000 auswärts angeworbene Arbeiter von der Aufnahme der Arbeit abgehalten beziehungsweise zur Abreise aus Winterthur bewegt werden.[17]

Pflegten ansonsten in den Streikdiskursen wie gezeigt die Arbeitgeber und die sie unterstützende bürgerliche Presse eine scharfe Abgrenzung zwischen „Einheimischen“ und „Fremden“ vorzunehmen, so war es nun an den Gewerkschaften, eine möglichst eindeutige Differenzkonstruktion vorzunehmen. Gemäß mehreren Dokumenten aus der Feder der Streikkommission handelte es

---

[12] Vgl. Stadtarchiv Winterthur GB 44 Polizeiprotokoll 1910, S. 135.

[13] Staatsarchiv Zürich P 193: a: 2: 6 K. u. k. österreichisch-ungarisches General-Konsulat Zürich an Statthalteramt Winterthur, 18. 3. 1910.

[14] Schweizerisches Sozialarchiv (Zürich), Ar 21.20.1 Zirkulare; ebd. Plakat „Svarilo! Zidarij in tezaki pozor!“; Schweizerisches Sozialarchiv (Zürich), Ar 21.20.2 Arbeitersekretariat Winterthur an Wilhelm Buchsegg, Gewerkschaftssekretär in Agram, 22. 2. 1910; ebd. Handzettel, April 1910.

[15] Schweizerisches Sozialarchiv (Zürich), Ar 21.20.2 Bulgarischer Gewerkschaftsbund an Arbeitersekretariat Winterthur, 29. 10. 1909.

[16] Schweizerisches Sozialarchiv (Zürich), Ar 21.20.2 Streikkommission an die österreichischen Bruderorganisationen, ohne Datum [Frühjahr 1910].

[17] Schweizerisches Sozialarchiv (Zürich), Ar 21.20.1 Text der Streikkommission zum Streikabbruch, Juni 1910.

sich bei dem so genannten „Streikbrechergesindel“[18] um „Lumpenproletarier erster Güte“[19], die entweder aus „kulturell noch rückständigen Ländern“[20] stammten oder sich aber aus dem „minderwertige[n] Element“[21] anderer Industriestaaten rekrutierten.

Namentlich in internen Diskursen verschmolz die angebliche Unzivilisiertheit der ausländischen Streikbrecher mit deren miserabler Behandlung durch die Unternehmer. So schrieb der Winterthurer Arbeitersekretär mehrfach an seinen Kollegen in Zagreb, die Streikbrecher aus Kroatien und Galizien befänden sich „in einer recht traurigen Lage“, würden „wie die Hunde in einer elenden Hütte untergebracht & wie die Hunde gefüttert“ und „von den Läusen beinahe aufgefressen“.[22] Die in solchen Beschreibungen enthaltene Anklage an die Adresse der Unternehmer indessen wurde durch Aussagen relativiert, die diese Behandlung als den Streikbrechern an sich angemessen erscheinen ließ. So hielt der Arbeitersekretär fest, „dass der ganze Hof in dem sich diese Leute aufhalten einer Mistgrube gleichsieht & es in der Bude drinnen vor lauter Gestank kein zivilisirter Mensch fünf Minuten lang aushalte. Wie wir Ihnen ja seiner Zeit mitteilten sind der größte Teil dieser Streikbrecher wieder abgereist & sind nur ein paar Lumpen die Ihren Judaslohn in Alkohol umsetzen noch hier geblieben.“[23] Die Unzivilisiertheit der Streikbrecher betonte das Arbeitersekretariat auch in einem anderen Schreiben zu einem abgefangenen Transport von 14 Arbeitern aus Serbien und Makedonien: „Wir mussten sie aber trotz der Läuse die sie mitbrachten, eine Nacht hier behalten um sie am andern Tag nach Zürich zu spedieren.“[24]

Öffentlich zeichnete ein ähnliches Bild von den ostmittel- und südosteuropäischen Streikbrechern etwa das sozialdemokratische Witzblatt „Der Neue Postillon“ in einem Gedicht mit dem Titel „Eines Winterthurer Streikbrecheragenten Leid und Freud“ (Der Neue Postillon, 19. 3. 1910):

---

[18] Schweizerisches Sozialarchiv (Zürich), Ar 21.20.2 Arbeitersekretariat Winterthur an Wilhelm Buchsegg, Gewerkschaftssekretär in Agram, 1. 2. 1910.

[19] Schweizerisches Sozialarchiv (Zürich), Ar 21.20.2 Arbeitersekretariat Winterthur an Wilhelm Buchsegg, Gewerkschaftssekretär in Agram, 22. 2. 1910.

[20] Schweizerisches Sozialarchiv (Zürich), Ar 21.20.3 Arbeiter-Union Zürich, 30. 11. 1909.

[21] Schweizerisches Sozialarchiv (Zürich), Ar 21.20.1 Text der Streikkomission zum Streikabbruch, Juni 1910.

[22] Schweizerisches Sozialarchiv (Zürich), Ar 21.20.3 Arbeitersekretariat Winterthur, 5. 10. 1909; ebd. Ar 21.20.2 Arbeitersekretariat Winterthur an Gewerkschaftssekretariat für Kroatien & Slowenien, 18. 10. 1909.

[23] Schweizerisches Sozialarchiv (Zürich), Ar 21.20.2 Arbeitersekretariat Winterthur an Wilhelm Buchsegg, Gewerkschaftssekretär in Agram, 1. 2. 1910.

[24] Schweizerisches Sozialarchiv (Zürich), Ar 21.20.2 Arbeitersekretariat Winterthur an Wilhelm Buchsegg, Gewerkschaftssekretär in Agram, 22. 2. 1910.

„Bald bin ich im Tirol
Im Schönen Zillertal
In Böhmen und Slowenien
Kennt man mich überall. [...]

Komm ich in eine Stadt
Geh ich in d'Herberg nein
Ruf ich: Wer will nach Winterthur
Will jeder der erste sein.

Dann muss vorerst bezahlen
Ich Bier, Wein, Brot und Schnaps
Und wenn die Bande besoffen ist
Hab ich selbst einen Schwaps.

Bring ich sie dann zur Bahn
Will jeder Vorschuss noch
Und haben die Lumpen ihren Teil
Blamieren sie sich doch.

Gelingt's mir oft mit Müh
Doch einen Fang zu tun
Steigt die Bande aus in Winterthur
Und beginnt gleich auszuruhn!

Die größten Lumpen all
Die ich auftreiben kann
Sind nicht wert, dass man sie spediert
Doch ich brauch jedermann."

Das in der Arbeiterpresse und internen gewerkschaftlichen Texten vorzufindende Streikbrecherbild verband die gängigen west- und mitteleuropäischen Vorstellungen über den Balkan und seine Bewohner mit den zeitgenössischen Zivilisationsdiskursen. Die Streikbrecher aus Südosteuropa wurden als schmutzig, verlaust und faul beschrieben. Zugleich wurden sie mit dem west- und mitteleuropäischen „Lumpenproletariat" auf eine Stufe gestellt, das sich offenbar nicht nur durch ein mangelndes Klassenbewusstsein, sondern auch einen starken Hang zum Alkoholismus auszeichnete. Diese semantische Parallelisierung zwischen „fremder" und „einheimischer" Alterität war indessen kein Spezifikum der Arbeitskämpfe mit südosteuropäischen Streikbrechern. 1906 etwa hatte die sozialdemokratische Zeitung „Volksrecht“ im Kontext eines Aufsehen erregenden Metallarbeiterstreiks in einem Zürcher Vorort seitens der (schweizerischen) Streikbrecher „Gejohl“, „als käme es aus den Kehlen der afrikanischen Wilden“ vernommen und Angreifer auf die Streikposten mit „Kannibalen“ verglichen (Volksrecht, 29. 8. 1906 und 30. 6. 1906). Offensichtlich manifestierte sich hier eine spezifisch sozialistische Variante der zeitgenössischen Zivilisationsideologie.[25]

Allerdings blieb es im Winterthurer Bauarbeiterstreik nicht bei verbalen Attacken. Verschiedentlich kam es zu Schlägereien zwischen Gegnern und Befürwortern des Streiks. Eine besondere Zielscheibe der Streikenden waren die Quartiere der Streikbrecher. Wiederholt bedrohten Streiksympathisanten Wirtinnen, die den „Arbeitswilligen“ Quartier gewährten.[26] Auch stürmten Streikende und Streiksympathisanten mehrfach Arbeiterbaracken.[27] So drangen am 9. Mai 1910 kurz vor Mitternacht zwischen 75 und 100 Mann in die Baracke der Firma Häring ein, um die zumeist kroatischen Streikbrecher einzuschüchtern.[28] Auch hier scheint allerdings zwischen einheimischen und ausländischen Streikbrechern kein wesentlicher Unterschied gemacht worden zu sein.

Bei den Unternehmern, auf der anderen Seite, führte die Abhängigkeit von ausländischen Streikbrechern nicht im Geringsten zu einer internationalistischen Haltung. Vielmehr waren sie bemüht, die Herkunft der Streikbrecher möglichst zu vertuschen. So schrieben die Winterthurer Baumeister in einer Eingabe an die Stadtregierung im März 1910, die „Arbeitswilligen“, „welche z. Zt. in der großen Hauptsache aus *Schweizern* bestehen“, hätten „Anspruch darauf, ungehindert ihrem Berufe nachzugehen und ihr tägliches Brot zu verdienen, ohne sich vorher einen Freibrief beim italienischen Streikkomitee holen zu müssen“ (Akten 1910: 32 f.). Da der massive Einsatz ausländischer Streikbrecher nicht in die von der Arbeitgeberseite gerne verbreitete Dichotomie zwischen faulen, ewig streikenden Ausländern und arbeitswilligen Schweizern passte, wurden die „Arbeitswilligen“ kurzerhand zu Schweizern umgedeutet.

---

[25] Vgl. grundsätzlich dazu Koller 2005 und Fisch 1992.

[26] Vgl. Stadtarchiv Winterthur, GB 44 Polizeiprotokoll 1910, S. 132 und 180; ebd. B 2: 163 Stadtrats-Protokoll, 7. März 1908 - 21. Juni 1910, S. 617.

[27] Schweizerisches Sozialarchiv (Zürich), Ar 21.20.4 Bezirkanwaltschaft Winterthur: Verfügung betreffend Teilnahme an Nötigung, böswilliger Eigentumsbeschädigung, Hausfriedensstörung, 7. 6. 1910.

[28] Vgl. Stadtarchiv Winterthur, GB 44 Polizeiprotokoll 1910, S. 260 f.; Staatsarchiv Zürich P 193: a: 2: 6 Spezialrapport Polizeikorps Zürich, 10. 5. 1910; Schweizerisches Sozialarchiv (Zürich), Ar 21.20.4 Bezirksanwaltschaft Winterthur: Verfügungen betreffend Anstiftung & Teilnahme zu bezw. an Nötigung, böswilliger Eigentumsbeschädigung und Hausfriedensbruch, 30. 5. 1910, 31. 5. 1910, 7. 6. 1910; Neues Winterthurer Tagblatt, 10. 5. 1910.

13 Jahre und einen Weltkrieg später, beim sechsmonatigen Basler Holzarbeiterstreik von 1923, war die Situation dann einfacher (vgl. Brügger 1979: 55–60; Gschwend 1983: 37–39; Degen 1991: 186–190; Koller 2009: 331–344). Wiederum versuchten die Bestreikten mit unter anderem in Südosteuropa angeworbenen „Arbeitswilligen“ die Ausständigen in die Knie zu zwingen. Als im August 1923 aber die ersten vier kroatischen Streikbrecher in Basel eingetroffen und von Streikposten über den Arbeitskampf informiert worden waren, legten sie selber die Arbeit nieder. Die Arbeiterpresse konnte dies als Triumph der internationalen Solidarität feiern (Basler Arbeiter-Zeitung, 10. 8. 1923; Bau- und Holzarbeiterzeitung, 16. 8. 1923), während es den Arbeitgebern im Folgenden erspart blieb, die Anwesenheit von Streikbrechern aus dem Balkanraum mit ihren anhaltend ausländerfeindlichen Streiksdiskursen in Einklang zu bringen zu müssen.

Fazit

Insgesamt war die Rekrutierung von Streikbrechern in Südosteuropa für den Einsatz in Arbeitskämpfen im schweizerischen Baugewerbe im frühen 20. Jahrhundert ein zwar quantitativ unbedeutendes, sozial- und kulturhistorisch aber dennoch interessantes Phänomen. Es zeigt einerseits den hohen Grad an Transnationalität, den die Streiktätigkeit um die Jahrhundertwende erreicht hatte. Streikbrecheragenten begaben sich wie frühneuzeitliche Söldnergeneräle grenzüberschreitend auf Rekrutierungstour und wurden dabei, ebenfalls wie frühneuzeitliche Söldnergeneräle, zuweilen in Südosteuropa fündig. Die Gewerkschaften, auf der anderen Seite, verfügten über ein transnationales Korrespondenznetz, zunehmend auch internationale Dachorganisationen, und schickten manchmal auch eigene Leute auf die Reise, um den Streikbrecheragenten zuvorzukommen.

Aus kulturhistorischer Sicht interessieren vor allem die wechselseitigen Perzeptionen und Interaktionen vor Ort. Während sich die Quellen über die Erlebnisse und Erfahrungen der Südosteuropäer leider ausschweigen, lassen sich zumindest für den Fall des Winterthurer Streiks die schweizerischen Wahrnehmungen und Reaktionen relativ gut rekonstruieren. Sie verdeutlichen die Prominenz von Eigen-Fremd-Konstruktionen in schweizerischen Streikdiskursen und zeigen gewissermaßen eine Umdrehung der üblichen Positionen. Während ansonsten die Arbeitgeber gegen die „fremden“ Streikenden Front zu machen pflegten, wandten sich hier die Arbeiterorganisationen gegen die „fremden“ Streikbrecher. Allerdings sind die Alteritätskonstruktionen nicht exakt spiegelbildlich. Die Arbeitgeber pflegten als Unterscheidungskriterium zwischen Eigen und Fremd auf die Nationalität zu rekurrieren, während sich die Arbeitnehmerorganisationen unter Wahrung ihres internationalistischen Anspruchs auf die „Zivilisation" beriefen. Dadurch verschmolz die den Balkan als rückständig betrachtende west- und mitteleuropäische „mental map" mit dem sozialistischen Klassenbewusstsein und Fortschrittsoptimismus: Menschen vom Balkan erschienen auf der gleichen Stufe wie „Lumpenproletarier" aus den Industriestaaten - allerdings im eigenen Erwartungshorizont nur für den Moment.[29]

Im Vergleich zu schweizerischen Wahrnehmungen südosteuropäischer Immigranten im späten 20. und frühen 21. Jahrhundert fallen sowohl Kontinuitäten als auch deutliche Unterschiede auf. Während das Bild insgesamt negativ und stark stereotypisiert blieb, änderte sich die Bedrohungswahrnehmung deutlich. Ganz anders als etwa die Italiener, die um die Wende zum 20. Jahrhundert als notorische Ruhestörer, Messerstecher und anarchistische Umstürzler betrachtet wurden, erschienen Menschen vom Balkan in den Streikdiskursen zwar als faul, schmutzig und unzivilisiert, aber nicht wirklich unmittelbar bedrohlich. Dies sollte sich gegen Ende des 20. Jahrhunderts ändern. Parallel zum quantitativen Gleichzug der Südosteuropäer mit den Italienern in der Schweiz und zur zunehmenden Respektabilisierung der letzteren in der helvetischen Wahrnehmung seit den 1970er Jahren wurden, gefördert von Boulevardpresse und rechtspopulistischer Propaganda, zahlreiche Stereotypen von den „Tschinggen" auf die „Jugos" und andere „Balkanesen" transferiert - nicht zuletzt die Vorstellung von einer kulturellen „Überfremdung" der schweizerischen Eidgenossenschaft.

Literatur

Aarburg, Hans-Peter von, Sarah Barbara Gretler 2008: Kosova-Schweiz: Die albanische Arbeits- und Asylmigration zwischen Kosovo und der Schweiz (1964–2000). Wien: Lit.

Akten betr. den Streik der Maurer und Erdarbeiter in Winterthur 1909 und 1910 (Vom Stadtrate veröffentlicht gemäß Beschluss vom 8. März 1910). Winterthur: Stadtrat.

Boškovska, Nada 2000: „Jugoslawen" in der Schweiz: Soziale, kulturelle und ethnische Herkunft, Integrationsprobleme. In: Schweizerische Ärztezeitung 81, 47: 2647–2651.

Buomberger, Thomas 2004: Kampf gegen unerwünschte Fremde: Von James Schwarzenbach bis Christoph Blocher. Zürich: Orell Füssli.

[29] Vgl. zu den theoretischen Positionen der internationalen Sozialdemokratie zur „Balkanfrage" und ihrer Verortung in den eigenen Fortschritts- und Zivilisationsdiskursen Koller 2005a: 300–320, ferner MacDonald 1939.

Brügger, Helen 1979: Die Basler Arbeiterbewegung nach Gründung der KPS. Universität Basel, Lizentiatsarbeit, Historisches Seminar.

Bundesamt für Migration 2009: Bestand der ständigen ausländischen Wohnbevölkerung nach Staatsangehörigkeit Ende 2007 und Ende 2008. URL: http://www.bfm.admin.ch (eingesehen: 8. 4. 2009).

Čičić, Zvonimir 1982: Die Kroaten in der Schweiz. Zürich: Eigenverlag.

Dahinden, Janine 2005: Prishtina - Schlieren: Albanische Migrationsnetzwerke im transnationalen Raum. Zürich: Seismo.

Degen, Bernard 1991: Abschied vom Klassenkampf: Die partielle Integration der schweizerischen Gewerkschaftsbewegung zwischen Landesstreik und Weltwirtschaftskrise (1918–1929). Basel: Helbing & Lichtenhahn.

Egger, Franz 1982: Der Bundesstaat und die fremden Zigeuner in der Zeit von 1848 bis 1914. In: Studien und Quellen 8: 49–71.

Fisch, Jörg 1992: Zivilisation, Kultur. In: Otto Brunner et al. (Hg.), Geschichtliche Grundbegriffe 7. Stuttgart: Klett, 679–774.

Gruner, Erich 1968: Die Arbeiter in der Schweiz im 19. Jahrhundert: Soziale Lage, Organisation, Verhältnis zu Arbeitgeber und Staat. Bern: Francke.

Gschwend, Urs Felix 1983: Die Basler Arbeiterbewegung in den 1920er Jahren. Universität Basel. Lizentiatsarbeit, Historisches Seminar.

Hirter, Hans 1988: Die Streiks in der Schweiz in den Jahren 1880–1914: Quantitative Streikanalyse. In: ders. et al. (Hg.), Arbeiterschaft und Wirtschaft in der Schweiz 1880–1914: Soziale Lage, Organisation und Kämpfe von Arbeitern und Unternehmern, politische Organisationen und Sozialpolitik, Bd. II/2. Zürich: Chronos, 837–1008.

Hoffmann-Nowotny, Hans-Joachim 1973: Soziologie des Fremdarbeiterproblems: Eine theoretische und empirische Analyse am Beispiel der Schweiz. Stuttgart: Enke.

Huonker, Thomas, Regula Ludi 2001: Roma, Sinti und Jenische: Schweizerische Zigeunerpolitik zur Zeit des Nationalsozialismus. Zürich: Chronos.

Kämpf, Philipp 2008: Die Jugo-Schweiz: Klischees, Provokationen, Visionen. Zürich: Rüegger.

Kieser, Hans-Lukas 2003: Turkey's Elite Diaspora in Switzerland (1860s to 1920s). In: Meropi Anastassiadou (Hg.), Médecins et ingénieurs ottomans à l'âge des nationalismes. Paris: Maisonneuve et Larose, 349–382.

Kieser, Hans-Lukas 2005: Vorkämpfer der „neuen Türkei“: Revolutionäre Bildungseliten am Genfersee (1870–1939). Zürich: Chronos.

Koller, Christian 2004: Coulissenschieber, Spitzelhunde und Dunkelmänner – Verschwörungstheorien im schweizerischen Streikdiskurs vor dem Ersten Weltkrieg. In: Traverse 11, 3: 73–84.

Koller, Christian 2005: Eine Zivilisierungsmission der Arbeiterklasse? Die Diskussion über eine „sozialistische Kolonialpolitik" vor dem Ersten Weltkrieg. In: Boris Barth, Jürgen Osterhammel (Hg.), Zivilisierungsmissionen: Imperiale Weltverbesserung seit dem 18. Jahrhundert. Konstanz: Universitätsverlag, 229–243.

Koller, Christian 2005a: Fremdherrschaft: Ein politischer Kampfbegriff im Zeitalter des Nationalismus. Frankfurt: Campus.

Koller, Christian 2006: Wer ist ein echter Schweizer? Doppelbürger, „Secondos", Ein- und Auswanderer in der Nati. In: Beat Jung (Hg.), Die Nati: Die Geschichte der Schweizer Fußball-Nationalmannschaft. Göttingen: Werkstatt, 51–62.

Koller, Christian 2007: Wildwest in Winterthur: Ein Bauarbeiterstreik und seine Folgen. In: Jahrbuch Winterthur 54, 136–141.

Koller, Christian 2008: Zwischen Secondo-Goalgettern und Kebab-Boykott: Prolegomena zu einer schweizerisch-türkischen Beziehungsgeschichte im Medium des Fußballs. Basel: Forschungsstelle Schweiz-Türkei.

Koller, Christian 2008a: La grève depuis le Moyen Âge: 600 ans de conflits du travail en Suisse. In: Ralph Hug, Stefan Keller (Red.), La grève, ça paie! Les conflits du travail en Suisse depuis la grève générale de 1918. Bern: Schweizerischer Gewerkschaftsbund, 42–51.

Koller, Christian 2008b: Fußball und Immigration in der Schweiz (1945–2008): Identitätswahrung, Assimilation oder Transkulturalität? In: Stadion 34, 261–284.

Koller, Christian 2009: Streikkultur: Performanzen und Diskurse des Arbeitskampfes im schweizerisch-österreichischen Vergleich (1860–1950). Münster-Wien: LIT.

Koller, Christian 2009a: Local Strikes as Transnational Events: Migration, Donations and Organisational Co-operation in the Context of Strikes in Switzerland (1860–1914). In: Labour History Review 74, 305–318.

Kury, Patrick 2003: Über Fremde reden: Überfremdungsdiskurs und Ausgrenzung in der Schweiz 1900–1945. Zürich: Chronos.

Leimgruber, Walter et al. 1998: Das Hilfswerk für die Kinder der Landstraße: Historische Studie aufgrund der Akten der Stiftung Pro Juventute im Schweizerischen Bundesarchiv. Bern: Schweizerisches Bundesarchiv.

MacDonald, Malcolm 1939: Karl Marx, Friedrich Engels, and the South Slav Question. In: University of Toronto Quarterly 7, 452–460.

Mäder, Lukas 2007: Jugoslawische Landarbeiter bei Schweizer Bauern: Die Kollektivrekrutierungen des Schweizerischen Bauernverbandes in Jugoslawien 1964–1974. Universität Zürich. Lizentiatsarbeit, Historisches Seminar.

Meier, Thomas D., Rolf Wolfensberger 1998: Eine Heimat und doch keine: Heimatlose und Nicht-Sesshafte in der Schweiz (16.–19. Jahrhundert). Zürich: Chronos.

Mikić, Dejan, Erika Sommer 2003: Als Serbe warst du plötzlich nichts mehr wert: Serben und Serbinnen in der Schweiz. Zürich: Orell Füssli.

Mikić, Dejan, Erika Sommer (Hg.) 2007: Jugoslawien - Schweiz einfach: 20 Erfolgsgeschichten. Zürich: Orell Füssli.

Nuić, Tihomir [o. J.]: Auf der Suche nach Freiheit und Brot: Spuren der Kroaten in der Schweiz. St. Gallen: Ivo Ledergerber.

Riedi, Anna Maria, Katharina Haab 2007: Jugendliche aus dem Balkan: Migration und Integration als Herausforderung für die Jugendhilfe. Zürich: Rüegger.

Rovere, Giovanni 1977: Testi di Italiano Popolare: Autobiografie di lavoratori e figli di lavoratori emigrati: Analisi sociolinguistica. Rom: Centro studi emigrazione.

Schneider, Willi 1960: Die Geschichte der Winterthurer Arbeiterbewegung. Winterthur: Genossenschafts-Buchhandlung.

Staikov, Zvetelina 2005: Bulgarien. In: Historisches Lexikon der Schweiz (elektronische Publikation), Version vom 11. 2. 2005.

Steffen-Gerber, Therese 2008: Jugoslawien. In: Historisches Lexikon der Schweiz (elektronische Publikation), Version vom 4. 2. 2008.

Tanner, Jakob 1994: Nationalmythos und „Überfremdungsängste“: Wie und warum die Immigration zum Problem wird, dargestellt am Beispiel der Schweizer Geschichte des 19. und 20. Jahrhunderts, in: Udo Rauchfleisch (Hg.), Fremd im Paradies: Migration und Rassismus. Basel: Lenos, 11–23.

Tezgören, Olivier 2008: Von „Pseudo-Touristen“ zu „Pseudo-Asylanten“: Die Einwanderung aus der Türkei in die Schweiz 1960–1990 im Fokus der Eidgenössischen Fremdenpolizei. Universität Zürich. Lizentiatsarbeit, Historisches Seminar.

Vuilleumier, Marc 2006: Ausländer. In: Historisches Lexikon der Schweiz (elektronische Publikation), Version vom 21. 9. 2006.

Ethnologia Balkanica 13 (2009)

Migration as Reflected in Narratives Written by Migrants Self-Identification and Presentation for Posterity

Biljana Ristovska-Josifovska, Skopje

Abstract

By exploring a number of Macedonian migrants from the western border-region of Macedonia through their written records, the present research attempts to study the expression of self-identification and presentation for posterity. The presentation of these profiles aims to display the similarities and differences between people's notions of certain actual historic events. Studying today's storytelling becomes important if we take into consideration the dynamics of migration movements in the region that continues to produce migrants to this day.

The movement of peoples is a political, social, economic and cultural process that has occurredcontinues since ancient times. The Balkan region has a long history of population movements – including emigrations, immigrations and forced migrations – which have varied over time in scope and intensity. In the contemporary context, discussions regarding issues related to migration have acquired great importance. The analysis of present trends in trans-border mobility reveals a variety of types of mobility. In Macedonia, different terms have been used to describe migration in different historical periods, among them most prominently the terms *gurbet* or *pečalba*, used to refer to economic migration involving temporary residence away from the native country (migrations thatwhich would often become permanent), and the term *Gastarbeiter* ("guest -worker") denoting workers migrating for temporary employment abroad from the 1960s onwards (cf. Vrazhinovski 2001: 6 f.; Stojanovik-Lafazanovska 2008: 27–31).

This paper focuses on migrations from the Mijak region as part of the western border -region of the Republic of Macedonia, and especially on the records of individual migrants from this area.[1] Population movements have been a dominant factor in the region's history. A combination of economic instability and persistent violence in this area resulted incaused a number of mass migrations of Macedonians, especially during the 19th century. The consequences of these

[1] See Smiljanic 1924: 61; Cvijić 1931: 166–178; Palikruševa 1996: 14; Petreska 1998: 7–25; Ristovska-Josifovska 2008a: 457–466.

migrations included confessional and ethnic changes such as Islamisation or Albanization and Turkicization (Limanoski 1984: 12–61; Trifunoski 1988: 59–70). In terms of their destination, these population movements included internal migrations in Macedonia – primarily to the regions of Veles, Kičevo, and Bitola – as well as external migrations in search of a better life in Serbia, Bulgaria, Romania, Egypt, etc.[2]

Occurring over a long period of time, these migrations developed in stages and varied in scale and duration according to whether they involved the departure of individuals or entire families. Initial migrations were typically undertaken by short-term migrants without their families: seasonal labourers, herdsmen and craftsmen, for example, or groups of construction-workers. Later on, some of these migrants came to settle permanently with their families (Cvijić 1922: 200 f.), causing significant changes in their language, folklore, customs, and clothing as they adapted to new cultural environments. Such adaptation was facilitated with the help of previously migrated populations who provided support for the newcomers. Macedonian emigrants typically socialized by forming cultural and educational associations and often by developing vigorous publishing activities in Macedonian or in the languages of the countries of residence.

The records of migrant authors and writers

With regard to the methodology employed in compiling this paper, I have not restricted my historical research to archive materials. Rather, in accordance with the approach of historical anthropology in which any form of testimony to human manifestation may constitute a valid historical source, and by employing methods of other disciplines in addition to those of history (cf. Dresel 1997: 90–96), this paper makes use of sources of information such as statistics, works on ethnography, folklore, history, and arts, etc. In particular, extensive use is made of the personal records of migrants and local writers in whose texts migration is reflected. In all these works, one can see the familiarity of the authors with migration as part of everyday life. Thus, with a view to elucidating a "migrational mentality", we ask how this mentality was articulated in the texts. As Aaron Gurevich maintained: "Every historian at some time encounters the socio-psychological side of history, since it is difficult to find any historical source which does not bear the stamp of the *mentalité* of its creators" (Gurevich 1992: 4).

---

[2] There were many customs related to migrating for work (see Smiljanić 1925: 67–68; Spirovska 1971: 259–263; Petreska 1998: 13–15).

The writings of selected authors and local writers, being the most immediate form of expression of those involved in the migration processes, are examined here as part of our endeavour to assess the ways in which different types of migration – i. e., internal migration, seasonal migration, emigration to neighbouring countries – are reflected in these texts and in the personal experience of authors who were often migrants themselves. The authors were selected partly on the basis of their having originated from the western part of Macedonia, a region in which migrational processes are particularly clear, partly on account of the link between their personal stories and migrations to other regions within or outside of Macedonia, and partly with regard to the diversity of their profiles. It is of particular importance for us that their works are immediate expressions of their personal opinions and feelings, as these authors were themselves amongst the people involved in the migratory processes. Although the records differ in respect of type and content, a common thread is found throughout the works that lies in the authors' aim of leaving a trace of themselves for future generations. These accounts, though individually expressed, constitute a part of a collective identity.[3]

The contents of the individual works analysed in this paper also serve as indicators of the situation throughout the region. Written from the point of view of people who participated in those processes in different ways, they reveal to us a number of motivations connected with the migrations of the population. In different works, regardless of whether they possess any artistic value or not, the movements and lives of migrants are reflected through narrations of their own experiences and those of people from the same region.

On the records of Macedonian migrants from the Mijak region

The notes and testimonies to be found in autobiographies and memoirs[4] provide insights into ideas and views. In writing about themselves and others, the authors relate to different aspects of the history of migrations, giving us specific information about events and people and dates, often presenting the migrant's philosophy from within.

Gjurčin Kokaleski (1775–1863), a rich cattle-breeder, gained a good reputation and became a famous landowner, tradesman and cattle-dealer. He was among the first organizers of a cattle-breeding organization (1801), a head of the region, a church- donor and the author of the first secular autobiographical text

[3] See Asmann 2001: 129–132.

[4] For autobiography in Macedonian literature see Avramovska 2004: 16–26.

in Macedonian literary history, “Narration” *(Nakazanie)*. His autobiographical text (Matkovski 1959: 107–116), written most probably around 1823/24, contains references to a number of historical and cultural trends in the Macedonian part of the Ottoman Empire. We cannot consider this autobiography a work of literary art; nor did the author intend it to be as such. Kokaleski simply created a kind of *manual* intended to advise his descendants as to how to proceed if they wished to emulate his success. With regard to events in the Mijak region, it is interesting to analyse Kokaleski’s work in terms of how his testimonies of individual professional activities present his autobiographical profile and his personal identity (Ristovska-Josifovska 2008: 305–313) as compared to the stories told by his present-day descendants (Hristov 2008: 314–322). The text can be analysed from different vantage points as a cultural indicator of the general situation in the Mijak region articulated through his life story. With regard to Kokaleski’s basic motivation to write his autobiography, the authorial dedication to his ‘sons, grandsons and all relatives’ at the beginning sheds some light on the subject and is highly significant. As a matter of fact, the whole text seems to be a narration with a utilitarian value, a kind of instructive manual for posterity.

In his autobiography we can follow a typical route of (seasonal and internal) labour migrations. Kokaleski used to migrate to work (in *Debar, Katerino,* and *Voden*). He narrates his life story with great precision and relates, how he worked and learnt various handicrafts over the years, but still stayed poor (Belich 1935: 278). Later on, he began to breed and sell sheep and became very rich *(“khaja”)*. Together with a partner and a number of hired workers, he regularly travelled to towns such as *Ber, Salonika,* and *Prilep* (Belich 1935: 283). Cattle-breeding was one of the primary activities in the Mijak region, but in time, as a result of the insecurity (there were frequent thefts and murders of stockbreeders), migration for work became one of the primary ways of providing for the family.

The work of Kokaleski offers an opportunity to study economic relations in Ottoman society through data recording various transactions and bills of sale of cattle and properties, as well as through descriptions of how work was organized, how rent relations (the hiring of people and property) operated within the law and in accordance with common law. Kokaleski relates, for example, that he used to travel to Thessalonika *(Solun)* with partners and together with people from Galičnik and Platičani, where they would sell sheep wool with the help of a middleman (Belich 1935: 283). He gives detailed information about the winter quarters for livestock *(zimovnici)*, numbers and values of sheep, and information about people (by name and by origin), etc.

Beside Kokaleski we place *Isaija R. Mažovski* (1852–1925), an anti-patriarchate and exarchate activist with an emphatically Slavophile orientation who believed in Russian support, an advocate of the idea of a joint Macedonian-Albanian anti-Ottoman struggle, and an emigrant who expressed his personal ideas and striving in his “Memoirs”. What we can draw from his writings, and which can serve not only as indicative of the village of Lazaropole in the 19th century but of the Mijak region and wider Macedonia, is a large number of snapshots of everyday life (customs, holidays, the symbols and iconography of village flags), accounts of historical events, his own ideology and political activities. Throughout his “Memoirs”, internal or external, economic or political migrations form a motif. The author also tries to present the historical movements of the peoples in separate stories, thus producing a written history based on his own experiences and on tales and folk memory. Several historical points are highlighted from earlier history in order to confirm the place of Macedonians in comparison with others, in relation to the times when they settled (Mažovski 1922: 6–8, 14–19, 22).

The movements of Mažovski himself through the Balkans and Russia were largely politically motivated, aiming at the realization of political goals. Mažovski’s “Memoirs” include a detailed and vivid description of his visits to Russia, using every possibility to ask for Russian help. The significance of this account lies not only in the insights it provides about his direct contacts with Russia, but also in the information it gives us about the organization of revolutionary activities, including his participation in the Macedonian Committee (1886) in Sofia (Ristovski 1985: 37) and his contacts with leading Albanians (Mažovski 1922: 29–34, 41–52). The accounts are vivid and detailed, giving precise names and data. Mažovski further broadened his activities by seeking political solutions to the situation in Macedonia. At the beginning of the 20th century, at the time of the Young Turks, Mažovski also contacted Macedonian emigrants in Sofia, among them the Debar Brotherhood. Believing that Russia and the Russian tsar would also help in the liberation of Macedonia, he travelled and established contacts with the most prominent people, including the Russian tsar himself, with the purpose of explaining to them the unbearable security situation that had arisen from the attacks of Albanian *kačaks*, and of promoting the idea of the liberation of Macedonia. At the same time, he never missed an opportunity to point out the famous Macedonian past.

Mažovski included little data about his childhood and his personal life in his autobiography, although one can see that he had intended otherwise when one reads the title. Nevertheless, he left some data about his work migration (as entrepreneur, seasonal worker). After having been employed as an entrepreneur in Pleven (Bulgaria), he took his family there (Mažovski 1922: 48), but even when he mentions his own family he pursues his basic idea of describing political activities. Besides data regarding his own family we also find data about other families from the Mijak region.[5] He also writes about a number of fellow countrymen, work migrants and emigrants, rebels and political activists.[6]

The genealogies of certain families record histories and lives affected by constant movements and sometimes give a clear picture of events and especially their causes and directions, providing a more direct presentation of migrations. We now turn our attention to the unfinished manuscript "The Genealogy of the Čuparov Family" by *Nikola D. Čuparov* (started around 1924), a seasonal labourer and emigrant. He is one of the *Čuparovi (Čupovski) brothers* who worked abroad and were active among the Macedonian emigrants in Bulgaria[7] and Russia. The author's life ended in 1925 in Sofia before he could finish his manuscript. "The Genealogy of the Čuparov Family" is rich with data about this family originating from the village Lazaropole in the Mijak region (Debar area). Their main occupation was cattle-breeding, although they sometimes also worked as masons. They first migrated from Lazaropole to Kruševo, fleeing from Albanian violence, and then settled in the village of Papradišta (Ristovski 1978: 53–81).[8] The author gives a detailed account of the family genealogy, starting from his great grandfather *Kuzman* (names, occupations, family history and personal fates). He writes about the tradition and folk narratives, the everyday life of the population and the situation in the Mijak region, including the history of the migrations. Resulting from the violence in the Mijak region, the migration to other regions of Macedonia began as early as in the second half of the 18th century, mostly to Novo Smilevo and Kruševo in the district of Bitola, to the village of Oraše in the district of Veles, to Papradišta in the district of Babuna, and to other places.

"The biography of my father Nikola Dimov Čuparov", written in Sofia in 1919 by his daughter after the author's dictation, also belongs toin this group of texts. This account of the migration of the Čuparov kin from Lazaropole to Papradišta confirms the stories about the Mijak migrations (Ristovski 1978: 51–53). The descriptions in both manuscripts abound with information that gives a clear picture of the situation, of local history, conditions and everyday life in the villages, of identity, migrations and their causes. It is noteworthy that the

---

5 For example, he writes about relatives coming from Lazaropole migrated to the Enidze-Vardar region (who owned over 2000 sheep and 40 horses) (Mažovski 1922: 7).

6 See the information about some of the participants in the so-called Ohrid conspiracy in Macedonia (1881) as well as about Zafir Belev (Mažovski 1922: 36).

7 In the documents we find them among the founders of the Mijak Oreše-Papradišta Cultural Brotherhood in Sofia (Ristovska-Josifovska 2004: 176 f.).

8 A historical source that confirms the information is the autobiography "From my biography" written by one of the brothers, Dimitrija Čupovski (Ristovski 1978: 89–108), which contains additional data about their life as emigrants.

information about some events or individuals overlaps. When the author writes in *Genealogy* about the population of the Veles region he quotes another work migrant, Georgija Pulevski, a man he felt a connectionconnected with because of their common origin from Mijak and their professional affiliation as masons. It is very likely that he used Pulevski's manuscript "Slavic-Macedonian general history" (Ristovski 1978: 57–58).

Georgi M. Pulevski (1822/23–1893) was a lexicographer, grammarian, historian, collector and publisher of folklore materials, as well as an ethnographer, poet, *komitadži* leader and revolutionary – and himself a work migrant to Romania and Serbia who died as an emigrant in Sofia in 1893 (Ristovska-Josifovska 2008b: 22–46, 185–207). He writes about the Mijak region in his "Dictionary of three languages" (Belgrade 1875) and, in more detail, in his "Slavic-Macedonian general history". In the latter, he gives a review of events as well as valuable ethnographic data for the entire Balkan Peninsula (Ristovska-Josifovska 2008b: 128–139). He writes about the places where the Mijaks lived and their migrations, locating them in "Dolna Reka and Malareka in the Gorni Debor district, and the village of Ehlovec in the Kičevo district", "in Novo Smilevo and in Kruševo in the Bitola district", and in "the Veles district" in "the village of Oraše and in Papradišta in the Babuna district", as well as in other places. Pulevski also gives the approximate date of the migration of the Macedonian population to the Veles region ("a hundred years ago"), and records how people looked upon the migrants: "Those who left are not considered part of the living" (Pulevski 2003: 911). These data correspond to those in the works of Kokaleski and Čhuparov about migrations to neighbouring areas. Such examples can be found in various writings, confirming each other.

Through these aspects and his ethnographic description, Pulevski also depicts the situation in the region. He singles out the mass departure of Slavic inhabitants in the 17th century, headed by the patriarch of Peč, Arsenie Crnoević, as an important historical event. As a result of this migration of the Slavic population, he says, leaving only the workers working for the beys, the land remained empty and Arnauts[9] settled there (Pulevski 2003: 914). His ethnographic review shows not only his views on the spread of the Albanian population in the Balkans, and especially in Macedonia, but also the ways in which they settled. In his ethnographic accounts, Pulevski writes about the Albanian population in the Western parts of Macedonia towards the end of the 19th century as newcomers.

[9] Albanians were called *Arnauts*, a term also used for Turks. Pulevski writes: "And the above said name Arnauts is not known why it is called thus, but Arnauts call themselves Shkipitars, as their language is pronounced *shkip*" (Pulevski 2003: 914).

Often one can also gain some idea about the life of migrants from completely accidental and, at first sight, insignificant data. Regarding the display of migrational mentality, it is important to underline remarks written in the country of residence of the author. For example, in his foreword to the "Dictionary of four languages" (Belgrade, 1873), Pulevski discloses in passing the details of his stay in Belgrade as a work migrant and, in explaining why he wrote the book, points out that knowing more languages is something everyone needs, among them "the worker, the craftsman, and anyone else who stays abroad, and communicates with other nations and wants to be able to reply as regards his task" (Rečnik 1873: I). He explains this necessity as follows: "We need to know, now we are staying abroad, even more languages than there are here" (Rečnik 1873: I). This directly points to the life of work migrants and their needs connected with the adjustment to the new environment: the changes resulting from migration and reflecting the place of emigration are present in the lifestyle and customs of the migrants as they try to adapt to the new environment in their new place of residence in order to operate more successfully.

Important data about migration is also provided in the recently published manuscript "Debar and the Debar area in the past" by *Krsto Kostov*. The manuscript was kept as a treasure in the family until it was published (Skopje 2004). The author, himself an emigrant to Sofia, actually writes about the history of his region, the population, customs and culture.[10] He writes exhaustively and in great detail about the life of migrants in their homes and about work migration as a part of life in his homeland. In the historical presentation he also pays attention to internal migrations of the population moving to the neighbouring areas within Macedonia, and later outside as well. In detail he writes about the life of Macedonian migrants, particularly about migrants from the Debar region who went to work in Thessalonika as tailors, construction workers, dairymen, etc. (Kostov 2004: 125). As well-known masons they travelled in groups through the Balkan countries, mostly Serbia, Romania and Bulgaria.[11] Writing a number of biographies and family histories, Kostov left significant data about the lives of migrants in the new environment and about how they organized themselves economically, culturally and politically. In particular, he discusses at length the

[10] He also describes the food culture in the Debar region, a region known for its bakeries and inns (Kostov 2004: 166). A confirmation of these occupations can be found in the testimonies about migrants from Macedonia to Bulgaria that were remembered as bakers and innkeepers.

[11] He also mentions Nikola Čuparov from Papradišta among the more prominent construction workers in Sofia (Kostov 2004: 123).

issue of organizing the Macedonian emigrants from the Debar region in Sofia, himself being a direct participant.[12]

With regard to reflection on personal impressions of migration, it is important to turn attention to the autobiographical story of the author titled "Memories from my early childhood". In it, he writes about his kin *(Bakovci)*, about his great-grandfather born in the 18th century, and about the directions of migration (mostly to Bulgaria and Romania). He vividly describes his family, a typical migrating-for-work family, as well as migrations in general in his region (causes, directions, customs, seeing migrants off, farewells, occupations). His short autobiographical text is particularly significant, however, in helping us understand the phenomenon of work migration and the personal turmoil experienced by the migrant himself. Kostov presents the reader with his own personal drama as a migrant and an outcast of his native village, a fugitive running from deadly threats. The tragedy of separation from home is expressed in his description of the place where the work migrants were sent: "There is no other place where there are nearly as many tears as there are in this place every year when hundreds of migrants for work are being seen off" (Kostov 2004: 273). The author's narrative supports the conclusion that migrations in Macedonia were a complex process determined by a number of factors and that migration for work was not only due to economic factors, but often also a result of security issues and of political factors.

Expressions of self-identification and presentation for posterity

The personal memories related in these texts (from details and notes to complete stories) provide an opportunity to analyse the objectivity of the historical accounts, although one must keep in mind that oral history is always told in part by taking a certain position (Portelli 1995: 57 f.). In spite of their necessary subjectivity, however, individual accounts of events, whether anonymous or authorized, can provide direct and specific narratives which, in relation to other sources of information, can illuminate a historical moment.

Special attention should be given to the works of collectors of folkloric and ethnographic materials and genealogies, as they present vivid reports and personal testimony about the region. Collecting and nurturing the cultural heritage depicting the life and work of the Macedonians was an important task in everyday lives of the people (Mironska-Hristovska 2005: 178–180), particularly in

[12] He discusses the cultural activities of migrants, e. g. the Debar Brotherhood in Sofia as well as the drama works and the theatre in Sofia (Kostov 2004: 354–366, 374–379).

view of the fact that neither a Macedonian state nor Macedonian institutions existed at that time. This was aptly expressed by Vasil Ikonomov from the village of Lazaropole, himself a migrant, a collector and publicist who wrote: "our life as a nation is mostly described in our folk songs and customs. Under the pressure of circumstances and the position in which our nation has often found itself, it lost all its scholars, lost a lot of their works, and there was no-one left but the folk singer to preserve the threads of our way of life from ages past. As a result, collecting and printing our songs and customs is of the greatest necessity, and is the only source in studying our past as a nation" (Ristovski 1985: 85).

The descriptions of the Mijak region by individuals from that region, analysed from a historical point of view, reveal some differences with regard to the presentation of data, differences which correspond with the historical and ethno-cultural changes that took place in this region. While the authors of works dating from the 19th and early 20th centuries simply recorded events (from ethnographic, folkloric and traditional descriptions to chronicles and memoirs) that intensified the emigration of the Macedonian population or the ethno-cultural and religious changes in the region, later authors until today write from a perspective of recollection and draw conclusions about the reasons for the present situation. From the point of view of historiography, where exact data is of particular importance, the older works could be considered to be more reliable testimonies – with due caution as regards possible subjective material mistakes. Later works, although sometimes reflecting a tradition created in time, must be analysed not only as verifications of earlier writings, but also as indicators of the influence of historical developments on the idea of the Mijak region in the minds of those who had already left it. In the selection of our sources it was especially important that the texts had either been published recently or were even unpublished, or that they had been studied little or not at all. Namely, the full text of Pulevski's manuscript (Slavic-Macedonian general history) was published in 2003, 110 years after the author's death, while Kostov's work (Debar and Debar area in the past) was published by his descendants in 2004.

The views of the authors are a direct expression of their personal positions and feelings. The accounts are completely different in terms of character and content, but if we try to condense the above-mentioned works to determine what they have in common, it is the strong emotions of the writers and the most direct expression of one's self in their autobiographical accounts and memoirs. At the same time, the authors' motives for writing these works are to leave a trace to future generations: the ancestors' successes and the memory of what remained and what could be lost – the Mijak region, a whole way of life that once existed. But what furthermore emerges from each text, almost without exception, is the authors' intent to explain to future generations that this loss or transformation is a direct consequence of the migrations; at the same time they point out the reasons that led to this situation, namely the insecurity and the violence caused by *kačaks* and various other groups or individuals before they settled permanently.

Exploring several Macedonian historical personalities from the western border-region of Macedonia through their written accounts about their lives as migrants provides insights not only into the historical situation, but also into their self-identification and their wish to inform future generations. From today's perspective and on the basis of fieldwork in the region, one can notice some changes in the stories told by present-day descendants living abroad. If one compares the written accounts and the present recollections, one can notice identical elements as well as changes in tales and in elements that have, over time, lost significance or gained new content and explanatory power. Studying today's storytelling becomes important if we take into consideration the dynamics of migration movements in the region that continue to produce migrants to this day.

Literature

Asman, Jan 2001: Kulturnata pamet. Pismenost, pamet i političeska identičnost v rannite visokorazviti kulturi [Cultural memory. Literacy, memory and political identity in the early high-developed cultures. Transl. from German: Ana Dimova]. Sofia: Planeta-3.

Avramovska, Nataša 2004: Avtobiografijata vo makedonskiot literaturen XIX vek [The autobiography in the Macedonian literary 19th century]. Skopje: Institut za makedonska literatura.

Belić, Aleksandar 1935: Galički dijalekat [Galichnik dialect]. In: Srpski dijalektološki zbornik [Serbian dialectological collection]. VII. Beograd-Srem. Karlovci, 275–305.

Dressel, Gert 1997: Istoričeska antropologija. Văvedenie [Historical anthropology. Introduction. Transl, from German: Kristina Popova]. Blagoevgrad.

Gurevich, Aaron 1992: Historical anthropology of the Middle Ages. Cambridge: The University of Chicago Press. Polity Press.

Hristov, Petko 2008: Collective Identity and the Myth of a Local Civiliser-Hero: Family narratives in modern European perspective. In: Elena Marushiakova (ed.), Dynamics of national identity and transnational identities in the process of European integration. Cambridge: Cambridge Scholars Publishing, 314–322.

Hristovska-Mironska, Valentina 2005: Prosvetitelstvoto vo Makedonija [The enlightenment in Macedonia]. Skopje: Institut za makedonska literatura.

Limanoski, Nijazi 1984: Islamizacijata i etničkite promeni vo Makedonija [The Islamisation and the ethnic changes in Macedonia]. In: Makedonci Muslimani (materijali od Prviot naučen simpozium odrzhan na 3 i 4 oktomvri 1981 vo Kičevo i od drugite kulturni i naučni sredbi na Makedoncite muslimani) [Macedonians muslims (Materials from the first scientific symposium held on 3th and 4th October 1981 in Kichevo and from other scientific meetings of the Macedonians Muslims]. Skopje: Kulturno naučni manifestacii na Makedoncite muslimani, 12–61.

Kostov, Krsto 2004: Debar i Debarsko vo minatoto [Debar and Debar area in the past]. Skopje: Pro Littera.

Matkovski, Aleksandar 1959: Gjurčin Kokaleski 1775–1863/Prilog kon prašanjeto za sozdavanje na selska, stočarsko-trgovska bur oazija vo Makedonija [Gjurchin Kokaleski 1775–1863. Contribution towards the foundation of the rural, cattle-breeding and trade aristocracy in Macedonia]. Skopje: Institut za nacionalna istorija.

Mažovski, Isaija Radev 1922: Vzpominanija na Isaija Radev roden na 9 mart, 1852 godina, v selo Debarsko-Makedonija [Memoirs of Isaija Radev born on March 9, 1852, in the village of Debarsko, Macedonia]. Sofia.

Petreska, Vesna 1998: Proletnite običai, obredi i veruvanja kaj Mijacite [The spring costums, rituals and beliefs among the Mijaks]. Skopje: Institut za folklor "Marko Cepenkov".

Portelli, A. 1995: What Makes Oral History Different, In: The Death of Luigi Trastulli and Other Stories: Form and Meaning in Oral History. Albany NY: Suny Press, 51–58.

Pulevski, Georgija M. 2003: Slavjansko-makedonska opšta istorija. Podgotovka Blaže Ristovski, Biljana Ristovska-Josifovska [Slavic-Macedonian general history. Ed. by Blaže Ristovski, Biliana Ristovska-Josifovska]. Skopje: Makedonska akademija na naukite i umetnostite.

Rečnik, 1873: Rečnik otă tri jezika. 1. Srpsko-Albanski. 2. Arbansko-Arnautski. 3. Turski. 4. Grčki. Skrojena i napisana otă Gjorgja M. Puljevski, arhitekta u Galičnik okru ije Dibransko 1872 godine [Dictionary of three languages. 1. Serbian-Albanian. 2. Arbanian-Arnautian. 3. Turkish. 4. Greek. Prepared and written by Gjorgja M. Pulevski, an architect in Galichnik, Debar area from 1872]. I-va chastă. Belgrade: Štamparija N. Stefanović i Družine.

Ristovska-Josifovska, Biljana 2004: Gjorgija M. Pulevski sred makedonskata emigracija vo Sofija [Gjorgija M. Pulevski among the Macedonian emigration in Sofia]. In: Glasnik, 48, 1–2, Skopje: Institut za nacionalna istorija, 176–177.

Ristovska-Josifovska, Biljana 2005: The Terror in Galichnik through Its Writers' Eyes. In: Terrorism, Intellectualism – Balkan troubles, Blagoevgrad: Ju. Z. U. "Neofit Rilski", 29–39.

Ristovska-Josifovska, Biljana 2008: Personal and Collective Identity (One historical profile in modern European perspective). In: Elena Marushiakova (ed.), Dynamics of National Identity and Transnational Identities in the Process of European Integration. Cambridge: Cambridge Scholars Publishing, 305–313.

Ristovska-Josifovska, Biljana 2008a: Migracii i promeni vo Mijačkiot kraj vo Makedonija [Migrations and changes in the Mijak region in Macedonia]. In: Tranziciite vo istorijata i kulturata [Transitions through history and culture]. Skopje: Institut za nacionalna istorija, 457–466.

Ristovska-Josifovska, Biljana 2008b: Georgija M. Pulevski: revolucioner i kulturno-nacionalen deec [Georgia M. Pulevski: Revolutionary and cultural and national activist]. Skopje: Selektor.

Ristovski, Blaže 1978: Dimitrija Čupovski (1878–1940) i Makedonskoto naučno-literaturno drugarstvo vo Petrograd [Dimitria Chupovski (1878–1940) and the Macedonian scientific-literary society in Peterburg]. Vol. I. Skopje: Kultura.

Ristovski, Blaže 1985: Vasil Ikonomov (1848–1934). Prilog kon pručuvanjeto na makedonskiot kulturno-nacionalen razvitok [Vasil Ikonomov (1848–1934). Contribution to research in the Macedonian cultural and national development]. Skopje: Institut za nacionalna istorija.

Stojanovik-Lafazanovska, Lidija 2008: Migracija i habitus. Makedonskata emigracija vo Germanija [Migration and habitus. Macedonian emigration in Germany]. Skopje: Institut za makedonski folklore "Marko Cepenkov".

Trifunoski, Jovan 1988: Albansko stanovništvo u Makedoniji [Albanian population in Macedonia]. Belgrade: NIRO "Knji evne novine".

Vražinovski, Tanas 2000: Makedonskoto iseleništvo – sostojbi i perspektivi vo negovoto proučuvanje [Macedonian emigration – conditions and perspectives of research]. In: Prv megjunaroden naučen sobir "Iseleništvoto od Makedonija od pojavata do denes" [First international scientific meeting "Emigration from Macedonia from its beginnings till today"]. Skopje, 5–21.

Ethnologia Balkanica 13 (2009)

Socio-Political, Religious, and Economic Reasons for Macedonians' Movements to Turkey

Vladimir Karadžoski, Prilep

Abstract

The massive movement of the Islamic population from Macedonia to Turkey started immediately after the Liberation, to reach its culmination in the early 1950s. Migration was the most actual question in almost all places inhabited by Muslims (mostly Turks and Islamized Macedonians). This movement was due to the new political and social changes in Socialist Yugoslavia and its communist system. The attitude of the new authorities toward religion endangered religious freedom, which enjoyed full respect by the State until World War II. For Muslims, their Islamic rules were far more important than the new rules established by the Government, e. g. regarding political, national and sexual equality, etc. Another reason was the new economic policy, i. e. the transformations of land and property relations that started with the agrarian reforms. The State's relation toward private ownership, collectivity, and other such issues affected big landowners, private owners, tradesmen and craftsmen, who were not willing to give up their properties. Affected by the economic measures of the Government, afraid of losing their religious freedom and of disintegration of patriarchal family life by the forced unveiling of women, Islamic people were looking for solution in migrations.

The socio-political and economic history of the Balkans and Macedonia in the 19th and 20th centuries was in great measure a result of movements and migrations of population, not only in times of war and economic crises, but also in relatively peaceful periods.

The emigration of Turks and other adherents of the Islamic religion from the Balkans started with the dissolution of the Ottoman Empire and had varying amplitudes in different periods, depending on the concrete internal or external political situation. Through the Balkan Wars (1912–1913) and World War I (1914–1918), the Ottoman Empire was finally expelled from the Balkan Peninsula after five centuries of rule. Macedonia was forcibly partitioned among the neighboring Balkan states: Greece, Serbia, Bulgaria and Albania. As a result of the newly created social, political and territorial circumstances, the migrations that had begun in the 19th century continued with even greater intensity. It is thought that over 2 500 000 inhabitants from the Balkans migrated in a time span of only one decade (Djordevic 1989: 115–130).

A great part of migrations took place on the ethnic territory of Macedonia, which led to dramatic changes of ethnic composition in some of its regions, particularly in those that came under Greek rule. From the Treaty of Lausanne, signed in 1923 by Greece and Turkey, it can be seen that migration included not only Christians but also Muslim population. The exchange of population was based on religious criteria, and the number of Muslims who migrated from Macedonia and Trakia toward Turkey reached about 350 000 (Ortakovski 1996: 149–151). Following this wave, until 1941, migration processes from the Balkans had a lower intensity. During World War II the migration was temporarily stopped, but the strong desire of the representatives of the Turkish minority to migrate to Turkey was not eliminated.

Macedonian people from the Vardar part of Macedonia took an active part in the great anti-fascist front during World War II. Thereby they won the right to become a constitutive subject of the new Yugoslav state – a federal community of equal peoples, and proclaimed the People's Republic of Macedonia. Immediately after the War, massive works to build the destroyed country were undertaken, both in infrastructure and economy.

The government and party authorities paid special attention to ethnic and inter-ethnic relations and to various religious confessions, especially to relations between Islam and Christianity. In the sequence of demographic and ethnic changes in the present-day territory of the Republic of Macedonia after World War II, the migration of Turks and other citizens of Islamic religion was regarded as a special phenomenon. As reported above, migrations to Turkey were also known in previous decades, but after 1945 they acquired new dimensions and specificities, with the establishment of the new communist authority in Yugoslavia and implementation of major social-economical and political changes in the Republic of Macedonia.

The reasons for migration of this people, former citizens of Macedonia, to Turkey in the period 1951–1960 and the problems they had during this process are considered in this paper[1]. The reasons for the new migration wave lie in the socio-political situation in the country, and also in the fact that Muslim believers could not accept quickly the radical social transformations and emancipation that undermined the old patriarchal establishment. They were afraid of losing the religious liberty they had enjoyed during the Kingdom of Yugoslavia and they strongly believed that "religion without a king" was something impossible.

1 The Turkish national minority mainly inhabited the villages, especially in the Ovče Pole basin, particularly along the Bregalnica River, the Polog basin (Tetovo), the Tikvesh plain and in the regions of Veles, Bitola, Prilep, Debar and Radovis. A part of them settled in the towns (Bitola, Skopje, Ohrid, Kumanovo, Prilep, Tetovo) and smaller groups were found in other parts of the present-day Republic of Macedonia.

Thus, the majority of Turks remained passive toward the National Front regime and even more toward the organs of the Communist Party and the atheism proclaimed by its members (Todorovski 1996: 105–118).

One of the most important reasons for migration from Macedonia to Turkey was the attitude of the communist regime toward religion, which the Muslim population saw as a threat to their religious freedom. However, the communist party of Macedonia, despite their declared atheism, was aware of the strong roots of Islam in the country. Therefore it did not take radical steps to abolish religious practices and institutions (mosques and churches), but it simply separated religion from the state. At the same time, the Communist Party led a broad campaign against religion and "religious prejudice" in the scope of its activities to emancipate the population through such means as ensuring gender equality, increased literacy, and improved culture of living. Still, this campaign was misunderstood by religious leaders, especially Muslim ones, because they were afraid of losing their believers. The atheist propaganda contributed a lot to the increasing resistance among this population against the authorities in general and particularly toward the ruling Communist Party of Macedonia. For Muslim believers, the Islamic laws were far more important and acceptable than the new rules of life imposed by the government.

The migration process was also influenced by the intensive foreign propaganda (e. g. the *Yucel* organization), which provoked additional tensions in the relationship between Turks and Macedonian authorities. Of equal importance was the internal influence of the illegal Turkish reactionary organization, headed by Ata Hodza and his closest associate Feta Rauf. The group had its own reliable persons in the organs of government through which it channelled attitudes and opinions on various political social, cultural and educational questions, which were obligatory for the believers but which confronted the legal system of the state. The group insisted on opening schools (mektebs) in which Muslim children should attend religious classes instead of going to the compulsory state schools. Because of its perceived enemy activities against the People's Republic of Macedonia, the group was destroyed by the authorities (DARM-60, a. e. 7.1954).

The new economic policy and transformations of land and property relations that started with the agrarian reform, collectivization, expropriation and other state measures directly affected Turkish big landowners, owners of private properties, craftsmen and tradesmen who were not willing to renounce their claims to property. The biggest victims of agrarian reform (1945–1948), obligatory purchase, collectivization (1943–1953), land holding limitations to a maximum of 10 ha (1953), and private property nationalization were private owners, craftsmen and tradesmen in the towns, who were not able to adapt to the new conditions. In the beginning of the 1950s the migration groups predominantly consisted of the representatives of *esnaf* (guilds) and *čaršia* (bazaar), whereas farmers and peasants started to migrate more intensively from 1954. In the period before World War II, Turks had mainly worked as merchants in the towns. After liberation they were looked upon as speculators, war profiteers and capitalist residues of the old system and they could find employment only as shop assistants. The social composition of those who migrated to Turkey reveals that the majority of them moved there to find better possibilities for their private businesses, free of limitations imposed by the "socialist sector". They believed that Turkey, as their motherland, would offer them better opportunities, higher earnings, improved material status and a better quality of life (Todorovski 2001: 318–319).

The ultimate goal of the Macedonian government and of its policy of social and cultural transformation was to overthrow the patriarchal way of life. In efforts to create a "new man", the government carried out energetic actions against the old religious consciousness. One of these actions was the Law on Unveiling, i.e., requiring removal of the *zar* and *feredža, the* traditional veils of Muslim women. Among the Muslim population, this action was viewed as a direct offense against their national honor and pride. Equally strong resistance was shown against the law which forbade religious education, the law which regulated the practice of Muslim religious leaders (odza) and the law on compulsory education of female children.

Through legislative pressure and political propaganda, the authorities made efforts to change the perceived dehumanization marked by the above named *zar* and *feredža*, buying, abduction, etc. These phenomena in customary law practiced by a part of Islamic minorities constitute the most obdurate and humiliating customs regarding the Muslim woman. Although some of these practices were against the law, they were an untouchable zone for the legal structures of the state.

In conditions of rapid social change, Muslim women (especially of Turkish and Albanian origin) found themselves caught between the norms of customary and positive law and the new social requirements. On the other hand, the communists did not always make wise political movements in their actions for women's emancipation, which often led to adverse effects. A good example of this was the removing of *zar* and *feredža* – probably one of the most drastic political measures pursued by the communist authorities in the Republic of Macedonia after World War II (Ackoska 1992: 17–27).

The Women's Antifascist Front had an especially important role in the agitation campaign for unveiling, forming special commissions for minorities. These commissions were headed by some more progressive Turkish or Albanian women and their task was to accelerate the process of emancipation and to change the position of women in everyday life. Some women readily accepted this idea, unveiling themselves even before the law was put into force. The law went into effect in 1951 and was also translated into Turkish. Still, the majority of Muslim women were firmly integrated into traditional ways of life. They were secluded and focused on their own families and neighborhoods, rejecting the new values and changes in relationships between the sexes.

The emancipation of Muslim women was far from being completed by the mere removing of the *zar* and *feredža*. For a majority of them, however, it was an unimaginably huge step and they could not get used quickly to showing themselves unveiled. They were not allowed to walk out in public with their faces exposed. Thus, Muslim women rarely went outside the house, agricultural works were performed by male members of the family, and *zar* and *feredža* were replaced by scarf and overcoat. In this context we should mention the strong campaign for education of female children and the ban on selling and buying of women.

Many Muslims refused to live in accordance with the new rules and, afraid that they would be deprived of their identity and faith, sought salvation in emigration to Turkey (Ackoska 2003: 235–245). Another important social factor that contributed to migration of Turks from Macedonia was their family relations. Many had relatives who had migrated to Turkey before the First and Second World War. This caused the chain migration of whole families (Palikruševa 1998: 131–136).

In short, the Islamic population was threatened by the government's economic policy and people were afraid of losing their religious liberty. They also felt that the old patriarchal system of family relations was jeopardized by the forced emancipation of women. For these reasons, a large number of the population, most of them Turks, chose migration as the only solution.

According to the existing data and documentation, all the people who migrated from Macedonia to Turkey were recorded under the same nationality – as Turks, although this did not correspond to reality, because other Muslim minorities (Albanians and Macedonian Muslims) were also part of these migrations (Trifunovski 1956: 145–147). This can be explained by the fact that people who wanted to move to Turkey were compelled to declare themselves Turks in order to receive permission to leave Yugoslavia and settle in that country. According to some data, the approximate number of Turks who migrated from Macedonia after World War II was 200 000 (Limanovski 1985: 99). This figure also includes the people who came to Macedonia from other parts of Yugoslavia, hoping to acquire the permission for migration to Turkey more easily.

At the beginning, the migration of Muslim citizens from the People's Republic of Macedonia in the 1950s was very difficult. One of the major problems in this first period was to obtain release from citizenship of the Federal People's

Republic of Yugoslavia (FNRY). The authorities refused to give release from Yugoslav citizenship to those who wanted to migrate to Turkey. It was considered that the policy of national equality, brotherhood and unity created a new environment which should be a good reason for them to stay in the country. Moreover, in that period the migration of Muslims was considered a hostile act. This attitude of the government contributed a lot to mass defections from the Yugoslav Army and escapes across the border.

The attitude of the authorities toward the migration process changed gradually and it became much easier to obtain a release from citizenship. This can be attributed to the improved relations between Yugoslavia and Turkey in that period. As a result of this, the interest in migration to Turkey increased to an even greater extent (Vražinovski 2005: 20–26). In the beginning of this second period, however, the procedure for release from citizenship was still quite complicated and many documents were required. Although later on they were reduced, it often took more than a year to complete all documents. Peasants were also faced with problems, since all adult members of the family had to go to the municipality office at least three times: first to submit their applications, than to announce it in the press, and finally to receive the document for release from citizenship (DARM 1.427.49, 35/307–308).

The migrations began around 1951 and reached their culmination in 1955. In the period from 1955 to 1959, the number of migrants to Turkey gradually decreased. This is mainly due to the fact that the majority of well-situated persons able to start some private business in Turkey had already gone and only the poorer people, who could not afford to pay for release from citizenship, stayed in the country.

The Law on Nationalization of Buildings for Rent and Building Lots (1958) remarkably contributed to the decrease of migration intensity, because this act forbade the owners to sell their land (DARM a. i. 5, 24. 8. 1959). By the late 1960s, however, economic and political conditions in Yugoslavia and Macedonia became much more relaxed and restraints from the side of the state were not so tight. In such an environment, the improved material status allowed the Turkish national minority to have a decent living, and they were successfully incorporated into the social and economic life of the country, no longer fearing loss of their faith and nation.

Literature

Ackoska, Violeta 1992: Emancipacijata na muslimanskata žena i meždunacionalnata ravnopravnost [Emancipation of Muslim women and international equality]. In: Glasnik na INI, XXXVI/1–2.

Ackoska, Violeta 2003: Bratstvoto i edinstvoto 1944–1974 pome du harmonija i disharmonija [The brotherhood and unity 1944–1974 between harmony and disharmony]. Skopje: Institut za nacionalna istorija.

Djordevic, Dimitrije 1989: Migrations during the 1912–1913 Balkan wars and World War One. In: Migration in Balkan History. Belgrade: 115–130.

Državen arhiv na Makedonija [The state archives of the Republic of Macedonia]. k-60 a. e. 7. commission on national minorities, 1954.

Državen arhiv na Makedonija [The state archives of the Republic of Macedonia]. 1.427.49, 35/307–308.

Državen arhiv na Makedonija [The state archives of the Republic of Macedonia]. a. i. 5, Information for the migration of the Turkish minority from Macedonia, 24. 8. 1959.

Limanovski, Nijazi 1985: Islamskata religija i islamiziranite Makedonci [The Islamic religion and islamized Macedonians]. Skopje.

Ortakovski, Vladimir 1996: Meždunarodnata položba na malcinstvata [The international position of minorities]. Skopje, 149–151.

Palikruševa, Galaba 1998: Procesite na etničkite prestruktuiranja na Torbešite, Pomacite i drugite vo R. Turcija, kako model na prestruktuiranje na nekoi etnički zaednici na Balkanot [The processes of ethnic restructuring of the Torbeshi, Pomaks and others in Turkey as a model for restructuring some ethnic communities in the Balkans]. In: Zemaljski muzej (Sarajevo) 6–7: 131–136.

Todorovski, Gligur 1996: Osvrt na verskiot i opštestveniot život na muslimanite vo Makedonija meždu dvete svetski vojni i po osloboduvanjeto [Reference to the religious and social life of Muslims in Macedonia between the two World Wars and after the liberation]. In: Glasnik na INI vol. 40, no. 2: 105–118.

Todorovski, Gligur 2001: Demografskite procesi i promeni vo Makedonija od početokot na Prvata balkanska vojna do osamostojuvanjeto na Makedonija so poseben osvrt na islamiziranite Makedonci [Demographic processes and changes in Macedonia from the beginning of the First Balkan War to the independence of Macedonia, with special reference to the islamized Macedonians]. Skopje: Institut za nacionalana istorija - Matica Makedonska.

Trifunovski, Jovan 1956: Za torbešite vo bitolsko-prilepskata kotlina [The Torbesh in the Bitola-Prilep basin]. In: Godišen zbornik na Filozofskijot fakultet na Univerzitetot vo Skopje, prirodno-matematički oddl (Skopje) 9, 11: 145–147.

Vražinovski, Tanas 2005: Iseluvanjeto od Makedonija vo Turcija [The emigration from Macedonia to Turkey]. In: Vsekidnevnata kultura na bălgarite i sărbite v postsocialističeskija period [The everyday culture of Bulgarians and Serbs in the postsocialist period]. Sofia, 17–26.

Rotation, Integration, and Social Exclusion
Discourse and Change in/of Migration Policies in Austria[1]

Stefanie Mayer, Vienna

Abstract

Although (labour) migration is an important topic of political debate, scholarly literature on migration discourses and policies in Austria is still lacking. This paper, which is an outcome of a research cooperation between Vienna-based LBI for European History and Public Spheres and Malmö University, combines discourse analysis and institutional approaches in order to produce a more complete picture of the developments spanning over roughly the last 50 years. Special emphasis is placed on the analysis of "integration discourse" starting to evolve in Austria in the early 1970s as a pro-migrant (if not necessarily pro-migration) discourse, and which since then has been developed into a weapon in the arsenal of anti-immigration policies. By means of this diachronic approach, the analysis points out omissions and blind spots in contemporary immigration and integration debates. I conclude that "immigration debates" in Austria are not so much concerned with the presence of foreigners within the country, but with the granting of a long-term perspective and social and political rights.

Introduction

Migration issues are important topics of political debate in many European countries. In Austria they figured prominently in recent election campaigns and are regularly invoked by right-wing politicians to stir public support. "Integration" – or rather the alleged lack of integration on the side of (especially Muslim) immigrants – became one of the most important notions in this respect. In this paper I reconstruct the evolvement of the policy field "immigration" and related discourses in Austria. The analysis points out omissions and blind spots in contemporary immigration and integration debates.

This case study in Austrian political discourse combines discourse analysis and institutional approaches in order to produce a more complete picture of the developments spanning over roughly the last 50 years. The analysis shows

---

[1] The results presented in this paper stem from a research cooperation between Malmö University and the Ludwig Boltzmann Institute for European History and Public Spheres in Vienna. A comparative volume was published in winter 2009 (Mayer/Spång 2009).

the persistence of certain discursive strands and positions as well as changes, but it also demonstrates certain difficulties in conceptualizing the relationship between discursive and institutional developments. My perspective on political discourse is informed by critical discourse theory and analysis (cf. Wodak 1998, Jäger 2001), which conceptualizes discourse as socially constituted but at the same time productive. In this perspective, quotations taken from the material should not be regarded as describing a pre-established reality but as constructing "foreign labour", "immigration" and other subjects as fields of political concern and regulatory endeavours. My methodical approach was inspired by Martin Wengeler's *topoi analysis* (2003), which allowed us to systematically consider topoi,[2] denominations and the intertwining of different strands of discourse. With regard to the material analysed, I concentrated on the political discourse. Primary sources for analysis were:

- Parliamentary debates about "foreign labour" from 1960 to 1975 and about the 2004 EU-enlargement in connection with the "transitory measures" which served to keep the national labour market closed for citizens of "new" member countries.[3]
- Publications from social partner organizations on these topics.
- Early literature by social scientists on migration issues from the beginning of the 1970s.[4] These early studies were often undertaken on behalf of the social partners or strongly influenced by their discourses. The publications analysed were explicitly meant to influence politics and are therefore taken as an expression of political discourse.

This choice of material reflects some of the defining features of the Austrian political system. Politics in Austria can traditionally be characterized as neo-corporatist and consensus-oriented. Even though these long-standing patterns have

---

[2] Topoi analysis focuses on argumentative patterns that keep reappearing within specific discourses. These topoi may link different topics or different strands of discourse in a seemingly self-evident way (e. g. migration and security-discourses). When applying different levels of abstraction, topoi analysis offers the possibility to identify the dominant rationale in migration discourse at a certain point in time without concealing the differences between political actors.

[3] For a discussion of the genre "political discourse" and of parliamentary debates more specifically, see van Dijk (2000). The Austrian parliament was traditionally dominated by two major parties (Social Democrats, SPÖ, and Austrian People's Party, ÖVP). The Freedom Party (FPÖ) which represents the (far) right-wing of the political spectrum became an important political player during the 1990s, when its share of the votes rose from around 5 % to nearly 27 %.

[4] The three publications analysed were: Österreichisches Komitee für Sozialarbeit (1971), Arbeitskreis für ökonomische und soziologische Studien (1973) and Beirat für Wirtschafts- und Sozialfragen (1976).

to some extent been eroding since the 1990s, the social partner organizations representing either labour or employer interests are still important political actors. In the field of labour migration the Austrian Federation of Trade Unions, which is closely connected to the Social Democratic Party, and the Economic Chamber, closely connected to the conservative People's Party, have traditionally been the most important players and their influence should still not be underestimated (cf. Tálos 2006).

Recruiting foreign labour

The decade of the 1960s witnessed the slow development of the policy field "immigration" out of labour market policy. This development was closely linked to the more general economic context of Western Europe. During the late 1950s and early 1960s Austria – in the wake of the West German "Wirtschaftswunder" – lived through an unprecedented economic boom. Scarcity of labour became the major economic problem, and the emigration of Austrian workers to Germany and Switzerland was a much-discussed topic. In this context foreign labour was called for by employers' representatives, while trade unions lobbied for an active labour market policy directed at Austrian natives. In the end a compromise between the social partner organizations was reached, which formed part of the so-called Raab-Olah Agreement that also institutionalized the social partnership in its advanced form.[5]

From 1962 on the social partners agreed on "contingents" for foreign labour every year, which established maximum numbers of workers to be recruited for different economic sectors and regions. As long as these "contingents" were not exceeded employers did not have to prove that no Austrian national was willing or able to do the job in question, but received the necessary employment permits easily. These agreements were meant to provide provisional regulation until a law which was already being negotiated between the social partners could be passed.[6] However, this "interim arrangement" lasted for 15 years as the sole mechanism of regulation. The agreements themselves were rather complex, with a multitude of subdivisions, but in practice labour was desperately sought for and hard to attract, and therefore the administration of permits was handled liberally.

[5] The institutionalization of the social partnership was a complex process, which cannot be dealt with in this paper.

[6] Until 1976 the employment of foreign labour was formally regulated by a German decree from 1933, which had been transferred to Austrian law in 1945. The "contingent-agreements" – like the social partnership in general – operated without a legal basis.

Official recruitment procedures were a domain of the Economic Chamber, which opened recruitment offices in Istanbul as well as in Zagreb and Sarajevo even before official agreements between Austria and the Turkish/Yugoslav governments were signed in 1964 and 1966 respectively. In fact, the practice of recruitment makes a good case for the "relative autonomy of migration" as postulated in migration research (cf. Bojadžijev 2008, Karakayali 2008), because within a few years the overwhelming majority of labour migrants came via different semi-official routes, often using their own networks. Many were either "recruited" by friends or family members already working in Austria (Bauböck/Perchinig 2006: 730), or just entered the country as tourists, "repairing" their legal status later on. This claim can be substantiated with available data,[7] which shows that in 1964 a total of 4073 workers were recruited by the Working Group of the Economic Chamber, which nearly equals the increase in foreign labour. In 1965 only about 50 % of the growth of foreign labour can be attributed to these official recruitment procedures, and in 1967 the proportion went down to 12.5 % (Parnreiter 1992: 72-73). At the beginning of the 1970s a survey among Turkish "guest workers" in Austria[8] proved the importance of social networks. According to this survey, 56 % of the workers taking part in the study came to Austria because friends or family members had "recruited" them. Some 41 % had contacted Turkish labour market authorities beforehand and 3 % had come to Austria on their own initiative (Arbeitskreis für ökonomische und soziologische Studien 1973: 24).

The practice of "tourist employment" was always a source of dispute between trade unions and employers' representatives.[9] For example, Social Democrats' voiced criticism in the parliamentary debate about the *Aliens' Employment Act* in 1975, when some MPs tried to equate "tourist employment" with undocumented work relations. This assertion was fiercely opposed by conservative MPs and the Economic Chamber (Stenographisches Protokoll BR 340, 4. April 1975).

This semi-official migratory strategy, however, does not only make a case for the "autonomy" of migration but also shows the vulnerability of labour immigrants with regard to institutional practices. When during the 1970s legal regulations tightened and the possibility to "repair" one's status once within the country was abolished through administrative measures, some of these former "tourists" found themselves in undocumented and unprotected labour relations.

---

[7] The numbers should only be understood as indicators of a certain trend. For reflections on the difficulties with regard to immigration data see Weigl (2009: 17).

[8] The survey was realized by Leopold Spira on behalf of the municipality of Vienna. A total of 252 Turkish workers participated.

[9] For the German case, which shows some similarities, see Karakayali (2008: 110 ff.).

Discussing foreign labour – the economic rationale

With regard to the institutional set-up it comes as no surprise that during the 1960s the discourse on labour migration was dominated by an economic rationale. Summarizing the discourse on the political level, a number of characteristic traits can be discerned:

1. The necessity of recruiting foreign labour was hardly ever questioned, although the "guest workers" were always regarded as a second-class replacement of Austrian emigrants. It is interesting to note that while Austrian emigration today hardly ever appears as a topic in immigration debates, it was inseparably linked to the discourse on foreign labour during the 1960s and 1970s.
2. Concerning the images of labour migrants created in political discourse, there was a strong tendency towards negative stereotypes, many of them linked to the assumed "backwardness" of the home countries or regions, which was set in sharp contrast to the Austrian self-perception as a modern, industrialized country.
3. Most importantly, debates about the regulation of foreign labour during the 1960s hardly ever left the realm of labour market policies. The only exceptions I found concerned housing and the perceived threat of diseases, but even these issues were mostly discussed with regard to employers' responsibility towards their (temporary) workers.
4. The regulatory idea of the "rotation system", in which "guest workers" should leave the country again after a few years of work, was not challenged on the political level, although it never complied to social reality. Neither were employers keen to exchange their workforce that often, nor did migrants themselves subject to these rules. Even if many had originally planned to "return" after a few years, this was often postponed for various reasons.

In 1963, the Austrian Federation of Trade Unions expressed the idea underlying the "rotation system" very clearly:

> "In view of the fact that Austrian employees with regard to income-level range on the last but one place of all European industrialized countries and furthermore a flooding of the Austrian labour market by foreign workers is not to be expected, the Austrian Federation of Trade Unions was able to form an agreement [with the Economic Chamber] whose defining function it is to close specific temporary gaps in the labour market by taking in foreign workers" (ÖGB 1963: I/67).[10]

---

[10] Original: "Angesichts des Umstandes, daß die österreichischen Arbeitnehmer hinsichtlich des Lohnniveaus innerhalb der europäischen Industriestaaten [...] an vorletzter Stelle ste-

The "contingent system" was a compromise between labour and employer interests which remained stable until the beginning of the 1970s, while the number of "guest workers" was rising, reaching its peak in 1973 with approximately 226000 (8.7 % of the total workforce) (Butschek/Walterskirchen 1974: 215). As was the case in many Western European countries, this compromise deteriorated when the economic context changed due to the crisis of the 1970s. Shifting political priorities – most prominently concerns about unemployment – led to a more restrictive approach towards labour immigration. This found expression in the more restrictive administrative handling of permits, a reduction of "contingents" (Davy/Gächter 1993: 166) and in the *Aliens' Employment Act* (BGBl 218/1975) that was passed in 1975 and finally provided a legal basis for the social partners' handling of labour immigration in line with the "rotation system". However, alongside these institutional changes the first half of the 1970s also saw the beginning of an integration discourse, which for the first time challenged the assumptions of the "rotation system" and introduced immigration as a field of political regulation beyond the scope of labour market policies.

Although the political aims of these two distinct developments seem antagonistic, the analysis also shows points of convergence. On the one hand, legal and administrative restrictions had the unintended effect of forcing immigrants to decide whether to leave the country without knowing if they would be allowed to return, or to settle in Austria and try to bring their families. On the other hand, a specific "integration" discourse might just as well legitimize a restrictive approach towards further immigration. The plurality of developments on different levels – regulatory approaches sticking to the idea of "rotation", political discourse shifting towards integration and immigrants' strategies following their own rationales – provide a complex landscape for migration research.

Early integration discourse – from foreign labour to immigration

Focusing on the level of discourse, pronounced changes can be discerned during the early 1970s when the employment of "guest workers" began to be discussed outside the realm of economic and labour market policies. These changes are clearly visible in the following quote, taken from a labour union publication, in

hen, weiters mit einer Überschwemmung des österreichischen Arbeitsmarktes mit Fremdarbeitern nicht zu rechnen ist, konnte der Österreichische Gewerkschaftsbund ein Fremdarbeiterabkommen treffen, dessen eigentliche Aufgabe es ist, verschiedene vorübergehende Lücken auf dem Arbeitsmarkt durch Hereinnahme von Fremdarbeitern zu schließen." All quotations were translated by the author.

which the Austrian Federation of Trade Unions directly contradicts its stance taken a few years earlier towards foreign labour:

> "In the end one will have to pose the question in Austria, too, whether one views the foreign workers in the medium term as immigrants or as an alien presence. In experts' discussions one talks about the integration principle on the one side and the rotation principle on the other, in which foreign workers are sent to their homeland after a few years and are replaced by new foreigners. Within the unions the integration principle has for many reasons been taken as a starting point" (ÖGB 1973: 16).[11]

Among the topics now being discussed publicly and on the political level were schooling for the children of so-called "guest workers", "guest workers'" use of spare time, and their social position within Austrian society. With regard to the social position of those now reluctantly called "immigrants", the German term "Unterschichtung" was used to describe the process of social stratification which created a new underclass within the country. These developments were evaluated differently: On the one hand they were seen as a threat to social peace, while on the other hand this stratification along national/ethnic lines secured the relative advancement of Austrian nationals, including unskilled workers (cf. Arbeitskreis für ökonomische und soziologische Studien 1973). While the latter argument is highly dubious from an ethical point of view, what is more important for my analysis is the prominence of social considerations in this early integration discourse as opposed to today's integration debates.

In the publication by the Federation of Trade Unions cited above, an early example of a line of reasoning is to be found that would become a fixed part of social democratic positions towards immigration in the course of the following decades. Instead of arguing against immigration in general, the unions now held the view that it was in the best interest of all involved – not the least immigrants already in the country – to tightly control immigration and handle permits restrictively. In this context again the practice of "tourist employment" was criticized (ÖGB 1973a: 15/16).

Within these early debates we can already find traces of argumentative figures which occupy a dominant position in today's integration discourse that focuses on ethnicity, culture and – often inseparably linked – religion. Although

---

[11] Original: "Schließlich wird man sich auch in Österreich die Frage zu stellen haben, ob man die ausländischen Arbeitskräfte mittelfristig als Einwanderer oder als Fremdkörper betrachtet. In der Fachdiskussion spricht man hier einerseits vom Integrationsprinzip, anderseits [!] vom Rotationsprinzip, bei dem man die ausländischen Arbeitskräfte nach wenigen Jahren wieder in ihre Heimat zurückschickt, um sie durch neue Ausländer zu ersetzen. In Gewerkschaftskreisen ist man aus vielen Gründen vom Integrationsprinzip ausgegangen."

these arguments were of minor importance within the debates of the 1970s, they are worth analysing because of the discursive changes that become visible:

> "But even if they [the 'guest workers'] come to us with correct information, the adjustment for them is huge: working speed and working environment are totally different in Austria than in their countries of origin. The climate differs considerably from that of their home countries, too. Our eating habits are substantially different and the hygienic facilities also differ markedly. [...] A considerable part of our foreign workers comes from regions where the Mohammedan denomination is prevalent, a denomination that differs considerably from the Christian religion in its conventions and customs. However, communication problems – the language problem – by far surpass all these difficulties" (ÖGB 1973: 6–7).[12]

Even though I already found references to culture and religion in the early 1970s, their relevance was reduced to pragmatic problems – e. g., questions of food provision in factory canteens or prayer times during working hours. One rather humorous example for worries related to religious differences can be found in an early social science-oriented publication on "guest workers",

> "... that more than half of the Turks [in Austria] still stick to the religious ban on alcohol in Islam; this considerably complicates their participation in Austrian conviviality" (Arbeitskreis für ökonomische und soziologische Studien 1973: 51).[13]

Gender issues, which are at the forefront of contemporary debates about the integration of Muslim migrants, only played a minor role in early integration discourse. Labour migration of women was acknowledged as a fact at a rather early stage by trade unions and the Economic Chamber alike (cf. ÖGB 1966), but was hardly ever debated specifically. In publications from the early 1970s there are a few references to Turkish women who – according to the authors –

---

[12] Original: "Aber selbst wenn sie mit richtigen Informationen zu uns kommen, ist die Umstellung für sie außerordentlich groß: Arbeitstempo und Arbeitswelt sind in Österreich ganz anders als in ihren Ursprungsländern. Auch das Klima unterscheidet sich deutlich von dem ihrer Heimatländer. Die Eßgewohnheiten sind bei uns grundsätzlich unterschiedlich, und auch die hygienischen Einrichtungen differieren stark. [...] Ein erheblicher Teil unserer ausländischen Arbeitskräfte kommt auch aus Gebieten, wo das mohammedanische Religionsbekenntnis vorherrschend ist, das in seinen Sitten und Gebräuchen sich doch wesentlich von der christlichen Religion unterscheidet. All diese Schwierigkeiten werden aber durch die Probleme der Verständigung – durch das Sprachproblem – bei weitem übertroffen."

[13] Original: "... daß mehr als die Hälfte der Türken sich noch an das religiöse Alkoholverbot des Islam halten; das erschwert ihnen die Teilnahme an österreichischer Geselligkeit beträchtlich".

especially appreciated the greater freedom of women in "Western" societies (Österreichisches Komitee für Sozialarbeit 1971: 79; Arbeitskreis für ökonomische und soziologische Studien 1973: 56). On the other hand, sexist assumptions about women being "easier to handle" than men and more likely to put up with the strict order of "guest workers' quarters" were voiced (Arbeitskreis für ökonomische und soziologische Studien 1973: 29). Another line of thought that, due to the legal situation of that time, appears exclusively in relation to "guest worker-girls" is the possibility to "integrate" into Austrian society through marriage to an Austrian citizen, because thereby they would immediately be granted Austrian citizenship (Arbeitskreis für ökonomische und soziologische Studien 1973: 55).[14]

Especially Turkish men were sometimes described as sticking to the alleged authoritarian traditions of their home regions. The paternalistic and stereotypical image of "guest workers" created within these texts is very explicit in the following quote:

> "Turks in many respects seem to adapt more easily to the Austrian way of life. It stands them in good stead that they are more inclined to submission, more immune to excessive alcohol consumption, and, because of their familiarity with ritual ablutions more likely to achieve a higher level of personal hygiene [than Yugoslavs]" (Arbeitskreis für ökonomische und soziologische Studien 1973: 56)[15].

But – according to the Austrian authors – this was not the only way in which the alleged authoritarianism of (Turkish) labour migrants could benefit them:

> "Given that for the advancement into lower leading positions a more authoritarian view of life as it is still prevalent among guest workers (especially among Turks) is favourable, there might result specific competitive advantages for guest workers" (Arbeitskreis für ökonomische und soziologische Studien 1973: 67).[16]

[14] Until 1983 women were immediately entitled to citizenship after marrying an Austrian citizen, while men had to settle in Austria for five years before they could apply (Fassmann/Münz 1995: 12/FN 5).

[15] Original: "[...] daß sich Türken überhaupt in vielen Beziehungen leichter an die österreichische Lebensweise anzupassen scheinen. Ihnen kommt dabei zugute, daß sie stärker zur Unterordnung tendieren, vor exzessivem Alkoholkonsum besser gefeit sind und durch die Gewöhnung an rituelle Waschungen leichter ein höheres Niveau an Körperpflege erreichen."

[16] Original: "Da für einen Aufstieg in die unteren Führungspositionen eine eher autoritäre Lebensauffassung, wie sie unter Gastarbeitern (insbesondere unter den Türken) noch weit verbreitet ist, förderlich wirkt, könnten sich für die Gastarbeiter spezifische Konkurrenzvorteile ergeben."

Although the above quotations resemble contemporary discourse to some degree, the explanations given for the presumed differences between Austrians and "guest workers" relate them to the "backwardness" of the migrants' home countries or regions. While not explicitly stating it, the authors seem to assume that such differences will vanish in the course of capitalist development – frequent comparison to the state of the Austrian countryside a few decades ago strongly point to that interpretation. Differences therefore seem to be a product of different circumstances rather than of fixed "identities" or "cultures". The downside of this notion is that whenever the term "integration" is used in relation to individual immigrants, it is used synonymously with assimilation. In one of the publications analysed there is a four-step definition of integration:

> "step 1: assimilation at the workplace; step 2: development of an Austrian life pattern; step 3: incorporation into an Austrian system of contacts; step 4: complete assimilation" (Beirat für Wirtschafts- und Sozialfragen 1976: 41).[17]

It was precisely against this equation of "integration" with "assimilation" that the idea of multiculturalism was formed later on, which fostered its own problematic implications, among them the notions of "identity" and "culture" as fixed entities that not only could, but even should be preserved. For my topic, however, another difference seems more important at the moment. While today "integration" denotes first of all a demand – and one could add: an impossible demand (cf. Bauman 1992) – directed at individual immigrants, in these early discussions it was primarily directed at the Austrian state, which was called upon to adopt new policies to address the failure of the "rotation system". One example is the question of naturalization, which in 2007 in the course of the reform of the respective law was defined as the "culmination of a successful integration process" (cf. Çilek 2007). In 1976 the authors of one of the social science surveys understood Austrian citizenship as "the basic condition for full integration" and the regulation that mandated a ten year residence in Austria for its acquisition was deemed an obstacle to integration (Beirat für Wirtschafts- und Sozialfragen 1976: 56/57). As citizenship is the key to equal rights in the political and the social domain,[18] the difference between these two concepts pro-

[17] Original: "Stufe 1: Anpassung an den Arbeitsbereich; Stufe 2: Entwicklung eines österreichischen Lebensmusters; Stufe 3: Eingliederung in ein österreichisches Kontaktsystem; Stufe 4: völlige Angleichung".

[18] Of course the situation differs according to the legal status and the duration of residence in Austria among other factors. See for example the failed attempt by the Vienna City Council to grant Third Country Nationals the right to vote on the city district level in 2002. (Bauböck/Perchinig 2006: 739, Valchars 2007: 129).

foundly alters the meaning of "integration". Integration in today's discourse becomes a task to be managed by (individual) immigrants, which in the end may or may not be evaluated positively by the Austrian state, but it does not entail the right to take part equally or even change the society one should "integrate" into.

From labour market to border control

The early integration discourse is also a good example of the contingent relationship of discursive and institutional changes, because (mainly due to the economic crisis of the mid-1970s) changes in discourse did not translate into changes in policies until the late 1980s – and even then they did so only reluctantly.[19] Instead, the *Aliens' Employment Act* of 1975 kept the most important principles of the rotation system. In fact the new law allowed for the perpetuation of most of the practices already developed and most importantly provided a legal basis for the social partners' involvement in the policy field. Although in hindsight the *Aliens' Employment Act* looks like an important cornerstone in the development of a restrictive immigration policy, it was not understood to be of such significance at the time of decision making.[20] The law was rather seen as a "legalization" of the status quo and an "Austrification" of existing regulations. As one MP put it:

> "In truth things are hardly being changed. What is actually happening is the Austrification of a formerly German law. One could just as well say: The legalization of present conditions" (Stenographisches Protokoll NR 140, XIII. GP, 20. März 1975).[21]

In terms of content, the *Aliens' Employment Act* was built upon the former legal regulation from the 1930s as well as upon the aforementioned agreement of the social partners (cf. Matuschek 1985: 184 f.). Besides establishing the possibility for individual applications by presumptive employers, the *Aliens' Employment Act* provided a basis for the practice of "contingents" (§ 12), thereby legalizing the routine of the last 15 years. Ironically, the importance of these "contingents" diminished markedly in the course of the following years. As this paper focuses on the relationship of discourse and institutions I will not provide a detailed ac-

---

[19] Legal changes in 1988 for the first time privileged immigrants already settled in Austria over "newcomers".

[20] It should also be noted that important restrictions – including the ban on "tourist employment" – had already been enforced on the administrative level in 1974.

[21] Original: "In Wahrheit werden die Dinge fast nicht verändert. Was geschieht, ist eigentlich die Austrifizierung eines ehemals deutschen Gesetzes. Man kann wohl auch sagen: Die Legalisierung derzeitiger Zustände."

count of the law itself, but instead turn to the parliamentary debate preceding the decision.

With regard to the actors of this debate, I briefly want to note a few important and lasting features of their arguments: The discourse of the Social Democrats (SPÖ) resembled that of the trade unions cited above in a pronounced way. They both tended to create an antagonism between the needs of immigrants residing within the country and further immigration. "Integration" thereby became a moral legitimation for the ever stricter control of immigration. One example from the debate of the *Aliens' Employment Act* reads as follows:

> "This demand [for a full liberalization of the Austrian labour market] was of course always rejected by us, namely with regard to the safeguarding of the jobs of domestic workers, and not least because of the foreign workers; to prevent helplessly exposing the workers who came to Austria as tourists to the arbitrariness of individual employers and landlords" (Stenographisches Protokoll NR 140, XIII. GP, 20. März 1975).[22]

This line of argument has been used by Social Democratic speakers in migration debates ever since. In my analysis I found it again, for example, in debates about the EU enlargement in 2004 and the so-called "transitional measures" which allowed Austria to keep its labour market closed for citizens of "new" member states (cf. Stenographisches Protokoll NR 55, XXII. GP, 24. März 2004).

One MP from the oppositional People's Party (ÖVP) related the question of the integration of "guest workers" to the historic experience of the integration of ethnic Germans after the Second World War and to migration within the Habsburg Empire, times when, according to him, integration did not pose a social problem despite language difficulties and national borders. In contrast, he saw the integration of the "armies of guest workers" ("Gastarbeiterheere") as problematic for various reasons, among them language, qualification and missing knowledge as well as the missing will to integrate on the part of all persons involved. He concluded:

> "The difficulties will in the end always have the result – this might sound inhuman, this may be regrettable – that the guest worker is obviously only employed for as long as he is needed. This position, and this must be stated clearly, is evidently unanimously shared by unions, entrepre-

---

[22] Original: "Dieses Verlangen wurde selbstverständlich von uns immer abgelehnt, und zwar schon im Hinblick auf die Sicherung der Arbeitsplätze der inländischen Arbeiter und nicht zuletzt wegen der ausländischen Arbeitskräfte, um die als Touristen nach Österreich gekommenen Arbeitskräfte nicht der Willkür einzelner Arbeitgeber und Quartiergeber hilflos auszusetzen."

> neurs and – as this bill and its explanatory document show – by the state and its labour market authorities" (Stenographisches Protokoll NR 140, XIII. GP, 20. März 1975).[23]

On the side of the Freedom Party (FPÖ), which today is well known for its racist campaigns, a uniform stance can be discerned, which was already developed in the debates about the *Aliens' Employment Act*. Their wish to reduce the number of "guest workers" in the country and their ideologically rooted rejection of "integration" – in 1975 one of their MPs explicitly stated that the party wished for the "anchoring of guest workers in their own inherited national folklore [angestammtes Volkstum]" (Stenographisches Protokoll NR 140, XIII. GP, 20. März 1975) – did not prevent them from arguing for a simplification of administrative procedures in favour of Austrian enterprises wishing to employ foreign labour on the basis of a "rotation system". This line of argument resembles the position taken by the FPÖ in the 1990s and 2000s with regard to seasonal workers. In their view Austrian enterprises should be able to hire seasonal workers without bureaucratic effort, but these workers should not have the possibility to gain any social rights or a long-term perspective within the country (cf. Stenographisches Protokoll NR 23, XX. GP, 22. Mai 1996).

One might conclude that even though "integration" was not a major topic of the debate on the *Aliens' Employment Act* in 1975, some aspects of this new discourse were taken up. Especially the emphasis that speakers from the major parties put on "human questions" must be taken into consideration. In comparison to earlier parliamentary discussions a much broader range of questions was addressed, but still one cannot fail to see that the familiar topos of the protection of Austrian workers remained at the centre of the debate.

With regard to institutional developments, an important shift in institutional relations can be dated to the early 1990s, when a change of discourse, which now – in the course of highly exaggerated fears after the fall of the "Iron Curtain" – related immigration, asylum, insecurity and criminality went hand in hand with institutional changes (cf. Zuser 1996). With a number of reforms of asylum and immigration regulations – most notably the *Asylum Act 1991* (BGBl 8/1992), the *Residence Act* (BGBl 466/1992) and the *Aliens' Act* (BGBl 838/1992) – the Austrian Ministry of the Interior took over the leading role in

[23] Original: "Die Schwierigkeiten werden im Ergebnis immer zur Folge haben – das mag nun unmenschlich klingen, das mag zu bedauern sein –, daß der Gastarbeiter offenbar nur so lange beschäftigt wird, als man ihn braucht. In dieser Haltung, das muß man auch deutlich machen, treffen sich offenbar die Gewerkschaften, die Unternehmer und – wie sich aus diesem Gesetz und seinen Erläuterungen ergibt – auch der Staat und seine Arbeitsmarktverwaltung recht einmütig."

the regulation of immigration and the regulatory focus shifted from control of the labour market to border control. With the *Residence Act* a specific law governed long-term residence for the first time (Davy/Gächter 1993: 259). Reforms in the following years[24] tended to further restrict the possibilities for legal immigration.

Since these reforms of the early 1990s, Austria has established a complex double system of various permits for residence and settlement on the one hand and a variety of permits for labour market access on the other hand. Both systems operate with different maximum quota and are hierarchically structured for choosing immigrants according to the needs of the Austrian economy. Until now the EU accession of Austria has not entailed any fundamental alteration of the system with regard to Third Country Nationals, and the equal treatment of EU citizens was postponed for as long as possible for citizens of the "new" member states. Today immigration mainly consists of EU citizens and family members of long-term immigrants or Austrian citizens. Besides, a decreasing number of asylum seekers is reaching the country. On the other hand, seasonal workers who are neither granted social rights nor given a long-term perspective within the country, are being employed in increasing numbers (Bauböck/Perchinig 2006: 737). This policy of hiring seasonal workers is the flip side of the official doctrine of "integration before immigration", which produces a class of labour migrants who are not considered "real" immigrants.

Conclusions

Reviewing the analysis of the discourse on foreign labour/immigration in the 1960s and 1970s and relating it to contemporary debates, I find a number of similarities as well as differences. The findings point to the perpetual importance of labour market issues for immigration debates in Austria (cf. Sedlak 2000). One basic and lasting feature of these debates, which can be made visible through a diachronic comparison of the topoi used, is the unquestioned focus on the needs of the Austrian economy and the domestic labour market. Notwithstanding this broadly shared consensus I found a characteristic divide between parliamentary actors, with the economy-oriented People's Party on the one side and the labour-oriented Social Democrats on the other. The slogan "Austria first!" that was put forward by the Freedom Party in an anti-immigration campaign could also be understood as the unspoken background of the Social Dem-

[24] It is impossible to list the frequent changes of these immigration laws within this paper. Note that between 1988 and 1998 the *Aliens' Employment Act* alone was reformed no less than eleven times.

ocrats' focus on the protection of Austrian workers and the People's Party's concentration on the Austrian economy. In recent debates the Green Party (in parliament since 1986) partially departed from this consensus by pressing for the rights of immigrants and for fairness of treatment. Nevertheless the party does not explicitly challenge the assumption that immigration should first of all benefit Austrian interests.

Until today immigrants themselves are rarely heard in public debates, though the tendency is slowly rising. The representation of immigrants, foreign-born Austrians, and the so-called "Second" or "Third Generation" in democratic institutions is still far from adequate. This can partly be explained as an effect of the restrictive approach towards naturalization and – probably more importantly – as an effect of the social exclusion of "foreigners" that is relatively independent of their citizenship.[25] This social stratification is perpetuated as it often entails disadvantages for children with an immigration background with regard to education.

A factor that became increasingly important in immigration debates in the course of the last decades was the perceived attitude of the Austrian population. It is not surprising that this argument has especially been brought forward by the Freedom Party as it is in line with the party's populist stance. However, in the parliamentary debates on the "transitional measures" accompanying the EU enlargement of 2004, the topos of the "anxieties and fears" of the Austrian population became consensually shared "knowledge" that even critical speakers had to relate to (Stenographisches Protokoll NR 55, XXII. GP, 24. März 2004).

Arguably, this widely shared perception of immigration as a threat to Austrian society obstructs the acceptance of immigration as a normality for every European society and thereby prevents the self-definition as an immigration country. The perception of immigration as a disturbance to the alleged stability of native society was reinforced by "forgetting" Austrian emigration which, as stated above, was an important topic during the 1960s and 1970s. Today migration therefore appears to be something only "others" do and not an option within "normality".

The change of discourse from labour immigration being (despite all prejudices against the "guest workers") perceived as something ultimately necessary and beneficiary to a view that focuses mostly on the threats thought to come with it, is a development that can be traced over the last two decades. Of course, the changing economic situation and the end of full employment played an important role in this context, but my analysis points to the distinct evolvement of an

[25] This phenomenon is linked to the Austrian understanding of "nation", which is still strongly connected to ethnicity.

"integration"-discourse as yet another important factor. I followed the development of the notion of "integration" from its assimilationist beginnings to its contemporary form where it functions as an obligation for individual immigrants. As such, it has strong culturalist undertones and tends to obliterate the social positioning of labour migrants within Austrian society. I argue that this specific discourse hinders participation rather than fostering it and that it strengthens prejudices and resentments on the side of "native" Austrians.

The other side of this specific version of "integration" is the discourse on, and the institutional set-up of, seasonal employment. Today's model of seasonal work, which deprives these workers of social rights, shows a number of analogies to the old "rotation" approach, though in a modernized and more restrictive version. In this specific discourse the economic rationale again prevails, problems of competition on the labour market do not seem to arise and long-term perspectives for the workers are legally prevented as far as possible. It is hardly coincidental that this form of temporary employment – in sharp contrast to immigration issues – has not stirred public debate.

Especially with regard to this last issue I would like to conclude that tight immigration regulations are not designed to prevent the presence of foreign labour within the country, but to restrict permanent settlement and the granting of rights. Given the results presented above, and besides all ethical and fundamental political concerns, I also remain sceptical as to the efficiency of this strategy in avoiding the problems that became associated with immigration. The history of migration policies and migration discourse in Austria rather points in the opposite direction. It indicates that the social segregation of society and labour markets politically constructed along ethnical/cultural lines is to a large degree an effect of the legal and social discrimination of immigrants and their descendants. And it is this segregation that lies at the bottom of many of the problems that are today being discussed as "problems of integration".

Literature

Arbeitskreis für ökonomische und soziologische Studien 1973: Gastarbeiter. Wirtschaftliche und soziale Herausforderungen. Wien: Europaverlag/Österreichischer Wirtschaftsverlag.

Bauböck, Rainer, Bernhard Perchinig 2006: Migrations- und Integrationspolitik. In: Herbert Dachs et al. (eds.), Politik in Österreich. Das Handbuch. Wien: Manz, 726–742.

Bauman, Zygmunt 1992: Moderne und Ambivalenz. Das Ende der Eindeutigkeit. Hamburg: Junius.

Beirat für Wirtschafts- und Sozialfragen 1976: Möglichkeiten und Grenzen des Einsatzes ausländischer Arbeitskräfte. Wien: Ueberreuter.

Bojadžijev, Manuela 2008: Die windige Internationale. Rassismus und die Kämpfe der Migration. Münster: Westfälisches Dampfboot.

Butschek, Felix, Ewald Walterskirchen 1974: Aspekte der Ausländerbeschäftigung. In: WIFO-Monatsberichte 47, 4: 214–224.

Çilek, Dinar 2007: Integration vor Einbürgerung: die Staatsbürgerschaftsrechtsnovelle 2005. In: Heinz Fassmann (ed.), 2. Österreichischer Migrations- und Integrationsbericht 2001–2006. Klagenfurt/Celovec: Drava Verlag, 41–46.

Davy, Ulrike, August Gächter 1993: Zuwanderungsrecht und Zuwanderungspolitik in Österreich. In: Journal für Rechtspolitik 1: 155–174, 257–281.

Fassmann, Heinz, Rainer Münz 1995: Einwanderungsland Österreich? Historische Migrationsmuster, aktuelle Trends und politische Maßnahmen. Wien: Jugend & Volk.

Jäger, Siegfried 2001: Kritische Diskursanalyse. Eine Einführung. Duisburg: DISS.

Karakayali, Serhat 2008: Gespenster der Migration. Zur Genealogie illegaler Einwanderung in der Bundesrepublik Deutschland. Bielefeld: Transcript.

Matuschek, Helga 1985: Ausländerpolitik in Österreich 1962–1985. Der Kampf um und gegen ausländische Arbeitskraft. In: Journal für Sozialforschung 25, 2: 159–198.

Mayer, Stefanie, Mikael Spång 2009: Debating Migration: Political Discourses on Labour Immigration in Historical Perspective. Innsbruck, Wien, Bozen: Studienverlag, transaction press.

Österreichische Komitee für Sozialarbeit 1971: Gastarbeiter in Österreich. Referate und Berichte der 3. Österreichischen Konferenz für Sozialarbeit, 16.–18. November Wien. Wien, München: Jugend und Volk.

Parnreiter, Christof 1992: ... alle Arbeitskräfte des Erdrunds. Über den Import ausländischer Arbeitskräfte nach Österreich und ihren Nutzen für die Wirtschaft. In: Thomas Prader (ed.), Moderne Sklaven. Wien: Promedia, 70–91.

Sedlak, Maria 2000: You really do make an Unrespectable Foreigner Policy ... Ethnic Issues in the Austrian Parliament. In: Teun van Dijk, Ruth Wodak (eds.), Racism at the Top. Klagenfurt/Celovec: Drava Verlag, 107–168.

Tálos, Emmerich 2006: Sozialpartnerschaft. Austrokorporatismus am Ende? In: Herbert Dachs et al. (eds.), Politik in Österreich. Das Handbuch. Wien: Manz, 425–442.

Valchars, Gerd 2007: Wahlrechte von NichtstaatsbürgerInnen in Österreich. In: Heinz Fassmann (ed.), 2. Österreichischer Migrations- und Integrationsbericht. 2001–2006. Klagenfurt/Celovec: Drava Verlag, 127–131.

van Dijk, Teun A. 2000: Theoretical Background. In: Teun van Dijk, Ruth Wodak (eds.), Racism at the Top. Klagenfurt/Celovec: Drava Verlag, 13–30.

Weigl, Andreas 2009: Migration und Integration. Eine widersprüchliche Geschichte. Innsbruck, Wien, Bozen: Studienverlag.

Wengeler, Martin 2003: Topos und Diskurs. Begründung einer argumentationstheoretischen Methode und ihre Anwendung auf den Migrationsdiskurs (1960–1985). Tübingen: Max Niemeyer Verlag.

Wodak, Ruth, Rudolf de Cillia, Martin Reisigl et al. 1998: Zur diskursiven Konstruktion nationaler Identität. Frankfurt: Suhrkamp.

Zuser, Peter 1996: Die Konstruktion der Ausländerfrage in Österreich. Eine Analyse des öffentlichen Diskurses 1990. Wien: his (Reihe Politikwissenschaft/Political Science Series no. 35).

ÖGB 1963. Tätigkeitsbericht 1962 des Österreichischen Gewerkschaftsbundes. Wien

ÖGB 1973. ÖGB-Rednerdienst: Ausländische Arbeitskräfte in Österreich. Oktober 1973, Wien

Stenographisches Protokoll NR 140, XIII. GP, 20. März 1975

Stenographisches Protokoll BR 340, 4. April 1975

Stenographisches Protokoll NR 23, XX. GP, 22. Mai 1996

Stenographisches Protokoll NR 55, XXII. GP, 24. März 2004

BGBl 218/1975 - Aliens' Employment Act (Ausländerbeschäftigungsgesetz)

BGBl 8/1992 - Asylum Act 1991 (Asylgesetz 1991)

BGBl 466/1992 - Residence Act 1992 (Aufenthaltsgesetz 1992)

BGBl 838/1992 - Aliens' Act (Fremdengesetz)

Ethnologia Balkanica 13 (2009)

Migratory Marginalities: Making Sense of Home, Self and Mobility

Petruţa Teampău, Cluj, and Kristof Van Assche, Minnesota

Abstract

We set out to explore, in this paper, the concept of migratory marginalities. Marginal social identities, partly linked to marginal places, can be transformed, renegotiated in migration. Receiving places and people, their lack of familiarity with the migrant, contribute to this partial openness for redefinition, yet a complete rewriting is unlikely to take place. In the process of redefinition, at different points in time, in different situations, identities can be silenced, hidden, re-interpreted, other identities can be invoked, combined, intertwined, hybridized, and the process is further complicated by the act of moving through spatial scales (embedding different identities) and the act of moving pure and simple (changing the context of identity construction). In the context of Sulina, a small town on the edge of the Romanian Danube Delta, we analyse the history of migration (in and out) in a site of marginality. Sulina proves to be a place of multi-layered marginalities, with a cherished period of temporary centrality, still marking the narratives of self and place (Teampău, Van Assche 2009). Against this backdrop, we analyse two narratives of migration in order to reveal the intricate dialectics of local-global in coping with an identity of marginality.

Geography and historical context

The most eastern locality of Romania, Sulina is a small town at the end of one of the Danube's three branches; it has no land connection to neighboring localities and, being surrounded by waters, has the appearance and the air of an island. Moreover, Sulina is unique in that it is both a river harbour city and a sea harbour city. The city has, according to the current official discourse, a long and fascinating history. However, the recorded history is not continuous, but punctuated across centuries by several data, with Sulina vaguely mentioned in some documents and maps. Most documents record Sulina as a pirates' nest, a place where anything is possible, a place which cannot be avoided on the route upstream the Danube. During the 19th century, the political-administrative authority in Sulina belonged, in turn, to the Ottoman and the Russian Empire, which encouraged, or at least tolerated, a very flexible state of affairs. Practically, it was a no man's land, where the rules were made up along the way. By the middle of the 19th century, the economic interests of the great European powers transformed the problem of the Danube into an issue of international politics. Following the Crimean War, through the Peace Treaty in Paris (March 18/30, 1856), they established the European Commission of the Danube (with representatives from France, England, Austria, Prussia, Russia, Sardinia, Turkey). Sulina became its headquarter, for an initial mandate of two years. This "European Union" *avant la lettre* governed the mouths of the Danube for more than a century, organized the navigation on the river and, in the process, transformed Sulina into a flourishing harbour and a pleasant city. In spite of the beneficial presence of CED, the communist regime (1948–1989) forbade any mention of this period of "imperialism", and many memories of it were lost. This city, born for a specific mission (supervising and ensuring the navigation on the Sulina channel), is today a rather isolated place (for most of the year), with low incomes and high unemployment rates, a fascinating history and uncertain future. New business networks, new places and new power relations are being inscribed on pre-existing spaces, while abandoned industrial landscapes are being reinterpreted.

Much like in most places in Romania, in Sulina, the fall of communism came together with exacerbated hopes (often unrealistic) about "change", about a different future, about opportunities never before imagined. One can assume that here, more than anywhere else, was the place to be for easy money in the early nineties, and many managed to find it. In the two decades since the revolution, sources of income and other resources have changed rapidly for the people of Sulina, but they seem to have adapted to each subsequent mutation (for an overview of the post-communist evolution of Sulina, see Teampău 2010, forthcoming).

Officially, there is a worrying 40 % unemployment rate in Sulina, one of the highest in the country. Unofficially, almost every family has at least one member working abroad (mainly in Spain and Italy), or serving as crew for a foreign ship, which pays a good salary in euros. Or, one is involved in fishing (more or less legally), in hosting tourists during the summer (no taxes paid), in taking those tourists for quite expensive trips "into the Delta" or cooking them "traditional" dishes, such as fish soup. However, this tourism frenzy only started to developonly after the late nineties. Before that, a few years after the revolution, "no one was coming here, and the summers were very much like the winters".

In fact, this tourism "business" has radically transformed the lives of the locals. During the summer, the whole place swarms with people in shorts and flip-flops, coming or going to the beach, looking for a place to drink or eat, or just walking up and down the first street in the warm evenings. However, the lights and sounds gently dissipate as you pass along the second street, while from the third street onwards there are only stars and frogs.

Off season, during winter, life has a different rhythm. People spend more time in their homes, trying to "do things for themselves", things they have been postponing throughout the summer. Somehow, during the winter, Sulina has a different atmosphere, it is like a family getting together after all the annoying guests have left. In the words of L., the local photographer, life in Sulina has two distinct cycles: the summer one, and the rest of the time, with different rhythms, different activities, different time frames. "During the summer, we feel like holiday guides", everything is oriented towards tourism, and sometimes, with thousands of tourists (like in the peak year of 2007, when some of them had to sleep in the park because they could not find housing), the population of the town almost doubles.

Space and social encounters

Borrowing concepts from non-representational geographers (Sarah Whatmore, Doreen Massey, Nigel Thrift), and from their ubiquitous source of inspiration, Deleuze and Guattari, we analyse two stories that started in Sulina, and led to many other places. Deleuzian concepts are incorporated in a narrative anthropology. We will enrich the picture with narrative fragments from other lives in Sulina.

C. and S., the two main characters of our stories, have interesting life histories, in which the theme of migration, of moving around, seems to be recurrent. Both in their thirties, they share a spirit of adventure, which they justify by appealing to the "special place" Sulina is and to its (semi-)official tradition of "piracy". Both started as fishermen (a customary local occupation), engaging in heavy drinking as often as possible, and then they tried their luck around the world, always coming back with new hopes and plans. C., who is an artist, received a higher education in Bucharest and Cluj, but returned to Sulina to paint. In fact, during the summer he is a very active tourist operator; he even has fixed "working hours" that coincide with the schedule of the incoming ships, and has specialized in backpackers or foreign young tourists (his own negligent looks help: he has pierced ears and short hair and is always riding a bicycle as if he has nothing better to do). Then he spends his winters "working": he paints, for the sake of painting (even though some of those works will be sold to tourists the following summer). S., a Lipovan, has worked all over Europe, returning with hopes of opening his own *pension* one day. When home, both C. and S. spend their time drinking and "fishing" for tourists. Their narratives focus on the specificity of Sulina, viewed in a contradictory manner as being both a place of opportunities and a place of no hopes, which forces them to leave, and yet to always come back, thus illustrating the underlying problem of migration: people who leave for a better life, but still dream of being able to "make it" at home.

A semiotic analysis of mobility seems in place, a non-binary inquiry into the meanings of home, of being away, and the consequences certain articulations of home, migration and the wider world might have for the constructions of self and place. We see migration/mobility as a means of making and remaking self and place. The meanings of places are constantly being redefined and renegotiated, and practices, experiences and conceptions of moving around/mobility can have consequences for place. In other words, we intend to describe how "people weave stories into and out of place so as to construct identities" (Mitchell *apud* Williams 2006: 34).

On the one hand, home can be seen as a tedious space, a place of the ordinary, of repetitive actions, where "abroad"/"away" always holds the promise of a real development, of the excitement of adventure, of a complete fulfillment of the self (home as the place to be when you have nothing better to do, in the words of Margaret Thatcher). Mobility itself is coded sometimes as adventure, an initiatory journey intended to shape the self, a dys-placement (moving in/out of place); it builds on a commitment to change. As some authors suggest, "movement is not just the experience of shifting from place to place, it is also linked to our ability to imagine an alternative. The dream of a better life and the nightmares of loss are both expressed by the metaphor of the journey" (Papastergiadis 2000: 11). Leaving, moving, going "away" means following a dream, a desire, the design of a better or new life.

It has also been noted that "the masculine tradition in travel literature casts the home as a blank and empty space and connotes travel experience with adventure and excitement. It is as if the home is the place of the mundane running order which keeps mind and body together, but 'abroad' is the place one looks for peak experience and real development" (Roger, Urry 1997: 16). Seamon, among others, discusses "the dialectic relationship between movement and rest", while Relph emphasizes "a dialectic experience of place", i. e., "balancing a need to stay with a desire to escape" (Gustafson 2006: 23).

World on the move: going away, moving around, coming home

Mobility can be largely defined as "the movement of 'peoples, objects, images, information and wastes'" (Urry 2000: 1) within and across the boundaries of national societies. People, products and information circulate freely around the world, problematizing concepts of national boundaries, home, dwelling, stasis, structure and social order (Urry 2000, McIntyre 2006: 4). It is also "the means by which people optimize access to their network of activities in various life domains: work, leisure, health, education, family etc." (McIntyre 2006: 4). There are indeed many forms of mobility, and many meanings for different people.

Studies show that for some individuals mobility is associated with “life, health and activity”, for others it means “variation, new experiences and new social contacts” and can also be connoted as “curiosity and open-mindedness”, or even “courage, initiative and adventurousness” (Gustafson 2006: 20).

According to some authors, “migration is never a spontaneous gesture. It presupposes some knowledge of the other side, a guide, a map or, at least, a rumour. The obvious difference between the places of departure and arrival, as well as the tangible distance between them, belies the complexities of motivations and hopes that fuel these journeys” (Papastergiadis 2000: 25). Moreover, mobility has become so much part of the life of modern individuals that the need or the incentive for it sometimes go unquestioned. Among these, “consumption of landscape” and various “leisure opportunities”, not to mention job prospects, rank quite high (McIntyre 2006: 6). Generally speaking, “circulation no longer represents an interruption of ordinary, settled life, but constitutes a normal condition for many people”, as “modern forms of dwelling, working, and leisure involve circulating through a geographically extended network of social relations and a multiplicity of widely dispersed geographic places” (McIntyre 2006: 8). However, this increasing circulation of people, goods and ideas that we have come to label globalization, has unexpected consequences on “our experience of home and away and ultimately [on] how we go about constructing our identities and anchoring our sense of who we are and where we belong” (Williams 2006: 47, Bouma- Prediger 2008).

Making place, making self

For Deleuze and Guattari, life is essentially *becoming,* ever changing, and an individual life is an entering into ever changing relationships with other people, but also places, objects and ideas, forming different *assemblages,* enabling different desires to be produced (Braidotti 2002, 2006). Place from a Deleuzian perspective is the necessary milieu for a living being, as the relatively stable block of space–time that results from a regular repetition of its constituting forces (Deleuze, Guattari 1987: 313). At the same time, a place is also a confluence of stories, a momentary configuration of trajectories of living and non-living objects, with a potential to form assemblages, with each other, and with people and objects faraway, with other places. From a Deleuzian perspective, therefore, places are made and places have their own individuality, an individuality that is reproduced perpetually by the actions of human and other beings.

Places are interconnected with identities: “the social processes of place creation reinforce individual identities and shape and support collective identities” (Stokowski, 2002: 369). Places must be constantly produced, inscribed with values, imagined, designed and shaped. They are not only mediums of social and collective memory, but also contexts of social interactions. Social relations are constituted, constrained by and mediated through space. The consequent landscapes may be said to be a product of a socio-spatial dialectic (Dear, Flusty 2002: 3).

Proshansky, Fabian and Kaminoff introduce the concept of "place-identity" (*apud* Groat 1995: 87), referring to "memories, ideas, feelings, attitudes, values, preferences, meanings and conceptions of behaviour and experience which relate to the variety and complexity of psychical settings that define the day-to-day existence of every human being". Place-identity influences our experiences with the environment, serving as a "cognitive backdrop, or perhaps better said, as a physical environment 'data-base' against which every physical setting can be 'experienced' and responded to in some way" (*apud* Groat 1995: 96). As individuals, we differentiate ourselves in this respect through "the specific pattern of cognitions of places, environment skills, and person/physical setting relationships that underlie the place-identity of the person" (*apud* Groat 1995: 111).

For Deleuze, not identity but difference is the basis of reality, but he does analyse the construction of identity, the seeming stability of personal identity, social identity and place identity, as the production of molar and rigid entities, constricting the continuous development of difference, often in the name of State, Reason or God. Identities restrict the flow of forces that leads to new assemblages, to creative thinking. Fixed identities suffocate rhizomatic thinking. For Deleuze and Guattari (1987: 10), the rhizome is a concept that describes thought that is prolific and creative, establishing connections between things, peoples and thoughts that are not obvious, but transversal.

The rhizome describes affective change, and it produces affective change: through a contact of previously isolated things, now affecting each other, it functions as an assemblage machine for new affects, new concepts, new bodies and thoughts (Deleuze, Guattari 1987). Places are the context of rhizomatic activity, and they are part of the rhizome. In constant flux, affected by the trajectories of all bodies that create it, it nevertheless offers opportunities for those bodies to enter into unexpected transversal relations.

If places are always in a process of (re)definition, then we can also argue that "practices, experiences and conceptions of mobility and attachment among the 'users' of a place may have important consequences for the place itself – how the place is designed and physically shaped, how the place is used by its permanent inhabitants as well as by temporary residents or visitors, and how the place is invested with meaning and value" (Gustafson 2006: 31). If place-identity serves as a kind of "cognitive backdrop" for all our spatial experiences, it makes sense to suggest that where they came from, how they were attached to "home", can play an influential role in defining the itinerant experience of migrants. This is just one side of the coin. The other side refers to how "home" itself (by which we understand a whole set of concepts, feelings and practices) is transformed by the very incident of mobility. At this point, a discussion of Doreen Massey's view of places can be helpful.[1]

According to Massey, "what gives a place its specificity is not some long internalized history but the fact that it is constructed out of a particular constellation of relations articulated together at a particular locus" (Massey 1994: 154). She argues for a "progressive sense of place" which "can only be constructed by linking that place to places beyond" (Massey 1994: 156). Thus, places are not to be conceived anymore as bounded entities, but "they can be imagined as articulated moments in networks of social relations and understandings" allowing for "a sense of place which is extroverted, which includes a consciousness of its links with the wider world, which integrates in a positive way the global and the local" (Massey 1994: 154 f.).

It is not only that places do not have boundaries in a classical sense, but, moreover, their definition can come, in part, precisely through the particularity of linkage *to* that "outside" which is therefore itself part of what constitutes the place. This understanding of places as being constituted out of the tension between inside and outside and out of their link *to* (and not difference from) outside can be very useful in integrating the mixed experience of local – global of the mobile person. And Massey does indeed progress in this view. Thus, she argues, "The specificity of place is continually reproduced", and this specificity "derives from the fact that each place is the focus of a distinct *mixture* of wider and more local social relations. There is the fact that this very mixture together in one place may produce effects which would not have happened otherwise. And finally, all these relations interact with and take a further element of specificity from the accumulated history of a place, with that history itself imagined as the product of layer upon layer of different sets of linkages, both local and to the wider world" (Massey 1994: 156).

These insights, developed further in a series of books, among which Massey 2005 should be noted, develop an event-based theory of space, a theory that nevertheless does not subsume space under time. Place has an identity here, even if this is changing all the time; it has an identity as an unrepeatable confluence of trajectories of bodies, and an unrepeatable set of linkages with other places, ideas, bodies in an ever-evolving rhizome (Buchanan, Lambert 2005, Massey 2005, Massumi 1992). As a theory of difference and change, Deleuze's

1 "If places can be conceptualized in terms of the social interactions which they tie together, then it is also the case that these interactions themselves are not motionless things, frozen in time. They are processes" (Massey 1994: 154).

perspective on identity usually privileges metaphors and figures of mobility: the line of flight, the nomad, deterritorialization. The figure of the nomad, positively contrasted with the sedentary world of parcelled land and rigid ideas, does not primarily refer to wandering tribes, but rather to a lack of boundaries that are predetermined and/or fixed by an external or transcendental authority (Deleuze 1984).

Nomadic law for Deleuze is a principle of individuation: identity is formed without reference to external criteria; "it judges immanently" (Deleuze 1994: 37). The principle itself leads to context-specific criteria for assessment: science or art or philosophy should not be judged according to external goals, but rather, by the standard of maximum performance and maximum effect. Does this work of art lead to new ways of seeing (Deleuze and Guattari 1994)?

Nomadic space, with Deleuze, is produced through its own distribution, not through an external rule. Nomadic space therefore cannot be described before a concrete distribution, through concrete activities and networked relations. It has no intrinsic properties defining relations; rather, it is the movement itself that produces space, activities produce identities. Using a space, moving through a space, filling it with ideas and desires, creates that space. Other groups wandering through the territory will bring their own space, bringing it to bear on the physical environment. In this creation of space, people and communities are transformed in the process. Belonging in this perspective cannot be determined by the State; its monopoly on social identification should be broken and moving through physical, social and conceptual landscapes, in rhizomatic meanderings, can open up new affective allegiances, as well as new conceptual horizons (Patton 2000, Massey 2005, Buchanan 2005).

Migratory marginalities

Molz Germann has argued that "the emblematic figures of a world where being at home has become impossible are those of peripatetic homelessness; the exile, nomad, traveler, alien, or global soul best reflect the postmodern inability to find one's way home or to feel *chez soi* in a world of unrelenting physical and virtual movement" (Molz Germann 2008: 2). However, even though she argues for an impossibility of home in a world of restless mobility (whether physical or virtual), she does admit that home is always "an absent presence in narratives of travel and mobility", as the stable point (or the illusion of stability) in which all stories are anchored.

As Shurmer-Smith and Hannam underline, "home is a particularly powerful term in the English language, encompassing a multitude of meanings from the concrete to the metaphoric, including 'bricks and mortar, kinship, tradition, contentment, regional loyalty, duty, community, nationalism, return, aspiration'" (*apud* McIntyre 2006: 6). As a consequence, it is never easy to define or to discuss "home"; it is an even more delicate topic for individuals who leave (or return) home. People willingly leave home in order to fulfill a dream or to follow an idea, a plan, a necessity (or all of the above).

In many versions of postmodern thought, including Deleuzian theories, home is a problematic, even suspect, construct. Home smells like stability, taxonomy, fixed identity, state-sanctioned immobility, imaginary roots and everything that is despicable for theorists of difference and mobility. Home is often represented as a product of nostalgia, another usual suspect for an academia fond of demystification. Some authors came in defense of both home and nostalgia (Wheeler 1994), arguing that both concepts have productive and restrictive versions. We argue that a Deleuzian-inspired anthropology of mobility and migration can very well embrace an analysis of home-making. In the very real world of desire and affect, people do long for anchoring points in time and space. Nevertheless, the meaning of home from a Deleuzian perspective cannot be a stable construct, but rather a shifting product of a dialectics between individuals, groups, places, objects and ideas.

We want to argue that in the case of our two narratives, what stands out is the dialectical construction of "home" and "away". In Sulina, local identity is largely underlined by recurrent narratives of piracy and cosmopolitanism (Van Assche, Teampău 2008), and by taking pride in breaking the laws of a centre one does not identify with. The often-quoted local saying "we are the first to see the sun and the last to see justice" expresses a deeply felt marginality, both geographical and political. Sulina, as the former seat of the European Danube Committee (CED), boasts of a history of international connections and local ethnic diversity. Thus, for the people of Sulina, Europe represents a return and a replacement, but also, like for any other Eastern Europeans, the glamour and the lure of a better life, and the locus of preconceived concepts (democracy, freedom, good life etc.; Teampău, Van Assche 2007).

Against this general background, for C., home is a place for the full, complete realization of self, while "going away" has rather existential stakes for his wanderer's soul. For S., on the other hand, home is a place for anchoring all the hopes and dreams of a better future; even though he is also an adventurer in his own way, he wants to "make it at home". He seems to be more pragmatic, even though quite skeptical about "putting yourself willingly in the mouth of the sharks" (if he ever wanted to start a business in Sulina).

C. explains his trips to Europe as something deliberate: *I wanted to eat something special that is not accessible to everyone here; when I left for Europe I had the impression that I was eating something in a five-star restaurant.* Europe enjoys a special imagery: he still preserves from his childhood during communism the image of the golden fishing hooks of the German tourists, glittering in the sun, as opposed to the ugly dark-brown Russian ones, that broke easily. For him, this image remained the essence of the glamour and glitter of Europe.

In reality, post-experience, Europe came to mean a lifestyle he could not really agree with:

> "People are obsessed with money and live their lives as if they are looking through glass, as if you see what is happening through a glass, you do not feel what you are doing. While here in Sulina and in other isolated places you really feel life. You do not have the instruments to do what you want, but you improvise to make ends meet. In Europe they have everything, but do not know how to use it."

He seems to value this *savoir-vivre*, living life to extremes (even those of poverty). "When I came back, I felt like I was in heaven, I was mastering my own life again, which I couldn't do in Europe, where I did not know anyone." C.'s story is a story of freedom, looking for a complete fulfillment of the self, which in the end can only be realized at home.

For both men, "abroad" was primarily an idealized and homogenized "Europe" that could not but disappoint. In their desire for a better life, they imagined a Europe that was very different from their home in Sulina, while hoping, sometimes assuming, that it would feel like home, because of Sulina's "European" past. A distance and a proximity were created simultaneously, and that paradox had to produce negative experiences when travelling. Both men experienced the dismissal in Europe of the European roots/claims of Sulina, and the maltreatment of East European immigrants (mostly illegal in their case, in their formative travels before 2007, before Romania's EU accession).

Both men experienced dissatisfaction with the pecuniary gains of European migration, low salaries, high living expenses and a lacking network for low-income survival. They also found out that the Law does not protect everyone in Europe: S. was not paid for the long hours he worked in a kitchen in southern Italy. When he complained he was beaten up. Injured and with no health insurance, he wound up back in Sulina worse of than before. C. shared similar experiences in Germany. Still, the European dream, the European home was not shattered, partly because in recent years, Sulina's European orientation was emphasized even more, and tourism from Western Europe increased significantly.

The two men had to make their living in various places in various European countries, and their respective Odysseys are hard to reconstruct in detail. Despite, and maybe partly because of, the generalized home of Europe, no particular European place felt like home to them. The "look through glass" mentioned by C. articulates the distance felt, the homelessness, lack of hospitality, and the lack of networks of friends and relatives. The act of moving, of migration, did not amount to the nomadism revered by Deleuze and his followers. The moving matrix of the rhizome did not accompany C. and S. routinely. New insights came from the work and travel in Europe, but often pre-existing ideas and routines were confirmed and reinforced. On many occasions, they felt they had to resort to "auto-pilot", "just working, (drinking), sleeping, working, moving on", in the words of S. The lines of flight, escapes from restrictive schemes of thought and feeling presumably prevalent in a nomadic lifestyle, were sometimes more literal escapes from the police.

Citizenship laws in most European countries did not recognize them as acceptable entities, and everything had to happen under the radar. This impacted their activities in daily life. It prevented the full experience of Europe, as well as an inclusion of European places in their affective worlds, in other words, home-making. Productive assemblages of man and place were not likely to form in that oppressive environment. State and Law predefined and sanctioned forms of belonging, and excluded both men from the territory of the various nation-states they crossed. Since they travelled without family, and usually without girlfriends, the affective link with places was generally weak.

Still, this general narrative does not capture the dialectics of home and away in its subtlety; "Europe" was not a stable source and site of disappointment. From their stories, it becomes clear that S. and C. travelled with new expectations every time, that their visions of Europe, of self, home, and of the place shifted along with their trajectories through Europe, and their encounters with other people, places, ideas and objects. "Home" followed them, and took on different shades every step. The perceived limitations of Sulina as a place to live; its marginality followed them as well. A history of marginality, led both of them to a desire to leave, either to come back and "make it", or to give it a try while travelling.

For S., the shifting horizons of migration were meant to be temporary, ephemeral; they were not supposed to touch him in the core, to affect his identity, to identify his affections. In order to come back well, one needs to come back with the trappings of success as seen in Sulina. A distance from the problems in Sulina (the "sharks" among others) implies a proximity, an adherence to the local criteria of success, success in Europe. For C., the journey itself, the very shifting of horizons, the continuous transformation of self in contact with other places, seemed to be the object of desire. His view of life as an openness, as a flow of affections, as an eternal becoming, comes close to the Deleuzian idealized nomad, but his life was/is hard, and the continuous change, his own history of marginality in his travels as in Sulina, clearly left marks. It is unclear whether the professed "home", the place of full realization of self, ever came close. Regardless of the perspective one has of his drinking habits, there is an element of flight, of unhappiness, and in many conversations, C. did share his desire to be somewhere else, to travel, acknowledging that travelling without money, a job or connections, takes its toll.

The physical isolation of Sulina, separated by swamp, river and sea from the rest of the world, makes it easier to imagine it as a remote hell, and as a safe haven. The difference with the surroundings can easily be articulated, a territory can be easily staked out. In Deleuzian terms, a territory is a home, a product of forces creating identity. A territory is a thing and its place, an individualized assemblage (Deleuze, Guattari 1987: 316; Buchanan, Lambert 2005) In this perspective, it is only natural that the home follows man, that a person cannot but stake out a territory. For Deleuze, the dialectics between deterritorialization and reterritorialization decouples and bundles flows of forces, erasing identities and recreating others. Both of them can be constructive and destructive; deterritorialization can be found in the creative line of flight, and in total destruction, while reterritorialization can be both home-making and subjection to a colonizing discourse.

In migration, and certainly in a tough voyage from and to a marginal position, the full spectrum of deterritorialization and reterritorialization can be felt, experienced. The disruptive powers of changing places, people, objects, the subjection to continuous transformation, heightened by relatively little knowledge of the new places and people, and by a spirit of adventure, an initial openness to transformation through migration, played out both positively and negatively for both C. and S., but in all extremes. During their travels, and in between, in Sulina, the presence and the memory of the pressures on identity, made them think, drink and go on "automatic pilot". "Home" responded to those pressures, and followed a parallel trajectory, assuming all the colours of new encounters, and absorbing the often contradictory desires triggered by often contradictory forces in the long journeys from and to Sulina.

For Deleuze, time can never be recaptured, and home can never be a place frozen in time. A real home can be a place of relationships, where those relationships with other people and with non-humans (the house, to name one thing) can be rekindled, reinvented. The time and the place, the now and the where of the meeting of the home, is constituted in the meeting, in the actual revisiting. Home, in that sense is a time-space that has to be reinvented all the time. Not doing so, implies remaining stuck in a territory that will lead to obvious disappointments later in time, and, to quote Massey (2005: 125) "deprives others of their stories". For C., the Sulina he imagines as home is not so much the golden-era Sulina of the CED, nor the idealized and westernized Sulina of the future – despite his occasional rhetoric of "a new Palm Beach".

Home is the place that is multi-layered in its meanings, but that semiotic complexity is possible exactly because things are made more predictable; chance encounters are rarefied. Places as interrelated stories, as multiple becomings, are challenging, and an imaginary home tends to be a less challenging site. Also for Deleuze, a territory is a natural thing, and deterritorialization is only conceivable in conjunction with reterritorialization. "The world" or "Europe" as a home can only have a shallow meaning therefore; it is the practice of home-making that becomes more complex in a larger world. Both C. and S. bring routines with them in their travels, habits and rhythms, as far as conditions allow.

Their storytelling about Sulina, about leaving, and about an eternal return, became part of the routines. However commodified their storytelling might be in a place with growing reliance on tourism – a tourism industry dictating the rhythm of their daily lives in summer, waiting for boats, picking up tourists – it served other purposes as well. Storytelling for them recreates home continuously, with an admirable flexibility. It seems that the routine of the storytelling itself gives a grounding to them, becomes home. For S., there is the recurring idea of starting a business back in Sulina, with Sulina as the spatialized home, but his evolving plans seem to include less and less time in Sulina, and the conditions under which he would like to start a business locally seem very far away from the current situation. Clearly an intelligent man, S. seems to immerse himself more in the stories about the business for several reasons, among which can be noted a desire to "have a story", to "have a plan" for outsiders and for himself, a surface layer of narrative that can give way easily to a myriad of new thoughts, plans, travels and homes.

The marginality of Sulina drove C. and S. to migration, and it followed them every step along the way. Both C. and S. are keenly aware of the limitations and the lure of Sulina: "man, look at this place!" and "damn, what are we doing here" oscillate in an affective equilibrium that is highly unstable. The same oscillation is a continuous questioning of self, a continuous confrontation with the possibilities and the threats of an open identity. Sulina, "at the end of the world", allows them to reinvent themselves freely, to toy semi-ironically with various labels for identification ("artist", "fisherman", "traveler", "businessman"), but its marginality also creates obstacles for careers in any of the designated fields. Creating a home by choosing a profession and adopting a relatively stable identity, is therefore very hard, and Sulina pushes and pulls men like a film noir *femme fatale*.

Both leaving and coming then are imbued with profound ambiguity: deep alienation abroad, and feelings of failure in Sulina, alternate. Home-making abroad is impeded by the marginality internalized in Sulina: especially S., in his descriptions of encounters with women abroad, testifies to this. A strong drive to reinvent himself, to "become different, to be good to her, and to settle there" sits uneasily with a disbelief in the possibility of ultimate success, a lack of confidence in home-making that became engrained in Sulina.

Conclusion

P. F. Thomese once wrote that every time you take a step, the whole world collapses underneath your feet, and there is no real way back. Thus, when you leave, "home" collapses and you have to take what you can with you and reconstruct it upon return. In the end, C. prefers to define his own concept of freedom, according to his own self/place and not to prevailing conceptions. Sulina, as a home, offers indeed an open definition of the self: one can be an artist, a cook, a fisherman, a free-floating spirit and a tourist operator, sometimes all at once. The Deleuzian deterritorialization, a freeing up of the fixed relations that make up a body, unleashing the creative powers of an assemblage, either physical, mental or spiritual (Deleuze, Guattari 1994: 68), is a lifestyle for C., and the open identity implied seems to work for him. He does take the toll of a Deleuzian life in an almost literal sense.

For S., the journey, the movement itself, is not the goal, and the pressures breaking open identity are experienced more as an unfortunate given, sometimes a threat, often an anticipated obstacle, to be defied with grace, elegance, sometimes daring and boldness. The relative stability in his image of home, in Sulina, with all its ambiguities, sharks and promises, does not undermine a Deleuzian interpretation of migration, place and self. Rather, it points at the necessity of middle-range theories, to bridge Deleuze's ontologies and an anthropology of memory and migration. We argue that Deleuzian-inspired geographies, like Massey's, can certainly help in bridging the gap.

An explicit link with anthropology offered by Massey (1994, 2005) is the presentation of places as evolving conglomerates of stories, all with their own rhythm and intensity, all potentially affecting each other, and anyone passing. Identity, as eternal change, as continuous aggregation and disaggregation of forces and series of events, will enter relations with places that can be conceived as a formation of new stories, some short-lived, some with a longer lease in new contexts. Massey (2005: 189), qualifying spaces as "multiplicities of stories-so-far", says elsewhere (175): "We are always, inevitably, making spaces and places. The temporary cohesions of articulations of relations, the provisional and partial enclosures, [...] these spatial forms are the necessary fixings of communication and identity." We could add, that "home" is in all probability the most necessary fixing of identity, albeit one that will shift continuously, in new encounters with people, places and objects. A Deleuzian-inspired anthropology should avoid the trap of a new orthodoxy overly celebrating marginality, hybridism, marginality and nomadism (see Pratt 1999 already, for a similar warning). A relational construct of home might be less stable, less useful for mythologies of origin and stasis, it can still speak to the richness of identity, and its need for forms of grounding (Bouma-Prediger 2008).

Literature

Bouma-Prediger, Steven, Brian Walsh 2008: Beyond Homelessness. Christian Faith in a Culture of Displacement. Grand Rapids: Eerdmans Press.

Braidotti, Rosi 2002: Metamorphoses. Towards a Materialist Theory of Becoming. Cambridge: Polity Press.

Braidotti, Rosi 2006: Transpositions: On Nomadic Ethics. Cambridge: Polity Press.

Buchanan, Ian, Gregg Lambert (eds.) 2005: Deleuze and Space. Toronto: University of Toronto Press.

Buchanan, Ian (ed.) 1999: A Deleuzian century? Durham: Duke University Press.

Deleuze, Gilles, Felix Guattari 1987: A Thousand Plateaus: Capitalism and Schizophrenia. Minneapolis: University of Minnesota Press.

Deleuze, Gilles, Felix Guattari 1994: What is Philosophy? New York: Columbia University Press.

Deleuze, Gilles 1964: Proust et les Signes. Paris: PUF.

Deleuze, Gilles 1983 (1965): Nietzsche and Philosophy. London: Athlone Press.

Deleuze, Gilles 1984: Kant's Critical Philosophy. London: Athlone Press.

Deleuze, Gilles 1994: Difference and Repetition. New York: Columbia University Press.

Eco, Umberto 1976: A Theory of Semiotics. Bloomington: University of Indiana Press.

Groat, Linda (ed.) 1995: Giving Places Meaning. San Diego: Academic Press.

Gustafson, Per 2006: Place Attachment and Mobility. In: Norman McIntyre, Daniel R. Williams, Kevin E. McHugh (eds.), Multiple Dwelling and Tourism. Negotiating Place, Home and Identity. Cambridge: CABI, 17–31.

Hardt, Michael 1993: Deleuze. An Apprenticeship in Philosophy. Minneapolis: University of Minnesota Press.

Massey, Doreen 1994: Space, Place, and Gender. Minneapolis: University of Minnesota Press.

Massey, Doreen 2005: For Space. London: Sage.

Massumi, Brian 1992: A Users Guide to Capitalism and Schizophrenia: Deviations from Deleuze and Guattari. Cambridge: MIT Press.

McIntyre, Norman, Daniel R. Williams, Kevin E. McHugh (eds.) 2006: Multiple Dwelling and Tourism. Negotiating Place, Home and Identity. Cambridge: CABI.

Molz, Germann Jennie 2008: Global Abode. Home and Mobility in Narratives of Round-the-World Travel. In: Space and Culture: 1–18.

Papastergiadis, Nikos 2000: The Turbulence of Migration. Globalization, Deterritorialization and Hybridity. Cambridge: Polity Press.

Patton, Paul 2000: Deleuze and the Political. London: Routledge.

Pratt, Geraldine 1999: Geographies of Identity and of Difference: Marking Boundaries. In: D. Massey, J. Allen, P. Sarre (eds.), Human Geography Today. Cambridge: Polity Press.

Raffestin, Claude 1980: Geographie du Pouvoir. Paris: LITEC.

Rojek, Chris, John Urry 1997: Touring Cultures. Transformations of Travel and Theory. London: Routledge.

Stokowski, A. Patricia 2002: Languages of Place and Discourses of Power: Constructing New Senses of Place. In: Journal of Leisure Research 34, 1: 368–382.

Teampău, Petruţa, Kristof Van Assche 2007: Sulina: The Dying City in a Vital Region. Social Memory and Nostalgia for the European Future. In: Ethnologia Balkanica 13: 257–278.

Teampău, Petruţa, Kristof Van Assche 2009: Sulina, Sulina, when there's Water, there's no Light. Narrative, Memory and Autobiography in a Romanian Town. In: Identities: Journal for Politics, Gender, and Culture 7, no. 1/2: 33–70.

Teampău, Petruţa 2010: Pirates, Fish and Tourists. Sulina after Communism. In: Constantin Iordachi, Kristof Van Assche (eds.), Danube Delta: Nature, Histories, Policies. Budapest: CEU Press (in print).

Van Assche, Kristof, Petruţa Teampău, Patrick Devlieger 2008: Liquid boundaries in marginal marshes: Reconstructions of identity in the Romanian Danube Delta. In: Studia Sociologica 1: 115–138.

Van Assche, Kristof, Patrick Devlieger, Petruţa Teampău, Gert Verschraegen 2009: Remembering and forgetting in the margin: Constructing past and future in the Romanian Danube Delta. In: Memory Studies 2, 2: 211–234.

Van Assche, Kristof, Petruţa Teampău 2009: Layered Encounters: Performance of Multiculturalism and Urban Palimpsest in a Romanian Town. In: Anthropology of East Europe Review 27, 1: 7–19.

Wheeler, Wendy 1994: Nostalgia isn't Nasty: The Postmodernizing of Parliamentary Democracy. In: M. Perryman (ed.), Altered States: Postmodernism, Politics, Cultures. London: Lawrence and Wishart, 94–109.

Williams, R. Daniel, Susan R. Van Patten 2006: Home and Away? Creating Identities and Sustaining Places in a Multi-Centred World. In: Norman McIntyre, Daniel R. Williams, Kevin E. McHugh (eds.), Multiple Dwelling and Tourism. Negotiating Place, Home and Identity. Cambridge: CABI, 32–50.

Ethnologia Balkanica 13 (2009)

Urban Newcomers in a Hungarian Village

László Mód, Szeged

Abstract

The paper tries to interpret the specific urban-rural migration concerning a small Hungarian village. In the 1970s most of its houses were purchased by families who fled city life and discovered the cultural and natural values of the village and its surroundings. The new owners use their properties for recreational purposes and have thereby created a new form of organization of leisure time. It is in their interest to preserve this heritage because their own self-definition and motivation would suffer should the village be flooded by mass tourism and lose its unique character. The striving for continuity indicates the degree of identification with the village's past and at the same time it serves as a tool for the community to create a system of ritual customs throughout the year that can be used in the future to mark community boundaries, and express and strengthen community identity. The furnishings of the houses reflect a return to the past and the creation of an individually imagined and represented peasant world.

In my paper I make an attempt to interpret a special phenomenon of urban-rural migration concerning a small Hungarian village that was depopulated in the 1970s. The locals moved away and newcomers from the cities bought their houses and started to use the rural space in a different way. My analysis mainly focuses on the new settlers' activities. They revived and invented traditions and tried to interpret the village and its surroundings as a cultural heritage. This present paper presents only the most important findings of my research.

Orvar Löfgren has analysed the problem of second homes in his book about the history of vacationing. In the 19th century it was only a small elite that aspired to possess a summer house, but in the early 20th century there was a considerable increase in the social classes owning such houses. This culture has a distinctive rhythm: for most of the year the summer houses stand empty; the beginning of summer is marked by the ritual of moving out from the city. The past and the effort to achieve continuity are of central significance; the owners of the holiday homes want to discover the local history and traditions that allow them to become local in as much as this is possible. The immersion in an entirely foreign world can also be regarded as important, together with the cult of simplicity and naturalness, which often includes the rejection of the advantages offered by modern life (Löfgren 2002: 109–154).

According to some estimates, in the first half of the 1980s some 11 % of Hungarian families owned properties of this type. The conversion of village houses into summer houses was linked unequivocally to members of the intelligentsia who fled to the countryside to escape the harmful influences of the city (Fejős 1985: 32–58). In the 1970s and 1980s, the group on the northern shore of Lake Balaton, known by locals as "new settlers", used their leisure activities to express their opposition to the basic values of the political regime of that time. They consciously opposed the patterns of pre-packaged tourism for mass consumption and made an attempt to organize a new kind of leisure use that included the invention and revival of traditions and the transformation of the area into a national park (Szijártó 2002: 7–21).

My research is based on fieldwork in a Hungarian village called Kisújbánya or Neuglashütte, which is located in Baranya county in southern Hungary. It was founded in the 18th century by German families who mainly dealt with glass making. After the decline of this economic activity, the forests provided a living for the families who began to produce wooden forks. Cattle breeding also played an important role in the traditional economy. The families took sour cream and cottage cheese to the nearby villages and sold their products there. Despite the fact that milk production based on cattle breeding was still significant in the 1960s and 1970s, the residents of the village worked in the local cooperative, in the Forest Industry of Mecsek, the Coal Mine of Mecsek or the well-borer Company of Komló. Up to the beginning of the 1970s the population of around 200 to 300 persons remained roughly unchanged. In the beginning of 1973 there were still 148 persons living in the village, and by the end of the year the number of inhabitants had fallen to 109. In 1975 a total of 76 people were registered, and by the end of the year there were only 13 people left. Most of the families left their homes because of the commuting problems and the previous migration of the younger people.

The new community that steadily grew from the mid-1970s onwards was composed largely of city dwellers who, for different reasons, decided to buy a house in the village and spend part of their leisure time there. Many of them spend only the weekends in the village, others stay for the whole summer. It can be said about the new owners that with regard to their occupations a fairly diverse community began to be formed. Besides doctors, teachers, lawyers and engineers, skilled workers, mainly miners, bought houses there(Mód 2004: 107–112, 2007: 116–123).

What perhaps most distinguishes the former inhabitants from the new ones is the way they use the village and its surroundings, the plots of land, the dwelling houses and the farm buildings. Before the 1960s the livelihood of the original German families depended on their exploitation of the local natural resources: they used wood from the forests to make agricultural tools, footwear and implements, they cultivated the arable land around the village, they kept cattle in the barns for milk production, and they used the large plots of land as meadows. The new arrivals rediscovered the space in a different way: they did not use agricultural implements for their activities but transformed the production space into a "recreation" space. What does this mean in reality? One can answer this question briefly by saying that the new owners no longer use their environment as a source of livelihood, they do not cultivate the fields and do not harvest hay for their animals. They cut the grass on the plots around the houses not to provide fodder for their cattle but principally for aesthetic reasons, to give the impression of tidiness. In many cases they have converted the farm buildings into temporary residences, giving them an entirely new function. In the summer months sunshades appear in the yards, together with equipment for outdoor cooking, grills and barbecues. In theoretical terms, the activities of the urbanites transformed the concept of rural space from a concrete term to an abstract one, that is, the countryside no longer designates a place clearly definable by particular actions and social groups, but can be defined by the difference between the way in which the rural space is actually used and the notions formed of this space. With regard to the use of space the rediscovered countryside is now part of the urban networks as it is being shaped by different urban groups according to basically urban ideals.

The families buying houses or land in Kisújbánya tried to create a distinctive world that can best be grasped and understood with the help of the term musealisation, i. e., it can be interpreted principally as the effort to preserve the ideal values of things. As a mental and physical act this is always a matter of human decision. It turns the things into musealia, the objects take on a new quality: museality. Gottfried Korff has tried to define it as the expansive dynamism of our present-day culture. One reason may be that consumer goods become outdated very quickly, so that our society is overwhelmed by relics (Korff 2004: 18–27). In the village of Kisújbánya, musealisation can be observed at several levels, and individual as well as community forms can be distinguished. The former are created by families in their own holiday homes and dwellings, while the latter are linked to a higher level and are associated with aspirations affecting the entire village.

The new owners are trying to create a new model for the organization of leisure time: they invent and revive traditions, carry out intensive activities for the protection of the man-made and the natural environment (Bódi 2002: 22–39). The definition of the village and its immediate surroundings as "heritage" is determined not only by what is in the possession of the creators of the heritage, but in a way also expresses their identity. In this way the heritage can provide assistance in laying the foundations of the community's origin and in designating the group's place in time and space. The new owners represent the settlement and its immediate natural environment as special and unique, they link their own identity to it and often define themselves as the protectors and guardians of the "unique heritage".

Wooden forks and harnesses are placed on the outside walls of the houses, objects that used to be integral parts of farming, articles of practical use. I have been to houses in which such tools were even hung on interior walls. In other rooms the walls were decorated with wall hangings with German and Hungarian inscriptions. In one living-room the wall was covered with photographs of the family. For the new owners they recall their childhood, memories of their parents, the past, which they have tried to revive in the house that they bought in 1993 in Kisújbánya.

The rituals invented by the association[1] of the new owners since the 1980s play an important role in creating and shaping local identity and at the same time provide an opportunity for the new owners to inform the outside world about their own aims and motivations. On festive occasions the borders of the community become visible and perceptible, though only symbolically, but at the same time they also grow stronger. The invented or revived rituals include those that are connected in some way to the traditions of the former inhabitants, aiming at creating a kind of continuity in a symbolical way, thereby also expressing the new residents' search for identity. Perhaps the best example of this is the event associated with St Martin's day, which aims to recreate the feast of the patron saint.[2] The rite has now been held for four or five years and it seems to be gradually becoming a special occasion in the life of the local community. The most important part of St Martin's day is the mass held in the church, celebrated by an invited priest. A few elements of the feast that were originally linked to calendar customs, such as All Soul's Day, point to the conscious creation of tradition. The commemoration held at the heroes' monument in memory of deceased relatives, and the lighting of candles in the cemetery, definitely belong to this category. The mass held on 8 June 2002, for deceased relatives was intended to express community identity, as all the dead were residents or house owners of the village. The ritual occasion was thus intended to express symbolically that a community with its own dead also has a past and roots.

The village lost its population in the 1970s for several reasons. Most of its houses were purchased by urban families for recreational purposes. It is in the interest of the new owners to preserve this heritage because their own self-def-

---

1 It was founded in 1988 and in 1999 it was converted into a foundation. According to the documents its most important purpose is to preserve the ethnographical, cultural and architectural values and traditions of the village.

2 Former inhabitants celebrated a dedication feast which was a religious event in the ritual calendar.

inition and motivation would suffer if the village were to be flooded with mass tourism and it were to lose its unique character. The local association or foundation plays a major role in this regard, as it undertakes to represent the interests of the community, in part by building on the culture of the former inhabitants and in part by inventing new traditions to shape and structure a local identity. The striving for continuity indicates the degree of identification with the village's past and at the same time is a tool the community can use to create a system of ritual customs covering the whole year that can be used to mark community boundaries and to express and strengthen community identity. The furnishings of the houses reflect a return to the past and the creation of an individually imagined and represented peasant world.

Literature

Bódi, Jenő 2002: Kövek és képzetek. Az építészet szimbolikus funkciói a Káli-medencében [Stones and images. The symbolic function of architecture in the Káli Basin]. In: Zoltán Fejős, Zsolt Szijártó (eds.), Egy tér alakváltozásai. Esettanulmányok a Káli-medencéből [The metamorphosis of a place. Case studies from the Káli Basin]. Budapest: Néprajzi Múzeum, 22–39.

Fejős, Zoltán 1985: A falusi turizmus – a hagyomány utáni korszak alternatívája? [Rural tourism – Alternative of the period after tradition?]. In: Zoltán Fejős (ed.), Folklór és tradíció II [Folklore and Tradition]. Budapest: MTA Néprajzi Kutatócsoport, 32–58.

Korff, Gottfried 2004: A tárgykultúra múzeumi feldolgozásának nehézségei. A muzealizálás mint intézményeken túlmutató trend [The problems of the museological integration of material culture. The musealization as a trend indicative of institutions]. In: Zoltán Fejős, Zsófia Frazon (eds.), Korunk és tárgyaink – elmélet és módszer. Fordításgyűjtemény [Our ages and our objects – theory and method. Collection of translations]. Budapest: Néprajzi Múzeum, 18–27.

Löfgren, Orvar 1999: On Holiday. A History of Vacationing. Berkeley, Los Angeles, London: University of California Press.

Mód, László 2004: Migration, Depopulation, Repopulation. Citizens in a Hungarian Village – a case study. In: Miklós Cseri, Zoltán Fejős, Zsuzsa Szarvas (eds.), Touristic Construction and Consumption of Culture(s). Budapest, Szentendre: Néprajzi Múzeum, Magyar Néprajzi Társaság, Szabadtéri Néprajzi Múzeum, 107–112.

Mód, László 2007: "Kihaló faluból – üdülőfalu" Gazdasági-társadalmi változások egy dél-dunántúli kistelepülésen (1970–2005) [Economic and social changes in a south-transdanubian village (1970–2005)]. In: Zsuzsa, Szarvas (eds.), Migráció és turizmus. Migrációs folyamatok hatása a helyi társadalmak változásaira a mai Magyarországon [Migration and tourism. The effect of migration on the changes of local society in Hungary]. Budapest: L'Harmattan, 111–142.

Szijártó, Zsolt 2002: Turizmus és regionalizmus a Káli-medencében [Tourism and regionalism in the Káli Basin]. In: Zoltán Fejős, Zsolt, Szijártó (eds.), Egy tér alakváltozásai. Esettanulmányok a Káli-medencéből [The metamorphosis of a place. Case studies from the Káli Basin]. Budapest: Néprajzi Múzeum, 7–21.

Ethnologia Balkanica 13 (2009)

La deuxième vie d'Ada-Kaleh ou Le potentiel culturel de la mémoire d'une île disparue

Monica Bercovici, Bucarest

Abstract: The second life of Ada-Kaleh or, what to do with the cultural potential of the memory of a disappeared island

Ada-Kaleh was an island in the Danube, disputed over the centuries between two military powers, the Ottoman Empire and the Habsburg Empire. From the 18th century onwards, it was inhabited by a stable Turkish population, and after World War One it belonged to Romania. Due to its particular climate, which allowed oriental vegetation, and to the specifics of the Turkish community, the island became a famous travel destination. It was destroyed in the end of the 1960s in order to build the Iron Gate power plant, which caused the extinction of the local community through the migration of all individuals to different parts of Romania and Turkey. Today, the island has become a cultural stereotype. This research aims to study the particular case of the disappearance of a socio-cultural community and to find out what constitutes the island's image from the insiders' point of view. The study is part of an *emergency ethnology*, due to the advanced age of the former inhabitants of Ada-Kaleh. In our approach, we will try to find out which are the island's attributes in the contemporary imaginary and how the memories of it's existence are updated, starting with a case study of a former inhabitant.

L'île d'Ada-Kaleh a disparu il y a plus de quarante ans. Elle a été détruite (dans un contexte que nous expliquerons plus loin), et cela a conduit à l'évacuation de la population turque qui l'habitait. Entité culturelle unique dans l'espace roumain (une île habitée seulement par des Turcs, à peu d'exceptions près), la communauté turque aurait dû se reconstituer dans un autre espace. Cela n'a pas été possible, car ses membres se sont rapidement dispersés dans les différentes régions de la Roumanie et de la Turquie. Ce sont exactement cette atomisation de la cohésion du groupe et, implicitement, la disparition de la communauté turque en tant qu'entité culturelle, qui caractérisent le cas d'Ada-Kaleh.

Aujourd'hui, l'ethnologue qui veut étudier le cas d'Ada-Kaleh se retrouve face à une seule possibilité : celle de la reconstruction. Il peut apprendre à connaître l'île (d'un point de vue culturel) en menant des entretiens avec ses anciens habitants. Mais il ne peut pas aller sur le terrain (car l'île n'existe plus) et risque de manquer rapidement de « témoins », vu l'âge très avancé des anciens habitants. Par conséquent, la démarche de l'ethnologue doit être encadrée dans le domaine de *l'ethnologie d'urgence*.

Y-a-t-il une possibilité de récupérer la mémoire de l'existence de l'île ?

De quelle façon perçoit-on, aujourd'hui, l'île disparue sous les eaux ; quels sont les attributs de cette île dans l'imaginaire contemporain ; comment sont réactualisés les souvenirs de son existence ?

Voici les quelques questions que cet article abordera sans donner de réponses, car la recherche annoncée est seulement à son début.

La méthodologie de recherche a consisté dans l'emploi de l'entretien non-directif – le seul type d'entretien qui nous semble être capable, dans ce cas, de recueillir des données sur la vie de l'île et, en même temps, de donner à l'interlocuteur la possibilité de se souvenir et de montrer involontairement au chercheur les mécanismes d'un processus de remémoration. En ce qui concerne l'étude de cas d'un ancien habitant de l'île, par contre, nous avons utilisé les outils de l'histoire orale, ainsi que ceux de l'imagologie, tout en essayant d'analyser son discours.

Courte introduction historique

L'île d'Ada-Kaleh, sur le cours du Danube dans la région des Portes de Fer, près d'Orşova, mesurait presque 1,7 km de long et presque 500 mètres de large. Située à proximité de trois pays (la Roumanie, la Bulgarie et la Serbie) et à mi-chemin entre l'Empire Ottoman et l'Empire Austro-hongrois, l'île a toujours été disputée en raison de l'important enjeu stratégique que représentait sa position. Le caractère provisoire de son facteur humain, par ailleurs, dérive de cette situation. En effet, la population existante, lorsque le front devenait dangereusement proche, était évacuée, et une nouvelle population venait la remplacer et ce indépendamment du pays qui gouvernait l'île à ce moment-là. A travers les siècles, ce mouvement de population est resté constant, en connexion avec le pouvoir dominant. De ce fait, la population insulaire (représentée par des soldats) avait acquis un fort caractère militaire, étant imprégnée des conflits dont l'île se retrouvait captive. Et si les turcs de la région de Dobroudja sont originaires des villages anatoliens, les turcs d'Ada-Kaleh étaient originaires des bourgs et des villes citées, situées sur le rivage droit du Danube (Suliţeanu 1972: 260). Ce n'est qu'au XVIIIe siècle que la population turque devint stable et qu'elle commença à habiter l'île d'une façon durable en la transformant en une localité rurale, avec des maisons et des jardins, et, plus tard, avec une mairie, une école, un petit point sanitaire, un office de police, un restaurant, une bibliothèque, une maison culturelle avec un cinéma, etc.

Suite au changement permanent d'autorité dominatrice, différents noms ont été attribués à l'île au cours de son histoire : Saan, Ruşava, Cerne, Demir Kapu,

Photo no. 1 : Vue générale de l'île (Archive de L'Institut d'Ethnographie et de Folklore « C. Brăiloiu » - AIEF)

Poarta de Fier (La Porte de Fer), Carolina, Ada, Insula Orşovei (l'Ile d'Orşova), Orşova Nouă (Nouvelle Orşova), Ada-i kebir, Fortăreaţa (La Forteresse), Ada-Kale, Ada-Kaleh, ce dernier nom figurant dans les documents à partir de l'année 1788 (Roman 2005: s. p.).

En 1444, Iancu de Hunedoara a commencé à fortifier l'île. Ces fortifications ont été consolidées au cours du temps pour finalement acquérir, au début du XVIIIe siècle, sous domination autrichienne, la forme que l'on peut voir aujourd'hui (dans l'île Simian, où la cité a été transférée après la destruction de l'île d'Ada-Kaleh). Après 1739, l'île a abrité une population turque qui a transformé l'édifice du commandement en mosquée. Sous la protection de l'Autriche, l'île est devenue, en 1885, garnison ouverte et n'a plus eu un caractère de cité militaire. A partir de ce moment-là, l'île a commencé à avoir une autonomie administrative et une politique fiscale propres (en devenant porto franco), ce qui a favorisé le développement du commerce (Roman 2005: s. p.). Après 1919 (Traité de Versailles), Ada-Kaleh a été rattachée à la Roumanie et après la Première Guerre Mondiale, Ada-Kaleh a perdu ses privilèges, qui seront à nouveau gagnés plus tard, en 1931, après la visite du roi Charles II de Roumanie.

Photo no. 2 : Le centre de l'île (AIEF)

Par la suite, l'île s'est développée grâce à la franchise d'impôt, exploitée par les fabriques de lokoum, de tabac et de textiles. Parallèlement, commença un phénomène de transformation de l'île en tant que destination touristique. D'après la monographie de Raul Călinescu dont la première édition date des années '30, l'île était visitée chaque année par 15000–16000 touristes et par 50–60 écoles (Călinescu 1940: 21). Tous les produits que les habitants de l'île fabriquaient et vendaient, ainsi que la végétation méditerranéenne, donnaient à l'île « une pittoresque atmosphère orientale », expression que, à ce moment-là, était déjà devenue un stéréotype journalistique. Toujours selon Raul Călinescu, l'île comptait une population de 800 habitants en 1937. On y trouvait une école primaire (quatre premières classes), avec un enseignement en turc et en roumain, et, à partir de 1925, une école industrielle pour les filles, où on enseignait le tissage (à noter qu'en 1934 l'école comptait 44 élèves internes et 2 élèves externes qui étaient des habitantes de l'île). L'office de poste était placé sous la juridiction de la Mairie, mais en réalité, il fonctionnait dans les locaux d'un salon de coiffure, dont le patron était le père du facteur (bon exemple de la façon selon laquelle les institutions suivaient le modèle des relations humaines).

A la fin des années 1960, l'île a été détruite afin de pouvoir bâtir l'hydrocentrale des Portes de Fer (construction qui nécessitait une augmentation du niveau de l'eau de 40 cm), comme le témoigne le documentaire « Le dernier printemps sur Ada-Kaleh », réalisé en 1968 par le studio cinématographique Sahia. Ceci a conduit au transfert de quelques villages du côté du Danube. La forteresse a été désassemblée, pièce par pièce, et puis rebâtie dans l'Ostrov Simian.

Pendant la période communiste (1944–1989), l'île a acquis un fort caractère touristique, soutenu par une propagande politique selon laquelle le nouveau gouvernement avait transformé les habitants d'Ada-Kaleh dans des *nouveaux hommes*. « Les ruines des murs ont servi pour une bonne période de temps comme maisons pour les insulaires, appelées *kemerfs*. Jusqu'en 1944, 30 familles pauvres habitaient dans les *kemerfs*, menant une telle vie que l'on peut se sentir justifié de se demander en quoi elle était différente de celle des animaux. Après le 23 août 1944, l'Etat a pris des mesures dans ce sens, en bâtissant des maisons pour les habitants des *kemerfs* » (Purcaru 1961: 68). Quand les travaux à l'hydrocentrale des Portes de Fer ont commencé, des films ont été réalisés dans le studio cinématographique de l'Etat, *Sahia*, pour démontrer que ni la forteresse en tant que monument appartenant au patrimoine culturel matériel de la Roumanie, ni les habitants d'Ada-Kaleh en tant qu'individus, ni la communauté d'insulaires, n'allaient souffrir à cause de ce chantier. Ce que les autorités n'avaient pas prévu, c'est que la communauté, en tant qu'entité sociale et culturelle, n'a pas eu les moyens de se reconstituer et, par conséquent, elle s'est dissoute. En même temps, suite au déracinement, des histoires personnelles, des vies communes, des amitiés et des familles se sont désagrégées. Les objets mêmes, appartenant aux différents habitants d'Ada-Kaleh, sont devenus des pièces du Musée des Portes de Fer.

Les attractions touristiques – sources des stéréotypes discursifs

En commençant par la période de l'entre-deux-guerres, quand l'île est devenue une attraction touristique, nous avons assisté à un processus de création de stéréotypes discursifs, qui seront repris par la littérature fictionnelle (cf. bibliographie) et, malheureusement, par tout discours contemporain, soit-il un reportage journalistique (comme par exemple, un article paru dans la revue « Formula as », no. 565, année 2003) ou une étude sociologique. Nous considérons nécessaire d'énumérer ces stéréotypes, car ils font aujourd'hui partie d'une image de plus en plus véhiculée. Par ailleurs, ils ont été repris aussi dans les discours de quelques insulaires, même si, dans ce cas, ils apparaissent quelquefois plus nuancés. Ainsi, la mosquée, le tapis oriental, le bazar, la forteresse, le tombeau du saint local Miskin-Baba, étaient autant de symboles représentés sur les jolies cartes postales envoyées à la maison par les touristes, que de vrais outils maî-

Photo no. 3 : La mosquée et les murs de la forteresse (AIEF)

trisés par la communauté turque pour définir et soutenir sa propre identité religieuse, communautaire et locale.

L'une des principales attractions touristiques était le tapis qu'abritait, à l'époque, la mosquée de l'île. Ce tapis, offert aux habitants par le sultan Abdul-Hamid II en 1904, avait une longueur de 15 m et une largeur de 9 m et pesait 480 kg. Ces dimensions étaient vraiment très impressionnantes compte tenu de la petite taille de l'île d'Ada-Kaleh. Le tapis apparaissait en outre dans les légendes qui témoignaient des origines des insulaires et renforçait leur identité[1]. Dans la vision d'Ileana Roman, le tapis servait aussi pour définir l'espace insulaire, du fait qu'il avait le pouvoir d'augmenter la surface de l'île : en effet, même si grand, le tapis ne pouvait couvrir la mosquée dans son intégralité ce que, symboliquement, se traduirait par un espace insulaire suffisamment grand pour abriter tout un univers (Roman 2005: s. p.).

---

[1] Le saint Miskin Baba, qui apparaît très souvent dans le discours des anciens habitants de l'île, semble aussi représenter un facteur de renforcement de l'identité en tant qu'autorité divine. Autant les musulmans de l'île que les chrétiens, invoquaient son tombeau pour demander de l'aide.

Tous ces facteurs identitaires sont devenus, petit à petit, des stéréotypes discursifs. Ainsi, les monographies de l'île, les oeuvres fictionnelles comprenant des personnages insulaires, les écritures journalistiques, ont toutes adopté et utilisé le charme de l'île : « dans ce cadre de féerie, peut être vu le pittoresque Ostrov qui a fait tant vibrer l'âme de beaucoup d'écrivains » (Călinescu 1940 : 3) ; « sa romantique splendeur » (Călinescu 1940 : 3) ; « jardin de la patience et de l'attente » (Roman 2005 : s. p.) ; un *Ostrov fleuri, odorant, rêve qu'on veut avoir sans jamais nous réveiller, Eden, Paradis perdu* etc.

Etude de cas: Bob Gheorghe

L'Institut d'Ethnographie et de Folklore « C. Brăiloiu » de Bucarest avait conduit une recherche de terrain dans l'île d'Ada-Kaleh, en 1966. A cette occasion, le folklore musical turc fut enregistré. C'est la raison pour laquelle, en 2007, un ancien habitant d'Ada-Kaleh est venu à l'Institut. Il voulait consulter l'archive, mais aussi poser la question relative à la récupération du patrimoine oral d'Ada-Kaleh. Il fut le premier insulaire à être enregistré, racontant l'histoire de l'île dans le cadre de ses histoires personnelles (ce que l'ethnologie francophone appelle *les récits de vie*). Nous nous sommes rendus compte, que le sujet concernait le domaine de *l'ethnologie d'urgence*, car, une fois l'île disparue, les anciens habitants étaient devenus les seules personnes à pouvoir parler de cette vie insulaire singulière. Et si l'Ada-Kaleh n'existe plus depuis quarante ans, la simple arithmétique nous montre que les habitants de l'île sont aujourd'hui âgés.

Notre premier entretien (comptant plusieurs rencontres) a été avec Bob Gheorghe (n. 1942). Il est très important de noter que cette personne fait partie du petit nombre de roumains qui ont vécu sur l'île et que, malgré son appartenance ethnique, il est l'insulaire le plus actif dans la tâche de récupération de la mémoire d'Ada-Kaleh. Les personnes interviewées par la suite furent : Pervin Halimoglu (n. 1950), Emine Ahmet (n. 1946), Firuze Ahmet (n. 1948) et Ergun Hayri (n. 1950) qui, eux, vivent en Turquie.

Si l'image nous permet de reproduire et d'intérioriser le monde, de l'observer mentalement ou grâce à un support matériel, elle nous permet aussi de le diversifier et de le transformer jusqu'à produire des mondes fictifs, car elle s'expose aux projections affectives du sujet (Wunenburger 2004 : 9). Nous constatons, dans le cas de Bob Gheorghe, non seulement une idéalisation de l'image, mais aussi un refus d'y échapper, en restant emprisonné dans l'image qu'il a construite, et en luttant pour construire de manière permanente une nouvelle image de l'île (perçue par son auteur comme la seule correcte). Dans ce sens, il dit, par exemple, que les monographies font appel à un mensonge, quand elles qualifient les turcs comme pauvres ; qu'il n'est pas correct d'appeler la population de l'île « adakalezi », et qu'il faudrait les appeler « insulaires », etc. Sans le savoir, Bob Gheorghe devient l'avocat d'une île que sa propre mémoire a créée, en la défendant avec une sorte de patriotisme local, ayant le sentiment total d'appartenance à l'île et, par la suite, se sentant directement touché par chaque affirmation sur l'île, qu'il considère être fausse. Son image de l'île est rapportée, en même temps, à l'expérience passée - le temps vécu -, à la vie présente - ses préoccupations pour construire une image juste de l'île - et au futur - autant de plans pour matérialiser ces préoccupations. Elle comprend une forme visible, matérielle, aussi bien qu'une forme mentale.

L'image mentale mnésique (car l'île n'existe plus, donc on ne peut pas parler d'une image mentale perceptive) est rendue présente, dans notre cas, par une mémoire sensori-motrice (les facteurs externes et la reconnaissance automate, comme dans le cas des plantes qui lui rappellent la végétation insulaire, comme le figuier), par une mémoire sociale qui est déclarative et qui implique la reconnaissance du passé sous forme d'histoire racontée (Wunenburger 2004 : 50). L'image anticipation est un plan pour une possible future perception, essoufflée par le désir (Wunenburger 2004 : 52). La forme inconsciente de l'image se manifeste, dans notre cas, par le rêve et par la rêverie, car Bob Gheorghe rêve souvent de l'île, dans des différentes hypostases, et il est, même pendant les entretiens qu'il donne, accaparé par une rêverie involontaire ayant l'île pour sujet. Tout comme une image mentale, l'expression verbale connaît, dans le cas de Bob Gheorghe, une formalisation. Il utilise, dans son discours, des formules récurrentes : « Chaque fois que j'ai donné une interview sur l'île, j'ai dit les mots suivants, que j'ai conçus à partir de la reconnaissance que j'ai pour les lieux et pour les habitants de cet espace : « Je suis heureux et je remercie Dieu d'avoir passé mon enfance et ma jeunesse dans ce petit coin de *paradis*, d'avoir connu ces merveilleux gens - la majorité de nationalité turque - habitants de l'île d'Ada-Kaleh, terre des eaux, mais, malheureusement, couverte par les eaux pour toujours » (entretien avec Bob Gheorghe). Parfois il utilise même des formules consacrées, en les reprenant de manière inconsciente, comme c'est le cas de « l'île du rêve et de l'oubli » (Dan 1936 : 47 apud. Tulei 2007 : 336). Quant à l'image matérielle, il a gardé tout ce qu'il a pu collecter en liaison avec l'île: des objets, des photos, des cartes postales, des monographies, des enregistrements vidéo et audio, et il a même créé un jardin similaire à la végétation insulaire, comprenant des arbustes et des fleurs apportées d'Ada-Kaleh.

Cette courte analyse discursive nous aide à comprendre comment les situations exceptionnelles créent des réactions proportionnelles. Il n'y a plus d'Ada-Kaleh ? On la refait dans le jardin devant son immeuble, dans un quartier de Bucarest. Bob Gheorghe mange des aliments qui lui rappellent l'île; il connaît tous les anciens habitants qui sont encore en vie ; il lit tout ce qu'on écrit sur l'île; il va aux archives (folkloriques, militaires, historiques, etc.) pour trouver

Photo no. 4 : Le jardin crée par Bob Gheorghe

des nouveaux documents ; il propose au Musée des Portes de Fer d'afficher une photo aérienne de l'île prise à proximité de son ancienne position ; il aide les metteurs en scène qui veulent faire des films documentaires sur Ada-Kaleh ; il garde la liaison avec les insulaires émigrés etc. Et tout ça pendant la journée, car la nuit il rêve d'Ada-Kaleh. Bref, il vit *en* et *dans* Ada-Kaleh[2], en faisant preuve d'une inadaptation qui se retrouve dans le discours des autres insulaires (voir les entretiens avec les insulaires publiés dans la presse roumaine, par exemple : http://www.informatiadeseverin.ro/ids/reportaj/pribegii-din-ada-kaleh.html, article daté 13 octobre 2008), mais qui, dans son cas, est beaucoup plus accentuée.

[2] Dans le sens du mot roumain *întru*, dont Constantin Noica parle : « Întru signifie *vers* et *dans* ; donc, il dit *ni dedans, ni dehors*, et tous les deux ; il est une sorte de *ne pas être dans*, compris comme un *être dans* ; ou, plutôt, un *être dans*, compris comme un *devenir dans*. Il indique ainsi également le fait de *rester* et de *se bouger dans*, un repos qui est aussi un non-repos, comme il exprime une *ouverture* vers un monde *fermé*, déterminé au moins, ou, d'un autre point de vue, une *recherche* dans le sein de quelque chose *trouvé d'avance* » (Noica 1987 : 27 ; n. tr.).

Nous avons choisi de présenter une courte analyse discursive des entretiens avec Bob Gheorghe car son discours est tout à fait différent des discours des autres insulaires. Comme nous avons mentionné, il est le plus actif ex-habitant de l'île (avec beaucoup d'initiatives dans le sens de récupérer sa mémoire), mais il est, en même temps, le plus nostalgique. Nous voulons présenter un annexe avec la transcription des entretiens avec Bob Gheorghe et les insulaires émigrés en Turquie dans le prochain article, après l'archivage de ces enregistrements et après un approfondissement de la recherche, pour qu'une analyse comparative soit possible.

Epilogue (Esquisse d'une recherche possible)

Pervin Halimoglu nous a donné, au cours de l'entretien mentionné, une remarquable preuve sur la dimension subjective de l'espace : « les casemates [de la forteresse d'Ada-Kaleh], on ne les a pas toutes vues : on n'avait pas de route dans cette direction » (entretien avec Pervin Halimoglu, Mai 2009). C'est juste un exemple qui démontre que le regard *d'insider* est unique et imprédictible. Cette recherche, qui est justement à son début, a comme objectif de récupérer le plus rapidement que possible les souvenirs capables, en ce moment, d'offrir une image depuis l'intérieur sur la vie insulaire d'Ada-Kaleh, et de conserver ces informations, en essayant aussi d'offrir une vision plus complète, plus débarrassée des lieux communs et plus précise de l'île.

Qu'est-ce que le cas d'Ada-Kaleh individualise-t-il ? L'intérêt pour enregistrer – voire préserver – les récits de vie des anciens insulaires vient de la complexité de ce cas particulier. Premièrement, il porte sur l'insularité avec ses fascinantes particularités (du point de vue de l'ethnologue). Deuxièmement, l'île d'Ada-Kaleh a été habitée par une communauté turque. D'autres communautés turques existent en Roumanie, mais aucune n'est aussi bien isolée géographiquement (sur une île et, puis, à l'intérieur d'un fort qui, lui-même a plusieurs murs concentriques) que celle-ci. L'insularité et la population turque forment ensemble le troisième facteur, l'univers d'Ada-Kaleh : les institutions locales, la vie privée des insulaires, leurs croyances (les habitudes, les rites, la mosquée, le saint local), les cafés, le bazar oriental et toutes les boutiques où on commercialisait des produits locaux ou importés de l'Orient tels que différents types de cigarettes, du café, du rahat-lokoum, etc. Bref, tout ce qui est devenu représentatif de cette attraction touristique, et beaucoup plus. Dernièrement, et c'est l'aspect le plus important, il s'agit de la manière selon laquelle la communauté a cessé d'exister. Ce n'était ni à cause de catastrophes naturelles (inondations, tremblements de terre, etc.), ni de conflits armés, ni de confrontations religieuses, mais d'une migration forcée, qui n'a pas offert à la communauté la chance de se refaire (Bercovici 2008 : 67). Par l'émigration de quelques anciens habitants en Turquie (qui a nécessité, quelquefois, la scission des familles) et par la dispersion des autres dans différentes régions de la Roumanie, la communauté, comme entité culturelle, n'a plus pu exister.

L'histoire orale est aujourd'hui la seule en mesure de récupérer les traces de cette migration, la mémoire de l'existence de l'île (la modalité dont on perçoit aujourd'hui l'île disparue sous les eaux), pour voir quels sont les attributs de l'île dans l'imaginaire contemporain, la manière dont on réactualise les souvenirs de son existence. Est-ce qu'il y a des petites communautés d'anciens habitants qui se sont reconstituées dans les nouvelles régions adoptives? Est-ce que *l'insularité* est un attribut qui meurt avec l'île ?

Vu l'impossibilité d'accéder au terrain, la seule démarche possible aujourd'hui (dans le sens d'une recherche ethnologique d'Ada-Kaleh et d'une récupération de la mémoire de l'île) est celle des enregistrements des anciens habitants de l'île. Une analyse plus détaillée sur la façon de percevoir l'île aujourd'hui, sur ses attributs dans l'imaginaire contemporain, sur le discours des anciens insulaires (sur une perpétuation des stéréotypes véhiculés ou, au contraire, sur l'abandon de ceux-ci), permettra une récupération culturelle de l'île. Mais est-ce que la mémoire de l'île et de ses habitants, le patrimoine matériel existant et la communauté dispersée d'ex-habitants sont suffisants pour donner une deuxième vie à l'île d'Ada-Kaleh ? Ce sont des questions que nous laissons ouvertes, mais auxquelles nous essayerons de répondre lors d'une recherche plus approfondie.

Sources

Ali, Ahmet 1934 : Monografia insulei Ada-Kaleh [La monographie de l'île d'Ada-Kaleh]. Craiova: Scrisul Românesc S. A.

Bercovici, Monica 2008 : Ada-Kaleh ou le Paradis perdu. In : Anuarul Institutului de Etnografie şi Folclor « C. Brăiloiu ». Bucarest : Editura Academiei Române, 19.

Budi, Monica 1968 : Ada-Kaleh. Aspecte istorico-etnografice. A ezare – gospodărie [Ada-Kaleh. Aspects historiques et géographiques. Habitat – maison]. In : Revista de Etnografie şi Folclor 13, 5 : 409–420.

Bulzan, Carmen 2008 : Destinul insulei Ada-Kaleh. Încercare de reconstituire a vieţii sociale prin recuperarea memoriei colective [Le destin de l'île d'Ada-Kaleh. Essai de reconstruction de la vie sociale par l'entremise de la récupération de la mémoire collective]. In : Symposion. Revistă de Ştiinţe Socio-Umane, tom. VI, 1 (11).

Călinescu, Raul 1940 : Insula Ada-Kaleh. Schiţă monografică [L'Ile d'Ada-Kaleh. Esquisse monographique]. In : Revista Geografică Română, Bucarest, III : 156–181.

Dan, M. Ar. 1936 : Ada-Kaleh. Bucarest : Institutul de Arte Grafice Tipografia Românească.

Dianu, Romulus s. a. : Nopţi la Ada-Kaleh [Les nuits d'Ada-Kaleh], IIème édition. Bucarest : Naţionala–Ciornei S. A. [première édition 1932].

Noica, Constantin 1987 : Cuvînt împreună despre rostirea românească [Mot ensemble sur la prononciation roumaine]. Bucarest : Ed. Eminescu.

Purcaru, Ilie 1961 : Ev nou in ţara banilor [Nouvelle époque dans le pays des gouverneurs], Craiova.

Roman, Ileana 2005 : Viaţa şi opera insulei Ada-Kaleh [La vie et l'œuvre de l'île d'Ada-Kaleh]. Bucarest : Editions Prier [version électronique : http://ccm.ro/ada_kaleh/].

Suliţeanu, Ghizela 1972 : The Musical Genres of Ada-Kaleh. In : The « Iron Gate » complex atlas. Bucarest : Editura Academiei Republicii Socialiste România.

Tulei, Mariana-Claudia 2007 : Între conservatorism şi înnoire – obiceiuri şi tradiţii ale turcilor din Ada-Kaleh [Entre le conservatisme et le renouvellement – les habitudes et les traditions des Turcs d'Ada-Kaleh]. In : Studia Juvenum. Capitole reprezentative din lucrările de diplomă ale absolvenţilor Facultăţii de Arhivistică – promoţiile 2002–2007, II. Bucarest: Editura Internelor şi Reformei Administrative.

Wunenburger, Jean-Jacques 2004 : Filozofia imaginilor [La philosophie des images]. Bucarest : Polirom, 2004.

Ethnologia Balkanica 13 (2009)

Intercultural Encounters in Fatih Akın's Films

Çağla Karabağ, Ankara

Abstract

Fatih Akın, a German-born film director of Turkish descent, has made a number of films that concentrate on migrants' experiences of cultural conflict and living between two worlds. This article focuses on the intercultural encounters in Akın's films with the theoretical frame of Russian philosopher Mikhail Bakhtin's concept of *dialogism*. Bakhtin's theory of dialogism places a strong emphasis on the self and the other in the construction of knowledge in the realm of human sciences, which means that dialogue is the core of Bakhtinian thought. For Bakhtin the other is crucial in accomplishing individual consciousness, and it is impossible to construct a self out of a single consciousness. In the light of Bakhtin's concepts, this study attempts to analyse the intercultural encounters in Fatih Akın's films *Short Sharp Shock* (*Kurz und schmerzlos – Kısa ve Acısız,* 1998), *Head-On* (*Gegen die Wand – Duvara Karşı,* 2004), *The Edge of Heaven* (*Auf der anderen Seite – Yaşamın Kıyısında,* 2007).

Since the 1960s, films, directors and audiences have been analysed with different theoretical and methodological approaches in the field of film studies.[1] Analysing a film as a text is not only examining the narrative and the cinematic code, but such an analysis also makes it possible and even essential to use various theoretical and methodological perspectives of different fields ranging from political science to sociology, from history to anthropology, etc. In this article, the interculturality between the characters of Fatih Akın's films will be investigated through Mikhail Bakhtin's (1895–1975) dialogical approach. Such a study provides us the opportunity to discuss the perspectives that the concepts of interculturality, otherness, diasporic identity and hybridity suggest, through the dialogism of the characters of Fatih Akın's films.

---

[1] When film studies emerged as an academic discipline in the 1960s, it mainly encompassed the study of *"auteurs"* and their films (Turner 1998: 196). Film studies scholars focused on the historically conditioned nature of spectatorship in the 1980s and 1990s. The history of cinema, in this sense, became not just the history of films and filmmakers, but also the history of spectators (Stam 2008: 231).

After the translation of *Rabelais and His World* into English in 1968[2], the writings of Mikhail Bakhtin began to have an impact on Western thought. Since then, his influence has been enormous, not only in literary criticism but also in history, anthropology, linguistics, philosophy, communication[3] and feminist studies (Dentith 1994: x). Bakhtin's theoretical legacy has also been utilized in film studies, for example in Robert Stam's book titled *Subversive Pleasures: Bakhtin, Cultural Criticism and Film* (1989). However, I have not yet come across a study that employs the interculturality perspective with the Bakhtinian frame in film analysis.[4] Analysing the film characters in terms of interculturality, this study positions itself on the intersection between film studies and intercultural communication studies.

The scholarly field of intercultural communication's history began after the Second World War as an outcome of the studies at the Foreign Service Institute of the U.S. Department of State. The original paradigm of intercultural com-

---

2 Although Bakhtin's study on French writer François Rabelais was translated into English in 1968, it was first published in 1965. Prior to its publication, it was submitted as a doctoral dissertation to the Gorky Institute of World Literature in Moscow. The study was certainly so controversial with the Russian academy intimidated by Stalinism, that although the work was completed in 1940, it was not examined until 1947, no degree was awarded until 1951 (and that after some controversy), and it was not published as a book until 1965 (Dentith 1994: 63).

3 For instance, Horace Newcomb in his essay "On the Dialogic Aspects of Mass Communication" (1984), offered Bakhtin's dialogical approach for cultural studies when studying the relations between mediated texts and social practice as an alternative to structuralism.

4 Although the main focus is different, for a similar study see the article of Fujimaki Mitsuhiro titled "Answerability as Bearing Witness: Mikhail M. Bakhtin on Shoah" (2001). Mitsuhiro addresses the question of Communication ethics by problematizing the nature of representation in his paper. He takes *Shoah* (1985), a film directed by Claude Lanzmann on the Holocaust, as a case study in order to see how Lanzmann challenges the nature of representation and attempts to recuperate the *Other*. The author finds Bakhtinian dialogism useful to foreground Lanzmann's work, hence his paper incorporates Bakhtin's dialogism into its analysis of *Shoah* (Mitsuhiro 2001: 103). On the other hand, Dean McWilliams discusses the function of the language in film. For this purpose he analyses Spike Lee's *Do The Right Thing* (1989) by adopting Bakhtin's concepts of polyglossia, carnival, dialogism etc. in his essay "Bakhtin in Brooklyn: Language in Spike Lee's Do the Right Thing" (2001). Alexandra Ganser, Julia Pühringer and Markus Rheindorf employ Bakhtin's concept of the chronotope to examine the road films in their article "Bakhtin's Chronotope On The Road: Space, Time, and Place in Road Movies Since the 1970s" (2006). Azadeh Saljooghi also uses a Bakhtinian approach to analyse the film *Close-up* (1990) by Iranian filmmaker Abbas Kiarostami in her article "A Bakhtin Reading of Kiarostami's Film Close-up" (2008). According to her, "The cinematic discourse of Kiarostami allows one to apply heteroglossia to the image world and illustrate alternative possibilities emerging from a fantasy world that otherwise is non-existent" (2008: 189).

munication was based on the concepts of the anthropologist Edward T. Hall and others at the FSI in the early 1950s (Rogers, Hart, Miike 2002: 5). The term "intercultural communication" was used in Edward T. Hall's *The Silent Language* (1959), and Hall is generally acknowledged to be the founder of the field (Leeds-Hurwitz 1990).

Although the foundations of the intercultural communication paradigm were laid in the 1950s, a broader theoretical basis was developed in the 1970s and 1980s, mostly due to the efforts of William B. Gudykunst. One can say that most of the perspectives of intercultural communication came to be mainstream from the late 1980s onward. Only a few scholars have studied the issues of power and socio-historical context from a critical perspective such as Martin and Nakayama (2004) (Hibler 1998). In *Intercultural Alternatives,* Blasco and Gustafsson (2004) offer a selection of alternative approaches to the question of interculturality from a range of theoretical perspectives including hermeneutics, phenomenology, semiotics, dialogic philosophy and social constructivism. Other critical perspectives such as post-colonial theories have emerged since the 1990s.

Eungjun Min, who employs Mikhail Bakhtin's concepts as a strategy for scholars who want to move beyond the positivism of the behavioural tradition and be more concerned with interdisciplinary interests and discursive levels of analysis, finds Bakhtin's thoughts important for the study of intercultural communication. According to Min, "Bakhtin addresses one of the most perplexing problems of contemporary social theory – diversity and the dilemma of reconstructing intercultural constructs" (2001: 5).

The philosophy of dialogism uses a different approach to understand culture through its epistemological focus on intersubjectivity and its dynamic way of linking specific utterances to the "living tradition". The dialogic approach sees meaning as an emergent phenomenon, integrating aspects of both the immediate and the historical social contexts of performance. Besides providing a radical critique of essentialist theories of culture, it simultaneously implies a universal epistemological orientation towards wholeness that is common to both everyday life and to works of art. When seen dialogically, culture is not stable and given, but emergent and dynamic. Since the 1980s, "thinking culture dialogically" has been synonymous with thinking about culture in a way inspired by the works of Bakhtin (Bostad 2005: 1 f., 4).

In this article, I argue that intercultural stories and the multicultural characters of Akın's films support Bakhtin's anti-essentialist analysis of culture and his emphasis on otherness and interculturality in the construction of identity. The main questions of this study can be outlined as such:

- What kind of perspective does the Bakhtinian concept of dialogism suggest for intercultural encounters?

- What can be argued about the characters in Fatih Akın's films from this perspective?
- Analysed through Bakhtinian dialogism, what kind of perspectives does the reflection on the film characters in terms of the concepts of otherness, being in-between, hybridity, multiculturality and interculturality provide us?

In this study, I will analyse the interculturality of the characters of Fatih Akın's three films *Short Sharp Shock* (*Kurz und schmerzlos - Kısa ve Acısız,* 1998), *Head-On* (*Gegen die Wand - Duvara Karşı,* 2004), *The Edge of Heaven* (*Auf der anderen Seite - Yaşamın Kıyısında,* 2007) with the theoretical frame of Mikhail Bakhtin's concept of dialogism.

A dialogic perspective for intercultural encounters

The phenomenological model in which the person can express her/himself through the mediation of others and the subject can exist within an intersubjective relation is a practical starting point in order to see Bakhtin's study as a whole (Irzık 2001: 8). Bakhtin's theory of dialogism places a strong emphasis on self and other in the construction of knowledge in the human sciences. Dialogue is at the core of Bakhtin's thought, that is to say, "all Bakhtin's writings are animated and controlled by the principle of dialogue" (Holquist 2002: 15). In *Problems of Dostoevsky's Poetics* Bakhtin wrote:

> "Dialogue ... is not a means for revealing, for bringing to the surface the already ready-made character of a person; no, in dialogue a person not only shows himself outwardly, but he becomes for the first time that which he is - and, we repeat, not only for others but for himself as well. To be means to communicate dialogically. When dialogue ends, everything ends. Thus dialogue, by its very essence, cannot and must not come to an end" (1984: 252).

In his essay "Author and Hero in Aesthetic Activity", written in the 1920s and published posthumously, Bakhtin's starting point is the relationship between self and other, between I and Thou (Dentith 1994: 11). In this essay, he discusses the relations between writers and the characters they create. In 1970, in the Russian-language literary magazine *Novy Mir*, Bakhtin focuses on the relation between one's own society and the other cultures that are foreign to it in space or time. But in both cases Bakhtin's analytical model is the same: "he stresses the need first to use one's understanding to penetrate the other person or the other culture as deeply as possible; but then having done this, he stresses in both cases the no less urgent need to *return* to the perspective provided by our native self or native culture" (Holquist 2006: xii–xiii).

In the first case, in his essay "Author and Hero in Aesthetic Activity", Bakhtin says:

> "In life, we do this at every moment: we appraise ourselves from the point of view of others, we attempt to understand transgredient[5] moments of our very consciousness and to take them into account through the other ...; in a word, constantly and intensely, we oversee and apprehend the reflections of our life in the plane of consciousness of other men" (1990: 16 f.).

In the second case, while discussing the relation between one's own society and the other cultures in 1970, Bakhtin says, "There exists a very strong, but one-sided and thus untrustworthy, idea that in order better to understand a foreign culture, one must enter into it, forgetting one's own, and view the world through the eyes of this foreign culture" (2006: 6 f.). According to him, our goal should be the dialogic version of "creative understanding":

> "*Creative understanding* does not renounce itself, its own place in time, its own culture; and it forgets nothing. In order to understand, it is immensely important for the person who understands to be *located outside* the object of his or her creative understanding – in time, in space, in culture. For one cannot even really see one's own exterior and comprehend it as a whole, and no mirrors or photographs can help; our real exterior can be seen and understood only by other people, because they are located outside us in space and because they are *others*" (Bakhtin 2006: 7).

Dialogism ensures that nothing can be conceived without the perspective of something else. As Michael Holquist (2002: 18) has pointed out, "in dialogism, the very capacity to have consciousness is based on *otherness.*" According to Bakhtin, "in the realm of culture, outsideness is a most powerful factor in understanding". A foreign culture reveals itself fully and profoundly only in the eyes of *another* culture and a meaning only reveals its depth once it has encountered and come into contact with another, foreign meaning:

> "We raise new questions for a foreign culture, ones that it did not raise itself; we seek answers to our own questions in it; and the foreign culture responds us by revealing us its new aspects and semantic depths. Without *one's own* questions one cannot creatively understand anything other or

---

[5] Bakhtin borrows the term *transgredient* from German aesthetic thought and he uses it in a complementary sense to "ingredient" to designate elements of consciousness that are external to it but nonetheless absolutely necessary for its completion, for its achievement of totalization (Todorov 1984: 95).

> foreign (but, of course, the questions must be serious and sincere). Such a dialogic encounter of two cultures does not result in merging or mixing. Each retains its own unity and *open* totality, but they are mutually enriched" (Bakhtin 2006: 7).

To summarize, from Bakhtin's perspective, the encounter with the *other* both enables the questioning of one's own culture and the shifting of given cultural borders. This implies celebrating diversity and plurality rather than cultural distortion or collapse, as suggested by conservative or essentialist thoughts. The intercultural encounters of the characters in Fatih Akın's films will be analysed from a dialogic perspective in the next section.

Intercultural encounters in Fatih Akın's films from a Bakhtinian perspective

One can say that a new and continuous cinema of Turkish migrants in Germany, which is also called "third-generation cinema", "ghetto cinema", "Turkish-German cinema", "German-Turkish cinema", "German minority cinema" has emerged since the mid-1990s (Ulusay 2008: 174). The films of New German Cinema directors in the 1970s and the 1980s that represented the experiences of ethnic minorities can be seen as filmic antecedents to this cinema (Burns 2007: 4). Fatih Akın is one of the outstanding representatives of this cinema that stimulated German cinema and that was generated by the children of the generation of the 1960s who migrated to West Germany for work.

Film director Akın was born in Hamburg in 1973 to Turkish parents and grew up in Hamburg-Altona. While studying Visual Communications at Hamburg's College of Fine Arts, he wrote and directed his first short film in 1995 called *You're the One! (Du bist es! – Sensin!),* followed by *Weed* (*Getürkt*, 1996). In his first feature film, *Short Sharp Shock (Kurz und schmerzlos,),* he tells the dramatic story of three close friends, the Turk Gabriel (Cebrail), the Greek Kosta and the Serb Bobby. With this story, Akın "illustrates the multicultural social reality in contemporary urban Germany" (Hamm-Ehsani 2005: 106).

In this study I will focus on the two characters, Gabriel and his sister Ceyda, from a Bakhtinian perspective. As I mentioned before, according to Bakhtin, "in the realm of culture, outsideness is a most powerful factor in understanding" (2006: 7). Gabriel and Ceyda have the power of outsideness. "As the children of migrants, they are fully aware of their inter- or transnational status in Germany, but they do not perceive that as problematic for their self-definition" (Hamm-Ehsani 2005: 111). They can speak Turkish and German perfectly and their identities are shaped both by Turkish and German culture. The wedding ceremony at the beginning of the *Short Sharp Shock* represents Turkish culture with its foods, music, dance and the rituals. In this long wedding sequence, which provides information about Ceyda and Gabriel's cultural background, it is remarkable that they have friends from Serbia, Germany and Greece. They communicate in German amongst themselves. Both Ceyda and Gabriel are second generation migrants who are very different from the first generation. It is meaningful that one of Gabriel's best friends is a Serb and the other one is a Greek, because the nationalist and the historical hostilities amongst the nations are meaningless for these characters who meet in a multicultural sphere and share the common denominator of being foreigners. Cultural prejudices and hostilities are criticized ironically in the film. Deniz Göktürk indicates that the film not only focuses on ethnic groups, but also on marginal social positions, and in this sense she compares the film to *The Hate* (*La Haine,* 1995) (Ulusay 2008: 208).

Ceyda is represented as a young woman who lives her own life and her sexuality without the oppression and protection of her family. Her lifestyle is not approved by her family, because they know nothing about her life. Her brother Gabriel always supports her rather than adopting a patriarchal attitude, and instead of a relation of protection he builds up a friendship with her. This support is the key factor for Ceyda to live her life as she wishes. Gabriel and Ceyda are outsiders both to German culture, as they are the children of immigrants, and to Turkish culture, as they were born and have grown up in Germany. Being outsiders prevents them from becoming stereotypes and turns them into rich characters, and it provides them the opportunity to observe from the position of the "other". One can say that they are the consequences of the dialogism between different cultures or symbolic practices of meaning.[6]

In *Head-On,* Fatih Akın tells the relationship between Turkish-born German Cahit and the daughter of an emigrated Turkish family, Sibel. It starts as a matter of formality, but transforms into a relationship of real love and passion. *Head-On* is a love movie, but it is also a movie which sheds light on the dilemma of the conflicting cultures that have to coexist in the same space. Both Sibel and Cahit attempt to commit suicide: Sibel cuts her wrists as a symbol of rebellion against the totalitarian patriarchy at home, which completely suppresses her individualism, and lonely and alcoholic Cahit drives his car full speed against a wall – the title of the film – in order to escape his own misery caused by the death of his beloved first wife and his social decline since then (Rings 2008). Contrary to the character of Ceyda in *Short Sharp Shock,* Sibel is a young wom-

[6] Clifford Geertz (1973: 89) defines culture as "an historically transmitted pattern of meanings embodied in symbols, a system of inherited conceptions expressed in symbolic forms by means of which men communicate, perpetuate, and develop their knowledge about and their attitudes toward life".

an who is oppressed by patriarchal family structures. She dreams of getting her freedom by marrying Cahit, whom she meets after trying to commit suicide. When Sibel asks for help, Cahit accepts her proposal and his decision may be a way of giving sense to his life, which has become meaningless since the death of his wife. Thanks to the marriage, something that her family approves of, Sibel is able to leave home. She has tattoos and piercings and has a sexual affair with a man whom she met in a bar. Her body is, so to say, freed from captivity.

Let us focus on the main characters' families in *Head-On* and *Short Sharp Shock*. We cannot see the mother of Ceyda and Gabriel after the wedding sequence in *Short Sharp Shock*. We are only faced with the character of the father while he is performing *namaz* or inviting Gabriel to perform *namaz* together.[7] We are led to think that he, as a migrant worker in a culture that he does not know, escapes from secular matters and shelters in a spiritual world to overcome his alienation. Except for kindly inviting his children to worship, he never intervenes in his children's lives.

The father character in *Head-On* has religious devotions as well. He says that his daughter's suicide attempt is a sin and asks Cahit whether the chocolates he brought contain any alcohol. Guests at Sibel and Cahit's wedding are not served any alcohol.[8] Contrary to the father who has a moustache and wears a cap, the mother has a modern appearance with her blond hair, make-up and dressed-up style. Sibel is severely oppressed by her father and brother; she once had her nose broken by her brother when he saw her holding hands with a boy. The brother cannot have a dialogical relation to the culture of the country where he was born. Because of this, Sibel's life is in such turmoil that sometimes death seems like the only viable option. Sibel does not want to accept patriarchal oppression as her destiny. The only reason that prevents her from running away from home is her love of her mother. It can be said that the father and brother of Sibel are monological characters because of their adoption of conservative and patriarchal behavioural patterns. Sibel, on the other hand, is a dialogical character who does not submit to the oppression because she is aware of the sovereignty of young women on their bodies in the country where she has grown up. The father and the brother are imprisoned within the confines of the religious and masculine authority and cannot have a dialogue with a life-style which is exterior to these confines.

---

7 *Namaz* is the daily ritual prayer in Islam which must be performed five times a day at prescribed times.

8 Consuming alcoholic drinks is *haram,* and suicide are considered *gunah* according to the Islamic rules (*haram* refers to an action which is divergent and *gunah* refers to an action which is considered sinful in Islam).

In the second film of the Life Trilogy, *The Edge of Heaven,* Akın tells the story of six characters whose lives intersect in many ways. There are three episodes: "Yeter's Death", "Lotte's Death" and "The Edge of Heaven". The characters are retired first generation migrant worker Ali, his German language professor's son Nejat, Yeter, whose death is caused by Ali, the daughter of Yeter, Ayten, and Lotte, who has met Ayten in Germany to be her partner, and finally Lotte's mother Susanne.

The film highlights the status of being in-between and multiculturalism that blurs cultural boundaries. The fact that the son of a Turkish migrant worker is a professor of German language reverses the cliché of Turks in Germany and presents a striking example of positions that are indicated by Bakhtin as "otherness" and "being outsiders". As the son of a migrant worker, Nejat is an "outsider" both to German and to Turkish culture, as he was born and raised in Germany and became a professor of German language. The film director explains the transformation and "outsider" position of his characters and their destruction of essentialist identity concepts as follows:

> "My characters are all outsiders in a way – society outsiders like prostitutes and political refugees. Even being a German professor is kind of being an outsider. Being out of the society and not being in the mainstream makes them outsiders. All of them are moving on in a way and every character has to make a transformation. That was the idea. Characters begin with this certain state of mind and by the end of the film they have changed their opinions and positions. I think this explains me in a way; I've changed my mind so much. ... I think my identity is always changing and moving. Identity is not a treasure that once you find it you keep it for the rest of your life. Because of circumstances it's changing and I try to explain that" (Tehrani 2008).

Faith Akın's expression finds its parallel in the arguments of Stuart Hall. From his point of view, cultural identity is:

> "a matter of 'becoming' as well as of 'being'. It belongs to the future as much as to the past. It is not something which already exists, transcending place, time, history, and culture. Cultural identities come from somewhere and have history. But like everything which is historical, they undergo constant transformation" (Hall 1990: 225).

We can find another outstanding example of Bakhtinian dialogism in *The Edge of Heaven.* In a dialogue between Lotte and her mother, while discussing who does not want Ayten to stay at home, Lotte says that her mother's attitude was "very German". The very mentioning of the cliché of German individualism by a German can be seen as a reiteration of a prejudice, but actually it is an ironic criticism of prejudices. This dialogue can be taken to be an expression of seeing "oneself" through the eyes of "the other". In Bakhtinian dialogism, dialogue is not only a way of expressing oneself or understanding the other, but also the precondition for knowing oneself, manifesting oneself as a whole and a being.

Conclusion

In Fatih Akın's films, the characters go on a journey. They move not only physically and geographically, but also mentally. A journey is a search which basically corresponds to the search for personality and identity. Akın's films are about being German, being Turkish, being in-between, being multicultural, but moreover about being human. It can be said that Fatih Akın's films are themselves hybrid, besides their hybrid characters. As Ulusay points out, the narrative of his films covers many features, from melodrama to comedy, and from gangster film to the conventions of "art cinema" (2008: 225), and Burns (2007: 13) pointed out that "like geographical borders, linguistic and musical borders are constantly crossed or dissolved in Akın's films".

Having been awarded the Golden Bear in Berlin and Best Script in Cannes, Fatih Akın's films have been welcomed in the international film market, including Hollywood. The reason for this interest can be found in the contents of his films, which introduce a sense of universalism that is generated by dialogism and hybridity. Even in contexts of different meanings and practices, people make friends, fall in love, suffer from death and separation, they dream, feel sorry or happy. The possibility of knowing oneself and others emerges, cultural boundaries disappear or shift thanks to dialogue. Boundaries make the culture whatever it is in a particular historical moment, but these cultural boundaries are fluid since culture has a dynamic structure. Cultures and cultural identities do not have a lasting essence or core.

The essentialist approach to culture and identity is the anchor of nationalist ideologies. In his stimulating study, *Imagined Communities: Reflections on the Origin and Spread of Nationalism* (1991), Benedict Anderson has asserted that the nation can be understood as a construction. He defines the nation as "an imagined political community – and imagined as both inherently limited and sovereign". The diasporic identity and hybridity of Akın's characters' destroy this imagination, they change the clichés about nations and open up a "third space"[9].

[9] Post-colonialist theoretician Homi Bhaba uses the term *third space:* "The intervention of the *Third Space of enunciation*, which makes the structure of meaning and reference an ambivalent process, destroys this mirror of representation in which cultural knowledge is customarily revealed as *integrated, open, expanding code*. Such an intervention quite prop-

Literature

Anderson, B. 1991: Imagined Communities: Reflections on the Origin and Spread of Nationalism. New York, London: Verso.

Bakhtin, M. M. 1968: Rabelais and His World. Transl. by H. Iswolski. Cambridge, Mass: MIT Press.

Bakhtin, M. M. 1984: Problems of Dostoevsky's Poetics. Transl. by C. Emerson. Minneapolis: University of Minnesota Press.

Bakhtin, M. M. 1990: Art and Answerability: Early Philosophical Essays. M. Holquist, V. Liapunov (eds.). Transl. by V. Liapunov. Austin: University of Texas Press.

Bakhtin, M. M. 1994: The Dialogic Imagination: Four Essays by M. M. Bakhtin, M. Holquist (eds.). Transl. by C. Emerson & M. Holquist. Austin: University of Texas Press.

Bakhtin, M. M. 2006: Speech Genres and Other Late Essays. C. Emerson & M. Holquist (eds.). Transl. by V. W. McGee. Austin: University of Texas Press.

Bhabha, H. K. 1994: The Location of Culture. New York: Routledge.

Blasco, M., J. Gustaffson, (eds.) 2004: Intercultural Alternatives. Copenhagen: Copenhagen Business School Press.

Bostad, F. (ed.) 2005: Bakhtinian Perspectives on Language and Culture: Meaning in Language, Art and New Media. Gordonsville, VA: Palgrave Macmillan.

Burns, R. 2007: Towards a Cinema of Cultural Hybridity: Turkish-German Filmmakers and the Representation of Alterity. In: Debatte: Journal of Contemporary Central and Eastern Europe 15, 1: 3–24.

Dentith, S. 1994: Bakhtinian Thought: An Introductory Reader. Florence, KY: Routledge.

Ganser, A., J. Pühringer, M. Rheindorf 2006: Bakhtin's Chronotope on the Road: Space, Time, and Place in Road Movies Since the 1970s. In: Linguistics and Literature 4, 1: 1–17.

Geertz, C. 1973: The Interpretation of Cultures. New York: Basic Books.

Hall, E. T. 1959: The Silent Language. New York: Doubleday.

Hall, S. 1990: Cultural identity and Diaspora. In: J. Rutherford (ed.), Identity: Community, Culture, Difference. London: Lawrence and Wishart, 222–237.

erly challenges our sense of the historical identity of culture as a homogenizing, unifying force, authenticated by originary Past, kept alive in the national tradition of the People" (1994: 37).

Hamm-Ehsani, K. 2005: Screening Transnational Turkish Community in Fatih Akın "Kurz und Schmerzlos" (Short Sharp Shock). In: Kültür ve İletişim [Culture and communication] Summer 8, 2: 101–128.

Hibler, K. 1998: Inter/cultural Communication and the Challenge of Postcolonial Theory. In: The Edge: E-Journal of Intercultural Relations. 1, 2: 1–11. (URL: http://interculturalrelations.com/v1i2Spring1998/sp98hibler.htm).

Holquist, M. 2002: Dialogism: Bakhtin and His World. London, New York: Routledge.

Holquist, M. 2006: Introduction. In: Speech Genres and Other Late Essays. C. Emerson & M. Holquist (eds.). Transl. by V. W. McGee. Austin: University of Texas Press, xi–xxiii.

Irzık, S. 2001: Önsöz [Introduction]. In: Mikhail Bakhtin, Karnavaldan Romana [From carnival to novel], ed. and trans. S. Irzik. Istanbul: Ayrıntı, 7–32.

Leeds-Hurwitz, W. 1990: Notes in the History of Intercultural Communication: The Foreign Service Institute and the Mandate for Intercultural Training. In: Quarterly Journal of Speech 76, 3: 262–281.

Martin, J. N., T. K. Nakayama 2004: Intercultural Communication in Contexts. Boston: McGraw-Hill.

McWilliams, D. 2001: Bakhtin in Brooklyn: Language in Spike Lee's "Do the Right Thing". In: P. I. Barta, P. A. Miller, C. Platter, D. Shepherd (eds.), Carnivalizing Difference: Bakhtin and the Other. London, New York: Routledge, 247–261.

Min, E. 2001: Bakhtinian Perspectives for the Study of Intercultural Communication. In: Journal of Intercultural Studies 22, 1: 5–18.

Mitsuhiro, F. 2001: Answerability as Bearing Witness: Mikhail M. Bakhtin on Shoah. In: Intercultural Communication Studies 13: 103–135.

Newcomb, H. M. 1984: On the Dialogic Aspects of Mass Communication. In: Critical Studies in Mass Communication 1: 34–50.

Rings, G. 2008: Blurring or Shifting Boundaries? Concepts of Culture in Turkish-German Migrant Cinema. In: GFL 1: 6–39 (URL: http://www.gfl-journal.de/1-2008/rings.pdf).

Rogers, E. M., W. B. Hart, Y. Miike, 2002: Edward T. Hall and the History of Intercultural Communication: The United States and Japan. In: Keio Communication Review 24: 3–26.

Saljooghi, A. 2006: A Bakhtin Reading of Kiarostami's Film "Close-up". In: Critique: Critical Middle Eastern Studies 17, 2: 189–200.

Stam, R. 1989: Introduction. In: Subversive Pleasures: Bakhtin, Cultural Criticism, and Film. Baltimore, London: The Johns Hopkins Univ. Press, 1–25.

Stam, R. 2008: Film Theory: An Introduction. Malden, MA: Blackwell.

Tehrani, B. 2008: An Interview with Fatih Akın, Director of "The Edge of Heaven" (URL: http://www.cinemawithoutborders.com/news/127/ARTICLE/1569/2008-05-02.html).

Todorov, T. 1984: Mikhail Bakhtin: The Dialogical Principle. Transl. by W. Godzich. Minneapolis: University of Minnesota Press.

Turner, G. 1998: Cultural Studies and Film. In: J. Hill, P. C. Gibson (eds.), The Oxford Guide to Film Studies. New York: Oxford UP, 195–201.

Ulusay, N. 2008: Melez İmgeler [Hybrid Images]. Ankara: Dost.

Ethnologia Balkanica 13 (2009)

The Marketing Opportunities for "Traditional" and "Non-Traditional" Music by Turkish Immigrants in Vienna

Hande Sağlam, Vienna

Abstract

Over the past few decades, immigrant music cultures have become a very significant part of musical life in Vienna. Musicians from Turkey in Vienna produce and distribute their music, which is embedded in co-ethnic, inter-ethnic as well as trans-national relations. This paper examines the repertoires and marketing strategies/opportunities of Turkish immigrant musicians and entrepreneurs in Vienna. Marketing advantages and disadvantages of the "ethnic" or "traditional" coded products of musicians with Turkish immigrant backgrounds are analysed using tools and concepts of urban ethnomusicology.

Introduction

In this paper I examine the different marketing opportunities open in Vienna to immigrant musicians from Turkey. I focus primarily on the need to use "ethnicity" as a marketing strategy and the socio-economic reasons and consequences of this phenomenon in the diaspora. My analysis is based on two research projects which I worked on from 2005 until January 2009 in Vienna. The first was an ethnomusicological pilot project called "The Music Culture of Immigrants in Vienna: Research on their Musical Identities and Acculturation" on the musical identities of Turkish immigrants in Vienna. The second project was called "Embedded Industries – Cultural Entrepreneurs in Different Immigrant Communities of Vienna" funded by WWTF (the Vienna Science and Technology Fund). This was a multidisciplinary project combining research methodologies from sociology, ethnomusicology and ethnology, and analysed how immigrants' creative industries are embedded in co-ethnic, interethnic and transnational networks.[1]

Turkish immigrants in Vienna

Austria has the fourth largest Turkish population in Europe after Germany (approximately 60 % of the Turkish immigrants in Europe live in Germany), France

[1] For more information on the project see: http://www.mdw.ac.at/mediacult/en/main.html.

Photo 1: FPÖ election poster of 2005 "Vienna should not become Istanbul"

and Holland. According to the 2001 census, Vienna has around 1.6 million habitants. More than 400 000 (around 27 %) have migrant backgrounds and 248 264 of them (around 19 %) have foreign citizenship. Immigrants from Serbia and Montenegro are the largest minority group in Vienna (approx. 120 000 people). After these comes the Turkish community as the second largest minority group: around 70 000 people living in Vienna are originally from Turkey and 39 119 of them still have Turkish citizenship. Thus, about 3 % of the Viennese population has a Turkish background.[2]

Socio-political situation of immigrants in Vienna and Austria

The first Turkish guest workers came to Austria at the beginning of the 1960s. Shortly afterwards, for social and economic reasons, their families arrived and built a new home environment in Vienna. After the military putsch of 1980, numerous politically active intellectuals, writers, musicians and artists migrated to European countries and also to Vienna; approximately 10 % of the Turkish immigrants in Vienna now belong to this social group. Today, the second and even third generations are growing up there. There are also quite a number of Turkish students who have moved to Vienna for educational purposes. This diversity means that the Turkish immigrants in Vienna have various immigration backgrounds and are from different social surroundings, but most of them are "guest

[2] For details see: http://www.statistik.at/web_de/statistiken/bevoelkerung/volkszaehlungen/bevoelkerung_nach_demographischen_merkmalen/index.html.

Photo 2: FPÖ election poster of 2005 "'Home(land)' instead of Islam"

workers" and their children, the so-called "second generation". Since the Aliens Act *(Ausländergesetz)* of 1996 (see Kwok 2009) made it almost impossible for an immigrant to get a work permit, they had very limited opportunities in the job market. Students with foreign citizenship are definitely not allowed to work.[3] Political and social discrimination against *"Ausländer"* [foreigners], particularly against Turks and Muslims since the 1990s, and especially after 9/11, has made the situation for Turkish immigrants in Vienna very difficult.

Most of these immigrants have lived for more than 40 years in Austria without being considered part of the "Austrian" community. Xenophobia, especially against "Muslims"[4], is growing steadily. Immigrants and the integration of immigrants is a very popular topic, especially in politics. The leader of the right-wing extremist party FPÖ, H. C. Strache, has used this subject as an election campaign issue for years.

Much of the scholarly interest in immigrants in Austria has so far concentrated on the questions of integration in general,[5] labour market effects (e. g.

---

[3] Only students with EU citizenship are permitted to work in Austria. Even this permission is very limited.

[4] Most of the Muslims in Austria come from Turkey and this is why Turks in Austria are usually considered by the dominant community to be Muslims, regardless of whether they perceive and identify themselves as Muslim or not.

[5] E. g. Bauböck 1995, Fassmann, Stacher 2003, Fassmann 2007.

Gächter 1998, Biffl 2002) and ethnic businesses.[6] Ethnomusicological aspects of immigration to Vienna have been analysed at our institute, the Institute of Folk Music Research and Ethnomusicology at the Vienna University of Music and Performing Arts, for years now.[7] Nevertheless, the relationship between immigrant culture and the marketing opportunities for the immigrants' cultural products has not been analysed very deeply. In the project "Embedded Industries, Cultural Entrepreneurs in Different Immigrant Communities of Vienna", we tried to analyse this issue from the viewpoint of immigrant artists. I concentrated especially on the music productions of Turkish immigrants in Vienna. Regarding this issue, the term ethnicity plays a very important role because the cultural products of immigrants are normally positioned on the market as "ethnic" products. That is why it is necessary to define the meaning of ethnicity.

(Re-) Presentation of ethnicity

Perceiving others – representing one's own

A common definition of ethnicity is "a social group with a shared history, sense of identity, geography and cultural roots". Ethnicity is an ongoing social process of transformation which is influenced by the political, economic and cultural issues of the respective communities. Fredrik Barth (1969) focused on the role of social interaction in the development of ethnic boundaries, arguing that ethnicity is not a matter of shared characters or cultural unities, but rather of practices of classification and categorization, including both self-classification and the classification of and by others concerning "who" and "what" a group of people are. Barth shifted the analytical focus from cultural difference as the basis of ethnic identity to the social establishment of cultural difference. According to this perspective, ethnicity and ethnic categories are conceived not as static and immutable, but subject to transformation. Barth's standpoint has been perceived as pioneering what later came to be known as the constructionist view: "the claim that ethnicity is the product of a social process rather than a cultural given, made and remade rather than taken for granted, chosen depending on circumstances rather than ascribed through birth" (Wimmer 2008: 971).

To define ethnicity may not be that difficult, but to define the "social group", the ascertainment of its "shared history", "sense of identity" and their "cultural roots" is not very easy. Max Weber considered ethnicity to be an artificial issue because ethnic groups are based on a subjective belief in shared community and

---

6 E. g. Cakir 2004, Haberfellner 2000, Schmid et al. 2006, Enzenhofer et al. 2007.

7 E. g. Hemetek 1996, Hemetek 2001, Hemetek, Bajrektarević 2000, Hemetek et al. 2006, Hemetek, Reyes 2007, Hemetek, Sağlam 2007.

this belief does not create the group, but the group creates the belief (Banton 2007: 19–35). If we consider that this belief is also a process of self-classification of the "ethnic group" and classification by "others," and that immigrants are minorities who are less influential in their new environment, the dominant culture thus obtains the legitimation to define, analyse and present the differences between themselves and immigrants. Consequently, the immigrants are understood and presented primarily through the values of the dominant culture; sometimes positively and sometimes negatively, with prejudices. They are groups of people distinguishable from the dominant group for ethnic, cultural, social, religious or economic reasons. In this paper we analyse the ethnic images of an immigrant group. That is why we must take into consideration that immigrant communities are minorities in society and that they have been judged mostly by the so-called dominant community.

Integration policies are usually designed to bring about the cultural change of immigrants rather than cultural exchange between the different communities in a country, although integration actually means to be part of society, enjoying equal rights and respecting its values and norms. The integration process should include at least two partners cooperating with each other. "Integration ist also ein Prozess wechselseitiger Anpassung und Veränderung zwischen einer aufnehmenden und einer aufzunehmenden Gruppe" [Integration is thus a process of reciprocal adjustment between the group already living there and the group settling] (Bauböck 2001: 14).

The forty year-old migration history in Austria of communities from Turkey (as well as former Yugoslavia and black Africa) has been considered by most politicians and by the majority as a problem of disintegration. Legal and social discrimination and the economic, social and political conditions of immigrants mean that they remain marginalized and their integration blocked. The multiculturalist notion of exchange, of trying to accept "differences" and supporting the representation of "other" cultures and the acceptance of immigrants as a part of a country has not been pursued. Austrian policies on immigration and integration remain among the most restrictive in the European Union (Fassmann 2007).

In the educational system, the language problems of immigrant children are considered to be the fault of the children and their families and are therefore not solved through alternative educational methods. Many pupils with migrant backgrounds are sent to *Sonderschulen* (special schools for retarded children) because of their difficulties with the German language. Austria performs rather poorly with regard to the first stages of the educational track and largely fails to exploit the academic potential of the Turkish second generation. In Austria, the Turkish second generation has obviously been predestined by the educational system to form the working class, while access to white collar professions is largely withheld (Perchinig 2008). These conditions are far from an ideal basis for interaction and cultural transmission between the minority and majority communities in Vienna.

Ethnic classification or labelling by the dominant community without it coming into contact with immigrant communities results in the creation of ethnic clichés, regardless of whether those affected actually identify with them or not. Immigrants must develop their social networks, both within their own community and outside it with the dominant culture, and these ethnic clichés play a very important role if immigrants want to develop their social networks with the dominant culture. In this case, the representation of ethnicity is greatly influenced by these clichés even if the immigrant community does not agree with them.

The positive or negative perceptions, prejudices and clichés of the dominant society and the legal framework (especially problems with work permits) make the self-identification of Turkish immigrants in Vienna very different from that of Turks living in Turkey. Being considered a minority group causes them to think about their own culture in a different way. They view their own culture from a perspective which they were not familiar with when they were in their homeland. The second and third generations in particular consider their background culture to be not only different from that of their parents, but also different from that of young people in Turkey. This is also reflected in their musical language and their marketing strategies in the music business.

Five categories of music-making: scenarios[8]

In the Institute of Folk Music Research and Ethnomusicology we have carried out much research on the musical identification of various immigrants in Vienna. The following categories of music-making are a part of the results of this research. The musical world of immigrants is very multifaceted, and we have divided it into the following five categories: 1. Internal practice; 2. Transmission of music from the country of origin; 3. Public ghetto; 4. Creative exchange, and 5. "Mainstream" musical activities.

1. Internal practice: For example, musical activities such as those at weddings, henna nights, religious ceremonies and events with musicians from Turkey. These are organized and presented by community members for community members.
2. Transmission of music from the country of origin – cultural heritage: This takes place mostly in private music courses on folk and court music and folk

[8] See also Hemetek and Sağlam 2009: 209–221.

dances from Turkey. There are many immigrants' cultural organizations which aim to transmit the cultural heritage of their country not only to their second generation, but to Austrians as well.

3. Public ghetto: In Vienna one can find a large number of immigrant-owned bars, restaurants and cafes. These places seem to be open to everybody, but are visited almost exclusively by community members. The music at these locations is dominated by mainstream pop music and Turkish pop music.
4. Creative exchange "World Music":[9] The musicians in this category perform on mainstream stages and at music festivals and the audience is mainly from the dominant culture. Most of those musicians don't want to be labelled as "immigrant musicians", even though they are. In this category, the ethnic classification which is applied by Austrians plays an important role. Most of these musicians are second generation or have lived in diaspora for many years. Their music is mostly labelled as World Music, which sometimes offers them advantages and sometimes disadvantages.
5. "Mainstream" musical activities: In this category we find the musicians who play electronic, jazz or classical music. Self-classification of ethnicity is significant here, but their ethnic or religious background is not at the forefront of their musical language at all. They are part of a cosmopolitan area and they want to be considered a natural part of this area.

These five categories define the musical language and expressions of immigrant musicians. However, the expectations of their own community and the dominant community make the marketing process complicated. As the expectation of the target group must be considered and fulfilled, "a marketing strategy should be

---

[9] The term World Music in ethnomusicology refers the diversity of the musical activities and the diversity in the musical activities found all over the world. "Steven Feld in 1994 has described this by saying that World Music is sense signifies for many 'quite simply innocently musical diversity'. (...) The ethnomusicological sense of the term World Music was first institutionally manifested in the early 1960s, when the Wesleyan University in Connecticut inaugurated its Wesleyan World Music Program, which in turn led to the founding of similar teaching programs at other universities and non-academic establishments such as the Centre for World Music founded in 1970 in San Francisco" (Brusila 2003: 48). Today the most common meaning of World Music comes from CD companies. In this case World Music is a term used as a marketing strategy resource, in Vienna (like almost everywhere in Europe and USA) to describe the musical styles that cannot be place in any other category. In 1987 in Great Britain a meeting of representatives from some main independent record labels discussed different ways of achieving international/roots music in the retail trade, in the press and among the audience. It was decided that the term World Music would be used by all labels present to offer a new category for record shops, press, audience, concerts and so on. Apart from the traditional Afro-American music, but only from the USA and not from any Latin American countries, and everything which does not come from the so-called "western music style" was deemed World Music (Sağlam 2008).

centred on the key concept that consumer satisfaction is the main goal" (Baker 2008: 3).

Marketing of ethnicity: four marketing strategies

In our project we noticed that in addition to these five categories of music-making there are four different marketing strategies (and actually possibilities) for musicians with immigrant backgrounds.

1. Co-ethnic marketing strategies (keyword: intracultural): Marketing by using the ethnic codes (religious, ethnic or national) of the community via the self-identification of their ethnicity. This strategy addresses community members almost exclusively. It is evident that entrepreneurs and musicians who provide wedding saloons for Turkish communities, some music lessons on folk and court music from Turkey, Turkish discos and all second generation hip-hop singers belong in this category.

2. Exoticism as a marketing strategy (keyword: instrumentalisation of stereotypes): This is mostly understood as a particular form of the Eurocentric view of the ethnicity of immigrants. In this case, the main purpose is to present ethnic issues and characteristics as "exotic"[10]. In this field the "differences" and the "ethnic roots" of musical products within the context of "multiculturalism" are stressed. Very often, musicians place themselves under the label of World Music and emphasize their "otherness". Music industries are marked by the mobilisation of mostly inter-ethnic resources. Examples include the Turkish singer who sells her music as an enchanting fusion of East and West all along the *Silk Road – Gülay and her band* (http://www.guelay.com) – or a band which is called *Nim Sofyan* (http://www.nimsofyan.com).

The group Nim Sofyan was founded in 2003 in Vienna by the Turkish musician Alp Bora together with colleagues from other cultural backgrounds. Nim

---

[10] In this case what I mean by "exotic" is a superficial respect for and recognition of cultures and ethnic groups, an attraction which is caused by the "otherness" of the ethnic groups. The subject matter and the quality of something which is "exotic" tends to be less important than their being unfamiliar and different. Ethnicity has to do with a social group and its values and traditions, but exoticism means the view held by the majority about other ethnic groups and their values.

Sofyan won the *Austrian World Music Award*[11] in 2004. Alp Bora made the following statement after winning the prize:

> "Three years ago we were street musicians and we had difficulties with the police on several occasions because of complaints due to noise. Today we received two prizes at once. That means a new start for us. From now on we are going to work hard to make our music known in Vienna" (Aktüel Haber 17 December 2004).

That was five years ago. The unknown name Alp Bora and his band Nim Sofyan have become a trademark in Vienna. In an interview in 2007 which we made for our project, he described what his musical style and the term 'world music' mean for him:

> "I don't know exactly what 'world music' means although I was put into that category. But if I think about it I would say that world music is music with ethnic influences. I can't say anything more about it."

A short quotation from the website of the band Nim Sofyan describes this strategy and their target group much better:

> "(...) electrifying music of the Balkans and Asia Minor, garnished with the most interesting elements of Mediterranean and Western European World Music, plus an occasional pinch of funk and jazz (...) their impressive performances untiringly tear down the artificial borders between orient and occident. The leader of the group, Alp Bora, with his seductive oriental-soul voice, who knows how to tattoo folk songs from Armenia to Macedonia into the listeners' souls" (http://www.nimsofyan.com, translation by Sağlam).

Cultural products in this field are primarily a fusion or melange of diverse cultural traditions and are mostly called World Music. They are mainly addressed towards educated members of the mainstream society. It is assumed that something new will emerge through the encounter between East and West, between

---

[11] Since 2003 the International Culture and Communication Centre (IKKZ) has organized the "World Music Awards" which take place at "Porgy and Bess", one of the most important jazz clubs in Vienna. In the course of time, the Austrian World Music Awards have become an important part of Viennese musical culture. The intention behind them was described in the following text issued via the media: "There should be a possibility in Austria to give an opportunity to musicians with different ethnic origins to present their work. At the same time, audiences should have the opportunity to get to know new sounds and artists. What we want is originality, innovation and respect and knowledge for traditions" (http://www.worldmusicawards.eu/).

something familiar and something foreign. As in the case of Nim Sofyan, their music has been presented not only as a fusion of different musical genres such as "funk" and "jazz", but also of two musical heritages: Anatolian and Central European, Balkan and Mediterranean and Western European (Parzer, Kwok 2009).

The consumers targeted are primarily upper class mainstream society (mostly Austrians) who have liberal views of the "otherness" of minorities and are willing to show their open-mindedness and interest in the "exotic"; they are the so-called "new bobos" (from the combination of "Bohemian" and "bourgeois"). Nevertheless, this strategy uses clichés to reach the interests of the majority. The "originality" and "otherness" of the music is no more than colour and excitement, or in the description of Parzer and Kwok (2009: 12) "superficial manifestations of culture" for the mainstream society. This kind of marketing can also be dangerous for the musicians. Emphasizing cultural differences through their music or through their marketing strategy can lead them to a dead end. Being perceived in a superficial way can cause misunderstandings. Emphasizing the differences between cultural groups can help to reconfirm prejudices.

3. Refusing ethnic coding (keyword: avoidance of exoticism): Here the labelling as "immigrants' music" and emphasising their "otherness through their ethnicity" is explicitly rejected. The ethnic codes may exist, but they are not in the foreground. They prefer to emphasize the individual musical language and the quality of the music and musicians. Ethnic categories play an insignificant role and have sometimes been rejected due to the potential danger of labelling. In the field of marketing, the emphasis lies on the genre and on the quality of products, not on the ethnic category. Several second generation DJs, jazz, classical and electronic musicians who grew up and were educated bi-musically do not want to single out only their cultural origin but also their fusion and individuality as artists.

An example of this is the band *Coup de Bam*. Two musicians from this group are originally from Turkey and the third one is from Croatia. All three of them have been living in Vienna since their childhood. The music of Coup de Bam can be defined as electronic music with an oriental touch. As a Turkish-Austrian collaboration, Coup de Bam was founded with the aim of "perfecting their vision of polyglot groove-pop music" (http://www.couchrecords.com). They describe their intentions as follows: "We didn't get together to make a good mix but to make good music. There is an authenticity which speaks for itself. Our music cannot be compared with Turkish folk music which is considered in Austria as such" (Wiener Zeitung, 14 January 2006, transl.: author). They want to avoid being considered exotic and refuse to be ethnically coded. Özden Öksüz, one of the musicians in this band, told me in our interviews:

> "The influence of a thousand and one cultures comes together. But nobody needs a photo of the darbuka and a photo of the 'guest musicians' to recognize them. We don't want to be considered ethno-kitsch. (...) I want to be judged simply by the music I make, regardless of where I come from (...)" (interview with Özden Öksüz, 2008).

Coup de Bam do not want to be labelled "exotic", "Turks" or "second-generation guest worker musicians", which would most probably bring them more carrier and financial benefits in the World Music scene. In CD shops, their album is to be found only in the World Music category. Being defined by an ethnicity to which they do not really belong is a form of misidentification on the part of the dominant culture and also indicates integration problems which have played a very important role in the musical life of the second generation in Vienna. They get into marketing difficulties when they present their product[12] in the category which they would choose themselves.

4. Multiculturalism as a marketing strategy (keyword: cultural diversity): Here entrepreneurs and musicians emphasize and mix different cultural identities. Some private music classes fit into this group. A part of the "World Music" scene on some international music festivals like *Salam.Orient* (http://www.salam-orient.at) and *Balkan Fever* (http://balkanfever.at), and part of the mainstream music scene use this marketing strategy. Understanding differences and similarities between the communities is the main goal of these activities.

Especially the two music festival organisers (for Balkan Fever: Richard Schuberth and for Salam.Orient: Norbert Ehrlich) are working very consciously on this problem. A quotation by the organiser of the Balkan Fever music festival summarizes their attitude as follows: "The music scene has changed very fast in this country, both positively and negatively, since the time we started our festival. What was considered to be exotic a few years ago has become normal and natural. (...) Stylistic diversity, trans-nationality and quality are important to us" (http://www.balkanfever.at). They emphasise the problematic aspects of ethnicity in their events. When they began, their musical activities were considered to be something exotic, but over time, and through their marketing strategies, this changed. They avoid presenting themselves as part of "the others" or "the foreigners", but as a part of Vienna. Using all four marketing strategies mentioned above, they emphasise the problematic aspects of being "ethnic", "exotic" or "other". They try to present the musicians through their individual, personal musical language and avoid presenting them as part of "the others" or "the for-

[12] In this context the term product means the music or the musical event.

eigners", but as part of a cosmopolitan world. It seems to be an adequate approach to present different musical identities in a cosmopolitan city like Vienna.

Conclusion

This study was to show the current situation of the marketing of immigrants and ethnicity in Vienna. Without considering its advantages and disadvantages, ethnicity has become a resource for the pursuit of profits in the immigrant cultural milieu. But their ethnicity has been understood differently by the immigrant communities and the dominant community. My analyses demonstrate the problematic aspect of ethnicity as a marketing tool. Superficial interpretations of the term ethnicity can lead to communication problems (which is the case with Coup de Bam).

Utilising ethnicity in marketing strategies is not a purely economic act; it also relates to political discourses such as the discourses of multiculturalism, as well as to political practices and the perceptions of the dominant culture of immigrants and the second generation. That is why it is very important to create a basis for intercultural communication. But if ethnicity is mixed with exotism, this communication cannot work.

I mentioned earlier that the representation of ethnicity is deeply influenced by the clichés of the dominant culture. Therefore the development of social networks between immigrants or the second generation and the dominant culture plays a central role in solving identification and marketing problems. "Ethnicity" as a marketing strategy serves on the one hand to create better marketing opportunities, but it also reaffirms and emphasizes ethnic codes (and prejudices) which were created and "believed" by the dominant culture. Rejecting ethnicity is a kind of reaction to ignorance of their culture. One of our interview partners expressed it as follows: "It is important just to be seen as part of the culture; people live here, of course they have their roots, but the important thing is the product they create."

Today in Vienna people come into contact with very different cultures and members of these cultures do not want to be defined from a Eurocentric point of view. Immigration and integration are two issues which one cannot separate. For integration one needs two groups to communicate. As Bauböck (2001: 14) wrote: "Integration is thus a process of reciprocal adjustment between the group already living in a place and the group settling there."

Literature

Baker, Michael 2008: The Strategic Marketing Plan Audit. Cambridge: Cambridge Strategy Publications.

Banton, Michael 2007: Weber on Ethnic Communities: A Critique. In: Nations and Nationalism 13, 1: 19–35.

Bauböck, Rainer 1995: The Integration of Immigrants. Wien, Institut für Höhere Studien 15.

Bauböck, Reiner, Patrik-Paul Volf 2001: Wege zur Integration - Was man gegen Diskriminierung und Fremdenfeindlichkeit tun kann. Klagenfurt: Drava.

Barth, Frederick 1969: Ethnic Groups and Boundaries: The Social Organisation of Culture Difference. London: Allen & Unwin.

Biffl, Gudrun 2002: Integration der Ausländer in den Arbeitmarkt. In: Gudrun Biffl (ed.), Arbeitsmarktrelevante Effekte der Ausländerintegration in Österreich. Vienna: Österreichisches Wirtschaftsforschungsinstitut, 243–280.

Brusila, Johannes 2003: "Local Music, not from here". The Discourse of World Music Examined Through Three Zimbabwean Case Studies: The Bhundu Boys, Virginia Mukwesha and Sunduza. Helsinki: Finnish Society for Ethnomusicology, Publicationa no. 10.

Cakir, Erkan 2004: Ethnische Ökonomie am Beispiel des türkischen Kleingewerbes in Wien. Vienna University of Economics and Business Administration, unpubl. MA thesis.

Cohen, Ronald 1978: Ethnicity: Problem and Focus in Anthropology. In: Annual Review of Anthropology (Stanford: Stanford UP) 7: 379–403.

Enzenhofer, Edith 2007: Ethnische Ökonomien - Bestand und Chancen für Wien. Report commissioned by the Vienna City Government and the Vienna Chamber of Commerce. Vienna: L&R Sozialforschung.

Fassmann, Heinz, Irene Stacher (eds.) 2003: Österreichischer Migrations- und Integrationsbericht. Demographische Entwicklungen - sozioökonomische Strukturen - rechtliche Rahmenbedingungen. Klagenfurt/Celovec: Drava.

Fassmann, Heinz (ed.) 2007: 2. Österreichischer Migrations- und Integrationsbericht 2001–2006: Rechtliche Rahmenbedingungen, demographische Entwicklungen, sozioökonomische Strukturen. Klagenfurt/Celovec: Drava.

Gächter, August 1998: Die Integration der niedergelassenen ausländischen Wohnbevölkerung in den Arbeitsmarkt. Vienna: Institute for Advanced Studies.

Gebesmair, Andreas (ed.) 2009: Randzonen der Kreativwirtschaft. Wien: LIT-Verlag.

Haberfellner, Regina 2000: Ethnische Ökonomien als Forschungsgegenstand der Sozialwissenschaften. In: SWS-Rundschau 40: 43–61.

Hemetek, Ursula 2006: Musical Practice of Immigrants from the former Yugoslavia and Turkey in Vienna I: Methodology, Concepts, Background, Structuring. In: Ursula Hemetek, Adelaida Reyes (eds.), Cultural Diversity in the Urban Area, Explorations in Urban Ethnomusicology. Vienna: IVE, 51–61 (= Klanglese 4).

Hemetek, Ursula (ed.) 1996: Echo der Vielfalt. Traditionelle Musik von Minderheiten, ethnischen Gruppen. Wien: Böhlau.

Hemetek, Ursula, Sofija Bajrektarević 2000: Bosnische Musik in Österreich. Vienna: IVE (= Klanglese 1).

Hemetek, Ursula, Hande Sağlam, Sofija Bajrektarević 2006: Einwanderer-Musikkulturen in Wien. Bestandsaufnahme zu musikalischer Identität und Akkulturation. Endbericht zum Projekt des Jubiläumsfond für die Österreichische Akademie der Wissenschaften, Vienna: Institut für Volksmusikforschung und Ethnomusikologie. Unpubl. manuscript.

Hemetek, Ursula, Adelaida Reyes (eds.) 2007: Cultural Diversity in the Urban Area. Vienna: IVE (= Klanglese 4).

Hemetek, U., H. Sağlam (eds.) 2008: Music from Turkey in the Diaspora. Vienna: IVE (= Klanglese 5).

Hemetek, U. and H. Sağlam 2009: Transformationsprozesse in und durch Einwanderer-Musikkulturen: Transkulturation und Rekontextualisierung am Beispiel von Musik aus der Türkei in Wien [Transculturation and Re-contextualisation Using the Example of Music from Turkey in Vienna]. In: Gebesmair, Andreas, Randzonen der Kreativwirtschaft [Boundary Zones of Creative Industries]. Wien: LIT-Verlag, 209–221.

Kwok, Kim 2009: Rechtliche Rahmenbedienungen migrantischer Kulturarbeit in Österreich [Legal framework of cultural work of immigrants in Austria]. In: Andreas Gebesmair (ed.), Randzonen der Kreativwirtschaft. Vienna: LIT-Verlag, 123–136.

Parzer, Michael, Kim Kwok 2009: Commodifying Differences: On the Use of "Ethnicity" in Immigrant Music Industries in Vienna. Unpubl. manuscript.

Pécoud, Antoine 2004: German Turkish Entrepreneurship and Economic Dimension of Multiculturalism. In: Migration between States and Markets. Oxford: Ashgate, 119–122.

Perchinig, Bernhard 2008: A Short History of Turkish Immigration to Central and Western Europe. In: Ursula Hemetek, Hande Sağlam (eds.), Music from Turkey in the Diaspora. Vienna: IVE, 11–21 (= Klanglese 5).

Sağlam, Hande 2008: Austrian "World Music" Awards, a New Marketing Opportunity for Immigrant Musicians in Vienna. Manuscript.

Sağlam, Hande 2008a: Music as a Cultural, Social and Religious Transmission Element among Alevis in Vienna. In: Rosemary Statelova, Angela

Rodel, Lozanka Peycheva, Ivanka Vlaeva, Ventsislav Dimov (eds.), The Human World and Musical Diversity. Sofia, 180–185 (= Bulgarian Musicology Studies).

Sağlam, Hande 2008b: Cosmopolitans and Locals – Music Production of the Turkish Diaspora in Vienna. In: Ursula Hemetek, Hande Sağlam (eds.), Music from Turkey in the Diaspora. Vienna: IVE, 37–48 (= Klanglese 5).

Schmid, Kurt 2006: Entrepreneurship von Personen mit Migrationshintergrund, Study Commissioned by AMS Österreich. Wien: ibw, KMU Forschung Austria.

Turino, Thomas 2003: Are We Global yet? Globalist Discourse, Cultural Formations and the Study of Zimbabwean Popular Music. In: British Journal of Ethnomusicology 12/ii: 51–79.

Wimmer, Andreas 2008: The Making and Unmaking of Ethnic Boundaries: A Multilevel Process Theory. In: American Journal of Sociology 113: 970–1022.

References on the Web

http://www.statistik.at/web_de/statistiken/bevoclkerung/bevoelkerungsstruktur (last accessed on 11/20/2009).

http://www.mdw.ac.at/mediacult/en/main.html (last accessed on 11/20/2009).

http://www.salam-orient.at (last accessed on 11/20/2009).

http://www.balkanfever.at (last accessed on 11/20/2009).

http://www.couchrecords.com (last accessed on 11/20/2009).

http://www.nimsofyan.com (last accessed on 11/10/2009).

http://www.guelay.com/ (last accessed on 11/20/2009).

http://www.worldmusicawards.eu/ (last accessed on 02/12/2010).

Migration, Ritual and Ethnic Conflict
A Study of Wedding Ceremonies of Albanian Transmigrants from the Republic of Macedonia

Robert Pichler, Graz

Abstract

Unlike many other rural milieus in the former socialist countries of Eastern Europe, Albanian villages in Western Macedonia experienced a boom of lavish wedding ceremonies in the aftermath of socialism. During six weeks in summer, when the bulk of transmigrants return from Western Europe or the United States to their home villages, costly wedding festivities are held daily in restaurants, which mushroomed in the last 15 years mainly to earn their money from these rituals. On the basis of a case study carried out in one of these villages, this article sheds light on the complex relationship between migration, nationalistic mobilisation, and the importance of rituals for social cohesion. I argue that the increase of lavish ceremonies during times of ethnic conflict can be attributed to the notions of social prestige, reciprocal obligations, and the imagination to maintain a localized (patriarchal) social order which is actually fading away as a consequence of migration.

Introduction

This article is part of a larger study that was guided by the broad question of the ways in which ordinary Albanian labour-migrants from a village in Western Macedonia have established networks between their village of origin and their places of destination, how they have managed to maintain these networks and which relations they have established towards wider communities, like the village, the nation, and the state.[1] Within the framework of this research project particular attention was given to communal rituals like weddings, betrothals, circumcisions and the Muslim festival of the Bairam. In the aftermath of socialism most of these rituals experienced a boom, particularly weddings and cir-

[1] The study was carried out within the research project "Networks of Identity. Labour-Migration and Long-Distance Nationalism among Albanians from Macedonia" that was funded by the Austrian Science Foundation (ASF).

cumcisions. During six weeks in summer, when the bulk of transmigrants[2] return from Western Europe and the United States to their home villages, costly wedding festivities are held daily in restaurants which mushroomed in the last 15 years mainly to earn their money with these rituals. On the basis of a case study carried out in one of these villages I want to shed light on the complex relationship between migration, nationalistic mobilisation, and the importance of rituals for social cohesion. I argue that the increase of lavish ceremonies during times of ethnic conflict can be attributed to the notions of social prestige, reciprocal obligations, and the imagination to maintain a localized (patriarchal) social order which is actually fading away as a consequence of migration.

In order to understand the motives behind the increase in ritual activities, one has to take a closer look at the social dynamics of interethnic relations during socialism and thereafter. Ethnic Macedonians and Albanians were differently affected by socialist modernisation and nation-building. I therefore provide in the first section an overview on some structurally decisive features of ethnically distinctive developments by placing them into their historical context. Veleshta/Velešta[3], the village under study, in many ways reflects the overall developments of the last fifty years in Albanian-inhabited rural areas of western Macedonia.

I. The village and its setting

Veleshta, a village located in the vicinity of Lake Ohrid is, like many other Albanian (and Slavic-speaking Muslim) inhabited villages in this area, very much affected by migration to "the West". Of its 5834 inhabitants[4] approximately 2700 are currently living abroad, the majority of them returning home only during summer. The greatest number of migrants from Veleshta went to Switzerland and to Austria, a substantial part to Germany, to the USA and to Swe-

---

[2] In accordance with Jasna Čapo Žmegač I use the term *transmigrants* in order to avoid the ambiguities in the word *transnational*. The prefix *trans* stresses the fact that migrants are constantly moving through space and across borders (Čapo Žmegač 2003: 131).

[3] Hereafter only the Albanian version Veleshta will be used.

[4] This is the official number of inhabitants according to the census taken in 2002 (Kaso 2005: 351).

den.[5] This migration process, which had its roots in the Yugoslav politics of the 1960s,[6] transformed the village as a whole.[7]

A closer look at migration flows suggests that more ethnic Albanians and Slavic-speaking Muslims from rural areas went abroad as labour-migrants than did ethnic Macedonians. This can be attributed to the state- and nation-building processes within the Socialist Republic of Macedonia which decisively contributed to the development of ethnically divergent migration patterns. The major difference is that ethnic Macedonians were much stronger affected by industrialisation and urbanisation from the 1950s onwards than the Albanians. This process ran hand in hand with enormous internal migration flows from rural areas to the cities and towns of the country. The majority of the Albanians, on the other hand, were only slightly affected by the modernisation politics of the Yugoslav state.

The reasons for these ethnically divergent migration patterns are complex and still a matter of dispute. While ethnic Macedonians claim that Albanians were reluctant to modernisation due to their low educational standards and strong Muslim influence in the villages, Albanians refer to a deliberate policy of ethnic marginalisation which left little room for their social integration. Although the arguments of both sides cannot be dismissed, a comprehensive explanation would require more historical complexity.

Brunnbauer claims that a specific ethnic division of labour was already established during the process of agricultural collectivisation in 1947–8. The collectivisation aimed at making agriculture more productive and to set people free for the ambitious industrialisation and modernisation of the country (Brunnbauer 2004: 580–581). Ethnic Macedonian peasants joined the agricultural cooperatives in greater numbers than Albanians, who tended to stay in their villages and stuck to small-scale agriculture (Bokovoy 1998: 120). This ethnic division of labour was further enhanced by the prevailing policies of Macedonian nation-building. In line with these policies, leading positions in state institutions, administration and government were predominantly filled with people who were supposed to define themselves as Macedonians. For the recruitment of industrial

5 According to a count of migrants from the village, which was taken in 1999, almost 40 % stay in Switzerland and 26 % in Austria, 15 % in Germany and 13 % in the USA. 5 % settled in Sweden (Qyra 2000: 217–233). I could not get the exact numbers for those who are currently living abroad, but a reasonable estimate would be 2700 people.

6 Unlike other villages in the vicinity, Veleshta had no pronounced tradition of labour-migration (pečalba/kurbet) due to its position in a fertile plain.

7 The flow of people, money and social remittances (ideas, norms, practices, and identities) within these spaces is so dense, thick and widespread that non-migrants lives are also transformed, even though they do not move.

labour, clientilistic networks based on ethnic affiliation played an important role as well (Pichler 2005: 84–85).

Apart from the fact that Albanians did not have equal opportunities to participate in the project of socialist modernisation, they were also less eager to become part of it. Along with this social reality and the accompanying attitude of those who were in power, there was a pronounced Albanian mistrust of all sorts of state intervention.[8] In part, this situation was a legacy of the interwar period,[9] but it was also a consequence of enduring anti-Albanian hostilities due to their collaboration with the Italian and German occupiers during World War II. Additionally, the impact of the Stalin-Tito breach with regard to Yugoslavia's relations with neighbouring Albania played an important role for the political degradation of the Albanians. Albania became, at least ideologically, one of the fiercest opponents of the Yugoslav regime after 1948.

Another important aspect which contributed to the marginalisation of the Albanians was their low educational standards. Albanian villagers had had no formal education in their mother tongue prior to World War II.[10] What is more, state education after liberation was often met with reservations in Albanian villages, also because parts of the Muslim clergy, who were influential among Albanians, regarded schools as a hostile element. However, with the communist regime coming into power, schooling became compulsory for children and adults alike, and Hoxhas were banned by law from providing religious instruction to children. As a consequence, the literacy rate among Albanians increased sharply in the 1950s and 60s, but it remained considerably lower than among ethnic Macedonians. This overall Macedonian trend is reflected on the village level, as the following table impressively indicates.

Veleshta		**Labunište**	
Female	Male	Female	Male
25,9 %	60,2 %	76,7 %	97,5 %

Table 1: Literacy rate among Albanians from Veleshta compared to ethnic Macedonians from Labunište in 1961 (Source: Census 1961 [Halpern Collection]).

[8] This, in fact, was not unique to Albanians. Mistrust of state intervention was widespread among peasants, particularly in mountainous areas with long tradition of local self-administration. However, with the socialist takeover of power, among Albanians cultural and political reservations predominated and created an atmosphere of mutual distrust.

[9] During the time of Serbian hegemony Albanians were exposed to systematic marginalisation (Schmitt 2008: 189–210).

[10] Between 1927 and 1928 only 7 565 Albanian students were registered in primary school from the whole of the Yugoslav Albanian population. The children in the Albanian inhabited villages of Macedonia attended the "mektep" at the village mosque where they were taught the Koran by the Hoxha (Muslim priest) (Grossmith 1977: 71).

The ethnic difference in reading and writing skills between Veleshta and the ethnic Macedonian village quarter in neighbouring Labunište was striking. In looking at different age-groups it emerged that illiteracy among Albanian women older than 25 years was almost 100 %. Among the male population, on the other hand, the percentage of illiteracy increased sharply at the age group of 45 to 49 years (60.3 %). In the age group of 60 to 64 years, 84.4 % of the males did not command reading and writing skills. This difference between the sexes indicates the restricted access of women to language courses offered by the socialist administration immediately after coming into power. In the ethnic Macedonian village-quarter of Labunište, on the other hand, all the women up to the age of 39 years were able to read and to write. In the age group 55 to 59 the illiteracy rate reached 50 % and even 33 % of those who were older than 80 years knew how to read and write. Among the male ethnic Macedonians of Labunište, literacy in all age groups was prevalent.

The structural educational disadvantage certainly played an important role for the Albanians' comparatively moderate social mobility. The Muslim and patriarchal milieu which dominated the Albanian villages in the first decades after World War II also left little room for female emancipation. While ethnic Macedonian households were exposed to rural-urban migration, resulting among other things in the weakening of patriarchal values and the increase of female employment, Albanian households remained stuck in the rural milieu with almost no female wage labour. The weak social integration among Albanians additionally favoured the preservation of tightly knit patriarchal kinship relations and conservative values. The household remained the main source of social security. Under these conditions early marriage patterns and high fertility rates persisted for the Albanians. Coupled with improving health and hygiene conditions, which contributed to lower rates of infant mortality and increasing life expectancy, the Albanians experienced a sharp population increase during socialist times. While the mean birth rate had begun to decline already in the 1950s among ethnic Macedonians, it remained on a much higher level and declined in a much slower pace among the Albanians during the course of the following decades (Brunnbauer 2005: 569–570). This nation-wide trend is reflected on the village level as the following data demonstrate.

	1953	1961	1971	1981	1994	2002
Veleshta	2304	2730	3355	4265	5034	5834
Vevčani	2541	2672	2438	2558	2438	2411
Jablanica	1267	1483	1385	1148	736	545

Table 2: Demographic development of selected villages in the Republic of Macedonia 1953-2002 (Source: Kaso 2005).

Between 1953 and 2002 Veleshta experienced a 150.8 % increase of its population. This can be attributed mainly to high fertility. The two neighbouring ethnic Macedonian villages Vevčani and Jablanica show different demographic trends. Vevčani, which is located in the hills north of the town of Struga, was among the most influential villages in the region with a strong sense of political autonomy[11] and influential links to the socialist government. Economically Vevčani was much better off than many of the surrounding villages. The demographic development thus was shaped by declining fertility and comparatively moderate emigration. The size of its population remained constant during communism and thereafter. In Jablanica, a village a little further up in the mountains, emigration intensified in the 1970s and together with decreasing fertility led to a dramatic depopulation of the village since the 1980s. Currently mainly old people are living in the village. Jablanica thus reflects a more general trend among Macedonian villages situated in the area around Struga.

The rapid demographic development and the difficult economic conditions were important reasons why Albanians seized the opportunity to leave as labour-migrants for Western Europe. As designed in the bilateral agreements between Yugoslavia and the host countries, labour migration was to be of a temporary nature only. But as it turned out, migration for many of these *Gastarbeiter* became a life-long move between two or even more states. For the first-generation migrants, who left alone and returned regularly once or twice a year, the village remained the centre of their longing and the idea to return always nurtured their imagination. The idea of returning home and settling permanently in the village was upheld even by those who followed their relatives and friends abroad in the 1970s and 1980s. Only in the course of the last 20 years has a structural shift of migration pattern from temporarily-designed male migration to emigration of entire nuclear families been taking place.

In political affairs, Albanians in Macedonia always looked towards Kosovo. With the Yugoslav Constitution of 1974, Kosovo's political status shifted to an "Autonomous Province" which gave Kosovo *de facto* (but not *de jure*) republican status. With this constitutional upgrading, Kosovo gained the right to regulate independently its social and economic affairs and its political bodies (Petritsch/Pichler 2005: 71–81). Almost all Albanian intellectuals from Macedonia had gained their academic degrees at the university of Prishtina/Priština, which was founded in 1970. There a well-connected pan-Albanian elite developed which

---

[11] When Yugoslavia was breaking up in 1991, the people of Vevčani voted in a referendum with 99 % for the "Independent Republic of Vevčani". It was the aim of the self-proclaimed country not to get involved into the turmoil of Yugoslavia's disintegration. Vevčani had its own flag, its own coat of arms, its own passport and its own money, the Ličnik (The New York Times 2002).

pushed for republican status for Kosovo and for the inclusion of Albanian inhabited areas in Macedonia (and Montenegro) into one "Albanian republic".[12] When such demands were expressed in demonstrations in Kosovo and Macedonia in 1981, the authorities quickly restored order at the cost of many injuries and several lives. After the 1981 demonstrations, which had come as a surprise to the political leadership, a campaign against any rising Albanian nationalism was set in motion and the Albanian movement was labelled "counter-revolutionary" and "irredentist". The Albanian leadership in Kosovo was blamed for not being strict enough in fighting nationalism.

In the Republic of Macedonia the reaction of the authorities was even harsher. The challenge to the territorial integrity of the Macedonian Republic had caused serious concerns from the political leadership. Meeting such demands would have endangered the very existence of the Republic. The authorities, thus, reacted fiercely against rising Albanian nationalism. Apart from severe observation and persecution of "nationalistic elements", the authorities aimed at counteracting the "cultural alienation" of the Albanians by intruding into their cultural spheres. A provision was aimed at curbing the high birth-rate of Albanians by cutting down on free medical treatment and social security services for families with more than two children. Additionally, a law was enacted that restricted the ongoing sale of land to Albanians (Poulton 2000: 126–127). In the area of Tetovo and Gostivar, the Macedonian police tore down the walls of big Albanian farmsteads in order to gain better control of the seemingly impermeable family-networks (Troebst 2001: 45). Additionally, measures were taken in the fields of education and culture that aimed at purging syllabuses, textbooks and folksongs of nationalistic content.

In the period of economic decline and the ensuing disintegration of Yugoslavia the ethnically distinct socio-economic developments contributed to increased tension in interethnic relations. While the former socialist industries had already begun to decline in the 1980s, the transformation to a market economy made the situation even more complicated. With the collapse of the Yugoslav market, international sanctions against Macedonia's most important trading partner, the Federal Republic of Yugoslavia, and a temporary trade embargo by Greece the economic situation was seriously aggravated. At the same time the public administration underwent painful adjustments. Increasing unemployment and a continuous decline of real salaries led to dramatically falling living standards and a loss of economic security. Ethnic Macedonians were much harder hit by this economic decline than Albanians, who were grossly under-represented in

---

12 In Belgrade the claim for republican status was portrayed as a separatist desire and contributed to the re-awakening of Serbian nationalism.

public employment.[13] Certain segments of the Albanian community were able to prosper in spite of their exclusion from the public economy by building a lively informal sector. Relying on remittances sent home by the large number of migrants abroad, Albanians took advantage of economic liberalisation to establish small private businesses (ESI 2002: 6–7).

With the escalating conflict in Kosovo the Albanian transmigrants from Macedonia became influential political actors as well. By forming cultural and political associations and pooling money in support of the Kosovo Liberation Army (KLA) the migrants' engagement shifted from the local to the national. Albanian migrants from Macedonia increasingly became integrated into the strong networks of the Kosovo Albanian Diaspora, which acted as a strategic force in the regional conflict. Inspired by the KLA's "successful campaign", a Macedonian Albanian rebel army appeared and started attacking Macedonian security forces in spring 2001. In the course of this military confrontation the National Liberation Army (NLA) occupied large areas in the north-western part of the country, which they declared as liberated territory. Only swift international intervention prevented the conflict from turning into a full-scale civil war. International mediators of the EU and the US finally brokered an agreement (the so-called Ohrid Framework Agreement) that urged the Republic of Macedonia's main political parties to accept a compromise.[14] For the ethnic Macedonians, whose national identity was already challenged by their neighbours,[15] this threat from the inside further enhanced their feelings of insecurity and uncertainty. The widespread opinion among ethnic Macedonians that Albanians are disloyal citizens who pursue their own agenda of separation instead of integration seemed confirmed by these developments. The divergent patterns of social and economic development further enhanced mutual distrust between the two ethnic communities. The expansion of Albanian settlements, the ongoing population increase and their seemingly isolated cultural development contributed to the increase of reservations and anxieties among ethnic Macedonians. In the cli-

[13] Albanians, who made up 22.7 % of the population in 1994, accounted for only 10.2 % of the overall state administration. A similar pattern was visible in the former state-owned enterprises (ESI 2002: 5).

[14] The Framework Agreement at first aimed at ending the violent conflict. Its main political agenda contained constitutional amendments and changes to the legislation which guaranteed a stronger representation of the minorities – particularly the Albanians – in public administration, security and economy.

[15] Bulgaria did not recognise the Macedonian language and the existence of a separate Macedonian nation, the Serbian Orthodox Church refused recognition of the Macedonian Orthodox Church, and Greece voiced strong opposition against the name of the new state and its symbols.

mate of rising nationalism, cultural differences mattered because of their proximate political impact.

II. Migration, ritual and ethnic conflict[16]

Keeping these macro-political developments in mind I now want to shift my attention to the production of locality in a deterritorialized social community. Following Appadurai, I see locality not as a given place, but as a property of social life and as a value which is realised by the village community in various ways (Appadurai 2005: 180). I argue that the increase of ritual activities during times of ethnic conflict is proof of the fact that locality needs to be emphasised in viewing a fragile social order which is jeopardised as a consequence of ethnonational strife and ongoing emigration. I thus want to look at the strategies applied by the majority of the community to produce local order under conditions of uncertainty and social disintegration. Rituals gain particular significance for a community in need of reliable compatriots and a pronounced moral security. Rituals serve the (re)production of virtual neighbourhoods in a milieu that is marked by social dispersal.

The Albanians in Veleshta constitute 46 patrilineal exogamous kinship groups *(fis)* which preferably practise village endogamy. I do not have accurate numbers for the actual situation, but from personal accounts and observations I conclude that the degree of village endogamy is similar to that of 1961. At that time, 82 % of the married women who lived in Veleshta were also born there.

Although they are primarily patrilineal and patrilocal, a wife's and mother's kin have an important role in a person's kinship network. The people from Veleshta held a taboo against marrying relatives within the ninth generation. The villagers' genealogical reckoning is primarily agnatic, which requires a good knowledge of the network of relatives. In theory the tendency of village endogamy supports such knowledge because people are related very closely to each other. Village endogamy thus creates a tight network of kinship relations between the various patri-groups which fosters the establishment of a particular village identity.[17]

---

[16] This part of the study is based on long-term, multi-sited ethnographic investigations, including participant observation, oral history and theme-guided interviews. The study was carried out during several longer field-trips to the village, mostly during summers, in the period between 2006 and 2009.

[17] Village endogamy as pronounced as in Veleshta is not the rule among Albanian villages in the area. The fact that Veleshta has a strong tendency towards marital relations within its

The ninth-generation taboo, however, is no longer enforced today. This fact is, among others, the result of migration, since many villagers, particularly those of the younger generation, have only a sketchy knowledge of their genealogies. As long as they live in the village they know about their first, second, and even third cousins, but those who have left the village early in their lives are no longer knowledgeable about their exact kinship relations. It therefore often happens that young people from Veleshta meet at village festivals abroad or during summer on the beach of Lake Ohrid without knowing that they are related to each other. As a consequence, the ninth-generation taboo has been loosened and been reduced to a three-generation taboo.

The loosening of strict exogamy rules reflects also the diminishing influence of elders in their children's choice of marriage partners. Although parents still are able to block the choice of their sons or daughters and they often try to interfere in these affairs, the marriage decision has increasingly become a matter of individual choice. Here it is interesting to note that girls became very active in the initiation of relationships and it is often their initiative which leads to marriage arrangements. These decisions, however, are taken within a certain framework of normative rules which relate to traditional habits as well as to actual circumstances. Apart from the fact that the choice of a spouse has to conform to the social hierarchy within the village, particular attention is paid to the continuity of the village community as a whole. This means that the rule of village endogamy should be respected and, if it can not be fulfilled, the spouse should come at least from a neighbouring Albanian village. Marriages with Albanians from other areas within the Republic of Macedonia, from Kosovo or from Albania are difficult to arrange and are, in fact, very rare. Marriage relations with Muslims from other ethnic communities in the area are exceptional and restrained to a small community of Muslim believers in the village[18]. Marriages with ethnic Macedonians are lacking. In Struga, a city ten kilometres from Veleshta, an ethnic Macedonian married an Albanian woman from a nearby village. This case is exceptional and was presented to me as a curiosity which is interesting, but not desirable.

So why do people who live in many different countries often far away from the home village still stick to the principle of village endogamy? What very often occupies the minds of the elders and what is very much a concern for them is that a son or daughter might fall in love with a foreigner. The reasons for this

own community is related to its size – the village is the biggest in the area –, its dominant economic position and its distinct local self-confidence.

[18] There is no precise information available about this, but according to rumours there are marital relations of these religious believers with spouses from neighbouring Slavic-speaking Muslim villages.

worry are manifold, but it is first of all the idea that the beloved child, as they say, "might get lost for us".

A young male student from Veleshta who lives with his family in Vienna, which I call M., gave me the following explanation:

> "I'm 22 now, I'm living here in Vienna, a metropolis by European standards, I'm studying law and enjoy student life very much, but my parents always voice their concerns that I'm still unmarried. My friends are mostly Turks and my parents fear I could fall in love with a Turkish girl. They are very much concerned that I might get lost to them if I marry a woman from another culture. They urge me to find a girl from Veleshta. This would be so easy for them. Although they will never return to the village to live there they behave as if Veleshta is still our homeland."

Asked about his personal opinion he explained to me that he would like to finish his studies first and only then think about getting married. This is also what his father prefers, but the women in his family, his mother and his aunts, all are

> "obsessed with the idea of my marriage ... One argument they often stress in order to convince me is the age of my grandparents. They are very old now and they should still be able to see my wedding. I cannot say that this argument leaves me untouched."

Asked if he considers marrying a girl from Veleshta he stated that he has no objections against this.

> "Why not?! If I find a girl from the village whom I like she will be my first choice. It is funny, and you won't believe it, but I feel very familiar with people from Veleshta. When I meet someone from the village here in Vienna or when I'm at home during summer, it is always very special. Maybe it is our language, the jokes we make and the stories we share. We are different; we are even different from Albanians in nearby villages. We are also very self-confident ..."

As can be seen from this account, the student's objections against marriage with a woman from his native village concerns only the time frame. He sees no reason to withdraw from this traditional habit; on the contrary, he has many arguments in favour of it. I give this example because it provides insight into a number of considerations related to marriage decisions and because it offers a widespread opinion, expressed by someone who is in the midst of his university education. His status is certainly an exception, since the majority of the young emigrants from Veleshta are workers.

Another encounter with a 42 year old Albanian man from Veleshta offers additional arguments for the continuation of intra-village marriages. The man, whom I met for the first time in 2004, left the village with his family in 1990. We talked about his daughter, who was an excellent student in high school and now studies economics at the University of Vienna. I asked G. how he would react if his daughter should decide to marry an Austrian man. G. ruled out this option categorically.

> "I'm convinced that this will not happen. My daughter loves me the way I love her. I taught her to respect our Albanian culture and a part of this culture concerns the continuation of our traditions. These traditions are very important for us, they helped us to survive the Slavic oppression and they keep us together. My daughter knows this and since she loves me she will respect this customs."

G. was very active during the time of military conflict in Kosovo and later on in Macedonia. He was decisively involved in the foundation of a village association in Vienna with the aim to collect money for the KLA. G's frame of mind is very much imbued with nationalistic fervour. Almost all conversation I had with him revolved around the Albanian question. He is obsessed by the idea to keep the Albanian nation clean of foreign elements. When we met a friend of his, one of the few Albanian intellectuals from Macedonia who lives in Vienna, he was always teasing him for having a French girl friend. "Are you going to become French when you marry her?" Another guy on the table next to us was labelled by him as "a half Czech" because he owns a house in the Czech Republic.

Although he always expressed these comments as a joke, they reveal substantial and serious ethno-national ways of thinking. For G. the Albanian nation is an extension of a kin group, a community of blood which is struggling its way out of a century-long period of oppression and neglect. Migration to Europe is thus regarded as a dangerous phenomenon because it takes people away from their country of origin and it might alienate them from their native culture. As a consequence, G. stated, "One has to do everything in one's power to keep the local community together. Marriage within our community is a very important way to reach this goal".

These two accounts offer distinct but interrelated explanations for the strong community feelings which tie people together who live dispersed across different places and have no regular contact with each other. While G., a second generation migrant, expresses a pronounced political interest when he talks about the future marriage partner of his daughter, the young student M. basically refers to the worries of his parents that he might get lost if he marries someone not originating from the village. M. also pointed to a cultural affinity with his people which obviously gives him a feeling of belonging to a deterritorialised local culture. G's account expresses a strong patriarchal position which leaves lit-

Picture 1: Hotel Exclusiv, one of the expensive places where wedding festivities are held during summer (photo taken by the author, 2008).

tle room to his daughter for any alternative decision. This interpretation seems descriptively accurate, since the few reported cases of "out-marriage" concern young man from the village who lived abroad for several years and who married a foreign woman. These men, who do not return to the village during summer, are regarded as "lost for the community". Such cases were not reported to me regarding females.

I now want to turn to the wedding ceremonies that take place during six weeks in summer when the bulk of transmigrants return from abroad to their home village. The weddings are performed as lavish festivities which are held daily in two hotels and a number of restaurants which have mushroomed in the last 15 years. The weddings are very costly. The most expensive part is the evening gathering in the restaurant where, according to the financial capacities of a family, between 300 and 500 guests are invited.

The restaurants charge between 10 and 13 Euro per person. Additional costs are for the music, mostly performed by professional bands from Albania, for the photographers and the filmmakers, for the cake, and sometimes for a stretch

Picture 2: Evening gathering in Hotel Diplomat (photo by the author, 2008).

limousine. All together, the family of the groom has to calculate between 8000 and 12000 Euro for this event. It is obvious that this cannot be managed with an average local monthly income of 250 Euro.[19] The costs for the bride's family, who gather with relatives and friends at home and prepare for the daughter's leaving of the household, also increased because many families transferred this event from their house to a restaurant where lunch is prepared and a band plays for the guests. Additional costs are for the *trousseau* which consists of a completely furnished room for the bride, gold jewellery, and the wedding dress, which can, all together, amount to 6000 Euro.

The performance of these festivities is an important public event in as much as it offers the respective families the opportunity to demonstrate their achievements. The number of guests invited, the number of expensive cars involved in

[19] Although I did not come across such cases, I know from personal accounts that there are costly weddings also among people who have no support from relatives abroad. Families go into debt for years to pay back a bank loan or money borrowed from friends or relatives.

Picture 3: The bride's room in the husband's house (photo by the author, 2009).

the procession to take the bride, the category of the restaurant for the evening gathering, all these are symbols that express the economic power of the respective family, something which easily translates into prestige and social status within the village community. Transmigrants, when they return to the village, wish to demonstrate that it was worth the effort to leave and they wish to underline that they still belong to this village community, although they are not living there any longer. Both the performance of these lavish festivities and village endogamy are manifestations of this position.

However, what seems to be solely an expression of a strong communal identity also provokes disapproval and even rejection from people who live permanently in the area. For many ethnic Macedonians, this "new wealth" of the Albanians appears primarily to be a result of their endemic criminality. This widely held perception offers a convenient explanation for the relative prosperity of parts of the Albanian community. Albanians, on the other hand, are eager to demonstrate their material achievements in public. Wedding ceremonies thus can turn into political events when processions of luxury cars drive through Macedonian-inhabited areas. With loud music, honking horns and the Albanian

Photo 4: As part of the rituals on the wedding day relatives of the groom go in a car convoy to the house of the bride to take her to her in-laws` house where she moves to after marriage. (photo by the author, 2008).

national flag being waved, these processions are expressions of strong national self-confidence. The public space thus becomes a stage where social polarization is expressed in ethnic categories.

But critics come also from the side of local Albanians who try to make a living in the area. The pastry maker, for instance, a young man from Struga, complains about the behaviour of the Albanians who return home during summer.

> "I can't understand them. Why do they return more primitive than they had been when they left? Why don't they bring culture from abroad?! Why only this luxury, these cars, these weddings? Is this everything they can show to us? They think that we, who stayed behind, are backward and ignorant about the world. But they are wrong! We understand more than they can imagine, and we also have culture here, even more than they understand. We are living here and we respect the rules, not like they do, they come back and disrespect all the rules."

The opinion of the pastry-maker expresses in a few sentences some often mentioned issues raised by critical Albanians who live in the area. But the young pastry-maker offers also an interesting interpretation for the behaviour of his co-patriots. He stated:

> "I've been in Padua, for a short visit only. I wanted to meet a friend of mine and there I've seen how our people behave when they are abroad. They work in the construction industry and live at the lowest stratum of society. They are occupied with work all the time. There they behave in a disciplined manner, but as soon as they return, they do what they want."

The pastry-maker refers to the fact that some of the returning migrants disrespect the rules and behave as if there were no limits.[20] He draws a sharp moral line between returning migrants and locals. In emphasising the moral dimension, he tries to avoid every form of humiliation or degradation with regard to his, in comparison, worse economic situation. He praises the local culture and even provides an explanation for the behaviour of his co-patriots. For him, the migrants only compensate for the social degradation and powerlessness to which capitalism relegated them. This example shows, however, that the wedding culture as a migrant import is not accepted univocally. The sharp economic differences between the home and the host country create also discrepancies and conflicts which indicate that the efforts to keep the dispersed ethnic community together faces limitations when social hierarchies are transformed to the disadvantage of those who stayed behind.

Conclusion

This case study of the Albanian village of Veleshta sheds light on the way migration contributes to the construction and imagination of locality. Migrants are moving regularly between places and form a trans-territorial ethnic network. The migrants are caught in an interdependent relationship between physical absence, imagined social adherence and the longing for home. Although the social network has virtually expanded into the world, the tendency towards village endogamy is still pronounced. Simultaneously, different tendencies can be observed. On the one hand, a loosening patriarchal order and a trend towards individualisation can be observed, but on the other hand, enormous material re-

[20] Complaints about migrants who disobey the speed limit, park their cars on the pavement, let their children command their cars, throw their rubbish out of the window, etc. are often made by people who live permanently in the village. However, also migrants often complain about the moral decay among young returnees.

sources are invested in rituals which underline a strong sense of communality and ethnic belonging. However, nationalistic mobilisation is only one component and certainly not the key to explain the enormous expenditures. Wedding festivities and other ritual activities go along with much costlier investments into new houses that have been built in the village in the course of the last twenty years (Pichler 2009). All these investments give evidence of a powerful imagination of home(land) that is expressed in various ways. The imagination of locality as a property of social life nurtures the desire to return into a seemingly reliable social milieu that has been endangered by the turbulences of migration and the ethnic conflict in the homeland. The production of locality is thus a reactionary retreat, filled with primordialistic ideas and expectations of an authentic, well structured, safe, and deeply-rooted existence.

Literature

Appadurai, Arjun 2005: Modernity at Large. Cultural Dimensions of Globalisation. Minneapolis: University of Minnesota Press.

Bokovoy, Melissa K. 1998: Politics and Ideology in the Yugoslav Countryside 1941–1953. Pittsburg: University of Pittsburgh Press.

Brunnbauer, Ulf 2004: Fertility, Families and Ethnic Conflict. Macedonians and Albanians in the Republic of Macedonia 1994–1999. In: Nationalities Papers 32, 3: 565–598.

Čapo Žmegač, Jasna 2003: Dva lokaliteta, dvije dra ave, dva doma: Transmigracija Hrvatskih ekonomskih migranata u Münchenu [Two localities, two states, two homelands: Transmigration of Croatian labour-migrants in Munich]. In: Narodna umjetnost 40, 2: 117–131.

European Stability Initiative (ESI) 2002: The other Macedonian Conflict (Discussion Paper). Skopje. URL: http://www.esiweb.org/index.php?lang=en&id=156&document_ID=32.

Grossmith, Christopher J. 1977: Marginality and Reproductive Behavior among the Albanian Minority in Yugoslav Macedonia. Chapel Hill, PhD thesis.

Kaso, Sherafedin S. 2005: Vendbanimet me popullsi muslimane në Maqedoni [Settlements with a Muslim population in Macedonia]. Skopje: Logos-A.

Petritsch, Wolfgang, Robert Pichler 2005: Kosovo – Kosova. Der lange Weg zum Frieden. Klagenfurt: Wieser.

Pichler, Robert 2009: Migration, Architecture and the Imagination of Home(land). In: Ulf Brunnbauer (ed.), Transnational Socities, Transterritorial Politics. Migrations in the (Post)Yugoslav Area. Munich: Oldenbourg: 213–236 (= Südosteuropäische Arbeiten 141).

Pichler, Robert 2005: Makedonien im Dilemma ethnisch divergierender Entwicklungsprozesse. In: Michael Daxner et. al. (ed.), Bilanz Balkan. Wien: Verlag für Geschichte und Politik: 68–100 (= Schriftenreihe des österreichischen Ost- und Südosteuropa-Instituts Band 30).

Poulton, Hugh 2000: Who are the Macedonians? Bloomington: Indiana University Press.

Qyra, Zejnulla 2000: Veleshta në histori [Veleshta in history]. Tirana: Edlor.

Schmitt, Oliver Jens 2008: Kosovo. Kurze Geschichte einer zentralbalkanischen Landschaft. Wien, Köln, Weimar: Böhlau.

Troebst, Stefan 1992: Makedonische Antworten auf die „Makedonische Frage" 1944–1992: Nationalismus, Republiksgründung, Nation-Building. In: Südosteuropa 41, 7-8: 423–442.

Press article

Macedonia tolerates a "republic" in its midst. In: The New York Times. 6 January 2002. URL: http://www.nytimes.com/2002/01/06/world/macedonia-tolerates-a-republic-in-its-midst.html.

Migrant Memories: German-Turkish Marriage Ceremonies in Berlin

Gülsüm Depeli, Ankara

Abstract

This article examines ritual practices in the wedding ceremonies of a migrant social group of German-Turks, living in Berlin. The field research was conducted from March to October 2007. Rituals are conceived as an externalized and materialized form of cultural memory, which can be defined as a "created shared past" settling on territorial, linguistic, religious and socio-historical collectivities. However, this paper's guiding concept is Assmann's "communicative memory" rather than "cultural memory" with its dynamic and process-related content.

The aim of this article is to examine the ritualistic activities of migrant communities in terms of the wedding ceremonies of German Turks, focussing on the relationship of ritual contents to social memory and belonging. Data are taken from my dissertation. The field research was conducted in Berlin from March to October 2007 and comprised interviews with people from the wedding sector (20), families (20) and young people (30). Additional information was gained from 15 wedding videotapes recorded between 1984 and 2007 and participant observations were carried out in 12 wedding ceremonies. Theoretically inspired by the claim of Morley and Robins that "identity is a question of memory, and memories of 'home' in particular" (2002: 91), this article draws attention to the "living memory" of the "migrant communities" through the example of the wedding ceremonies of German-Turks in Berlin, in order to examine the relationship between the memory, home and belonging.

After the fall of the Berlin Wall in 1989, the economic situation in Berlin changed. Factories closed and the industrial entrepreneurs' factories left the city for countries where labour was cheaper. The economic vision of the city shifted strongly to the direction of service industries. The large empty factory buildings became the place for ceremonial events, but since about 90 % of the business was for marriage parties, they became known as "wedding salons" and over a short time, these salons mushroomed on the periphery of the city.[1] The large physical capacity of these ex factories made them especially appropriate

[1] Interview with Ahmet Ersöz (30. 8. 2007).

for Turkish-style wedding ceremonies. Today there are more than 30 wedding salons in Berlin. In particular it is the lower class German-Turks[2] that choose them for their wedding ceremonies, and it is possible to see marriage ceremonies with over 1400 guests in these kinds of salons.[3]

The German-Turkish salon weddings in Berlin are analysed here in order to show links between cultural memory and ritual performances of the migrant communities. In this context, there are two main questions. First, what kind of culture-specific peculiarities exists in the marriage ceremonies of German-Turks in Berlin? To answer this, a description will be given of the structural change in the ritualistic order of wedding ceremonies of German-Turks in Berlin from 1980 to 2007. The second question concerns how cultural memory functions in these ritual practices of the migrant communities. In other words, how does memory act in this ritual process?

Ritual, communicative memory and cultural identity

Rituals have been conceptualized as explicit components of cultural memory.[4] Existing as externalized and impressive cultural performances and also aesthetically appreciated materializations, rituals comprise in themselves many material and symbolic forms through which can be traced the processing of cultural memory. In addition, Geertz points to the exhibition nature of rituals, which also includes drama, "not as merely a spectacle to be watched but as a ritual to be enacted" (1973: 112–116). Similarly, Rothenbuhler (1998) emphasizes the communicative, performing and playful aspects of rituals. Therefore, ritual processes embody a fusion of the "world as lived" and the "world as imagined" (1973: 112).

Moreover, marked as *rites of passages*[5], ritual activities are considered to be guarantors of the social order, functioning as a way of conveying the self-approval and the self-image of cultural identity (Kansteiner 2002: 182). In this regard, Baumann gives an interesting example by claiming that when the Jews

[2] The German-Turkish migrants in Berlin generally come from East and Southeast Anatolia and the Black Sea region in Turkey. Thus, the migrant community is composed of economically, ethnically and religiously disadvantaged, lower class people, including Kurds, Turks, Sunni Moslems and Alevis (Interview with Kenan Kolat, 2. 6. 2007).

[3] This research field is concerned with "salon ceremonies"; however, there are hotel, restaurant and religious weddings (in the mosque), which are outside of the scope of this article.

[4] Assmann 2001, Halbwachs 1992: 54–84, Baumann 1999: 120–135, Appadurai 1996.

[5] See van Gennep 1909.

danced around the Golden Calf[6] they were in fact dancing around their collective identity. That is, through rituals the social groups transmit collective messages to themselves (1999: 129).

Before focussing on ritual contents of German-Turkish weddings, it is necessary to describe the concept of cultural memory. Assmann used the term cultural memory explicitly and put forward an analytical description of the concept in which he divided social memory into two categories: "communicative memory" and "cultural memory" as shown in Table 1 below.

Memory	Communicative Memory	Cultural Memory
Content	Personal biographies in context of historical experiences	Mythical history of origins or of non-reachable past.
Form	Non-official, semi-structured, natural, develops during daily communicative interchange	Planned, very well structured, ritualistic communication, for ex; religious festivals.
Means	Living reminiscences in actual organic memory, narrations of the narrated.	Clear objectification, traditional symbolic codification via words, images, dances etc.
Structure of time	Between 80–100 years, in contact with the present, time period framed with 3 or 4 generations.	Absolute past, a mythical past tense form.
Transporters	Unclear, witnesses of a remembering group.	Professionalized transporters/ mediators of traditions.

Table 1: Assman's division and description of cultural memory[7].

In the research which this article describes, the "communicative memory", in other words the "memory peculiar to generation" (Assmann 2001: 54) is limited to a life-span of 80–100 years, covering a maximum of four generations. This category shows cultural transfer in process, where the old and young generations act together. Although the older generations have more influence on the transmission of the cultural remembrances in the social group, it is hard to neglect the effects of spontaneous improvisations (Assmann 2001: 56–60), through which

[6] According to the Hebrew Bible, the golden calf was an idol (a cult image) made by Aaron to satisfy the Israelites during Moses' absence, when he went to Mount Sinai.

[7] Assman's schema (2001: 59) translated by the author from the turkish version of the book.

the boundaries of the generational hierarchies are blurred. Thus, in this process, learning, acquiring and practising are realized simultaneously.

In contrast to communicative memory, "cultural memory" is the category which embeds "culture as body". Cultural memory, socially institutionalized by definite rules, boundaries and actors, is something above living personalities. It is the memory of the collective, which existed before individuals were born, and will continue to exist after they die (2001: 54). Assmann places national, religious, and ethnic festivals and celebrations in this category as the characteristic indicators of cultural identity.

With regard to Assmann's categories, it is important to indicate that the focus of this article is positioned exactly within the category of communicative memory, because the ritualistic activities which are under the heading of cultural memory are also practised within this ambivalent communicative part of the memory. Thus, in Halbwachs' words, "while the collective memory endures and draws strength from its base in a coherent body of people, it is individuals as group members who remember" (Coser 1992: 22, from Halbwachs 1950: 48). In the process of realization of this cultural memory, which has a constructed and materialized nature, Halbwachs mentions the importance of the support of a group, which has recollections of a collective past to remember and is delimited in space and time. In this context, he suggests the terms of home and family, which have a direct relation to marriage as a social institution, to localize cultural memory.

In the global era of dislocating experiences neither home nor family can be considered to be in a stable position. Yet at the same time, paradoxically, the importance of the desire to be at "home" has been gaining ground in today's new and disorienting global space (Morley, Robins 2002: 87). Especially in the case of migrant communities, Morley and Robins claim that "the continuity of the identity is broken, too" (2002: 87). Supporting this idea of a "broken identity", Hall proposes a theoretical perspective to consider cultural identities as "non-unified, fragmented and fractured constructions, which are constructed multiply across different, often intersecting and antagonistic discourses, practices and positions" (1996: 4). In this complex process of "becoming" (rather than being) there appears a new acknowledged aspect, that is the imagination defined as a "property of collectives" (Appadurai 1996: 8). In this sense, Appadurai concentrates on the migrant social groups, which comprise an actual form of 'community of sentiments' via the new media technologies. In particular, his emphasis is on the evident circulations of mass mediated images, scripts, and narratives, which also play a part in the ritualistic practices of migrant communities as components of both memory and desire (1996: 4–9).

Looking at the working mechanism of memory can also be helpful for considering the peculiarities of remembering. Conceiving memory as a "plurality of interrelated functions" instead of being just storage enables us to see how memory continues to live in changing cultural selves and spatio-temporal conjunctures. According to Jedlowski,

> What we call "memory" is a complex network of activities, the study of which indicates that the past never remains "one and the same", but is constantly selected, filtered and restructured in terms set by the questions and necessities of the present. (...) Philosophically speaking, what we call "memory" can be described as the field of a complex temporal dialectic: while on the one hand the flow of life over time entails effects that condition the future, on the other it is the present that shapes the past, ordering, reconstructing and interpreting its legacy, with expectations and hopes also helping to select what best serves the future (2001: 30).

Considering the spontaneous aspects influencing the process of remembering, it should be kept in mind that emotions, connotations, narrative discourses, and idiosyncratic realities are also put into use simultaneously. In short, remembering becomes real at the point of intersection of variable reflections, which include the spontaneous actualisations and modifications of the recollections.

The anchoring of memory to communication and cultural identity (Assmann 2001: 51–69, Jedlowski 2001: 29–44, Hall 1996: 1–17), to home, family (Halbwachs 1992), and to the imagination (Appadurai 1996: 1–23) are summarized in Morley and Robins' claim that we can find our key concepts, memory, identity and home, in a well coordinated manner: "Identity is a question of memory, and memories of 'home' in particular" (2002: 91). In this article the relationship between memory, home and belonging is questioned through the "living memory" of the changing migrant communities of the global world, using the example of the wedding ceremonies of German-Turks in Berlin.

Marriage as embodying the above-mentioned characteristics of ritual activities exemplifies one of the main *rites of passage* in the lives of people, by transforming ordinary acquaintances to kin (Halbwachs 1992: 57). In Turkey as in many other countries the phrase "it is not the individuals, but the families who marry" is commonly heard.[8] So the participation of a large number of guests at a wedding serves to witness and approve the marriage of a couple and unites the families. Additionally, the number of guests in a wedding signifies the quality of the solidarity of the group and serves as evidence of the prestige and honour of the couples' parents. In order to maintain and share this prestige within their solidarity group, the parents take all of the responsibility to ensure the collective harmony in the salon. The food, music, dance and decoration which are chosen

[8] For an anthropological description on Turkish weddings see Schiffauer (1987).

by parents and marrying couples demonstrate the quality[9] of the wedding party and to celebrate the collectivity of the social group present at the wedding.

Considering this process in the context of German-Turkish social groups, the religious, regional, customary and traditional activities, material and symbolic contents of the marriage ceremonies, which have transferred from the past and from Turkey to Germany, the process of this transference, including the remembrances and re-inventions, will be described in the following sections in relation to the wedding ceremonies in Berlin. Before describing the history of the wedding ceremonies of German-Turks in Berlin, however, the socio-economic background of weddings in the Turkish community in Germany is presented.

Socio-economic background of Turkish marriage ceremonies in Germany

The official labour migration from Turkey to Germany began in 1961.[10] In their excellent book *Arbeitsemigranten*, Berger and Mohr (1976) tell the story of this migration through the metaphor of the "naked man", based on the idea that when the migrants were told to take off their clothes for the medical inspection they also removed their identities. Migrating mostly as single persons in the 1960s, when they crossed the border from Turkey their family, history, territory, national and cultural bounds were left behind in the spatio-temporal past. In this sense, a migrant was not Turkish, Kurdish, Alevi, or a Sunni Muslim anymore. Since the "family unit" was split, even his/her culturally bounded social role as a parent was also partly damaged. They would not be able to act as members of their "family units" until they returned to Turkey. Accordingly, in the host country, they did not live in homes but in a "heim" (dormitory).

These first migrants to Germany were just mechanical parts of a big industrial machine until the 1970s. For a long time, the Turkish community was forgotten in all kinds of cultural, political and economic "rights" and "representation" struggles. Even the leftist labour union pretended not to see them as the subjects of economic exploitation (Berger, Mohr 1976: 145). However, in the

[9] Quality does not refer to any professional criterion or competence here. The most important aspect is to meet the musical, customary, aesthetic expectations of the cultural group. For instance, in the 1980s the presence of a musician was more important than his/her musical competence.

[10] Until the second half of the 1960s, emigrants from Turkey to Germany were economically motivated. In the course of time, according to the political chaos in Turkey, some ethnic and religious groups, especially from poor regions were selected by the Turkish government to be sent to Germany. Moreover, the 1980 military coup forced a large number of people to leave Turkey, and this dramatically changed the emigration characteristics (see Abadan-Unat 2009, Wilpert, Gitmez 1987: 86–125).

early 1970s the migrants' situation changed. 1973 was the year of the oil crisis and marked the end of the active recruitment stage of migration history all over Europe. Accordingly, Turkish migrants in Germany had to decide whether to settle down in the host country or return to their homeland. Those who decided to settle in Germany brought their family members there under the terms of the Family Reunification Arrangement. As a result, the lives of the German-Turks changed from being single people living in dormitories to living in small family units. In those years, the Kreuzberg district next to the Berlin Wall, with its cheap, almost ruined apartments, became the German-Turkish enclave.

Despite the apparent end of recruitment, migration continued but in the form of family reunifications and marriage migrations. After the 1980 military coup in Turkey the nature of migration changed again because of the illegal and asylum migrations. All of these changes created a heterogeneous migrant profile. With new socio-economic and cultural motivations in the migrant society, infrastructural development began to materialize in the beginning of the 1980s. The first evidence was seen in the food market (Wilpert, Gitmez 1987: 99–105), with the opening of Turkish restaurants and grocery stores. At the same time, culture-specific entertainments began to appear in Berlin, and Turkish cafes and casinos opened in Kreuzberg.

The big "Turkish Bazaar" near *Bülowstraße,* created by first generation migrant entrepreneurs, has become an important place for German-Turks with its musicians, music and video film stores, restaurants, casinos and even belly dancers *(dansöz)*. Duru (2003: 230–231) mentions that in the 1980s there was a sign in the subway on which was written "Zum türkischen Basar" (to the Turkish Bazaar). It was to this bazaar that the first generation of German-Turkish men, the main wedding organizers in those years, came to buy food, find musicians and belly dancers and the like for their wedding ceremonies.[11]

The first wedding ceremonies began to be held at the end of the 1970s in family houses, some German pubs *(Kneipen)* and the salon of the hippodrome. In one of the video recordings from 1984, it is observed that the wedding was made in a factory hall.[12] In the early years the absence of infrastructure and professional support meant that the German-Turkish families arranged everything concerned with the wedding, even providing the chairs and tables to furnish the empty rented salon. The need for a specific, a special place for wedding parties became evident and towards the end of the 1980s the first real wedding salons, managed by German-Turk owners, appeared in Kreuz-Kölln.[13] These salons,

---

[11] Interview with Muharrem Doğan (2. 8. 2007).

[12] Video recording of F. T. and H. T. (1984). The interviews were coded using initials to protect the participants' privacy.

[13] The short name of the two urban quarters of "Kreuzberg and Neu-Kölln".

Burcu Düğün Salonu (Kreuzberg), *Gelin Düğün Salonu* (Neukölln), and *Körfez Düğün Salonu* appear to have been opened by semi-sectoral trade groups, especially by caterers and musicians from the Turkish Bazaar. Until 1989 there were no more than four wedding salons. However, some years after the fall of the Berlin Wall the number of these salons increased rapidly, occupying buildings in the city periphery and thus the wedding salons spread from Kreuzberg to the whole city.

Since the Second World War Berlin was supported economically by state subventions, and this continued after the fall of the Berlin Wall. However, in the middle of the 1990s this economic support ceased and Berlin, now lacking industrial enterprises, had to develop its service sector.[14] Obviously, the niche economies of German-Turk enclaves were not unaffected. In 1997, the number of wedding salons reached 17[15] and the secondary-sector like musicians (including religious song groups), photography and video stores, jewellery, trousseau and bridal wear shops expanded rapidly. The number of wedding salons slowly increased to 25 in 2007[16] and the secondary sector enterprises also expanded.

Historical description of marriage rituals of German-Turks in Berlin

Although the German-Turks have been arranging their wedding ceremonies in Berlin since the late 1970s, in the early years most of the community preferred to have their wedding ceremonies in Turkey so they could invite many more immediate and distant family friends and old neighbours. Those who decided to marry in Berlin had to rely on their "solidarity networks", in the 1970s defined almost solely by "being a migrant". In other words, the regional, religious, ethnic or kinship nuances had still not appeared as identity marking aspects. Thus, until the end of the 1980s the guest profile in weddings included people from different regions of Turkey, and Italians, Iranians, Yugoslavs, Greek migrants, and also a few Germans. In fact, the language of the announcements in the wedding was in both Turkish and German, and the structure of the wedding celebration was somewhat different in Berlin from what it would have been back in Turkey.

In wedding parties until the beginning of the 1980s there was not a full sit-down meal, but rather snacks such as nuts, sunflower seed, chickpeas were offered, and because of the lack of local sources these items were brought from

[14] Interview with Ahmet Ersöz (30. 8. 2007).

[15] Türkisches Branchenbuch 1997. Berlin: Concept Verlag.

[16] Türkisches Branchenbuch 2007. Berlin: Concept Verlag.

Turkey by individuals.[17] In wedding photographs and videos from the 1980s one can see chicken and salad or döner and salad on the tables, but no forks or knives or table napkins.[18]

Furthermore, the wedding cake, a vital ingredient of a wedding reception nowadays, did not yet exist in most German-Turkish weddings. Only in one video from 1988 do we see a small homemade cake, which was brought to the salon in the hands of a dancing woman, probably a relative of the bride. After a brief hesitation about what to do with this cake, she put it on the table of the couple[19] and there it remained until the end of the wedding, untouched.

The German-Turks had not discovered the economic advantages of transnational shopping in the 1980s. For example, they used to buy or rent the wedding dress in Germany at high cost. However, since the second half of the 1990s German-Turks bought the wedding dress, invitation cards and the gold jewellery in Turkey at relatively lower prices.

Observing the ritual practices in the weddings, it is possible to see that not only the suppliers but also the people were inexperienced. Celebrating together in urban and foreign environments, much less holding a public wedding, was a new experience. Therefore, until the second half of the 1990s, it was usual for various reasons to witness big quarrels in weddings;[20] sometimes because of the belly dancer, sometimes because of a problem between the families or because of a missed ritual practice. Furthermore, it was difficult to celebrate loudly until midnight in those years, because the wedding salons were located in city neighbourhoods and the police often warned the wedding celebrants about being too noisy.[21]

The ritual content of weddings was not very well known to the majority of the first generation migrant men. They tried to follow the correct ritual order by calling upon their remembrances of past marriage customs and traditions from their hometowns in Turkey. There were many questions about procedure, such as: How should the bride and groom enter the salon? Should the couple enter the salon before the drum and horn *(davul-zurna)* or after them? Should the face of the bride be veiled or not? Should the henna tray be turned around above the

---

17 Interview with Me. T. and Mu. T. (21. 8. 2007).

18 Video recording of Me. T. and Mu. T. (1988).

19 Video recording of Me. T. and Mu. T. (1988).

20 Interviews with L. T. and N. T. (2. 8. 2007); A. Tu. and B. Tu. (14. 10. 2007); Au. A. and K. A. (8. 8. 2007).

21 Interview with Muharrem Doğan (2. 8. 2007).

heads of marrying pairs before praying or after? Moreover, how many times should it be turned around?[22]

The performative content in wedding videos indicates that people were continuously remembering, relearning, constructing and inventing the ceremonial structure. In other words, as part of a natural "memory act", all was functioning at the same time. In those years, perhaps because they were unsure and confused about the ritual rules, on the photographs people looked serious rather than happy. Even the dances were enacted slowly and with a dignified expression. Furthermore, people did not dress up to attend the wedding. The music also was not chosen to entertain and create a joyous mood. Until the mid-1990s the music in weddings mostly consisted of sad and nostalgic folk songs.[23]

In the mid-1990s, chain-migration continued steadily, and there was a significant increase in the number of the German-Turkish population. In particular, the younger generation was gradually entering social life and for many young people who were between 1 and 15 years old during the Family Reunification in the 1970s, marriage was already on the agenda. The wedding ceremonies continued in a more or less similar way to those of the 1980s and the beginning of the 1990s. Over the years certain aspects of the wedding became regularised and the most important episodes of wedding preparations and ceremony were seen to be:

- Henna night (at home before the wedding).
- The bride and groom processing to the front of the gathering (in the salon).
- The gift ceremony (in the salon).

However, this plain ceremonial order changed, becoming much more complex and enriched in the following years, and ethnic-specific local nuances in customs and traditions became part of marriage practices. Since the middle of the 1990s two main elements appeared as determining actors of the coming transformations in the ritual contents of the weddings: the wedding services sector and the younger generation. In those years, the generational separation became visible. The young became "popular music" consumers of music transmitted from Turkey to Germany via international media technologies. As Greve (2003: 138–139) describes,

> The main innovation of the 1990s was the emergence of a Turkish youth culture. Musically, this new form was brought to the fore by some performers in the late 1980s. (...) Pop music was the first form of music in

[22] In the wedding video of S. V. and Y. V. (1990), a quarrel because of the ritual order was observed. At one point a man furiously pulled the veil off the bride, which made the bride cry. Fortunately, they did not dwell on the subject for long, and continued to dance.

[23] Interview with Ozan Ali Gürsoy (7. 9. 2007).

> Turkey, which was almost only listened to by a limited age group; namely the youth. (...) Until the 1980s, Turkish parents and adolescents essentially listened to the same music. For adolescents, there was no specific dress style and no typical youth language, a basic rebellion against the parents overall did not take place ...[24]

Related to this significant distinction between the generations, the wedding sector also experienced an explicit change, re-adapting itself to the new socio-cultural conditions by acquiring a new social role in the wedding ceremonies. At the end of the 1990s, this service sector positioned itself between the first and the second generation as an active conveyor of marriage traditions and customs, and salon managers began to serve as wedding consultants.[25] Thus, there was an intervention by the wedding service sector in memory transfer between the generations about the ritual order in wedding ceremonies. It can be said that the second generation voluntarily handed the task of organizing weddings to this commercial sector.[26] By "consulting" the community about the ceremonial content of weddings, the entrepreneurs put forward a standardized wedding programme with a fixed budget which included music, food and decorating accessories.

This kind of small sector formation, which Bourdieu termed "cultural intermediaries" in a capitalist economy (2002: 360), have always to be alert to the social changes. They arise from socio-cultural needs and are shaped by social life. By the same token, the commercial sector also shapes socio-cultural life in order to achieve the goal of maximizing its own interests. Thus, the wedding sector could not be indifferent to the younger generation gaining prominence in the early years of the twenty-first century.

Interestingly, in those years, the economic motive of the wedding sector was divided in two. Those who paid the money were the parents. However, the younger generation was the main target and the consumers who valued the entertaining elements of the wedding reception more than the first and second generations. Hence, even the ritual aspects gained an entertaining and spectacular quality in this period, with some of the venues changing their name from "wedding salon" to "event centre".[27]

The entertainment and consumer oriented wedding sector has been recalling some material objects from the cultural past since the second half of nineties.

---

[24] Translated from the German by the author.

[25] Interview with Ideal Event Centre (16. 6. 2007), Prestige Festsaal (2. 5. 2007), Festsaal Kotbusser (10. 4. 2007).

[26] Almost all the second generation families who were interviewed appreciated the role of the wedding sector because it released them from the burden of organizing the weddings.

[27] Such as: Ideal Event Centre, Gloria Event Centre, Neue Welt Event Centre, Royal Event Centre, Events 4 Stars (Türkisches Branchenbuch 2007: 137, 147).

For instance, nowadays, traditional clothing and accessories frequently appear in wedding ceremonies; these items include caftans, the Ottoman fez, regional ethnic garments, traditional house slippers, umbrellas, water pipes and the like. It is possible to see Kurdish or Turkish flags, hear ethnic music, or even observe representatives of political associations in wedding ceremonies as identity marking aspects of the social groups.[28] Even those involved in the wedding sector who had a strong nationalist bias during the interviews welcomed the appearance of these multicultural aspects.

There have been other reinventions, not only in the material content, but also in customary, musical and ritualistic arrangements. As expected, the commercial sector has been decisive in shaping the content of weddings by rearranging the ritualistic order. The actual ritualistic practices are stylized and new ritualistic and entertainment stages are invented. In the more recent wedding events, the main programme is as follows.[29]

- Henna night (two days before, in the salon),
- engaging in a spectacular motorcade round Kreuzberg,
- entrance of the bride and groom to the salon,
- first dance,
- dance competition between bride and groom,[30]
- binding the red strap of the bride (symbol of virginity),
- the gift ceremony,
- cutting the wedding cake,
- farewell of bride and groom for honeymoon (the couple are filmed/photographed saying good-bye).

Today, the standardised wedding ceremonies in Berlin encompass almost all the cultural plurality of Turkey, including Kurdish, Turkish and Alevi music, some local-specific customs and dance styles. Interestingly, while stressing these ethnic and religious local appearances in the weddings in Berlin, none of the interviewed families or the people from the wedding sector referred to wedding ceremonies in their hometowns. In other words, "traditional" and "customary" content was present in form in the Berlin weddings, but they did not comment on where this content originated. Speaking within a competitive rhetoric, they

---

[28] The Kurdish Red Crescent "Heyva Sor" participated in two weddings (Şato Eğlence Salonu – 27. 4. 2007; Gloria Event Centre 4. 5. 2007), Turkish Flag seen in two weddings (Ideal Event Centre – 17. 6. 2007; Prestige Festsaal 18. 5. 2007), an official speech held by the president of a hometown association in a wedding (Ideal Event Centre – 9. 9. 2007).

[29] This sequence is given according to the field notes of participant observations between May – October 2007.

[30] In this amusing show, the bride and groom perform a dance separately, adjudicated by the musician; the winner is the member of the couple who gets the most applause.

compared their weddings in Berlin with those in Istanbul, Izmir or Antalya, the major cities in Turkey.

The participation of the younger generation is generally encouraged and appreciated by the grandparents. The young guests try to maintain the collective harmony in the wedding event by adjusting their behaviour in accordance with the rules of the older generation; they take part in traditional dances voluntarily, are mostly careful about not smoking or having alcoholic drinks within sight, show respect to the older guests by kissing hands and chatting with them about school or family issues etc.[31]

As noted before, the younger generation's impact is especially noticeable in the choice of music at the wedding receptions. Turkish pop music is played, although the youngsters listen to some special ethnic dance music and participate in traditional dances like *Çepki* and *Horon*. With the shift from the old towards new music styles and repertoires, also the dances *(halay)* are changed. In comparison to the traditional dances of the 1980s, today they dance in a much more dynamic way. Dances are hybridized with figures of pop music, rap, hip-hop and some other musical inputs. To meet the expectations of the younger consumers, salon managers have installed dance-floors with special stage lighting systems.

The tendency towards entertainment rather than ceremonial content brought with it some new entertainment, such as a cooking demonstration,[32] stand-up performances and releasing doves in the wedding salon. Since 2005, the commercial sector functions almost as a dream factory by exploiting and manipulating the material aspects of the cultural memory of the German-Turkish social groups, and their impact on communicative memory is noteworthy. In one wedding you can see the bride and groom in Ottoman clothing, in another the bride wears a copy of Lady Diana's wedding dress. It is possible to witness a wedding ceremony where the couple enters the salon on horseback "just like ancient Turks"[33]. However, luxurious limousines are also offered by the wedding sector. During the field research a salon manager explained that he was trying to complete the last official procedures for the bride and groom to come to the salon by helicopter.

Photography and filming have been part of wedding ceremonies since the end of the 1970s, but by the beginning of the 21st century the arrival of new

---

[31] Field notes from a wedding (April 2007 – Neue Welt Event Centre) and a Henna Night (10. 5. 2007 – Melodie Festsaal).

[32] In a wedding in Villa Müzikhol (April 2007), a chef prepared a special Chinese dish for the couple in front of the guests. As instructed by the salon manager, he turned this into a show by playing with the spectacular flames coming from the plate.

[33] This term is used by the Interviewee P. D. (Interview with P. D. and E. Ç. 20. 7. 2007).

electronic media and the Internet have brought new ways to add to the spectacle. Big screens on the walls of the salons were used to display the actual wedding event and also videos/photos of the couple and their families. The wedding can also be broadcast live via Internet, thus enabling family and friends who are far away to join in the celebrations. At the same time the people enjoy watching themselves while performing and acting in the wedding ritual. For the migrant social groups, the effect of watching themselves can be interpreted as the rehabilitation of self-approval and as marking cultural identity.[34] The spectacular nature of these modern wedding events can be summed up as the appearance of enthusiastically self-displaying and transnationalized collective identity practices.

Conclusion: building bridges between micro description and macro conceptions

In this article, rituals are considered as the material, externalized forms of cultural memory. The research concerning the German-Turks in Berlin explored the transfers of customary and traditional contents of wedding celebrations between generations and the reproductions in their socially acquired practices. The aim has been to make visible the relationship between collective ritual activities and cultural memory.

Regarding the changing content of the celebrations, the increasing role of commercial sector entrepreneurs and the development of electronic media have been among the most significant factors in transnationalizing the material, psychological, representative and imaginative aspects of cultural identities. It should also be kept in mind that all three generations of Turkish migrants still meet in the wedding celebrations. Thus, the cultural memory of the German-Turkish social group in Berlin is steadily being formed in a communicative and multilayered spatio-temporal manner.

The ceremonial texture, which is enacted by the first generation migrants, commercial enterprises and the younger generation, is not merely imported from past stored memory. On the contrary, it is produced and reproduced actively in the present, in other words, in the process of communicative memory, which is determined as being unclear and unreliable by Assmann (2001: 54–60). References to the past, the socio-economical conditions of the present and future-oriented imaginations about marriage are all in juxtaposition in the symbolic and material components of current ceremonial practices of the weddings.

[34] For research concerning the functions of watching old video recordings by the women of migrant communities see Koltyk 1993: 435–449.

In this respect, the migrants keep the customs of the ceremonial contents of marriage ceremonies alive while reproducing their content via remembrances, repetitions and imitations. At the same time, recalling Jedlowski's claim, this ritual content has been interpreted and changed steadily according to the "field of temporal dialectic" (2001: 30), in which the new actors, here the young generation, the commercial sector and the power of imagination as a daily activity, play an important role.

Another important point is the association of the wedding ceremonies to home and memory. As mentioned above, the marriage ceremonies in Berlin include many local or regional aspects imported from Turkey, in regard to language, customs and music. However, in comparison with the wedding ceremonies in the large cities of Turkey, those in Berlin have their own peculiarities. First, the ceremonial content of weddings in Berlin is strongly hybridized and they have become extravagant events, which is not seen in salon weddings in Turkey. Although the customary and traditional practices of wedding ceremonies are very much appreciated, the references to their meanings or origins are not linked to the hometowns. Thus, in terms of Halbwachs work on the connection of memory and locality, it is interesting to consider what the term 'home' means for the German-Turks.

Today, the transnational route and life spheres in which the German-Turks travel include mostly the large cities of Germany with higher German-Turkish populations (Berlin, Munich, Stuttgart, Cologne) and the large, especially touristic cities of Turkey. Even though specific homelands live in the imaginations and in self-realizing identity practices in a remarkable way by making use of many material aspects and symbolic meanings transported from the short-past and historical past, discourses on wedding ceremonies in the field reveal that they reflect mostly the general sphere and travel route. With the contribution of the electronic media, transportation opportunities for relevantly cheaper prices and the commercial entrepreneurs' manipulations of material aspects of cultural life, "home" is not far away any more, which had been the source of homesickness. The migrants can find in Berlin almost everything they had in their hometowns in Turkey. In this sense, it can be said that "nostalgia" has disappeared. However, the participation of the younger generation in the collective wedding celebration activities and their general motivation in displaying their cultural identity appears to be evidence of the continuing existence of a homeland in remembrances, in the imagination. Most of the young people who were interviewed defined themselves as being both from Berlin and from their hometowns in Turkey. They possess identity defining aspects from both places and this is evident in their hybridized, multidimensional performances in the wedding celebrations.

Literature

Abadan-Unat, Nermin 2009: Turks in Europe, 1957–2007: From Guestworker to Transnational Citizen. New York: Berghahn Books.

Assmann, Jan 2001: Kültürel Bellek [Cultural Identity]. Transl. by Ayşe Tekin. Istanbul: Ayrıntı.

Appadurai, Arjun 1996: Modernity at Large. Chicago: University of Chicago Press.

Baumann, Gerd 1999: The Multicultural Riddle: Rethinking National, Ethnic and Religious Identities. New Work, London: Routledge.

Berger, John, Jean Mohr 1976: Arbeitsemigranten: Erfahrungen, Bilder, Analysen. Transl. by Nils Lindquist. Hamburg: Rowohlt.

Bourdieu, Pierre 2002: Distinction: A Social Critique of the Judgement of Taste. Transl. by Richard Nice. Massachusetts: Harvard University Press.

Coser, Lewis 1992: Introduction: Maurice Halbwachs 1877–1945. In: Levis A. Coser (ed.), On Collective Memory. Chicago: University of Chicago Press, 1–34.

Depeli, Gülsüm 2009: Almanyalı Türklerde Evlilik Törenlerinin Dönüşümü: Kültürel Bellek, Kimlik ve Aidiyet [The transformation of the marriage ceremonies of German-Turks: Cultural memory, identity and belonging]. Ankara: Ankara University, Sosyal Bilimler Enstitüsü (unpubl. PhD thesis).

Duru, Sezer 2003: Berlin Berlin. In: Gültekin E. (ed.), Türk Edebiyatında Berlin. [Berlin in Turkish Literature] Istanbul: YKY, 228–235.

Geertz, Clifford 2000: The Interpretation of Cultures. NY: Basic Books.

Greve, Martin 2003: Die Musik der imaginären Türkei: Musik und Musikleben im Kontext der Migration aus der Türkei in Deutschland. Stuttgart: Metzler.

Hall, Stuart 1996: Introduction: Who Needs Identity? In: S. Hall, P. du Gay (eds.), Questions of Cultural Identity. London: Sage, 1–17.

Halbwachs, Maurice 1992: On Collective Memory. Chicago: University of Chicago Press.

Jedlowski, Paolo 2001: Memory and Sociology: Themes and Issues. In: Time and society 10, 1: 29–44.

Kansteiner, Wulf 2002: Finding Meaning in Memory: A Methodologic Critique of Collective Memory Studies. In: History and Theory 41: 179–197.

Koltyk, Jo Ann 1993: Telling Narratives Through Home Videos: Hmong Refugees and Self Documentation of Life in the Old and New Country. In: The Journal of American Folklore 106, no. 422: 435–449.

Morley, David, Kevin Robins 2002: Spaces of Identity: Global Media, Electronic Landscapes and Cultural Boundaries. London, New York: Routledge.

Rothenbuhler, Eric W. 1998: Ritual Communication: From Everyday Conversation to Mediated Ceremony. Thousand Oaks, CA: Sage.

Schiffauer, Werner 1987: Die Bauern von Subay: Das Leben in einem türkischen Dorf. Stuttgart: Klett-Cotta.

Türkisches Branchenbuch, Berlin-Brandenburg 1997–2007. Berlin: Concept Verlag.

Van Gennep, Arnold 1909: The Rites of Passage. Chicago: University of Chicago Press.

Wilpert, Czerina, Ali Gitmez 1987: A Micro-Society or an Ethnic Community? Social Organization and Ethnicity amongst Turkish Migrants in Berlin. In: J. Rex, D. Joly, C. Wilpert (eds.), Immigrant Associations in Europe. Aldershot: Gower, 86–125.

Field References

Interviews with

Ahmet Ersöz (30. 8. 2007 – Member of "Turkisch-Deutsche Unternehmervereinigung Berlin-Brandenburg" [Association of Turkish-German Entrepreneurs of Berlin-Brandenburg].

Kenan Kolat (2. 6. 2007 – Head of "Türkische Gemeinde Deutschland" [Turkish-German Community in Germany].

Muharrem Doğan (2. 8. 2007, Father of L. T.).

Ali Gürsoy (7. 9. 2007, Musician).

Me. T. and Mu. T. (21. 8. 2007).

L. T. and N. T. (2. 8. 2007).

A. Tu. and B. Tu. (14. 10. 2007).

Au. A. and K. A. (8. 8. 2007).

Ideal Event Centre (16. 6. 2007).

Prestige Festsaal (2. 5. 2007).

Festsaal Kotbusser (10. 4. 2007).

P. D. and E. Ç. (20. 7. 2007).

Fieldnotes of participant observations in weddings and Henna nights in

Şato Eğlence Salonu (27. 4. 2007).

Gloria Event (4. 5. 2007).

Ideal Event Center (17. 6. 2007).

Prestige Festsaal (18. 5. 2007).

Ideal Event Center (9. 9. 2007).

Neue Welt Event Centre (April 2007).

Melodi Festsaal (10. 5. 2007).

Villa Müzikhol (April 2007).

Video recordings of
F. T. and H. T. (1984).
Me. T. and Mu. T. (1988).
S. V. and Z. V. (1990).

Food and Migration: The Case of Bulgarians in Munich

Evgenia Krăsteva-Blagoeva, Sofia

Abstract

This article considers the transformation of migrants' food tastes in the context of their integration into the host society. Fieldwork with several groups of first generation Bulgarian migrants was conducted in Munich. Because of the emotional, sensory and mnemonic effects of the consumption of native food, bringing food items from Bulgaria appeared crucial for immigrants' nutritional practices. Different levels of preservation and transformation of the "original Bulgarian taste" were shown, depending primarily on the social and marital status of the immigrants. The great importance of ritual food and the role of cuisine as a signifier of origin and identity are clearly shown in the text. The conscious treating of foreign guests to Bulgarian dishes reflects the capacities of food as an instrument of self revelation (deliberate or even involuntary). Differences between Bulgarian and German attitudes towards cooking and eating result in an active cultural exchange, in which Germans borrow much more Bulgarian food items and nutritional practices than vice versa.

It is well known that food habits are deeply embedded in the personalities of individuals; they are stable and long lasting. Perceptions of what is tasty and what is not are culturally determined. Despite being conservative and long lasting, food practices are also subject to change (Opare-Obisaw et al. 2000: 145). The reasons for changes are to be found in processes of cultural globalization and the resulting homogenization of food. Migration also causes inevitable changes in food practices. Immigrants, especially those of the first generation, experience transitional cultural dilemmas of resistance and change (Koc, Welsh 2001: 3). Different stages and levels of enculturation, assimilation and integration in the host society are reflected in the fluidity of immigrants' cultural identity. Food changes among them also may be viewed as an example of cultural diffusion or borrowings of elements from a foreign culture. New eating habits, new behaviours, new experiences and tastes of the immigrants are due not only to their cultural and spacial transition, but are deeply influenced by cultural globalization as well. And because globalization presupposes hybridization (Pieterse 1995), their food practices (like their culture as a whole) are more or less being hybridized – they are a specific mixture of "native" dishes and "foreign" borrowings (in our case most of them are not German, but Italian, French, etc.).

Food choices are no longer limited to the social and cultural contexts of either the home country or the host country (Bouchet 1995, Cook, Crank 1996).

Yet first generation migrants are frequently very resistant to dietary change. According to Bourdieu's *habitus* theory, this resistance is due to the fact that individual taste is a result of the *initial capital* of a person, which includes factors such as one's social status in the past, family, ancestors and the like. Habitus is an orientation towards certain tastes, which is inherited, long lasting and sometimes even unconscious – it stems from the family context and it is not subject to change even in case of social (and presumably spacial) individual mobility (Bourdieu 1990: 130–131). Another explanation is found in the so-called "principle of incorporation": because food is being absorbed, it crosses the border between the "outside" and the "inside", so it touches upon the very nature of a person. This is the reason why some migrants retain certain food habits when language and other cultural expressions tend to be forgotten (Fischler 1988: 275, Scholliers 2001: 8). Using Fernandez' concept of "returning to the whole" (Fernandez 1986), David Sutton acknowledges that through food the past is embodied into the present – "the memory of taste and smell leads to the *emotional* effect and the sense of *emotional/embodied plenitude*" (Sutton 2001: 82). Food, memory and the construction of identities are strongly interconnected. Food has certain mnemonic qualities – it evokes memories of time, place and belonging (Kravva 2001: 141). Eating could be seen as a "sensory point of entry into a web of sentiments, memories and fantasies, which largely constitute the sense of identity" (Goddard 1996: 213).

In this context, the main aim of my research among the Bulgarians in Munich was not simply to trace changes in their food practices, but to examine the way their taste is being transformed. Having in mind classical concepts of food as signifier, classifier and identity builder (Bourdieu 1984, Levi Strauss 1997, Douglas 1999), I was interested in the relation between this alteration of taste and transformations of their individual and collective identity. As we shall see below, Ferda Erdinc's statement that "Taste memory travels with you in such a way that awareness of it is usually discovered in the absence of that taste in real life" (Erdinc 2001: 93) is valid for many immigrants, too.

My research among Bulgarian immigrants in Munich consisted of 25 semi structured in-depth interviews with people who migrated to Germany in different periods of time.[1] Two of them are old people, who "escaped" from communist Bulgaria in the 1960s and 70s. Thirteen are students or recently graduated

[1] The fieldwork was done in January – February 2008 during my visit as an Erasmus teacher in the Institute für Volkskunde/European Ethnology, Ludwig-Maximilians-University Munich. I want to thank Profs. Klaus and Juliana Roth for their help and support.

young people working in Germany; four are middle-aged women with successful careers. Members of the staff of a Bulgarian restaurant, visitors to the Bulgarian church and the Bulgarian priest in Munich were also interviewed. All the respondents are first generation migrants, except for one, who was born in Germany in the family of a German father and Bulgarian mother. Some indirect data about the children of the respondents (representatives of the second generation migrants, most born in Germany or living there since childhood) were also collected. My concentration was on the first generation migrants, who according to anthropological literature were expected to stick to their native dishes and flavours or to experience different stages of hybridization in terms of food. As a rule their children, the second generation, are the ones to import the food practices of the dominant culture into their homes (Fischler 1993: 103, Levenstein 1997: 469). As we shall see below, neither of these two "rules" proved absolutely applicable to the case of Bulgarians in Munich.

"Returning to the whole" via food

According to data for the 2004–2005 academic year, the number of Bulgarian students in Germany (12456) is the highest of all students from Europe; on a world scale it concedes the first rank only to the number of Chinese students (Liakova 2008: 46). There is an inner differentiation within this group. The students who came earlier – in the early 1990s, when there was no established Bulgarian student community in Germany – are more open to the host society. There is a clear tendency of ethnic closing among those who came in the last three or four years, when such a community had already been institutionalized (Liakova 2008: 56). The "isolationists" do not wish to have any contacts with Germans and segregate themselves within the boundary of their Bulgarian circle. As a group, most of them perceive Germany as a country for making money and they do not plan to live there long. Those who came earlier are willing to be integrated into German society, some of them have married Germans, they have started successful careers and most of them are planning to live in Germany in the future. This differentiation among the Bulgarian students and young people who have already graduated from German universities is a rough starting point for examining their eating habits. In accordance with expectations, the "isolationists" tend to cook predominantly Bulgarian dishes, they do not wish even to taste any German meals because they are convinced not only that Bulgarian cuisine is the most tasty, but that even the dishes of exquisite restaurants are not good. Here is part of the interview with a young girl working in such a restaurant with a group of Bulgarian colleagues:

> "It is a very expensive restaurant, their dishes are quite exquisite and it was very interesting for me to taste some of them. All the other Bulgarian students working there were always spitting at the dishes, saying 'Oh, have you tried that, its disgusting; who is this cook, let him come and try my wife's moussaka in order to understand what a real meal is'."[2]

Food conservatism of these young people is similar to that of one of the oldest respondents. He came to Germany in 1977 and for all these years he did not like even one German meal, at all:

> "Nothing of their food is tasty, absolutely nothing. My mother used to cook predominantly vegetarian dishes and this is what I ate my whole life. I tried almost nothing of German cuisine. In German restaurants I order only vegetarian garnishes such as potatoes. I ate beans yesterday and the day before yesterday and I have some beans left for today and tomorrow."[3]

He himself is not able to answer the question why such monotony is not boring for him. This is an example of the cultural, habitual and archetypal nature of taste as something not constructed or figured out, but deeply coded in the very essence of self.

Those students who are more "open" towards the host society also share the idea of the "superior Bulgarian taste", but they have experienced more or less significant taste transformations. Many of them declare that after coming to Germany their diet became more varied and healthier, with less fat. For some students the level of food security (defined as access by all people to safe and adequate food – Campbell et al. 1988) has increased. Although they consider local fruits and vegetables tasteless, they are more accessible to them than in Bulgaria.[4] In Germany they tried for the first time such exotic fruits as mango, papaya and the like, which in Bulgaria were too expensive for them. The cultural shock of the initial enculturation was combined with the fact that for the first time in their lives some of these young people were supposed to cook for themselves. In Bulgaria cooking was their mothers' task. So, in the beginning (for a period of several months to one year) they used to live on French fries, spaghetti and more simple Bulgarian meals, constantly asking their mothers on the phone how

---

[2] Informant V. M., born 1982 in Sofia. She lives in Germany since 2002 and recently married a German.

[3] Informant G. M, born 1923 in the town of Lukovit. He has no wife to cook for him, but even when he was married to a Bulgarian woman he ate almost the same. From all the respondents he is the only one to remember the first Bulgarian restaurant in Munich.

[4] Informant I. B., born 1986 in the village of Dorkovo, student.

exactly to cook them. In the course of time they started borrowing recipes from their fellow students, but mainly Italian, Chinese etc., and a considerable variety appeared in their meals. For them Bulgarian cuisine is a good option among many others. Some cases of slow acceptance of German food products, initially considered not tasty, were registered. For example, when given for the first time a drink of apple juice and carbonated water, a young girl thought "how disgusting it is" and now, a few years later, she even likes it and drinks it regularly.[5] "Weißwurst", the typical Bavarian sausage, is still not accepted by many Bulgarians. On the whole, after a certain period of time (which differs among individuals), immigrants start eating German food due to new habits they acquire. Yet all of them are more or less nutritionally homesick. They miss certain food items and associate the image of their home country with the smell and the taste of baked peppers, salads and cheese, traditional pastry and other favourite products and dishes. Sutton calls this "burning desire that is satiated through a sensory experience, evoking local knowledge" (Sutton 2001: 81).

In comparison with other immigrant communities, for which accessibility but not availability of native food items was the major concern (because of the distance, time and price paid for accessing these items – Koc, Welsh 2001: 8), in my sample availability is the bigger problem. Compared with Bulgarian products, the local ones are considered inferior in terms of taste: although native recipes are followed, the dishes are quite different from their Bulgarian equivalents.[6] Nevertheless, respondents of all groups try to adjust local culinary context to their flavour and to recreate the original Bulgarian taste they like best Because it is expensive and time consuming, some people cook this way only when they have enough time – once or twice a month. Many others, belonging to different groups, stick to the Bulgarian cooking "because this is the best for me", or "out of habit, not because I am insisting my cooking must be exactly Bulgarian".

The adjustment to "Bulgarian taste" is sought in two main ways. The first is to stick to original recipes and try to find local substitutes for the ingredients. The best cooks (two middle aged women with Bulgarian husbands and successful careers in Germany) compensate for the "tastelessness" of German products by using Bulgarian spices. Some of these species are brought from Bulgaria, because local ones are considered no good. The second way of adjusting local food to the Bulgarian taste is to improvise and to prepare international meals which taste Bulgarian. In this case informants follow their basic ideas about what suits

---

[5] Informant N. O., born 1986 in the village of Lesidren.

[6] Such a tendency of hyperbolization of tasteful native products is typical for other migrant groups too (Sutton 2001: 79).

what, i. e., what spices and dressings to use in order to achieve a certain effect. Such an approach is more creative and more unusual: "I am always changing something in the recipe, but its core is always Bulgarian, I want it to be so."[7] The first way is more direct and widespread – immigrants seek suitable products in German shops in order to prepare their native meals. This task is time-consuming, difficult, expensive and sometimes simply impossible, because the taste of German ingredients is quite different. Local vegetables and fruits, even the so-called bio products (which are more expensive) are not accepted at all. They are considered tasteless, artificial, "plastic". This is especially true for tomatoes.[8] All the respondents claim that they deeply miss tasty Bulgarian tomatoes:

> "It is absolutely impossible to find decent tomatoes here, the only ones which partially resemble our tomatoes are the Sicilian ones – they cost 10 euro per kilo. They only look like ours in shape and you imagine how it is supposed to be in terms of taste and you buy them, you make a compromise with yourself."[9]

Looking for the "original taste", various food items are bought from Balkan shops, where they are more expensive – white cheese from the Greeks, lamb from the Turks, vegetables and fruits from both types of shops. When one of the respondents went to buy cheese in a Greek shop and the shopkeeper started telling her how delicious this cheese was, she told him: "Please, don't explain this to me, I am Bulgarian." After a short pause he said: "It is as good as yours."[10] What is illuminating in this example is that he did not dare say "It is better than yours". Very rarely and for a short time some original Bulgarian vegetables appear in the big supermarkets and women are constantly checking what is available. They share information about where to go in order to find the most suitable products. Providing them is a very important task. Some of the narratives of seeking the most appropriate food items resemble quite a lot the discourses about searching for scarce products in the time of socialism. Shopping in Greek and Turkish shops is more expensive, so it is not accessible to everyone. Students prefer supermarkets because of the lower prices; but almost all the women with decent jobs and relatively good social status, who are able to afford shopping in Balkan shops, tend to buy there regularly.

---

[7] Informant I. N, born 1970.

[8] The qualities of Bulgarian tomatoes were acknowledged by many foreigners, too. Some of them, like Prof. Peter Black, for example (see footnote 31), even consider them best in the world, an assertion that might be resisted in other parts of the Balkans.

[9] Informant A. R., born 1958.

[10] Informant K. G., born 1975 in Sofia, living in Germany since 1995, married to a German.

Food migration

Because of the difficulty of finding suitable substitutes, a considerable number of foodstuffs are imported from Bulgaria by people travelling with regular busses from Sofia to Munich. There is no limitation to the weight of the luggage as on aeroplanes, but passengers are allowed to have only one bag for free, so this bag is deliberately chosen to be as big as possible.

> "This bag is, as my mother says, as big as an elephant's penis and it is full of food. Many times they stopped me at the borders and wanted to see what was inside. They were shocked and asked 'Are you going to open a storehouse?' It was a big shame, because I was carrying food not only for me, but also for my sister. For each of us – three big tin cans of cheese, six pieces of yellow cheese, all kinds of salami and traditional sausages and many jars with baked peppers, lyutenitsa[11] etc. – and you need three people to carry this bag."[12]

Not all the respondents were so lucky in transferring food. For example, some bus drivers established their own rules about how many pieces of cheese, yellow cheese, sausages and the like were to be taken in a bag. Exceeding their authority, they examined luggage and even sometimes just threw away products. In spite of all these problems, people still carry food items. Even sauerkraut is regularly carried by Bulgarian passengers, although Germany is famous for its sauerkraut. German sauerkraut is not considered good at all. It is too stiff, with vinegar, and it is cut into pieces, which is why it is not suitable for preparation for Bulgarian style stuffed cabbage leaves *(sărmi)*. Some respondents have tried several times to produce their own sauerkraut with no success,[13] maybe because of the lack of certain bacteria in Germany, the local sort obviously is quite different.

In the period before 2001, when the regulations for aeroplane safety were not so strict, the quantity of transferred food was even bigger. There are data on carrying half a pig, bred by grandparents in a village; of a whole lamb or of a handbag full of peppers. Nowadays carrying food is so widespread that many people usually travel by bus precisely for this reason. Aeroplane passengers usually put well wrapped up sausages or bottles of brandy between the clothes in their valises. It is worth noting that carrying foodstuff is typical of people of different social status, even members of higher classes. More differences in terms of class

---

[11] Lyutenitsa *(ljutenica)* is a traditional puree made of baked peppers and tomatoes.

[12] Informant K. G., born 1975 in Sofia, married to a German.

[13] Only one man with great culinary and gardening capacities managed to make his own sauerkraut, and the reason for his success remains a secret.

were registered in cooking. The most striking example of how important original food items are for Bulgarians is the case of a young girl studying in Munich whose parents work in Spain. She goes to Spain more frequently than to Bulgaria and her mother supplies her with sheets of the traditional homemade pastry *banica*. According to respondents, substitutes for these pastry leaves cannot be found in Germany. Many people use Greek ones, which are as thin as Bulgarian ones; Turkish ones are thicker, but they are also used when there is no other option. When going to Bulgaria, the mother provides herself with pastry leaves and keeps half of them for several months in Spain in order to give them to her daughter in Germany. Thus a food migration that follows the twists of human migration was registered. In Sutton's words "eating food from home becomes a particularly marked cultural site for the re-imagining of 'worlds' displaced in space and/or in time" (Sutton 2001: 84).

For many respondents the desire for native products diminishes over time. In the first years after their arrival to Germany, because of the process of adaptation, they felt the lack of their home cuisine more: „In time, sooner or later you give up and start cooking with local products."[14] The scope of transferred food products is diminishing and only the most important of them remain: some spices, cheese and pastry sheets, some traditional meat products and brandy. The high value of the pastry is found not only in its taste, but also in its capacity to fit all kinds of occasions.[15] The pastry is highly appreciated even by the respondent who has the strongest orientation towards integration into the host society. He is 27 years old and already has a decent job. He believes that integration has to be quick and easy, which is why he has deliberately rejected Bulgarian food and is the only one to declare that he likes and values German cuisine. The only thing which is "really Bulgarian" according to him is pastry, and he makes it himself on calendar feasts, following the tradition.[16]

The gradual diminishing of quantities of food items brought from Bulgaria is due not only to adaptation processes but also to the fact that the quality of Bulgarian provisions is deteriorating. During the socialist period there was no variety of foodstuffs, but most food products were considered good and it was much easier to judge and to choose a high quality product. With the industrialization and marketization of food production after 1989 there came a great variety of

---

[14] Informant I. G., born 1964, living in Germany since 1992.

[15] "It is festive and daily, it is suitable for breakfast, for dinner, for supper. I have treated so many people to *banica*, so many Germans – all of them like it very much" (Informant I. N, born 1970).

[16] Informant N. G., born 1981. What is interesting in his case is the fact that although he wants to "forget about Bulgaria" he is among the leading figures in the Bulgarian church in Munich.

products, and the choice is now much more difficult. As a whole, food quality in terms of taste has deteriorated. This was one of the expected results of the country's access to the EU – in the popular discourse the expectation that "when we become members they will make us produce their tasteless vegetables" was commonly heard.

> "Now you don't know what is good – during socialism there was one type of goat cheese – you take it and you know that this is a goat cheese. Now there are so many types of cheese that you really don't know which is the right one. Sometimes more expensive food is good, but not always – sometimes you can give big money for nothing."[17]

The problem with the Bulgarian production is its unpredictability. Usually a new trademark appears on the market with good quality, but after a short period of time, when people have started acknowledging it as good, it suddenly changes and becomes really bad. This is due to the lack of efficient state control and the wish of producers to make quick and big money by saving on raw materials or on technology. For example, the tasteful tomatoes migrants are longing for disappeared from the local Bulgarian market in the last two years because farmers are economizing on water, so tomatoes cannot grow red. That is why Bulgaria is importing tomatoes from other countries, mainly from Turkey. Being accustomed to the predictability and sustained quality of German products, immigrants are often annoyed and disappointed by the fact that they make such efforts in carrying products so far which finally turn out to be of poor quality: "In Bulgaria you never know what is inside the packing. I was cheated so many times when I brought expensive things here with incredible efforts and found out that they were bullshit and I had to throw them away."[18] But the same happens with the official export of Bulgarian production. For example, German firms importing Bulgarian wine prefer the white wines, because the percentage of low quality among them is lower. The problem with Bulgarian red wines (which are more famous in Europe) is that there are big differences between the shipments of one and the same trademark.[19]

Selling Bulgarian food in Munich

Although interest in Bulgarian provisions among the migrants is continuing, there is only one shop providing such products in Munich. It was not established

[17] Informant M. R., born 1971 in a family with German father and Bulgarian mother.

[18] Informant K. G., born 1975.

[19] Informant G. M., born 1973, working in a German firm importing Bulgarian wines.

as a Bulgarian shop, it is just that some of the "precious" food items are sold there. For unknown reasons it is not very popular among the immigrants; the owner says that the clients are not as many as he expected, maybe because of the prices. So his main activity is to provide supplies to the Bulgarian restaurant "Rila". A woman who owns a travel agency for trips to Bulgaria is selling *lyutenitsa*, waffles, tinned goods and brandy in her office. These products are arranged on a shelf inside the room and are not visible from the outside, even though they are legally imported.[20] According to the owner, students really enjoy sorts of waffles, those typical of the socialist period. Russian and Ukrainian students are also looking for these wafers, because they were imported into the USSR in the past. Some Germans used to buy Bulgarian goods, too. They especially like lyutenitsa; one lady even came with an empty jar and asked for "20 of these". The owner says that this product is like a narcotic: it is so delicious that after trying it once, one gets addicted and cannot stop eating and wanting it. Yet most of the respondents do not buy food from this place (or from the above mentioned shop, which is located nearby). In addition to disliking the informal nature of this trade (they consider selling food in a travel agency rather strange and "too rustic"), they claim that prices are high. The owner enjoys an extraordinary food supply line for her own needs from Bulgaria, because she works with the regular bus companies. That is why for her there is no limitation to the quantities she can get, and people are angry because of this: "She acts as if this is her own bus." Maybe the envy over the fact that she is able to cook predominantly with original products is also a motivation for not buying food from her. For example, she does not make traditional pastry, because her mother makes it for her and sends it by the bus – "after 20 hours it is not cooled down yet and we eat it".[21] Having real homemade pastry in Germany is a luxury. Many respondents dare only to dream of receiving a frozen prefabricated version, which is not so delicious at all. It is most frequently mentioned by many of them as a meal they miss very much.

Bulgarian restaurants – selling "authenticity"

Bulgarian restaurants are crucial for the marketization of the national cuisine. Eating out is a main characteristic of urban culture; restaurants are not only economic phenomena, they are important social places, institutions – some authors even consider them a type of mass media (Girardeli 2004: 311). The me-

[20] Although some informants suspect that the owner is not officially allowed to sell such products and that this is why they are hidden indoors.

[21] Informant A. R., born 1958, married to a Bulgarian.

diating function of "foreign" restaurants is intensified – they are mediators between "our" and "their" culture. Selling "authenticity", Bulgarian restaurants reaffirm the image of Bulgarian food as "ethnic" and "exotic". Such a label was attached to Bulgarian cuisine in other Western countries, too (Kassabova 2008). Which cuisine does and which does not get labelled "ethnic" (and "exotic") in the frames of contemporary global culture is a problem for a separate study. What is clear is the fact that, especially in multicultural societies, the dominant cuisine is usually not considered "ethnic".

As mentioned above, there is a considerable number of foreign restaurants in Munich and as a rule they are cheaper than German restaurants. The local public is very open to all kinds of experiments. In this context a Bulgarian restaurant is one of numerous options. For immigrants, going there is a way of celebrating national and religious feasts. The old restaurant "Sofia Grill" was closed several years ago because of the death of its famous owner. She also was a fugitive from communist rule and all the respondents remember her as a great cook and a nice person. She prepared a wonderful grill and she used to pander to visitors' taste, making rare and cheap but beloved dishes such as hominy with cheese or cracklings. Because of the good food and low prices, many Germans working nearby used to go there for lunch. In the evening and especially on weekends it was impossible to go there without making a reservation. There is a big difference between this restaurant and the new one, "Rila". People dislike it because of the high prices and bad service. Many complaints in this respect were registered. Problems arise because of some notorious practices, typical for restaurants in Bulgaria, which have been transferred to Germany. Students are not allowed to stay there if they order only French fries and Coca Cola. Oriental *chalga* music[22] is played when most of the public is Bulgarian, but many people dislike this kind of music. When they politely asked to have it turned off, the waiter said that it was the music of the boss. Many respondents ceased going there precisely because of this music:

> "I was at a party there and when this music started I could not stand it. My husband came to take me home (he is German) and I was ashamed, I went outside to meet him because I didn't want him to see what was going on ... If this is Bulgaria, I am ashamed of it. This was the last time I went there."[23]

The most indicative example of transferring "bad Bulgarian practices" to Germany was an unsuccessful attempt at advertising the restaurant. The owner made

---

[22] Oriental-style new folk music, very popular in Bulgaria.

[23] Informant V. P., born 1950.

a deal with the travel agency to attach leaflets to bus tickets, promising that whoever comes with this leaflet to the restaurant would receive a free beer. When people began asking for this beer, problems occurred. They were accused by the waiters of not saying in the beginning that they had such a leaflet. Logically enough, clients showed the leaflets while waiting for the bill. When the woman from the agency received complaints about this matter, she proposed that the waiters should ask in advance whether customers had such a leaflet or not. The owner disagreed, saying that he was not interested in them showing these leaflets at all, he was interested only in them paying big bills. This was the end of their common business.[24] It remains unclear why the owner started such an advertisement if he was not inclined to follow his own rules. Again the desire for quick and big money while avoiding regulations is one of the possible explanations.

The bad image of "Rila" is the reason why some people regularly visit the Croatian restaurant "Zagreb". Its cuisine is considered the same as in "Sofia Grill", and what is more, the chef there used to work with the late owner of the old Bulgarian restaurant. Older immigrants go to the "Zagreb" after Sunday liturgy in the Bulgarian church, but they visit "Rila" too, even though it is an expensive place. For a woman who migrated when she was very young and did not manage to cook the Bulgarian way, going to these restaurants for years has been her only contact with her native cuisine. It is interesting that her grandson is more capable of cooking certain Bulgarian dishes than she herself is.[25]

Rituals and guests

The gradual diminution of usage of original products during the integration process into the host society has led to a slow decrease in the scope of Bulgarian dishes prepared at home. Many people "eat Bulgarian" predominantly in the "Rila" and "Zagreb" restaurants, which is rather expensive. At home only the most important cuisine, the festive one, is preserved as an integral part of the ritual system. Regardless of the extent of adaptation and socialization in German society, all first generation immigrants try to observe the key Orthodox feasts, Christmas and Easter, preparing appropriate ritual food. Usually original products brought from Bulgaria are kept especially for these events. Preparation of a table with an odd number of vegetarian dishes for Christmas Eve seems strange to Germans, "but I am still doing it because this is our tradition and I insist on following it, because I still consider myself Bulgarian".[26] Catholic and Orthodox

[24] Informant A. R., born 1958.

[25] Informant I. S., born 1925, immigrated 1947.

[26] Informant I. G., born 1964, living in Germany since 1992.

Easter are usually on different dates, and some immigrants celebrate the Catholic one (because the whole country has a holiday on this day), while others honour the Orthodox one. A few people celebrate both. This depends a lot on their family status and whether they have a German partner or not. Those celebrating the Catholic feast are still following culinary prescriptions of the Orthodox one.

Unexpectedly, many women prepare traditional Easter cakes, requiring hard kneading of the dough. Some of them only colour eggs red, a tradition which is almost forgotten in Bulgaria. In Germany it has been revived by immigrants of the first and second generations as a distinction from the local tradition of making multicoloured eggs: "My daughter (second generation migrant) is colouring the eggs in our family. Her boyfriend is German, but when I told her that our tradition is to colour red eggs only, she started doing it this way."[27] The same holds true for some of those who celebrate the Orthodox feast: "It was very difficult for me to explain to my children why there are no red eggs here in Germany. So I told them that we are Bulgarians, our Easter is not on that day and our eggs are red."[28] As an important part of the feast, ritual food is given distinctive meanings: it reaffirms and symbolizes not just religious, but even more, national identity (it is well known that both are interrelated). Another crucial emblem of Bulgarian identity is pastry with fortune slips inside, made for Christmas or New Year's Eve. Pastry sheets and cheese from Bulgaria are kept in the fridge for precisely this purpose. Rarely, in families with both Bulgarian partners, other Orthodox feasts with specific dishes like fish on St. Nicolas Day (6. 12.) and Annunciation (25. 3.) are celebrated. In some of these cases men are as good cooks as women. What is more, they transfer to Germany the old practices of making homemade brandy, wine, backed peppers, pickles, flat sausages, even honey. Some regional differences in the cooking of both partners are still preserved.[29]

As a rule, Bulgarian dishes are made for foreign guests, especially Germans. This is so because "food does not simply symbolize social bonds and divisions, it participates in their creation and recreation" (Sutton 2001: 84). Giving and receiving food is always connected with social status, and important guests are given highly prestigious food (Fenton 1997: 154). It was not easy for the respondents to explain why this demonstration of identity through food was so important for them. It is a kind of public acknowledgment of their origins. Bulgarian food is "the only thing which is really good in Bulgaria, it was preserved for

[27] Informant R. P., born 1938.

[28] Informant I. N., born 1970, with a Bulgarian husband.

[29] "In Bulgaria there are 50 kilometres between my birthplace and his town, but there are differences in the cuisine. It is seen in a simple salad – it is different depending on who has made it – me or him" – informant I. N., born 1970.

centuries unspoiled – it is real, it is ours and it remains"[30]. From a psycho-dynamic perspective food knowledge is very loaded emotionally, because it occurs in the passionate world of the small child.[31] As stated above, such an emotional attitude towards tasty food is kept for a lifetime, and not only among migrants. In immigration it is often intensified or consciously diminished, depending on personal wishes and the respective level of integration into the host society. In both cases deliberate efforts are needed.

A similar emotional attitude towards Bulgarian food was found in the case of a young woman with a German father and Bulgarian mother. Her German identity is undeniable, she rarely cooks something Bulgarian at home, but for her wedding party she chose catering from the Bulgarian restaurant: "This was something that I wanted, it was important for me. It is an emotional tie, not identity. I bought my ring from Bulgaria, too. I wanted the wedding food to be special and to be connected with me."[32] While the informant herself denies that this was an expression of her national identity, it is obvious that Bulgarian food was an instrument of her self-revelation. This was a conscious (or maybe unconscious) emotional demonstration of her connection to Bulgaria. What is more, it was a symbolic presentation of her personal identity, not restricted in national terms only. Even if unique, this case is interesting because it reflects some tendencies typical for second-generation migrants, although the woman in question is hardly considered such. As a whole, hybrid cultural practices of the first generation migrants are valid for their children, too. For the woman mentioned above and for only one person of first generation migrants,[33] the concrete place of consumption makes food tasty, too. According to them, everything is tasty where it developed. That is why they enjoy Bulgarian food in Bulgaria, German food in Germany, etc. The playful switching of cultural contexts, accompanying spatial mobility, is important in this respect. In contrast with the majority of respondents, they do not esteem so highly the sensory aspects of transferred food – for them it is tasty in Bulgaria, because it is part of the whole cultural experience of going back there.[34]

---

[30] Informant G. M., born 1973.

[31] I wish to express my gratitude to Prof. Peter Black, George Mason University, for this comment and for his valuable help in editing this text.

[32] Informant M. R., born 1971, with a German father and Bulgarian mother.

[33] A person quite open for all kinds of culinary experiments and foreign influences as a whole.

[34] "For me the place is important. I eat all these things in Bulgaria, here it is not right to say that I don't like them, but for me they are in a way connected with Bulgaria. When I go there I eat them a lot and I like them. I eat cheese and yellow cheese and lyutenitsa with the unhealthy white bread. I carry all these products here, but it is simply not the same, I don't know why. There I eat sausages, here I have one of them in my fridge for weeks. Here I

My data on second-generation migrants is partial and predominantly indirect, based on information provided by their parents, who were my key informants. Their culinary preferences correspond with worldwide tendencies of acquiring the majority food culture, but also maintain an interest in Bulgarian cuisine. The main difference from their parents is the fact that they like German dishes much more. At the same time they make some emblematic Bulgarian dishes, often consulting about recipes on the phone with their grandmothers in Bulgaria instead of their mothers in Germany. What is more, this is typical not only for women, but for men, too. This phenomenon needs separate study, but three possible explanations might be posed in advance. The first involves the need for "roots", which is typical of the second-generation migrants even though they have adopted a new national affiliation. They are still considered citizens of migrant origin and the question of where their parents came from is still relevant. There are some cases when the lack of certain cultural competences, associated with their origin, cause serious identity crises.[35] The second explanation leads to sensory aspects of food. Maybe Bulgarian dishes are made because they are still found tasty by the second generation immigrants. They are part of the hybrid immigrant lifestyle, yet a secondary part, because these meals are made mostly for feasts, while everyday cuisine is German or international. The third option points to the "exoticism" of this food; in a postmodern context ethnic culture is found interesting (Featherstone 2007).

"Us" and "them" in food choices

It appears that the concept of taste is not only cultural, that it is not only acquired during acculturation. Obviously there are certain "objective" sensory qualities of Bulgarian vegetables, fruits, cheese, lyutenitsa, etc. because many Germans find them tasty as well. As a rule Germans and especially Bavarians are open to foreign culinary borrowings. Maybe this is due to the fact that German cuisine is not highly prestigious for Germans themselves, which is why they

can make a shopska salad for sure, but I don't. And of course there are no such tomatoes here ..." – informant M. R., born 1971, with a German father and Bulgarian mother.

[35] Quite interesting is the case of two sisters. The older one had lived in Bulgaria till she was 12 years old, when their parents migrated to Germany, while the younger was born there, and when going to school, almost all her classmates were of migrant origin. She knew that she was Bulgarian, but she knew almost nothing about Bulgaria, so it was very hard for her to "prove" her origin. As a result an identity crisis occurred, and it coincided with her adolescent identity crisis: "I know pretty well who I am, but she doesn't. She was told that she was Bulgarian, but she doesn't feel so, because she never lived there" – informant L. K. (the older sister), born 1978 in Sofia, married to a German.

easily borrow foreign cookery and the number of ethnic restaurants, especially in Bavaria, is very high. On the other hand, "if you are married to an Italian or a French guy you will not be allowed to make even a simple Bulgarian pastry, because Italian and French cuisines are famous and considered best".[36]

Bavarians are very adaptive in accepting some Bulgarian culinary methods, too. For example, all the neighbours of the owner of the travel agency started baking peppers:

> "I bake about 30–40 kilos of peppers every autumn. I supplied all my German neighbours with Bulgarian devices for baking peppers and in September we all bake together. We import about 100 kilograms of peppers from Bulgaria with the bus and I give to each of them 10 kilos and our whole block of flats bakes peppers. I taught them how to do it. When I started baking they smelled the aroma and came to ask me what was I doing. I gave them a taste, they liked it a lot and I started giving them 5–6 kilos. In the beginning one of them was suspicious about the electric device, he was not sure that it was safe and well done, but then he understood that it was OK and now he is baking normally too. After baking they continue with putting peppers into marinade according their traditions, I simply freeze them."[37]

As stated above, most Bulgarians dislike German cuisine. They rarely visit German restaurants, and most of them have not included German dishes in their home menu. Bavarian meals are considered too heavy, while local ecological production is regarded as a commercial trick. There are some rare cases of adopting one or two German dishes, but mostly international influences were registered: women cooking Italian, French and Chinese meals. Some German deserts are highly esteemed, but again controversial opinions were registered.[38] The level of compromise with the local cuisine and conversely of sticking to Bulgarian recipes depends largely on the identity of the marital partner. As Klaus Roth has convincingly shown, food is an object of serious negotiations and even conflicts in bi-cultural marriages (Roth 2004, 2006). That is why Bulgarian women with German

[36] I am grateful to Prof. Juliana Roth for this comment.

[37] Informant A. R., born 1958.

[38] "Our sweets have nothing to do with theirs. I enjoy very much receiving syringes [Bulg. tulumbichki, Oriental sweets with sugar syrup] from Bulgaria. A Ukrainian woman made once a 'Napoleon' cake and told me 'Come and taste it, you are the only one to understand how great this cake is. Whoever German I gave it to, they always don't like it'. Wherever you go, even in their most expensive sweet shops, our garash cake is not there ..." – informant Y. R., married to a German husband.

husbands cook more internationally (although not with many German dishes) in comparison to those married to Bulgarians or other Balkan men.

There is a cultural difference in the very concept of cooking typical of Bulgarian and German cuisines. For Bulgarians food and eating are very important elements of everyday life, associated with social contacts, etc. (Krăsteva-Blagoeva 2001). "In Bulgaria eating is very important. Me and my sister, when we go to visit our parents, even before we go there they ask us in advance what do we want them to cook for us."[39] It is a question of prestige for guests to be stuffed with food. As a German wife of a Bulgarian man said, "The first Bulgarian word I knew when I went to Bulgaria was 'eat, please'"[40]. For Bulgarians eating is an inevitable part of communication – all conversations are made around the table and sometimes people eat only because they have to talk with their friends or relatives. They stay around the table for hours, pausing for smoking. According to several Bulgarian respondents, the German way of eating is quite different. It almost excludes personal communication: people are sitting at the table only to have their meal with no conversation. They eat quickly and hurry to do something else. Three Bulgarian daughters-in-law (one of them with a German father) report feeling uneasy when having meals with their German husband's parents because of this. Because of scarce and indirect information on the matter, it is not possible to estimate whether this is due to social status (the families mentioned are of peasant background) or is due to German upbringing and discipline, presupposing that eating is not to be mixed with other activities. What is important is that the consciousness of this fact is viewed as an important cultural difference between Bulgarians and Germans.

Another distinction is the fact that being very "modern", many Germans have abandoned cooking completely. That is why they enjoy being treated:

> „We have many German friends. All of them like to come to our place and to eat something fresh and homemade, because they themselves do not cook at all. Even a mother with two children does not make anything for them, only prefabricated frozen things."[41]

Because many Bulgarians still spend time on cooking, an image of Bulgarian cuisine as "traditional" or "pre-modern" is established. It corresponds with the advertising strategies of some Bulgarian restaurants in other Western countries, for instance, the 'Pleven' restaurant in Vienna (Kassabova 2008). The very idea of "fast" and "slow" cooking has changed. For instance, some of the simplest dishes like stuffed peppers are perceived by the migrants as difficult and time-

[39] Informant K. G., born 1975 in Sofia, married to a German.
[40] Informant K. M., born 1974 in Plovdiv.
[41] Informant K. G., born 1975 in Sofia, married to a German.

consuming, which is why they prepare them for special occasions. This is due also to the fact that German peppers are too stiff, so they need preliminary blanching in order to be cooked well.

Many migrants do not like stuffing themselves with food, which is typical of Bulgarian nutritional behaviour. Sometimes they eat very little for a few weeks before coming back to Bulgaria. There are two types of reaction in this respect. Middle-aged people with more conservative orientations are doing this because they know that they are going to eat a lot and they like doing so. They associate going to Bulgaria with eating a lot and eating tasty food. Young women, on the other hand, do not like eating too much, and they also do not share their mothers' habit of cooking for hours. Of course they enjoy common meals the first one or two days of their visit, but later they get bored. Yet boredom does not prevent them from the inevitable carrying of food to Germany. This is due to the taste of traditional Bulgarian products. It is illustrative that a young girl, watching TV at home in Munich, was given a piece of cucumber from behind by her mother. Not seeing what it was and still watching the screen, she took one bite and said "This is a Bulgarian cucumber".

* * *

The interconnection of food, taste and identity became obvious in this research. Because of the emotional, sensory and mnemonic effects of the consumption of native food, carrying food items from Bulgaria is crucial for immigrants' nutritional practices. Their constant search for the "original" taste evokes "returning to the whole" experiences of different strength and depth. It appeared that not only does taste encode memories of birthplace: "Eating these meals makes you feel at home"[42], but in some cases it is the opposite: the place of consumption makes the food tasty. Eating is a crucial part of both cultural contexts the migrants are living in. Their constant transition between here and there, "living here and dreaming of there", not knowing for sure where home is, is encoded in their food preferences and practices. Even when trying to suppress them for the sake of integration, they are still there. Different levels of their preservation and demonstration depend on the social and marital status of the immigrants. The intensity of their ties with the home country, especially with parents and grandparents, is also an important variable in accounting for the differences found in this sample, although there are some cases in which such ties have weakened but nostalgic food preferences are still alive. The continued consumption of ritual food and the conscious treating of foreign guests to Bulgarian dishes reflect the

[42] Informant G. M., born 1973.

potentials of food as an instrument of self-revelation, deliberate or involuntary. The contrast between Bulgarian and German attitudes towards cooking and eating results in an active cultural exchange. In its frames Germans borrow much more Bulgarian practices than vice versa. As a whole, as people change their cuisine as part of the assimilation process, they tend to preserve, albeit to different extents, their attitudes to food, cooking and eating.

Literature

Bouchet, Dominique 1995: Marketing and the Re-definition of Ethnicity. In: J. Costa, G. Bamossy (eds.), Marketing in a Multicultural World. Thousand Oaks, CA: Sage, 68–104.

Bourdieu, Pierre 1984: Distinction: A Social Critique of the Judgment of Taste. Cambridge Mass.: Harvard UP.

Bourdieu, Pierre 1990: Social Space and Symbolic Power. In: In other Words. Essays towards a Reflexive Sociology. Stanford, CA, 130–131.

Campbell, C., S. Katamay, C. Connely 1988: The Role of Nutrition Professionals in the Hunger Debate. In: Journal of the Canadian Dietic Association 49: 230–235.

Cook, Jan, Philip Crang 1996: The Worlds on a Plate: Culinary Culture, Displacement and Geographical Knowledges. In: Journal of Material Culture 1, 2: 131-153.

Douglas, Mary 1999: Deciphering a Meal. In: M. Douglas (ed.), Implicit Meanings. London: Routledge, 231–252.

Erdinc, Ferda 2001: Journeys through Smell and Taste: Home, Self, Identity. In: Food and the Memory. Proceedings of the Oxford symposium on food and cookery 2000. Ipswich, MA: Prospect Books, 91–99.

Featherstone, Michael 2007: Consumer Culture and Postmodernism. London: Sage.

Fenton, Alexander 1997: Prestige, Hunger and Charity: Aspects of Status through Food. In: Jürgen Teuteberg, G. Neumann, A. Wierlacher, E. Barlosius (eds.), Essen und kulturelle Identitat: Europäische Perspektiven. Berlin: Akademie Verlag, 154–163.

Fernandez, James W. 1986: Persuasions and Performances: The Play of Tropes in Culture. Bloomington: Indiana University Press.

Fischler, Claude 1988: Food, Self and Identity. In: Social Science Information 27, 2: 275–292.

Fischler, Claude 1993: L'Homnivoire. Le gout, la cuisine et le corps. Paris.

Girardeli, Davide. 2004: Commodified Identities: The Myth of Italian Food in the United States. In: Journal of Communication Inquiry 28, 4: 307–324.

Goddard, Victoria 1996: Gender, Family and Work in Naples. London: Berg.

Kasabova, Anelia 2008: Sred naj-ekzotičnite kuhni văv Viena – "restorantăt na istinskite bălgarski specialiteti". Meždu pazara i identičnostta [Among the most exotic cuisines in Vienna – The "restaurant of real Bulgarian specialties". Between market and identity]. In: Bălgarska etnologija 34, 3: 34–46.

Koc, Mustafa, Jennifer Welsh 2001: Food, Foodways and Immigrant Experience. Paper Written for the Multiculturalism Program, Department of Canadian Heritage and the Canadian Ethnic Studies Association Conference, November 2001. Halifax (manuscript).

Kravva, Vassiliki 2001: Food as a Vehicle for Remembering: the Case of the Thessalonikan Jews. In: Food and the Memory. Proceedings of the Oxford Symposium on Food and Cookery 2000. Ipswich, MA: Prospect Books, 136–144.

Krăsteva-Blagoeva, Evgenia 2001: Bulgarians and McDonalds. Some Anthropological Aspects. In: Ethnologia Balkanica 5: 207–218.

Levenstein, Harvy 1997: The Food Habits of European Immigrants to America: Homogenization or Hegemonization? In: Jürgen Teutenberg et al. (eds.), Essen und Kulturelle Identität. Europäische Perspektiven. Berlin: Akademie Verlag, 465–472.

Levi-Strauss, Claude 1997: The Culinary Triangle. In: Carole Counihan, Penny van Esterik (eds.), Food and Culture. A Reader. New York: Routledge.

Liakova, Marina 2008: Hibridnijat žiznen svjat na bălgarskite studenti v Germanija [Hybrid way of life of the Bulgarian students in Germany]. In: Kritika i humanizm 25, 1: 45–63.

Opare-Obisaw, Clara Docea, D. A. G. Fainu, Kezia Awadzi 2000: Changes in Family Food Habits: the Role of Migration. In: Journal of Consumer Studies and Home Economics 24, 3: 145–149.

Pieterse, Jan N. 1995: Globalisation as Hybridization. In: M. Featherstone, S. Lash (eds.), Global Modernities. London: Sage.

Roth, Klaus 2004: Streit ums Essen? Nahrungsverhalten in bikulturellen Ehen und Familien. In: Ene Kõresaar, Art Leete (eds.), Everyday Life and Cultural Patterns. International Festschrift for Elle Vunder. Tartu: Tartu UP, 171–191. (= Studies in Folk Culture, 3) = Spor za jadeneto? Hranitelno povedenie v bikulturni brakove i semejstva. In: Bălgarska etnologija 32, 3 (2006) 10–24.

Scholliers, Peter 2001: Meals, Food Narratives, and Sentiments of Belonging in Past and Present. In: Peter Scholliers (ed.), Food, Drink and Identity. Cooking, Eating and Drinking in Europe since the Middle Ages. New York: Berg, 3–19.

Sutton, David 2001: Remembrance of Repasts: An Anthropology of Food and Memory. New York: Berg.

Ethnologia Balkanica 13 (2009)

Zur sprachlichen Leistung von Migrantenkindern aus Südosteuropa nach dem bayerischen Modell der „Sprachlernklassen“ an deutschen Grundschulen

Eleni Peleki, München

Abstract: On the language acquisition of children of Southeast European migrants taught after the model of “language learning classes” at German primary schools

The paper presents the results of a research project on the language performance of elementary school children in Bavaria, Germany. Its aim was to evaluate the school model of the “Sprachlernklassen” (language learning classes) or nowadays “Deutschlerngruppen” (German language learning groups) and to answer questions concerning the language improvement of the children, especially of children with migrant backgrounds from Southeast Europe.

Die Migrationsthematik hat derzeit enorme Konjunktur, weil sie mit weitreichenden soziostrukturellen und politischen Veränderungen der Weltgesellschaft zusammenhängt und im Zeichen der Globalisierung neue Züge annimmt. Der Begriff der Migration hat seine Wurzeln im lateinischen Wort „migrare“ (wandern, wegziehen) beziehungsweise „migratio“ (Wanderung). Er hat sich in den letzten Jahren, beeinflusst durch das weltweit verwendete englische Wort „migration“, zumindest in der sozialwissenschaftlich geprägten Fach-, zum Teil aber auch in der („politisch korrekten“) deutschen Alltagssprache eingebürgert (vgl. Han 2005).

Mit der soziologischen Auseinandersetzung mit diesem Phänomen hat sich erst Treibel (1988) befasst. Sie bezieht sich auf unterschiedliche Aspekte, um den allgemeinen Begriff der Migration präziser zu fassen (2003: 18 f.). So werden bei den verschiedenen Typen von Migration folgende Aspekte unterschieden:
- der *räumliche* Aspekt unterscheidet zwischen Binnenwanderung und internationaler Wanderung,
- der *zeitliche* Aspekt zwischen temporärer und dauerhafter Wanderung,
- der *kausale* Aspekt, bezüglich der Wanderungsursache, zwischen freiwilliger Wanderung und Zwangswanderung und
- der *quantitative* Aspekt hinsichtlich des Umfangs der Migration zwischen Einzel-, Gruppen- und Massenwanderung.

Die Unterscheidung zwischen freiwilliger und unfreiwilliger beziehungsweise erzwungener Migration[1] führt Riek (1995) weiter, indem er betont, dass die Migrationsentscheidung einem multikausalen Determinantenkomplex unterliegt, der sowohl von subjektiver als auch von objektiver Natur ist. Demzufolge ist es schwer, für jeden Einzelfall eine klare Trennlinie zwischen Zwang und Freiwilligkeit festzusetzen. Han (2000) unterscheidet vier Dimensionen, die einen Einfluss auf den Migrationsprozess haben, nämlich die motivationale, räumliche, zeitliche und soziokulturelle Dimension.

Deutschland war in seiner wechselvollen Geschichte oft Anziehungspunkt für Migranten und hat demzufolge eine stetige und rege Erfahrung mit Zu- und Abwanderungen, so dass Migrationen und ihre Folgen keine neuen Erscheinungen sind, sondern kontinuierliche Momente der deutschen Geschichte. Zu den wichtigen ethnischen Minderheiten in Deutschland gehören die Arbeitsmigranten der 1960er Jahre aus den Anwerbeländern und ihre Kinder, die Übersiedler, die Spätaussiedler und Sinti/Roma sowie Asylsuchende und (Bürger-)Kriegsflüchtlinge. In gleicher Weise stellen die so genannten Vertragsarbeiter der ehemaligen DDR aus Vietnam, Polen, Kuba, Mosambik und Angola ethnische Minderheiten in Deutschland dar.

Heinz Kühn (SPD), der ehemalige Ministerpräsident von Nordrhein-Westfalen und erste Ausländerbeauftragte der Bundesrepublik, plädierte bereits 1979 dafür, Migranten und Flüchtlingen langfristig gesicherte Lebens- und Zukunftsperspektiven zu ermöglichen. Er forderte gezielte Fördermaßnahmen sowie Einbürgerungserleichterungen. Die Bundesregierung stellte sich gegen diesen ersten nationalen Integrationsplan.

Ab 1981 forderte die CDU/CSU-Opposition von der Koalitionsregierung aus SPD und FDP eine effektive Begrenzungspolitik. Die Bundesregierung beschloss im Juli 1982 Maßnahmen zur Förderung der Rückkehr ausländischer Arbeitnehmer. Die Bundesregierung wurde kurz drauf abgelöst durch eine Koalition aus CDU, CSU und FDP, in deren Programm die Ausländerpolitik einen Schwerpunkt bildete. Es wurde eine Kommission für „Ausländerpolitik" gebildet, die aus Vertretern von Bund, Ländern und Gemeinden bestand. Ein neues Ausländergesetz trat jedoch erst im Januar 1991 in Kraft. Obwohl das neue Gesetz die Integration durch mehr Sicherheit hinsichtlich des Aufenthaltsstatus erleichtern sollte, erfüllte es nicht die Anforderungen, die man an ein modernes Ausländergesetz stellen konnte, nämlich erleichterte Einbürgerung oder Doppelstaatsangehörigkeit.

---

[1] In der angelsächsischen Fachliteratur erscheint neben dem Begriff „migration" der Begriff „forced migration" beziehungsweise „impelled migration", der besser auf den Zwangscharakter vieler Migrationsentscheidungen hinweist und dem deutschen eher irreführenden Begriff der 'unfreiwilligen' Migration entspricht.

Eine besondere Stellung unter den Migranten nehmen die Aussiedler ein. Seit 1988 kamen jährlich über 200000 Menschen deutscher Volkszugehörigkeit nach Deutschland, vor allem aus Russland und Kasachstan, Nachkommen deutscher Siedler, die im 18. Jahrhundert nach Russland gezogen waren; viele von ihnen waren im Zweiten Weltkrieg nach Kasachstan zwangsumgesiedelt worden. In die Gruppe der Aussiedler fielen auch die Siebenbürgener Sachsen und Banater Schwaben aus Rumänien, Nachkommen deutscher Siedler aus dem 13. und 18. Jahrhundert. Diese Aussiedler, seit dem 1. Januar 1993 „Spätaussiedler" genannt, sind Deutsche im Sinne des Grundgesetzes (Artikel 116 GG); nach § 6 des Bundesvertriebenengesetzes haben sie einen Anspruch auf Einbürgerung. Als Basiskompetenz für ihre Aufnahme gilt die deutsche Sprache. Da die deutschen Sprachkenntnisse der einreisenden Aussiedler mit der Zeit aber immer schlechter wurden, führte die Bundesrepublik 1996 einen Sprachtest, später einen „qualifizierten Sprachtest" in das Aufnahmeverfahren ein. Der Anteil der Aussiedler, die den Sprachtest bestehen, sinkt seither ständig.

Mit dem Gesetz zur Umsetzung aufenthalts- und asylrechtlicher Richtlinien der Europäischen Union[2] ist das Aufenthaltsgesetz grundlegend geändert worden. Danach wird die Erteilung einer Aufenthaltserlaubnis zur Wahrung oder Herstellung ehelicher Lebensgemeinschaft an Ehegatten von Deutschen oder Ausländern davon abhängig gemacht, dass der Ehegatte sich zumindest auf einfache Art in deutscher Sprache verständigen kann. Für Ausländer, die zur Herstellung der ehelichen Lebensgemeinschaft zu ihrem deutschen oder ausländischen Ehegatten ins Bundesgebiet nachziehen möchten, bedeutet dies, dass sie vor der Einreise ins Bundesgebiet einfache deutsche Sprachkenntnisse nachweisen müssen. Damit möchte Deutschland sicherstellen, dass sich Ausländer im Bundesgebiet von Anfang an zumindest auf einfache Art in Alltagssituationen auf Deutsch verständigen und am gesellschaftlichen Leben teilnehmen können.[3]

---

[2] Ausgenommen vom Sprachnachweis sind nachziehende Ehegatten, die wegen einer körperlichen, geistigen oder seelischen Krankheit oder Behinderung nicht in der Lage sind, einfache Kenntnisse der deutschen Sprache zu erwerben. Gleiches gilt für Ehegatten, bei denen ein erkennbar geringer Integrationsbedarf besteht. Weitere Ausnahmen vom Sprachnachweis gelten für Ehegatten von hochqualifizierten Forschern, Firmengründern, Asylberechtigten, anerkannten Flüchtlingen, Daueraufenthaltsberechtigten aus anderen EU-Staaten sowie für Ehegatten von Ausländern, die wegen ihrer Staatsangehörigkeit für einen Aufenthalt visumfrei in das Bundesgebiet einreisen und sich darin aufhalten dürfen (Staatsbürger von Israel, Japan, Kanada, Südkorea, Neuseeland, USA); vgl. § 28 Abs. 1 Satz 5 und § 30 Abs. 1 Satz 1 Nr. 2 sowie die Ausnahmen in § 30 Abs. 1 Satz 2 und 3 des deutschen Aufenthaltsgesetzes.

[3] Siehe Integrationsportal des Bundesamtes für Migration und Flüchtlinge: http://www.integration-in-deutschland.de.

Migrantenkinder im deutschen Bildungssystem – Stand der Forschung Vorschulische Bildung

Die zunehmende soziale und kulturelle Heterogenität der Gesellschaft wirkt sich auch im schulischen Bereich aus. Kinder verschiedener Hautfarbe, mit verschiedenen Sprachen begegnen sich in Schulgebäuden, um sich dort durch gezielte Erziehung auf die gesellschaftlichen Anforderungen vorzubereiten. In den mehrsprachigen Klassen, die nicht mehr die Ausnahme sind, sondern der Regelfall, wird der Wissenshorizont der Kinder um authentische, über den eigenen Kulturkreis hinausgehende Handlungsfelder erweitert, denn „Menschen - und vor allem Kinder und Jugendliche - sind mit dem Bedürfnis ausgestattet, die Welt und alles, was darin ist, zu verstehen, um darin erfolgreich zu sein" (Speck-Hamdan 2004: 6). Aus „fremden Volksgruppen", die passiv aufgenommen wurden, sind aktiv Beteiligte im Austausch in einer mehrsprachigen Gesellschaft geworden (Allemann-Ghioda 1999: 85), wobei die Schule als zentraler Ort des interkulturellen Lernens dazu beigetragen hat.

Jugendliche in Deutschland haben zu 22,2 % einen Migrationshintergrund. In den einzelnen Ländern unterscheiden sich die Anteile, in Bayern ist das Verhältnis 79,5 % zu 20,5 %. Dort stellen die Jugendlichen mit türkischer Herkunft den größten Anteil. In vielen Ländern bilden die Jugendlichen, die mit ihren Eltern aus dem Ausland zugewandert sind (Zuwanderer) die größte Gruppe, nur in Berlin gibt es mehr Jugendliche, die in Deutschland geboren wurden, deren Eltern aber beide aus dem Ausland stammen (erste Generation).[4]

Mit Hinblick auf die Befunde der PIRLS und PISA-Studien zum engen Zusammenhangs von Schichtzugehörigkeit, Migrationshintergrund und schulischen Leistungen wird in der aktuellen Bildungsdebatte die Wichtigkeit der vorschulischen Bildung für den Abbau von schichtspezifischen Bildungsungleichheiten hervorgehoben. Besonders für Migrantenkinder wird die Ansicht geteilt, dass sich der Besuch von vorschulischen Einrichtungen günstig auf ihre späteren Bildungschancen auswirkt. Seit 2000 besuchen ausländische Kinder ab vier Jahren bis zum Schuleintritt zu über 80 % Kindertageseinrichtungen, die für sie zur „Regel-Einrichtung" geworden sind. Der Anteil des Kindergartenbesuchs der 3- bis 4-jährigen und 4- bis 5-jährigen ausländischen Kinder ist nicht wesentlich geringer als der der deutschen und ausländischen Kinder zusammen (47 % vs. 56 % beziehungsweise 76 % vs. 83 %), wobei die Partizipation ausländischer Kinder an Vorschuleinrichtungen in der Altersstufe der 5- bis 6-jährigen (86 % vs. 90 % insgesamt) besonders hoch ist. Nach Daten des Statistischen Bundes-

[4] Bayerisches Staatsministerium für Unterricht und Kultus (2003): PISA-E-2003. Die wichtigsten Ergebnisse des umfassenden Ländervergleichs.

amtes (2006) sind wichtige Determinanten für die Teilnahme von Migrantenkindern an den vorschulischen Betreuungseinrichtungen die berufliche Integration, die kulturelle Assimilation sowie das verfügbare kulturelle Kapital der Familien, während für die einheimischen Kinder insbesondere die sozioökonomischen Ressourcen des Elternhauses bedeutsam sind.

Schulbesuch

Die Bildungschancen unter den Migranten sind sehr heterogen. Im Jahr 1999 besuchte jeder zweite ausländische Schüler eine Schule, die zu keinem weiterführenden Abschluss führt: 41,7 % besuchten eine Haupt- und 6,4 % eine Sonderschule, während unter den deutschen Schülern nur 17,1 % eine Haupt und 3,9 % eine Sonderschule besuchten (vgl. Empfehlung der Bildungskommission der Heinrich-Böll-Stiftung 2004).

Die PISA-Befunde von 2003 zeigen, dass Schüler mit Migrationshintergrund, vor allem türkischer Herkunft, im Vergleich zu deutschen Schülern eine verzögerte Schullaufbahn aufweisen. Der Grund dafür liegt in der häufigen Zurückstellung bei ihrer Einschulung oder in Klassenwiederholungen. Dadurch steigt aber das Risiko der Überalterung der Kinder in der Grundschule, was oft zur Sonderschulüberweisung führt, so dass von den ausländischen Sonderschülern ca. 70 % eine Schule für Lernbehinderte besuchen, bei den deutschen hingegen nur ca. 50 % (vgl. Empfehlung der Bildungskommission der Heinrich-Böll-Stiftung 2004).

Nach den PISA-Ergebnissen sind Kinder und Jugendliche mit Migrationshintergrund insbesondere an den Gymnasien deutlich unterrepräsentiert (vgl. dazu Alba et al. 1994). Während 39,5 % der Schüler der Sekundarstufe I ohne Migrationshintergrund im Jahr 1999 ein Gymnasium besuchte, war es bei den Schülern mit mindestens einem Elternteil aus der Türkei, aus sonstigen Anwerbestaaten und der ehemaligen Sowjetunion nur ein Fünftel (19,2 %). Beim Besuch von Realschulen ist der Abstand zwischen den deutschen und ausländischen Schülern zwar weniger stark ausgeprägt, aber dennoch vorhanden (21,7 % der deutschen Schüler zu 17,5 % der ausländischen). Bei den Gesamtschulen hingegen ist der Anteil der Kinder mit mindestens einem im Ausland geborenen Elternteil mit 13,5 % höher als der Anteil der deutschen, der 8,9 % beträgt (vgl. Krohne et al. 2004: 373 ff.).

Schulabschlüsse und Übergang in die Berufsausbildung und Arbeitswelt

Hinsichtlich der erreichten Schulabschlüsse zeigt sich ein wachsender Bildungserfolg der Kinder nichtdeutscher Herkunft. Während in den 1970er Jahren mehr als die Hälfte ohne Schulabschluss blieb, sank zwischen 1983 und 1993 die Quote der Schulabgänger ohne Schulabschluss unter den ausländischen Jugendlichen von 31 % auf 19 %. Der Anteil ist ca. 2,5-mal so hoch wie bei deutschen Jugendlichen. 2003 schafften fast fünf von sechs mindestens den Hauptschulabschluss, und ein immer größerer Teil absolviert erfolgreich die weitführenden Schulen.

Nach der PISA-Studie von 2003 wurden 46 % der 15-jährigen nichtdeutscher Herkunft in Deutschland geboren, weitere 27 % sind bereits vor ihrem Schulbeginn und weitere 19 % noch während ihrer Grundschulzeit zugewandert. Der Anteil ausländischer Schulabgänger mit höheren Bildungsabschlüssen wie Realschulabschluss, Fachabitur und Abitur hat sich erhöht und zwar von 19 % im Jahr 1983 auf knapp 40 % 1999. Beim Abitur ist in den letzten zehn Jahren eine Erhöhung von knapp 4 % auf rund 10 % zu beobachten, was einen stark ausgeprägten intergenerationalen Bildungsaufstieg aufzeigt.

Bemerkenswert ist jedoch, dass Bundesländer, die beim Kompetenztest der PISA-Studie (2003) positiv bewertet wurden, in den offiziellen Schulstatistiken tendenziell am unteren Ende der Rangskala liegen. In Bayern und Rheinland-Pfalz zum Beispiel, die beim PISA-Kompetenztest gut abschnitten, dominieren die Hauptschulabschlüsse. Die beiden Bundesländer verfügen allerdings über relativ hohe Sonderschulquoten bei ausländischen Schülern, weisen die höchste Quote von ausländischen Schulabgängern ohne Abschluss auf und haben den absolut und relativ geringsten Anteil an ausländischen Schülern, die einen weiterführenden Schulabschluss erreichen. Es hat den Anschein, als ob in diesen Ländern die Diskriminierung im Hinblick auf den formalen Schulerfolg (gemessen an den Schulabschlüssen) am größten ist. Im Gegensatz dazu überwiegen weiterführende Schulabschlüsse in Nordrhein-Westfalen, das in der PISA-Studie 2003 im Mittelfeld liegt, sowie in Bremen, das bei PISA am Schluss rangiert (vgl. Hunger, Thränhardt 2004).

Das Ausmaß der Chancenungleichheit zwischen Jugendlichen mit und ohne Migrationshintergrund[5] beim Zugang zur beruflichen Ausbildung wird deutlich in der Hamburger Untersuchung der Leistungen, Motivation und Einstellungen zu Beginn der beruflichen Ausbildung (ULME) im Schuljahr 2002/2003.

Nach Lehmann et al. (2004) weisen ausländische Jugendliche hauptsächlich mit türkischer, iranischer und afghanischer Staatsangehörigkeit am Beginn ih-

[5] Der Migrationshintergrund wurde nach der Staatsangehörigkeit und Umgangssprache in der Familie gemessen.

rer Ausbildung (Berufsfachschule, Berufsschule) den niedrigsten Fachleistungsstand auf, während Schüler aus EU-Ländern, Russland und Südostasien hohe Leistungen erbrachten.

Die Wahrscheinlichkeit der Einmündung in die Berufswelt liegt bei deutschen Jugendlichen bei 40 % und bei Jugendlichen mit Migrationshintergrund nur bei 29 %. Bei einem mittleren Ausbildungsabschluss (bis zur Fachhochschulreife) steigt der Anteil bei Deutschen auf 47 %, bei Migranten dagegen nur auf 34 %. Bei guten oder sehr guten Mathematiknoten wächst die Quote auf 64 % beziehungsweise 41 %, d.h. dass sich die relativen Abstände vergrößern und Jugendliche mit Migrationshintergrund durchschnittlich bessere schulische Vorleistungen nachweisen müssen als ihre deutschen Altersgenossen.

An den Hochschulen machten 2003 die Bildungsinländer (ausländische Studierende mit deutschem Abitur) 3 % der Studierenden aus (vgl. StBA 2003b). In einer Pilotstudie von Heine et al. (2006), die erstmals den Einfluss des Migrationsstatus auf die Übergangsquote in den Hochschulbereich untersucht, wurde gezeigt, dass Studienberechtigte mit Migrationsstatus, die zu Hause kein Deutsch sprechen, die höchste Studierneigung aufweisen, wobei diese Gruppe die kleinste unter allen Studienberechtigten ist (1 %). In allen Migrantengruppen liegt die Übergangsquote bei jenen Studienberechtigten, die aus einem akademischen Elternhaus kommen, deutlich höher als bei jenen ohne akademischen Hintergrund. Deutlich wird, dass die Bildungsherkunft einen Einfluss auf die Übergangsquote hat.

Hinsichtlich der aufgeführten Ergebnisse ist allgemein zu beobachten, dass der Bildungsabstand zwischen deutschen Jugendlichen und denen mit Migrationshintergrund sich nicht wesentlich reduziert hat. Der Grund dafür ist, dass Unterschiede in der sozialen Herkunft in der Schule offensichtlich nicht kompensiert werden. Man kann annehmen, dass die Beherrschung der Verkehrssprache Deutsch überwiegend als familiale Verantwortung behandelt wird. Kinder mit Migrationshintergrund sind aufgrund des Sozialschichteffektes seltener an weiterführenden Schulen zu sehen, was für ihren Sozialisations- und Integrationsprozess erhebliche Folgen haben kann. Es ist ein Zeichen dafür, dass die dritte Generation von dem Bildungsniveau und dem sozialen und beruflichen Integrationsgrad der zweiten Generation abhängig ist.

„Sprachlernklassen“: Das bayerische Schulmodell zur integrativen Förderung von Kindern und Jugendlichen nicht-deutscher Herkunftssprache

Ein neueres Praxismodell für die intensive Förderung von Schulanfängern in Deutsch als Zweitsprache ist das seit dem Schuljahr 2002/03 in Bayern angewandte Modell der Sprachlernklassen. Zielgruppe sind Schüler, die zwar in Deutschland geboren, aber in den ersten Lebensjahren ohne intensiven Kontakt zur deutschsprachigen Umwelt aufgewachsen sind. Eine weitere Gruppe sind im Ausland geborene Kinder, die ohne Sprachkenntnisse nach Deutschland kommen, darunter auch Aussiedlerkinder. Schülern nichtdeutscher Herkunftssprache soll das Erreichen der Bildungsabschlüsse ermöglicht werden, die ihren Fähigkeiten und Leistungen entsprechen. Vorrangige Bedeutung haben hierfür der Erwerb und die Erweiterung der Kenntnisse der deutschen Sprache, die die Grundlage für eine erfolgreiche Teilnahme am Unterricht und für die schulische und gesellschaftliche Integration bilden. Demzufolge ist Ziel des Modells der Sprachlernklasse die Intensivierung sowie Förderung der sprachlichen und sozialen Integration dieser Kinder und Jugendlichen und ihre vollständige Eingliederung in eine Regelklasse nach ein bis zwei Jahren (KMS 11. 4. 2003). Das Lernen einer Sprache wird nach dem Lehrplan Deutsch als Zweitsprache (2002) im Wesentlichen bestimmt durch:

- die eigene Lernanstrengung des Lernenden,
- die gezielte sprachliche Förderung zur Optimierung des individuellen Sprachwachstums,
- die Verknüpfung vom Neuen mit dem bereits vorhandenen sprachlichen und kulturellen Vorwissen der Lerner,
- vielfältige Möglichkeiten der Anwendung bereits erworbener Handlungs- und Sprachmuster in der deutschsprachigen Umwelt.

Das Konzept der Sprachlernklasse basiert auf diesen Aspekten des Spracherwerbs. Der Unterricht wird zum einen durch die sprachliche Dimension und zum anderen durch die sozial-interaktive Dimension bestimmt. Die Schwerpunkte liegen in der intensiven Vermittlung der deutschen Sprache und der sprachlichen Interaktion mit deutschen Mitschülern. Das Besondere der Sprachlernklasse ist einerseits der kompakte Unterricht im Fach Deutsch als Zweitsprache, verknüpft mit den grundlegenden Fächern, und andererseits die intensive Kooperation mit der Regelklasse, in der der Sprachlerner Mitschüler ist und Gelegenheit hat, sich im Klassezimmer und in der deutschsprachigen Umwelt zu artikulieren.

Sprachlernklassen umfassen ca. 12 Schüler (nur mit Migrationshintergrund), die in ausgewählten Fächern, besonders auch in Deutsch als Zweitsprache, den Unterricht getrennt von ihrer Regelklasse (Schüler mit und ohne Migrationshintergrund) erhalten. In den übrigen Fächern nehmen sie am Unterricht ihrer Regelklasse teil. Der Unterricht in der Sprachlernklasse umfasst für die Jahrgangsstufe 1 mindestens 14 Wochenstunden und höchstens 17 Wochenstunden für die Jahrgangsstufe 4. Der individuelle Leistungszuwachs des einzelnen Schülers bestimmt die Eingliederung in die Regelklasse, die zu jedem Zeitpunkt im Schuljahr möglich ist. Grundlage für den Unterricht in der Sprachlernklasse sind der Lehrplan für Deutsch als Zweitsprache sowie der Lehrplan für die Grundschule. Den Unterricht in der Sprachlernklasse erteilt eine Lehrkraft mit Qualifikation im Fach Deutsch als Zweitsprache. Diese kooperiert eng mit den Lehrern der Regelklasse. Der Unterricht in der Sprachlernklasse dient vorrangig dem Erwerb und der Erweiterung der deutschen Sprachkenntnisse und bereitet auf die Regelklasse vor. Er darf sich daher nicht auf Sprachunterricht beschränken, sondern ist auch fachbezogen zu erteilen. Bei der Vermittlung fachlicher Inhalte orientiert er sich an den curricularen Vorgaben für die Fächer in der jeweiligen Schulform. Um einen möglichst problemlosen Übergang zu gewährleisten, soll der Unterricht in der Sprachlernklasse in enger Abstimmung mit dem Unterricht in den Regelklassen durchgeführt werden. Im Hinblick auf die zu erreichende Integration sollen die Schüler einer Sprachlernklasse von Anfang an in ausgewählten Fächern (zum Beispiel in musisch-kulturellen, in praxisbezogenen Fächern und im Sport) am Unterricht ihrer künftigen Regelklasse teilnehmen. Schüler, die eine Sprachlernklasse besucht haben, können bei Bedarf anschließend an einem Förderkurs teilnehmen.

Der Großteil bereits bestehender Sprachlernklassen in Bayern sind Klassen der 1. Jahrgangsstufe. Für Kinder, bei denen durch die Sprachstandsdiagnose im Rahmen der Schuleinschreibung für die Jahrgangsstufe 1 fehlende oder sehr geringe Deutschkenntnisse festgestellt werden, wird noch vor Schulbeginn in der Zeit zwischen Mai und Juli ein Vorkurs zur Deutschförderung auf freiwilliger Basis angeboten. Dies geschieht in Kooperation mit den Kindergärten im Einzugsbereich der jeweiligen Grundschule. Nach Angaben des Bayerischen Kultusministerium für Unterricht und Kultus gab es im Schuljahr 2004/5 in Bayern 215 Sprachlernklassen mit 2657 Schülern, im Schuljahr 2005/6 270 Klassen mit 3030 Schülern und im Schuljahr 2006/7 296 Klassen mit 3728 Schülern. Eine Evaluation dieser Integrationsmaßnahme steht noch aus; die vorliegende Studie will dazu beitragen (s. Peleki 2008).

Empirischer Teil: Fragestellungen und Forschungshypothesen

Ziel der vorliegenden Studie ist eine Antwort auf die Frage, ob das Modell der Sprachlernklasse das Erlernen der deutschen Sprache fördert (cf. dazu Peleki 2008). Dazu sind Hypothesen erstellt worden, die in operationaler Form lauten:
Hypothese 1: Die sprachliche Leistung der Kinder der Sprachlernklasse unterscheidet sich nicht von der sprachlichen Leistung der Kinder der Regelklasse.
Hypothese 2: Schüler mit Migrationshintergrund der Sprachlernklasse und der Regelklasse zeigen die gleiche Anzahl von Substitutionen bei Nomina wie die Kinder ohne Migrationshintergrund der Regelklasse.

Hypothese 3: Die lexikalisch-semantischen klassifikatorischen Fehler bei Nomina der Kinder der Sprachlernklasse unterscheiden sich nicht von denen der Kinder der Regelklasse.

Forschungsmethodik, Datengewinnung

Die den Kern der vorliegenden Studie bildende Gesamtstudie fand an zwei Grundschulen, die mir von den zuständigen Schulämtern zugeteilt wurden, im Raum München statt. Beide Schulen waren dadurch gekennzeichnet, dass sie das Modell der „Deutschlerngruppen" in der 1. Klasse bereits ein Jahr eingesetzt hatten. In den ersten zwei Wochen nach Schulbeginn habe ich den Unterricht in den untersuchten Klassen beobachtet, um das Vertrauen der Kinder für meine Untersuchung zu gewinnen.

Versuchspersonen und Untersuchungsbedingungen

Die Untersuchung wurde mit insgesamt 87 Kindern der 1. Klasse aus beiden Grundschulen durchgeführt. Die Sprachlernklassen besuchten 23 Schüler türkischer Herkunft und die Regelklassen 64 Schüler, darunter 14 Kinder mit und 50 ohne Migrationshintergrund.[6] Das durchschnittliche Alter der Kinder der Sprachlernklasse betrug 6,8 Jahre und der Kinder der Regelklasse 6,6 Jahre. Die Kinder der Sprachlernklassen verteilten sich jeweils auf zwei Regelklassen. Es handelte sich daher – in jeder Schule getrennt betrachtet – jeweils um eine Sprachlernklasse und zwei Regelklassen. Insgesamt waren zwei Sprachlernklassen und vier Regelklassen in die Untersuchung einbezogen. Die Sprachlernklassen bestanden jeweils aus 10 und 13 Schülern mit Migrationshintergrund.

Nach Fragebogen-Aussagen der Lehrer und Eltern lagen weder kognitive oder perzeptuelle Einschränkungen noch Sprachentwicklungsstörungen vor. Als Merkmal für den Migrationshintergrund wurde der Migrationsstatus der Familie definiert. Es wurden drei Gruppen unterschieden: Familien, in denen beide Eltern, ein Elternteil oder kein Elternteil in Deutschland geboren wurden. Die Informationen wurden mit Hilfe eines Elternfragebogens erhoben. Zu jedem der Untersuchungszeitpunkte war jedes Kind anwesend. Die Kinder wurden zur Messung ihrer sprachlichen Kompetenz von mir aus den Klassen wäh-

6 Die Sprachlernklassen werden ausschließlich von Kindern mit Migrationshintergrund besucht, die eine sprachliche Förderung benötigen. Die Regelklasse besuchen Kinder mit und ohne Migrationshintergrund, für die keine zusätzliche sprachliche Förderung erforderlich ist (s. Beschreibung des bayerischen Modells der Sprachlernklassen).

rend des Unterrichts einzeln herausgeholt und in einem Nebenraum getestet. Dadurch konnten die Untersuchungen einerseits ungestört von den anderen Kindern durchgeführt werden und andererseits konnten die Kinder nicht abgelenkt werden. Die Tests fanden morgens von 8 bis 10 Uhr statt, um allen Versuchspersonen die gleichen Voraussetzungen zu bieten. Vor allem im 1. Schuljahr zeigen die Kinder zu einem späteren Zeitpunkt Ermüdungserscheinungen, so dass sie nicht mehr konzentriert arbeiten können. Den Schülern wurde zu Beginn erklärt, dass es sich um ein Spiel handele; während der Durchführung der Tests schien das „Spiel" den Kindern Spaß zu machen. Die Gesamtstudie besteht aus zwei Teilstudien mit ergänzenden Daten aus einer Eltern- und einer Lehrerbefragung mit Fragebögen; aus den Daten des Elternfragebogens wurde die Einbeziehungsweise Zweisprachigkeit der Kinder festgestellt (s. Peleki 2008).

Empirische Studie zur lexikalischen Semantik: Instrument und Methode

Da die Kinder des 1. Schuljahres noch nicht lesen und schreiben konnten, dienten als Grundlage zur Messung der sprachlichen Leistung der Kinder der Sprachlernklasse und der Regelklasse Tests zum Benennen von Nomina anhand von Bildern. Benenn-aufgaben bei Kindern können angesichts des relativ seltenen Auftretens von Versprechern (Tip-of-the-tongue-Phänomen) als eine sinnvolle Methode eingesetzt werden, um Einblick in den Stand des semantischen und lexikalischen Wissens von Kindern zu erhalten (Kauschke 2007, McGregor et al. 2002).

Die Kriterien zur Konstruktion des Materials werden nun genauer dargestellt. Als Zielitems wurden Objektbegriffe ausgewählt, die prinzipiell bildlich darstellbar sind. Zunächst wurden linguistische Konstruktionskriterien festgelegt, um kontrollierte und vergleichbare Itemlisten zu gestalten. Die Nomina sind mono- oder polymorphematisch, da auch Komposita und Pluralformen ausgewählt wurden. Sämtliche Nomina sind Konkreta, die sich auf ganze Objekte beziehen. Die Nomensets bestehen zur Hälfte aus unbelebten Objekten (Artefakte), die sich aus Vertretern der semantischen Felder Kleidung, Musikinstrumente, Werkzeuge, Fahrzeuge, Haushaltsgegenstände und so weiter zusammensetzen. Die andere Hälfte besteht aus belebten beziehungsweise natürlichen Objekten wie Tiere, Pflanzen oder Naturphänomene. Damit die Tests inhaltlich valide und nicht bestimmte Kinder bezüglich des Lebenskontextes, des Wohnumfeldes und der Schichtzugehörigkeit benachteiligt sind, sollte die Aufgabenwahl eine repräsentative Teilmenge aus dem lebensnahen Wortschatz darstellen.

Als Testmaterial dienten die Schwarz-Weiß-Zeichnungen von Objekten von Barnhuser et al., die nach dem Lehrplan der 1. Klasse konzipiert sind und den oben erwähnten Kriterien entsprechen. Das Testmaterial wurde zur Überprüfung der Benennübereinstimmung 30 erwachsenen Personen vorgelegt. Items wurden dann verwendet, wenn mindestens zwei Drittel der befragten Personen zu einer übereinstimmenden Bewertung kamen.

Die Benenntests bestanden in einer einfachen Benennung nach Vorlage der einzelnen Bilder, wobei Elizitierungsfragen (bei Nomina „Was ist das?“) eingesetzt wurden. Dadurch konnte der expressive (aktive) Wortschatz der Kinder, das heißt, die Wörter, die produziert wurden, untersucht werden. Nachdem das Wort produziert war, wurde gegebenenfalls die Frage „Wo siehst du das?“ gestellt. Der Schüler wurde somit aufgefordert, das Objekt auf den dargestellten Bildern zu zeigen. Auf diese Weise konnte sein rezeptiver (passiver) Wortschatz kontrolliert werden. Man kann davon ausgehen, dass ein Kind die Wörter, die es produziert, auch versteht. Gab das Kind eine falsche oder gar keine Benennung, wurde das nächste Bild vorgelegt.

Zum Testmaterial gehörte außerdem ein Erzählposter (Wittkowske 2001: 71) zum Thema „Winter“. Das Buch, in dem das Erzählposter stand, wurde im Heimat- und Sachunterricht des 1. Schuljahres eingesetzt. Das Erzählposter wurde im Pretest von 30 Erwachsenen geprüft. Die Items wurden dann in die Hauptuntersuchung aufgenommen, wenn bei der Überprüfung der genannten Objekte zwei Drittel der Befragten eine übereinstimmende Benennung produzierten. Dabei wurde eine Liste mit den intendierten Nomina angefertigt, mit deren Hilfe bei der Testdurchführung protokolliert und aufgezeichnet wurde, ob die untersuchten Kinder die genannten Nomina produzierten oder nicht. Insgesamt wurden während des Schuljahres acht Benenntests in monatlichem Abstand durchgeführt, wobei der erste Nomentest zwei Wochen nach Schulbeginn stattfand. Das Testmaterial umfasste insgesamt 134 Prüfitems.

Auswertungsverfahren

Die Reaktionen der Kinder wurden während der Untersuchungen protokolliert und gleichzeitig aufgezeichnet, um Fehler bei der späteren Datenbearbeitung auszuschließen. Die Tests zur lexikalischen Benennleistung wurden unter quantitativen und qualitativen Aspekten ausgewertet.

Zur Untersuchung der Benenngenauigkeit sowohl für die einzelnen Bilder als auch für das Erzählposter erfolgte eine quantitative Bewertung der Antworten als richtig oder falsch. Als korrekte Antwort wurde das in der Benennübereinstimmung ermittelte Item gewertet. Selbstkorrekturen wurden akzeptiert. Bedeutungsgleiche Wörter (Synonyme, manchmal auch regionale wie zum Beispiel „Semmel“ für „Brötchen“) wurden als korrekt kodiert. Nach McGregor (1997) gelten als falsch Antworten jene, die keinen oder geringen Bezug zum Zielwort aufweisen, wie zum Beispiel gefüllte Pausen, Interjektionen, Lautmalereien. Nullreaktionen, „ich weiß nicht" Antworten wie auch der alleinige Einsatz einer Geste werden ebenso als falsch bewertet. Semantisch korrekte, jedoch artikulatorisch fehlerhafte Wortproduktionen, die von der deutschen Hochlautung nicht erheblich abweichen, wurden als korrekt kodiert, da es sich bei diesem Verfahren nicht um die Beurteilung der Aussprache handelte, sondern um ein Untersuchungsinstrument zum lexikalisch-semantischen Entwicklungsstatus.

In einem weiteren qualitativen Auswertungsschritt wurden alle inkorrekten Reaktionen genauer analysiert, da es unter semantischen Gesichtspunkten von Interesse ist, welche Verbindungen zwischen dem Zielwort und seiner verbalen Substitution bestehen. Zur Bestimmung der Fehlerart wurde ein Klassifikationssystem entwickelt, das sieben Kategorien enthält. Nach McGregor (1997) gelten im Rahmen der taxonomischen Klassifikation über- und untergeordnete und benachbarte Begriffe (Hyperonyme wie zum Beispiel Zielwort *Tulpe* mit Hyperonym Blume, Hyponyme wie zum Beispiel Zielwort *Tasche* mit Hyponym Rucksack und Kohyponyme wie zum Beispiel Zielwort *Bürste* mit Kohyponym Kamm) als falsch, ebenso wie die Benennung des Ganzen statt des Teils (Holonyme zum Beispiel Zielwort *Briefkasten* mit Holonym Post) oder des Teils statt des Ganzen (Meronyme zum Beispiel Zielwort *Briefkasten* mit Meronym Brief). Dieser strengen Richtlinie wird hier auch gefolgt.

Semantische Neologismen (Wortneuschöpfungen, wie zum Beispiel Futterstelle für *Futterkrippe*) und Wortartwechsel, die Produktion eines Nomens, das einer anderen Wortart als das Zielwort angehörte (Schi fahren statt *Schifahrt*), zählten ebenso zu den semantisch-klassifikatorischen Fehlern. Die Auswertung der über die beschriebene empirische Untersuchung erhaltenen Daten wurde mit Hilfe von SPSS durchgeführt.

Hypothese 1: Die sprachliche Leistung der Kinder der Sprachlernklasse unterscheidet sich nicht von der sprachlichen Leistung der Kinder der Regelklasse. Mit dieser Hypothese soll überprüft werden, ob sich die sprachliche Leistung der Kinder der Sprachlernklasse (nur Kinder mit türkischem Migrationshintergrund) von der sprachlichen Leistung der Kinder der Regelklasse (Kinder mit und ohne Migrationshintergrund unterscheidet. Dazu wurden zunächst die absoluten Häufigkeiten bzw. die Anzahl der richtigen Benennungen der Einzelbilder und der genannten Nomina des Erzählposters (siehe oben) für beide Gruppen zusammengezählt, die auch als Grundlage für weitere Analysen gelten.

Der Mittelwert (MW) der richtigen Benennungen der Einzelbilder und genannten Nomina des Erzählposters beträgt für die Sprachlernklasse ($n = 23$) 168,57. In der Regelklasse ($n = 64$) ist die Anzahl der richtigen Benennungen der Einzelbilder bzw. der genannten Nomina niedriger. Der Mittelwert (MW) beträgt hier 141,75; der T-Wert ist mit $p = 0{,}000$ signifikant, das heißt, die beiden Gruppen unterscheiden sich bezüglich ihres Mittelwertes der Anzahl aller richtigen Antworten. Die Kinder der Sprachlernklasse geben mehr richtige Antworten und schneiden bei den sprachlichen Tests besser ab als ihre Mitschüler der Regelklasse. Die Hypothese wurde somit widerlegt. Das erklärt sich dadurch, dass die Kinder der Sprachlernklasse einen systematischen Sprachunterricht im L2-Spracherwerb durch eine für Deutsch als Zweitsprache qualifizierte Lehrkraft erhalten. Außerdem wird nach Angaben der Lehrpersonen in den beiden untersuchten Schulen den Kindern der Regelklasse mit mangelnden Sprachkenntnissen kein hinreichender Förderunterricht angeboten. Der Grund dafür liegt im Mangel an qualifiziertem Personal; dieses wird in den Sprachlernklassen eingesetzt.

Betrachten wir die Ergebnisse des ersten Sprachtests, der zwei Wochen nach Schulbeginn durchgeführt wurde, ergibt sich, dass sich die Kinder der Sprachlernklasse (n = 23) mit einem Mittelwert (MW) von 22,2609 der richtigen Antworten und ihre Mitschüler in der Regelklasse (n = 64) mit einem MW von 20,3438 der richtigen Antworten signifikant voneinander unterscheiden (p = 0,026). Anhand dieses Ergebnisses ist eine unzutreffende beziehungsweise falsche Zuweisung in den oben erwähnten Klassen zu vermuten. Der Grund dafür könnte darin liegen, dass die Zuweisung in die Klassen aufgrund eines Testverfahrens erfolgte, das nicht standardisiert ist und deshalb sehr stark von der Erfahrung der ausführenden Lehrpersonen abhängt. Aufgrund dieser Ausgangslage überrascht das gute Abschneiden der Kinder der Sprachlernklasse bei allen sprachlichen Tests nicht so sehr, denn sie hatten von Anfang an bessere Voraussetzungen.

Hypothese 2: Schüler mit Migrationshintergrund zeigen die gleiche Anzahl von Substitutionen bei Nomina wie die Kinder ohne Migrationshintergrund. Mit dieser Hypothese soll die Anzahl von Substitutionen bei Nomina zwischen den Kindern mit Migrationshintergrund in Sprachlernklassen und Regelklassen sowie bei Kindern ohne Migrationshintergrund gemessen werden. Zur Überprüfung der Hypothese wird zunächst die Anzahl der Substitutionen der Nomina der Einzelbilder und des Einzelposters je nach Familientyp getrennt betrachtet.

Dabei ergeben sich folgende Kennwerte: Für die Anzahl der Substitutionen der Nomina der Einzelbilder ergibt sich für die Kinder mit Migrationshintergrund in beiden Schulklassentypen (Sprachlernklasse und Regelklasse n = 52) ein MW von 9,8 und beim Erzählposter ein MW von 3,97, zusammengefasst ein MW von 13,77. Bei den Kindern ohne Migrationshintergrund (nur Regelklasse n = 35) ergibt sich bei den Einzelbildern ein MW von 11,37 und beim Erzählposter ein MW von 5,11, für beide ein MW von 16,48. Bei Betrachtung der Anzahl der Substitutionen der Nomina der Einzelbilder ist ein T-Wert mit einem p = 0,005 signifikant, das heißt, die beiden Gruppen unterscheiden sich bedeutsam bezüglich ihres Mittelwertes der Anzahl der Substitutionen. Das bedeutet, dass die Kinder mit Migrationshintergrund in beiden Klassen (Sprachlernklasse und Regelklasse) weniger Nomina bei den Einzelbildern substituieren als ihre Mitschüler ohne Migrationshintergrund. Bezogen auf die Anzahl der substituierten Nomina des Erzählposters ist ein T-Wert mit einem $p = 0{,}000$ signifikant. Die Kinder mit Migrationshintergrund in beiden Klassen (Sprachlernklasse und Regelklasse) substituieren weniger Nomina beim Erzählposter. Die Kinder mit Migrationshintergrund machen weniger Gebrauch von Substitutionen, das heißt, sie treffen häufiger das Zielwort. Die Fehlerhäufigkeiten in Abhängigkeit zur Migrationsgeschichte des Familientyps lassen nachfolgende Rückschlüsse zu.

Die zugrunde gelegte Hypothese wird widerlegt. Auffallend ist das Ergebnis der beiden Gruppen: Kinder ohne Migrationshintergrund weisen im Allgemeinen größere sprachliche Mängel auf als ihre Mitschüler mit Migrationshintergrund, während die besuchte Schulklasse (Sprachlernklasse und Regelklasse) dabei nicht berücksichtig wird. Dieses Ergebnis könnte mit einer Intelligenzverteilung zusammenhängen; da mir jedoch aus Datenschutzgründen die IQ–Werte für beide Schulen nicht vorliegen, kann dies nur als Vermutung gelten.

Eine weitere Erklärung wäre, dass die Kinder mit Migrationshintergrund besser abschneiden, da sie bereits von frühem Alter an mit zwei Sprachsystemen konfrontiert sind. Bilinguale haben im Unterschied zu ihren monolingualen Altersgenossen ein höheres Sprachbewusstsein: Sie besitzen im Allgemeinen früher ausgeprägte Fähigkeiten zur semantischen Analyse struktureller und funktioneller Spracheigenschaften (Bruck, Genesee 1995, Pleh et al. 1987). Nach Holler-Zittlau et al. (2004) verfügen Kinder mit Deutsch im Zweitspracherwerb schon im Alter von 4 bis 4,5 Jahren über sprachliche sowie metasprachliche Kompetenzen in ihrer Muttersprache und nehmen die zweite Sprache vor dem Hintergrund dieser Kenntnis wahr.

Wiederhold et al. (1972) stellten in Tests fest, dass die Sprachentwicklung monolingualer Kinder bei Schuleintritt noch nicht abgeschlossen ist. Der Wortschatz wird nicht nur quantitativ, sondern auch qualitativ erweitert, u.a. durch den Erwerb abstrakter Begriffe und das Verständnis für den metaphorischen Sprachgebrauch. Das wäre eine Erklärung für die geringere sprachliche Leistung der Kinder ohne Migrationshintergrund.

Nach Wode (1993) unterscheiden sich der L1- und L2-Erwerb hinsichtlich der Wortklassen erheblich, da L2-Lerner ihre Vokabeln von Beginn an Wortklassen zuzuordnen scheinen. Diese müssen nicht erst gelernt werden, da sie bereits aus dem L1-Erwerb vorhanden sind. Das könnte sich dadurch erklären, dass es nach dem zweisprachigen Sprachproduktionsmodell von Poulisse und Bongaerts (1994) beim Wortabruf einen gemeinsamen Netzwerkspeicher für beide Sprachen gibt. Eine Erklärung des signifikanten Unterschieds in der sprachlichen Leistung der Kinder mit Migrationshintergrund bieten die Interdependenz-Hypothese von Cummins (1991) sowie der konzeptorientierten An-satz von Cromer (1968), Slobin (1973), Miller, Johnson-Laird (1976) und Clark (1973). Darüber hinaus verfügen bilinguale Kinder über eine größere kommunikative Sensibilität, da sie situationsbedingte Faktoren besser wahrnehmen und schneller darauf reagieren müssen, um Schematisierungs- und Verhaltensfehler zu korrigieren (Ben-Zeev 1997).

Hypothese 3: Die lexikalisch-semantisch-klassifikatorischen Fehler bei Nomina der Kinder der Sprachlernklasse unterscheiden sich nicht von denen der Kinder der Regelklasse. Mit dieser Hypothese soll überprüft werden, ob sich die Fehlermuster bei Nomina zwischen den Kindern in beiden Klassentypen (Sprachlernklasse und Regelklasse) unterscheiden. Zunächst wurden die Kennwerte aller Substitutionen der Nomina ermittelt und mittels eines T-Tests für unabhängige Stichproben auf signifikante Mittelwertunterschiede überprüft. In einem zweiten Schritt wurden die einzelnen lexikalisch-semantischen Fehlermuster analog analysiert. Die Mittelwerte aller substituierten Begriffe ergeben für die Sprachlernklasse einen Mittelwert von 8,96 und für die Regelklasse einen Mittelwert von 15,50. Dies bedeutet, dass von den Schülern der Regelklasse im Durchschnitt mehr Begriffe substituiert wurden. Die Tabelle auf S. 285 illustriert das Ergebnis.

Bei Betrachtung der Anzahl aller substituierten Nomina nach Klassentyp ergibt sich bei gleichen angenommenen Varianzen ein T-Wert mit einem $p = 0{,}200$, das heißt, die beiden Gruppen unterscheiden sich bedeutsam hinsichtlich ihrer Mittelwerte. Konkret bedeutet dies, dass die Schüler der Sprachlernklasse mit einem Mittelwert von 8,96 im Vergleich zu den Schülern, die ausschließlich die Regelklasse besuchen (MW = 15,50) weniger Nomina substituieren.

Da die Voraussetzungen für einen T-Test für unabhängige Stichproben hier nicht gegeben sind, wurde die verteilungsfreie, nichtparametrische Alternative des Mann-Whitney-U-Tests als Analysetyp gewählt. Als Ergebnis dieses Tests kann festgehalten werden, dass sich die Klassen hinsichtlich der *Holonymie,* der *Hyperonymie*, *Kohyponymie* und der *Meronymie* unterscheiden, wobei bei den Schülern, die nur die Regelklasse besuchen, diese semantisch-klassifikatorischen Fehlertypen statistisch bedeutsam häufiger auftreten. Während die Sprachlernklasse *Holonymie* (für Beispiele s. Tabelle) einen Mittelwert von 0,35 aufweist, beträgt dieser bei Schülern, die nur die Regelklasse besuchen 1,02. Das bedeutet, dass bei den untersuchten Kindern die Anzahl der semantisch-klassifikatorischen Fehler in Form der Holonymie in der Regelklasse ($p = 0{,}002$) von der der Sprachlernklasse signifikant verschieden ist, und zwar dahingehend, dass bei Kindern der Regelklasse diese Fehlerform häufiger auftritt.

Unter Berücksichtigung der *Hyperonymie* (s. Tab. 1) zeigte sich in der Sprachlernklasse ein Mittelwert von 1,39. Bei Schülern, die nur die Regelklasse besuchen, beträgt der Mittelwert 2,97. Das bedeutet, dass bei den untersuchten Kindern die Anzahl der semantisch-klassifikatorischen Fehler in Form der Hy-

Tabelle 1
Einige Beispiele für semantisch-klassifikatorische Fehler aus den Einzelbildern und dem Erzählposter

Zielwort	Hyperonym	Hyponym	Kohyponym	Holonym	Meronym	Wortneuschöpfung	Wortartwechsel
Semmeln	Brot						
Teddybär			Puppe				
Kaugummi			Kekse		Papier		
			Plätzchen				
Kinderwagen						Babyauto	
						Babywagen	
Tasche		Rucksack					
Schrank			Regal				
Tanne	Baum						
Zopf				Haare			
Kamm			Bürste				
Vogel Strauß	Vogel		Storch				
			Gans				
			Ente				
Fingernagel				Hand			
Glühbirne				Lampe			
Eierbecher						Eierglas	
Schlittenfahrt						Schlitten fahren	
Heu	Futter						
Tannenbaum	Bäume						
Kirche					Kapelle		
Eimer			Korb				

peronymie in der Regelklasse (p = 0,000) von der der Sprachlernklasse signifikant abweichend ist, und zwar dahingehend, dass bei Kindern der Regelklasse diese Form der Fehlerart häufiger auftritt. Die Untersuchung der *Kohyponymie* zeigt Folgendes: Bei den Schülern der Sprachlernklasse liegt der Mittelwert bei 2,26 und in der Regelklasse bei 4,00. Dieser Unterschied ist nach dem Mann-Whitney-U-Test bedeutsam signifikant (p = 0,000). Bei dieser Form der semantisch-klassifikatorischen Fehler zeigten die Kinder der Sprachlernklasse ein bedeutsam besseres Ergebnis, das heißt, diese Form trat im direkten Vergleich zur Regelklasse bedeutend seltener auf.

Ein weiterer bedeutsamer Unterschied zeigt die Analyse der *Meronymie.* In der Sprachlernklasse trat diese lexikalisch-semantische Fehlerform durchschnittlich in 0,09-mal auf, während sie in der Regelklasse im Mittel 0,38-mal auftrat. Das Ergebnis des anschließenden Mann-Whitney-U-Tests ist signifikant: p = 0,041. In der Regelklasse trat diese Fehlerform häufiger auf. Bei den verbleibenden semantisch-klassifikatorischen Fehlertypen, nämlich dem *Wortartwechsel* und der *Wortneuschöpfung* sind keine statistisch bedeutsamen Unterschiede festzustellen.

Die typischen Fehlerprofile stimmen zum Teil mit den erwähnten Studien von MacGregor et al. (2002) und D'Amico et al. (2002) überein. So stellte sich auch in der vorliegenden Studie heraus, dass die für Nomina charakteristische Fehlerstrategie in semantischen Substitutionen besteht. Nach der „Atomkügelchentheorie" von Aitchison (1997) wird die Dominanz semantisch-klassifikatorischer Reaktionen bei Nomina angesichts der klaren hierarchischen Gliederung von Nomina plausibel.

Nach der *Prototypen-Theorie* von Bowerman (1978) werden Merkmalansätze integriert, indem analytische Prozesse der Erkennung und des Vergleichs von Merkmalen zur Einordnung in Konzepte, die durch Nomina ausgedrückt werden können, und in Relationen (wie Über-, Unter- und Nebenordnung) angewendet werden. Es wurde berichtet, dass Kinder anfangs Begriffe der *basic-level*-Ebene produzieren, so dass der Begriff „Blume" vor dem Begriff „Rose" auftritt, was allerdings in der frühen Entwicklungsstufe des Kindes zu beobachten ist. Im Alter von drei bis vier Jahren treten Hyponyme (Unterbegriffe) in der Regel vor Hyperonymen (Oberbegriffen) auf (Waxman, Hatch 1992). Für die Kinder der Regelklasse scheint dies jedoch nicht der Fall zu sein.

Die Kinder der Sprachlernklasse machen signifikant weniger semantisch-klassifikatorische Fehler als ihre Mitschüler in der Regelklasse. Ein möglicher Erklärungsansatz könnte im Unterrichtsprozess der Sprachlernklassen legen, denn dort wird speziell auf die sprachliche Kompetenz der Kinder eingegangen. Die Kinder der Regelklasse, die zum Teil auch Kinder mit Migrationshintergrund sind, bekommen dagegen keinen spezifischen Deutschunterricht, der dem Modell der Sprachlernklasse entspricht. Ein zusätzlicher Förderunterricht wird aufgrund mangelnden Lehrpersonals nur begrenzt angeboten. Ein weiterer Grund wären die in der Regelklasse eingesetzten Lehrmaterialien, die die Lexikonentwicklung, die Organisation des semantischen Wissens der Kinder, die Ausdifferenzierung und Erweiterung semantischer Felder und ein wachsendes Wissen über sprachstrukturelle Gliederungsprinzipien und Hierarchien nicht genügend fördern. Das Ergebnis könnten Wort-speicherungsschwächen mit Übergeneralisierungen sein, wobei das konzeptuelle Wissen reduziert ist. Dieses Phänomen ist nach den vorliegenden statistischen Ergebnissen bei den Kindern der Regelklasse zu beobachten.

Implementierungen für die Praxis

Die Ergebnisse legen die Vermutung nahe, dass die Zuweisung zu den Klassentypen fehlerhaft ist. Die Zuweisung in die Sprachlernklasse beziehungsweise die Regelklasse erfolgte aufgrund eines Testverfahrens („Screening Modell für Schulanfänger" 2002), das nicht standardisiert ist und deshalb sehr stark von der Erfahrung der durchführenden Lehrpersonen abhängt. Zweifel an der Qualität des Instruments und seiner Anwendung drängen sich auf. Die Praxis braucht aber ein gutes formatives Instrument im Sinne einer Prozessdiagnostik, das die sprachliche Fähigkeit der Kinder erfasst und Hinweise auf eine passende Förderung gibt. Dieses Verfahren sollte nicht für selektive Zwecke eingesetzt werden, wie dies seit langer Zeit Gegenstand der Diskussion um die Schuleingangsdiagnostik ist und wieder verstärkt in den Blickpunkt des Interesses geraten ist. Als zentrales Element soll hierbei die gemeinsame diagnostische Arbeit im Team unter Lehrern gesehen werden. Da dem Lehrerurteil und damit der subjektiven Beurteilungskompetenz des Lehrers eine erhöhte Bedeutung zukommt, wäre die Teilnahme der Lehrkräfte an Fortbildungsveranstaltungen zur Aneignung von diagnostischer und prognostischer Kompetenz eine dringende Voraussetzung.

Die Ergebnisse zeigen außerdem, dass die Kinder der Regelklasse im Vergleich zu den Kindern der Sprachlernklasse quantitativ und qualitativ erhebliche Schwierigkeiten auf der semantisch-lexikalischen Ebene aufwiesen. Das wirft die Frage auf, wie Schüler gefördert werden können. Da Förderunterricht oft aus diversen Gründen nicht ermöglicht werden kann, sollte die Klassenlehrkraft die theoretisch postulierten Stadien des Bedeutungserwerbs mit entsprechenden methodischen Möglichkeiten kennen und sie bei der Wortspeicherung und dem Wortabruf praktisch verknüpfen können. Einerseits bilden dabei geeignete und gute Lehrmittel eine Basis, andererseits ist für die Unterrichtsqualität die Fähigkeit der Lehrkräfte entscheidend, Lernprozesse bei den Kindern zu unterstützen, auszulösen, zu verstärken und zu steuern. Denn Wissen ist nicht statisch, sondern entwickelt und verändert sich aufgrund sozialer, politischer und ökonomischer Einflüsse. Das eigene Wissen und Können laufend zu erweitern und zu aktualisieren, liegt in der Verantwortung der einzelnen Lehrkräften. Das muss laufend mit dem Auswerten und Reflektieren der eigenen Praxis geschehen, autodidaktisch mit der Einarbeitung in neue Lehrmittel oder in der Weiterbildung. Die Lehrerbildung steht vor der Aufgabe, den Lehrkräften nicht den Mythos einer einsprachigen, mono-kulturellen Mittelschichtschülerschaft zu vermitteln, sondern ihnen das grundlegende Wissen für eine erfolgreiche und qualifizierte sprachliche Förderung zwei- und mehrsprachiger Kinder in einer entsprechenden Unterrichtsentwicklung zu vermitteln. Danach entwickelte Förderpläne für jeden Schüler wären zwar sehr aufwändig, stellen jedoch ein gut fundiertes Konzept für eine weitergehende Individualisierung dar.

Es wurde gezeigt, dass Kinder mit Migrationshintergrund in beiden Schulklassentypen bessere sprachliche Leistungen hervorbrachten als ihre Mitschüler ohne Migrationshintergrund. Eine Erklärung dafür könnte sein, dass sie bereits vom frühen Alter an mit zwei Sprachsystemen konfrontiert sind. Zweisprachige Kinder haben im Unterschied zu ihren monolingualen Altersgenossen ein höheres Sprachbewusstsein: Sie besitzen im Allgemeinen früher ausgeprägte Fähigkeiten zur semantischen Analyse struktureller und funktioneller Spracheigenschaften. An dieser Stelle muss auch der Stellenwert der Herkunftssprachen und ihre Förderung für den Bildungserfolg betont werden. Es wäre wünschenswert, Lehrkräfte mit Migrationshintergrund in den vorschulischen Einrichtungen und in den Grundschulen einzustellen sowie eine Deutsch als Zweitsprache-Weiterbildung für alle praktizierenden Lehrkräfte obligatorisch zu machen. Es sollte auch angestrebt werden, die Schreib- und Ausdrucksfähigkeit der Kinder mit Migrationshintergrund in ihrer jeweiligen Muttersprache zu fördern (zum Beispiel in Form von Arbeitsgruppen). Es könnte dabei wertvoll sein, Kinder ohne Migrationshintergrund in diese Arbeitskreise zu integrieren, um damit einerseits ein gegenseitiges Kulturverständnis zu fördern und andererseits das Fremdsprachenangebot für Kinder ohne Migrationshintergrund zu erweitern.

Literatur

Aitchison, Jean 1997: Wörter im Kopf. Eine Einführung in das mentale Lexikon. Aus dem Englischen von Martina Wiese. Tübingen: Niemeyer.

Alba, Richard D., Johann Handl, Walter Müller 1994: Ethnische Ungleichheiten im deutschen Bildungssystem. In: Kölner Zeitschrift für Soziologie und Sozialpsychologie 46, 2: 209–237.

Allemann-Ghionda, Christina 1999: Schule, Bildung und Pluralität. Sechs Fallstudien im europäischen Vergleich. Bern u. a.: Lang.

Barnhusen, Friederike, Anette Pohl, Doris Fischer 2004: Logico Picolo Deutsch. Basisübungen 2. Wortschatzübungen und Begriffsbildung. Oberursel: Finken.

Ben-Zeev, Sandra 1977: Mechanism by which Childhood Bilngualism affects Understanding of Language and Cognitive Structures. In: Peter Hornby (Hg.), Bilingualism: Psychological, Social and Educational Implications. New York: Academic Press.

Bowerman, Melissa 1978: The Acquisition of Word-Meaning: An Investigation into some Current Conflicts. In: Natalie Waterson, Catherine Snow (Hg.), The Development of Communication. Chichester: Wiley.

Bruck, Maggie, Fred Genesee 1995: Phonological Awareness in Young Second Language Learners. In: Journal of Child Language 22: 307–332.

Clark, Herbert 1973: Space, Time, Semantics, and the Child. In: Timothy Moore (Hg.), Cognitive Development and the Acquisition of Language. New York: Academic Press, 65–110.

Cromer, Richard 1968: The Development of Temporal Reference during the Acquisition of Language. Harvard University. Unpubl. PhD thesis.

Cummins, Jim 1991: Interdependence of First- and Second-Language Proficiency in Bilingual Children. In: Ellen Bialystok (Hg.), Language Processing in Bilingual Children. Cambridge et al.: Cambridge UP, 70–89.

D'Amico, Simona, Simone Betrovato, Manual Gasparini, Daniela Constabile, Elisabeth Bates 2002: Timed Picture Naming in Italian Speaking Children and Adults: Differences between Nouns and Verbs. Paper presented at the IASCL-SRCLD conference in Madison, USA.

Empfehlung der Bildungskommission der Heinrich Böll Stiftung 2004: Schule und Migration. Heinrich Böll Stiftung.

Han, Petrus 2005: Soziologie der Migration. Erklärungsmodelle, Fakten, politische Kosequenzen, Perspektiven. Stuttgart: Lucius & Lucius.

Heine, Christoph, Heike Spangenberg, Dieter Sommer 2006: Studienberechtigte 2004. Übergang in Studium, Ausbildung, Beruf. Ergebnisse der Befragung der Studienberechtigten 2004 ein halbes Jahr nach Schulabgang im Länder- und Zeitvergleich. Hannover.

Holler-Zittlau, Inge, Wienfried Dux, Roswitha Berger 2004: Evaluation der Sprachentwicklung 4 bis 4½-jähriger Kinder in Hessen. Eine empirische Untersuchung der deutschen Gesellschaft für Sprachheilpädagogik (DGS) Landesgruppe Hessen e. V. im Auftrag des Hessischen Sozialministeriums. Wiesbaden.

Hunger, Uwe, Dietrich Thränhardt 2004: Migration und Bildungserfolg: Wo stehen wir? In: Klaus Bade, Michael Bommes (Hg.), Migration - Integration - Bildung. Grundfragen und Problembereiche. Bad Iburg: Grote (= IMIS Beiträge 23).

Kauschke, Christine 2007: Erwerb und Verarbeitung von Nomen und Verben. Tübingen: Niemeyer.

Krohne, Julia, Ulrich Meier, Klaus-Jürgen Tillmann 2004: Sitzenbleiben, Geschlecht und Migration. Klassenwiederholungen im Spiegel der PISA-Daten. In: Zeitschrift für Pädagogik 50, 3: 373–391.

Lehmann, Reiner et al. 2004: Untersuchung der Leistungen, Motivation und Einstellungen zu Beginn der beruflichen Ausbildung (ULME I). Hamburg.

McGregor, Karla 1997: The Nature of Word-Finding Errors of Preschoolers with and without Word-Finding Deficits. In: Journal of Speech, Language and Hearing Research 40: 1232–1244.

McGregor, Karla, Rena Friedman, Renée Reilly, Robyn Newman 2002: Semantic Representation and Naming in Young Children. In: Journal of Speech, Language, and Hearing Research 45: 332–346.

Miller, George, Philip Johnson-Laird 1976: Language and Perception. Cambridge: Cambridge University Press.

Peleki, Eleni 2008: Migration, Integration und Sprachförderung. Eine empirische Untersuchung zum Wortschatzerwerb und zur schulischen Integration von Grundschulkindern. München: Meidenbauer.

Pléh, Csaba, Alexandr Jaronvinskij, Alexandr Balajan 1987: Sentence Comprehension in Hungarian-Russian Bilingual and Monolingual Preschool Children. In: Journal of Child Language 14: 587–603.

Poulisse, Nanda, Theo Bongaerts 1994: First Language Use in Second Language Production. In: Applied Linguistics 15, 1: 36–57.

Riek, Götz–Achim 1995: Die neue Ost–West–Migration am Beispiel der Rußlanddeutschen in der Russischen Föderation. Neuried: Ars Una.

Slobin, Dan-Isaac 1973: Cognitive Prerequisites for the Development of Grammar. In: Albert Charles Ferguson, Dan-Isaac Slobin (Hg.), Studies of Child Language Development. New York: Holt, Rinehart & Winston, 185–214.

Speck-Hamdan, Angelika 2004: Wie Kinder lernen. Vom Entstehen der Welt in den Köpfen der Kinder. In: Television 1, 2004: 4–9.

Statistisches Bundesamt (Hg.) 2006: Datenreport 2006. Zahlen und Fakten über die Bundesrepublik Deutschland. Berlin, Bonn: Bundeszentrale für politische Bildung.

Treibel, Anette 1988: Engagement und Differenzierung in der westdeutschen Ausländerforschung. Eine Untersuchung ihrer soziologischen Beiträge. Stuttgart: Enke.

Treibel, Anette 2003: Migration in modernen Gesellschaften: Soziale Fragen von Einwanderung und Gastarbeit. Weinheim, München: Juventa.

Waxman, Sandra, Thomas Hatch 1992: Beyond the Basics: Preschool Children Label Objects Flexibly at Multiple Hierarchical Levels. In: Journal of Child language 19: 153–166.

Wiederhold, Karl-August 1971: Kindersprache und Sozialstatus. Eine empirische Unter-suchung zum Sprachstand und Sprachwandel bei Kindern des 1. und 2. Schuljahres. Ratingen.

Wittkowske, Steffen 2001: Das Auer Heimat- und Sachbuch I. 1. Aufl. Donauwörth: Auer.

Wode, Henning 1993: Psycholinguistik. Eine Einführung in die Lehr-und Lernbarkeit von Sprachen. heorien, Methoden, Ergebnisse. Ismaning: Hueber.

Addresses of authors and editors

Editorial Board

Authors and editors of volume 13

Monica Beatrice Bercovici
Institut d'Ethnographie et de Folklore "C. Brăiloiu"
rue Tache Ionescu, no. 25, Bucharest
bicajel@yahoo.com

Dr. Seher Cesur-Kiliçaslan
Acıbadem Mahallesi, Acıbadem Caddesi
İbrahim Ağa Konutları C1 A Blok, Daire No: 19, TR - 34718 Kadıköy, Istanbul, Turkey
sherk@hacettepe.edu.tr, seherck@gmail.com

Dr. Gülsüm Depeli
Hacettepe University, Faculty of Communication, TR - 06800 Beytepe Ankara
depeli@hacettepe.edu.tr

Dr Georgia Eglezou
Media School, Bournemouth University, Talbot Campus, Poole, Dorset BH12 5BB, UK
eglezoug@yahoo.co.uk

Çağla Karabağ
Hacettepe University, Faculty of Communication, TR - 06800 Beytepe Ankara
ckarabag@hacettepe.edu.tr

Vladimir Karadžoski
Institute for Ancient Slavic Culture, MAK - 7500 Prilep
vkaradzoski@yahoo.com

PD Dr. Christian Koller
Bangor University, School of History, Welsh History and Archaeology, College Road, Bangor (Gwynedd) LL57 2DG, UK
c.koller@bangor.ac.uk

Prof. Evgenia Krăsteva-Blagoeva PhD
Department of Anthropology, New Bulgarian University, ul. Montevideo 21, BG - 1618 Sofia
evgenia_blagoeva@hotmail.com

Prof. Leo A. C. J. Lucassen
Institute for History, Economische en Sociale Geschiedenis
Johan Huizingagebouw. Doelensteeg 16, NL - 2311 VL Leiden
l.a.c.j.lucassen@hum.leidenuniv.nl

Stefanie Mayer M.A.
IHS Wien
Stumpergasse 56, A - 1060 Vienna
stmayer@ihs.ac.at

Dr. László Mód
University of Szeged, Department of Ethnology and Cultural Anthropology
Egyetem u. 2, H - 6722 Szeged
modlaci@freemail.hu

Marios Papakyriacou M.A.
Habersaathstr. 54, D - 10115 Berlin
mariotzan@yahoo.gr

Dr. phil. Eleni Peleki
Lehrstuhl für Didaktik der deutschen Sprache und Literatur/DDaZ, Ludwig-Maximilians-Universität München, Schellingstr. 3 RG, D - 80799 München
eleni.peleki@germanistik.uni-muenchen.de

Dr. Robert Pichler
Department for Southeast European History
Mozartgasse 3, A - 8010 Graz
robert.pichler@uni-graz.at

Prof. Biljana Ristovska-Josifovska
Institute of National History
Grigor Prlicev 3, P. Box 591, MAK - 1000 Skopje
brjosifovska@yahoo.com

Hande Sağlam M.A.
IVE
Anton-von-Webern-Platz 1, A - 1030 Wien
saglam@mdw.ac.at

Petruţa Teampău M.A.
Str. Rasinari 1, ap. 8, RO - 400457 Cluj Napoca
mindrut_petruta@yahoo.com

Prof. R. Günsel Terzioğlu
Hacettepe Ünivesritesi Merkez Kampüsü
D Blokları Aile ve Tüketici Bilimleri Bölümü, 7. Kat, TR - 06100 Sıhhiye/Ankara
gterziog@hacettepe.edu.tr

Prof. Kristof van Assche, PhD
Land Use Planning, St. Cloud State University
Stewart Hall 337, 720 4th Avenue South, St. Cloud, MN 56301-4498, USA
kvanassche@stcloudstate.edu

Instructions to Authors

Ethnologia Balkanica is a refereed journal. We welcome submissions by ethnologists, folklorists, ethnographers, cultural and social anthropologists as well as scholars from related disciplines working on the ethnology of Southeast Europe. Submissions should meet the criteria below. The decision about acceptance or rejection rests with the editorial board. When a manuscript has been accepted the full text incl. notes, references, and summaries must be forwarded as a printout and as a data file on diskette or by e-mail. Data files should contain no styles and a minimum of formatting. Authors should send their full postal and e-mail addresses as well as their affiliation together with their paper to the editors.
Length: Articles should have a minimum of 4500 and a maximum of 9000 words.
Languages: Manuscripts can be submitted in English, French or German. Authors who are not writing in their mother-tongue must have their text checked by a native speaker of the language of the text. Titles of publications in southeast European languages must be followed by a translation in the language of the text in brackets [ ].
Abstracts: All manuscripts must be supplied with an English summary of 150 words that summarises the main arguments and findings of the article.
Spelling: Though we prefer British spelling for texts in English, American spelling is also acceptable. In any case the spelling must be consistent.
Transcription from Cyrillic alphabets should follow the scientific style (ISO standard). Do not use ch, zh, sh, iya but č, ž, š, and ija (see transcription list on next page). If your programme does not know these letters, use the popular form of transcription but mark all letters that require diacritical marks with a "*". Romanian names must be written in the original, i. e., with all diacritical characters.
Citations and References: Citations should be in Harvard style, author, date and page as follows (Verdery 1983: 27); if there are two or more authors, separate authors with commas. This applies also to footnotes. No comma after the author's name. Don't use p. or pp. Always cite page numbers where you are quoting or paraphrasing from a specific part of a text, and avoid too much citation where a work in its entirety is referred to. Avoid the use of ibid. and op.cit, but if you do so, make sure you use them correctly. Note that "cf." means "compare to", not "see also"; if you mean the latter, say so. If a cited scholarly work is not (yet) published, use for example (Smith forthcoming) if the work will be published with certainty. References to archival sources should be given in footnotes, particularly when they are lengthy. Make sure that you use dashes between numbers and dates, for example April – May, 22–30, and not hyphens (-).

All references cited, and only these, should be listed under the heading "References" or "Literature", according to the style indicated below. Always give page numbers for papers in edited volumes or journals. Do not forget to mention the publisher.
For all questions of style, format, headings, quotation, notes, and references please take earlier volumes of this journal as a model. Other styles are not accepted.
Pictures and diagrams: Please always send photographs, graphics, and diagrams separately, never imported into the text. Photographs should be saved in the TIF format; please avoid all compressed formats such as JPEG. Resolution should be from 300 dpi (photographs) up to 800–1200 dpi (drawings, caricatures). If you send pictures taken with a digital camera please adjust to maximum resolution and minimal compression.
The author will get one free copy of the journal and a free supply of 10 offprints.

Table: Transliteration of south slavic cyrillic characters (ISO standard):

а	a	к	k	ф	f	ю	ju
б	b	л	l	х	h	я	ja
в	v	м	m	ц	c	ђ	đ, (dj)
г	g	н	n	ч	č	ѕ	dz
д	d	о	o	ш	š	љ	lj
е	e	п	p	щ	št	њ	nj
ж	ž	р	r	ъ	ă	ћ	ć
з	z	с	s	ы	y	џ	dž
и	i	т	t	ь	j	ѣ	ě
й	j	у	u				

Ethnologia Balkanica

Journal for Southeast European Anthropology/Zeitschrift für die Anthropologie Südosteuropas/Journal d'anthropologie du sud-est européen

Editor-in-chief: Prof. Klaus Roth, Co-editor: Dr. Ulf Brunnbauer

Klaus Roth; Ulf Brunnbauer (Eds.)

Region, Regional Identity and Regionalism in Southeastern Europe

Part 2

The contributions to this second volume focus equally on tangible and intangible dimensions of Southeast European regions. They represent the region both as a territorial unit and as a mental construct laden with symbolic meaning. The papers demonstrate that regions, be it the entire Balkan Peninsula or be it a small area somewhere in the mountains, can become palpable, visible, and audible. They can produce culture and they can, at the same time, be products of culture: regions can be constructs of those who inhabit them - or of spatial planning from "above". In any case, both the physical and the symbolic regions are a very relevant issue in Southeast Europe, serving purposes of spatial, ethnic, religious or even professional identification, or of politically motivated border-drawing.

Bd. 12, 2009, 272 S., 29,90 €, br., ISBN 978-3-643-10107-5

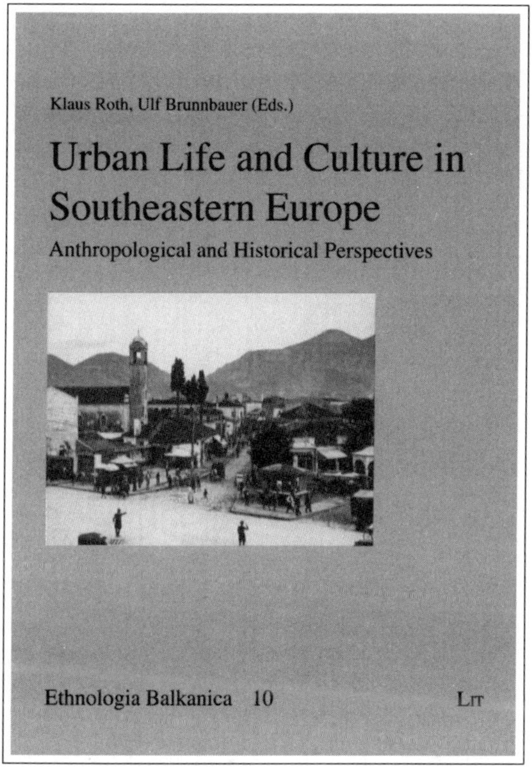

Klaus Roth; Ulf Brunnbauer (Eds.)

Urban Life and Culture in Southeastern Europe

Anthropological and Historical Perspectives

Urbanization in Southeastern Europe displays significant idiosyncrasies. While the region was predominantly rural long into the 20th century, cities grew rapidly after WWII, causing deep socio-cultural changes which gained in momentum after the end of socialism. The articles in this volume, originally presented at the conference 'Urban Life and Culture in Southeastern Europe' in Belgrade, May 2005, explore these changes past and present, focusing on urban culture, social topography, urban planning, and urban-rural relations.

Bd. 10, 2007, 368 S., 29,90 €, br., ISBN 978-3-8258-9903-5

LIT Verlag Berlin – Münster – Wien – Zürich – London

Auslieferung Deutschland / Österreich / Schweiz: siehe Impressumsseite

Balkan Border Crossings
Contributions to Balkan Ethnography
edited by Vassilis Nitsiakos (University of Ioannina, Greece)

Vassilis Nitsiakos

On the Border

Transborder Mobility,
Ethnic Groups and Boundaries
on the Albanian-Greek Frontier

LIT

Vassilis Nitsiakos
On the Border
Transborder Mobility, Ethnic Groups and Boundaries along the Albanian-Greek Frontier
The flow of emigrants from Albania to Greece, being one-sided, indicates a relation of inequality between the two countries. Indeed, the violence with which the collapse of the regime is effected and the subsequent opening of the border and the, as a rule, undocumented way of entering Greece, makes this relation even more asymmetrical and places the moving ones in a much more powerless position, as they live and work illegally: their "outlaw" status deprives them of all rights. Legalisation improves their position but does not cancel the structural inequality that characterises the phenomenon of immigration any way, as well as the quality of the immigrant. In any case, the effort of the immigrants to present aspects of identity that would facilitate their position and residence (proofs of Greek roots or Christian faith, changes of names, etc.) demonstrates, precisely, how they experience this unequal relationship, which is further aggravated by factors pertaining to their otherness.
Bd. 1, 2010, 504 S., 49,90 €, br., ISBN 978-3-643-10793-0

LIT Verlag Berlin – Münster – Wien – Zürich – London
Auslieferung Deutschland / Österreich / Schweiz: siehe Impressumsseite

Balkanologie

Beiträge zur Sprach- und Kulturwissenschaft
hrsg. von Thede Kahl, Michael Metzeltin, Gabriella Schubert und Christian Voss

Thede Kahl
Hirten in Kontakt
Sprach- und Kulturwandel ehemaliger Wanderhirten (Albanisch, Aromunisch, Griechisch)

Die Hirtengesellschaften Südosteuropas haben durch ihre Wanderungen zur Ausbreitung zahlreicher kultureller Phänomene in weiten Räumen Südosteuropas beigetragen, gleichzeitig aber durch die Geschlossenheit ihrer Gesellschaften die eigene Kultur gut bewahren können. Die Wanderhirten unterliefen durch die Aufgabe ihrer ausgedehnten Herdenwanderungen im 20. Jahrhundert einen tiefgreifenden Wandel. Einerseits kam es zum Abbruch der gewachsenen Kontaktsituationen, andererseits entstanden durch Sesshaftwerdung und berufliche Neuorientierung zahlreiche neue Konstellationen des Kulturkontaktes. Die hierbei ablaufenden Prozesse stehen im Zentrum des Interesses. Nach einer kulturgeographischen und ethnolinguistischen Dokumentation des albanisch-griechischen Grenzraums erfolgt eine Beschreibung der Kontaktsituationen, die für Wanderhirten charakteristisch waren, eine Darstellung der Sesshaftwerdung und eine kommentierte Analyse der Hirtenterminologie in den untersuchten Sprachen und ihren regionalen Dialekten. Obwohl die untersuchten Sprachen – Albanisch, Aromunisch und Griechisch – unterschiedlichen Sprachfamilien angehören, sind sie durch zahlreiche Gemeinsamkeiten miteinander verbunden. Da es besonders viele verbindende Elemente in der Kultur der Wanderhirten gibt, berührt die Untersuchung eine der Kernfragen der Balkanologie. Due to their migrations the pastoral societies of South East Europe have contributed to the spread of numerous cultural phenomena across wide swathes of East Europe, while at the same time the closed nature of their societies has enabled them to successfully preserve their own culture. As a result of giving up their extensive nomadism and transhumance in the 20th century the pastoral nomads have experienced far-reaching change. On the one hand, contact situations which had existed from time immemorial were broken off, on the other, sedentarisation and vocational reorientation have resulted in numerous new constellations of cultural contact. This study will focus on the processes which have taken place in this context. A cultural-geographic and ethno-linguistic documentation of the Albanian-Greek border region will be followed by a description of the contact situations which were typical for nomadic pastoralists, an account of the process of sedentarisation and an analysis of the pastoral terminology in the languages under consideration and their regional dialects. Although the languages studied – Albanian, Aromanian and Greek – belong to different linguistic families, they do share a number of common features. Given the very many connecting elements in the culture of the pastoral nomads, the study touches one of the central questions of Balkan studies.

Bd. 2, 2008, 384 S., 29,90 €, br., ISBN 978-3-8258-0944-7

LIT Verlag Berlin – Münster – Wien – Zürich – London

Auslieferung Deutschland / Österreich / Schweiz: siehe Impressumsseite